opera
and
ballet
in australia

To MUM,
   On your Birthday!,

Lots of Love,
Alison-Jo Anne
   x x x x x x x

(10th April 1978.)

opera
and
ballet
in australia

john
cargher

cassell australia

For Penelope
because as a child she preferred Die Kluge and Il Tabarro to The Beatles

Endpapers:
Jose Varona's costume designs for The Tales of Hoffman.
Left, Dapertutto; right, Pittichinaccio

CASSELL AUSTRALIA LIMITED
31 Bridge Road, Stanmore, New South Wales
30 Curzon Street, North Melbourne, Victoria
Copyright © 1977 Cassell Australia Limited
First published 1977
Edited by Jane Morgan
Designed by Michele Withers
Jacket photograph Philip Morris

Set in 11/12 Garamond, 9/10 Helvetica by
Savage & Co Pty Ltd, Brisbane
Printed and bound by Singapore National
Printers (Pte) Limited
F.1077

National Library of Australia
Cataloguing in Publication Data
Cargher, John.
    Opera and ballet in Australia.

    Index.
    ISBN 0 7269 1360 x.
    1. Opera — Australia. 2. Ballet. I. Title.
782.10994

opera contents

ballet contents

acknowledgements

A great number of people have assisted me by supplying information and facts without which this volume could not have been written. If the result is somewhat longer than expected, the fault is theirs; one thing led to another and there is nothing worse than an enthusiastic author abetted by a sympathetic publisher. Thank you, David C. Field, for putting up with unkept deadlines and not forcing cuts in spite of rising costs.

I accept full responsibility for all this book contains, E. & O.I. (errors and omissions included). The following did their best to keep me on the straight and narrow in my quest for operatic truth and I acknowledge their help gratefully and in alphabetical order: Ronald Dowd, Stephen Hall, Judith Jacks, Mary Lewis, Alan Light, Harold Love, Justin McDonnell, Joan Maslin, Prudence Neidorf, Therese Radic, John Winther, Elizabeth Wood and John Young.

My special thanks to Celia Winter-Irving, who placed her incomplete history of opera in Australia at my disposal. Her efforts to present the social, economic, political, ideological and geographic influences on the art in this country cover different aspects from my own audience-cum-critic treatment. But her manuscript steered me in many different directions and I found it of immense help. Perhaps my book will encourage more detailed volumes about the subject to be published. If so, I hope Celia gets a share of the cake.

The writing of the ballet section proved to be a more difficult task than I had anticipated and it would have been impossible without the assistance of the Australian Archives of the Dance and their Archivist, Edward H. Pask. Ted has been a most patient and inexhaustible source of information, allowing himself to be telephoned at all hours of the day and night and invariably coming up with the right answers. Material from The Australian Ballet and the Archives was made available by kind permission of the Administrator of the Australian Ballet.

The history of the Australian Ballet itself has been so much better chronicled than that of the Australian Opera that I thought bringing it into some kind of order would be simple. It has not proved to be so, and I have had to call on the recollections of many people, who have contributed to a larger or lesser extent by making themselves available for sometimes lengthy interviews; the spectacle of John Cargher manipulating microphones among the dishes (and glasses) in the Florentino Restaurant in Melbourne will, no doubt, be remembered with glee by its waiters.

My principal thanks must go to William Akers, Kathleen Gorham, Geoffrey Hutton, John Lanchbery, Noel Pelly, Margaret Scott and Dame Peggy van Praagh, especially the last, the discomforts of whose hospital bed would not have been eased by my questions.

Illustrations necessarily play a large part in any book on ballet and I express my deep appreciation to William Baxter for permission to use so many of his superb photographs, which give such a true feeling of the dancers' work.

I would also like to thank Jane Morgan for the help she gave me in editing both parts of this book. If it were not entirely a case of making order out of chaos, it must have seemed so to her at times; there always has been madness in my method.

JOHN CARGHER
Melbourne 1977

Richard Bonynge Musical Director of the Australian Opera Company.

introduction

Football has as much to do with ballet as the Sun Aria has with opera.

Now there is a nice controversial sentence to start the ball rolling. Is he flattering football or is he running down the Sun Aria? Alternatively, is he raising ballet to the level of mass entertainment, or is he putting down opera into the provincial song-fest league? Actually, I am not doing either, I am trying to establish the lack of values which exists in a country which has no heritage in either art.

We are, let us be honest, newcomers in the fields of opera and ballet, and simple faith that we are excelling in both is not enough. We may very well be in the top leagues of both, but if we are – and are we? – we don't know why. Most of us couldn't care less; some of us feel it is our patriotic duty to storm the Gallipoli of culture; a few have acquired some kind of love for either art; and a tiny minority have clasped them both to our many-sized bosoms.

Writing a book on opera and ballet (or ballet and opera) is a kind of literary suicide. Cross-fertilization between the only two musical arts in the theatre is not the done thing in Australia; it rates somewhere between incest and test-tube babies in the popularity stakes. Balletomanes at the opera are there to be seen more often than to see; you find them at first nights rather than on subscription nights. As for opera, because some soprano, donkey's years ago, gave her name to a kind of peachy sweet, this art has been nurtured in the broad midsts of our society matrons for years. In the absence of a dancing Melba, there is no earthly reason why they should patronize the ballet. (I am still puzzling myself, why the simple meringue is known as a 'Pavlova' only in Australia, which, in the main, has been violently anti-ballet until very recently.)

What on earth, then, has caused the publishers to lump together two different and, in the eyes of many, opposing arts within a single book? No, it isn't greed; unless you consider that engaging in one of the riskiest business ventures of all, publishing, is greed. The fault is the author's, who happens to have fallen in love with both arts at a tender age by an accident which may be worth retelling.

It happened back in 1936 when I was young and nimble enough to climb endless stairs at Sadler's Wells and, less frequently, at Covent Garden, to go to the opera. Less frequently at the Garden because it cost two shillings in the gallery, while fourpence was enough if there were any 'late door' seats in the gods at the Wells. For the price of my lunch (cup of tea and a ham roll for fourpence) I saw *Rigoletto* and *Faust* and *Hugh the Drover*. At that age missing lunch two or three times a week was of less moment than to be enraptured by, say, Ruth Naylor or Arnold Matters, of whose Australian backgrounds I had no idea.

Sadler's Wells offered seven performances a week, five of opera and one night and the Saturday matinee of ballet. I never went to the ballet, that sissy art. Turn down a cuppa and a ham roll for the ballet? No effing fear, as we used to say in the factory when we didn't want to use a four letter word now in common usage.

And then came the fatal day when I turned up at the Wells with a girl named Millicent to see *Rigoletto*. I remember nothing about Milly except her name and the fact that she was not upset when we found we had mixed our nights up: it was the Vic-Wells Ballet and not *Rigoletto*. Milly had been to the ballet before and had enjoyed it. (She would; she was a girl!) If memory serves me right, I had a whole shilling of my own that day, and in those days girls paid their own way. To cut a long story short, I went to the ballet to please Milly and promptly forgot her in favour of the ballet. Cross my heart, I remember that night as though it was yesterday, and I can still recite most of the cast, let alone the ballets, by heart: *Le Baiser de la fée* (Ashton-Stravinsky) with Pearl Argyle and Harold Turner; *The Rake's Progress* (de Valois-Gordon) with a spectacular performance by a not yet knighted 'Bobbie' Helpmann and Elizabeth Miller; and *Casse noisette, Act 2* (*Nutcracker* to you) with Harold Turner and Mary Honer. But curiously enough, the dancer who stuck in my mind, who finally convinced me that ballet was for me, was no great star, but one Claude Newman who danced the *Trepak* and proved that male dancing is not necessarily effeminate. Two years later I founded a ballet company!

Fairly obviously I didn't turn my back on opera. Equally obviously, I believe that other opera lovers can come to love ballet and vice versa. And that, not the profit motive, decided the final form of this book.

Having apparently (have I?) caused you to forget the outrageous statements which started this chapter, I will now return and complete my assault on the intelligence of some of my readers. I know very well that it is wrong to generalize – that there have always been some Australians (I shall not insult them by calling them cultured Australians) who have enjoyed opera or ballet, or both. In all fairness they will admit that until recently they have hardly had the opportunity to get to know either art very well and it is the attitude of their fellow-citizens which has been largely responsible for this.

It is hard to blame a people 24,000 kilometres from what used to be known as civilization for failing to adopt something which came to them only at second-hand, and which was second-rate when it did come. The pioneers of the early nineteenth century were hard-working artisans who enjoyed what was presented to them as ballet or opera for the popular entertainment it was in those days in every part of the world, 'cultured' or not. The only thing missing here in Australia was continuity.

It is very easy to go to an 'entertainment' and to have a good time. I don't subscribe to the theory that you have to know a lot about the background and technique of entertainment to enjoy it. I believe that all art is a form of giving people pleasure, or entertainment.

'To entertain: to amuse, divert.' Perhaps diversion is a better word. 'Diversion: relief from work or absorption, amusement.' Do we really go to the ballet to be educated? Do we go to the opera to be uplifted? Surely not, whatever our teachers may say; and I say 'teachers' guardedly, for our critics and writers on these subjects and any other matters of art are much too inclined to treat us all as children.

I am sure we all have one thing in common: the memory of being taught in school how important, how beautiful or (dreaded expression) how 'good for us' such-and-such was. Do we, as adults, not have the right now to make up our own minds? I hardly class myself as a novice in opera or ballet, but I fail to be uplifted when I see *Swan Lake,* and after umpteen performances of *Fidelio* I still haven't learnt its 'meaning', whatever that may be. I get pleasure, pure and simple, by going to the theatre, and if that is uplifting or educational, fair enough, but I still go because it pleases me. If it didn't, I wouldn't. And if it doesn't please you, don't you go either! At least, don't go and see something you know is not to your liking, always remembering that opera and ballet are many things to many people.

There are ballets and operas I dislike intensely, but musical theatre as such is a constant source of pleasure to me. Let us say that I am a gourmet for this fare and that like any other gourmet I sometimes, even often, am not served too well. That's all part of the fun of the thing. If everything in the garden were lovely, there would be no bliss in beauty. Pleasure in art and pleasure in beauty are relative things and the height of pleasure and beauty is its contrast with the ugly, the mediocre, or the average. May the day of unimpaired excellence never come in these fields, or any other. It would leave us with no great memories to cherish.

Back to the fray! I diverge again. What does football have to do with ballet, or the Sun Aria with opera? Nothing at all. The Press, God bless it, loves the old ballet pro's gambit that footballers are athletes like dancers; that their jumping around is like ballet and that they practise an art of a sort. I have nothing against football, mainly because I have never played it or seen it played – except in glimpses of several thousand Saturday replays before switching the television off. I strongly suspect that I could easily become a football fan; that the excitement of the crowd would get to me and that I would cheer along with the best of them.

My only objection to football is the uncivilized manner of watching it. My fourpenny seat in the gallery at Sadler's Wells did allow me an uninterrupted view of proceedings with reasonable elbow room and company which was attentive both of the performance and of my rights to view it and pass comment. I have done my share of cheering and booing like any football fan, but I have done it in comfort and I propose to continue to do so.

As for the 'art' of playing football, it is a skill as much as ballet dancing is a skill, but there the resemblance ends. One is a skill used in competition, and rough competition it often is. I have no wish to become embroiled in the question of the showmanship of the blood-letting every Saturday afternoon, but however carefully choreographed it may be in advance, it is an instant happening which will never occur again in exactly that configuration. A ballet is a *planned* happening, carefully thought out and backed by many different talents. The ability of a dancer to jump as high as a footballer is but a small ingredient of the whole, and by the time you add up the components of football and ballet you will find the scales heavily weighted in favour of the latter.

If it were possible to choreograph an exciting football game and to restage it night after night, year after year, with different players for the same audience, then, and only then, would the sport have common ground with the art under discussion. Comparing football with ballet is good publicity and, like all good publicity, useful only to promote the sport, or the art. It is a dead-end exercise in every other way.

My statement that the Sun Aria has nothing to do with opera is more controversial, and that is why I have made it. (Be outrageous, make people furious, but make them think!) Is it truly so outrageous? It is not, you know. Admittedly, the Sun Aria (God bless it, may it continue for ever) is a competition in which young singers offer extracts from opera to prove their ability as singers, or potential singers. The Sun Aria, and the many other aria competitions in Australia, are a most valuable training ground for opera and their record of winners who make the grade in this field is indeed impressive. But we now come back to the football–ballet parallel. Footballers and ballet dancers both leap athletically and have highly trained bodies, yet no footballer will become a ballet dancer without further training and the same applies in reverse. The leap of the footballer can be paralleled by the aria of the singer.

The ability to sing an aria does not make a singer; that in itself is a truism. More to the point, a singer does not make an opera. Even if your Sun Aria winner happens to develop into a great star after learning not only singing, but musicianship, acting, mime, movement, fencing, dancing, make-up (and all the other things which distinguish an opera singer from a concert singer who stands stiffly before the Sun Aria judges) – unless that singer is surrounded by the planned happening of an opera performance, his or her contribution is worthless. Where is the connection between the recitation with piano of a five minute piece of music of operatic origin and the complex entity which represents the world's most expensive art form? It is a feeble link indeed.

From the practical, no matter how outrageous, to the impractical: the habits of Australian audiences. And let me hasten to say that we are very far from unique in our behaviour patterns. The trouble is that in a society starved (through no fault of its own) since it began of things which were daily fare in Europe, there was little scope for developing the kind of audiences that have kept opera and ballet alive in other countries.

When I sarcastically speak of 'our patriotic duty to storm the Gallipoli of culture' I do mean exactly what the phrase implies: anybody who believes that being cultured means 'being seen' at the ballet or the opera is doomed. He or she will never gain pleasure from the medium because the real purpose of the exercise is not to be seen but to see and, since it is a full-time job being seen at the opera, there is little time left to get anything out of the spectacle on stage. Until the early part of this century they kept the lights on in European theatres, so that those who came to be seen could be seen. Boxes in theatres were not designed for a good view of the stage, but for a good view of the other boxes. (I told you we were not unique in this field; in fact, we were, and are, as much amateurs in the field of social graces as in the more serious one of appreciating the art of our choice.)

If European audiences, even in living memory, even today up to a point, can beat our phony culture vultures at their own game, they also beat us in Elysian fields. While the ancestors of those bores, stared, and were stared at, night after night, performances continued on stage and some members of the audiences did not ignore everything presented to them. Slowly the focus of attention swung from the auditorium to the stage. The point was reached when even the overture, the intermezzo and the preludes to acts, which had been invented as a kind of musical warning bell while people cast their final pieces of gossip across to their friends and enemies, began to be a part of the enjoyable whole.

Nobody knows exactly who started to turn the lights out during performances, (some say it was Mahler, others Toscanini) but it was the one step which made it almost impossible to ignore the happenings on the stage. And what was actually taking place up there in those days has, both in opera and in ballet, come down to us in a recognizable form. I don't think anybody will deny that an audience exposed regularly to *Giselle* or *The Marriage of Figaro* will in the end find enjoyment in the quality of the performance.

Thus were born the audiences who kept the arts alive overseas, but we in Australia were denied this privilege. When we were charged with aesthetic indifference, we could, until recently, cry poverty with justification. Elsewhere in this book I shall demonstrate that what was seen here in the early history of Australia was not so far removed from what was seen in Europe. The point is that it was not seen here often enough to leave a lasting impact and the accursed villains of cost and inflation ultimately caused the local article to fail to keep up with the more sophisticated presentations of Europe and America. It is the middle twentieth century which lies at the root of our trouble, not the much extolled 'good old days', which were no better in Europe than they were here. Artistically they were lousy by modern standards. Let us not forget that to start with.

What it was that audiences did or did not see in Australia is the subject of this book and I make no claim that it is, or attempts to be, a definitive history of either art in this country: too much mitigates against it. Many years will pass before anybody will be in a position to have access to sufficient facts to be more authoritative than I can be. The hurdles to be overcome are considerable.

I once complained, in the course of a broadcast, about the immense amount of historical material on music in Australia which lies in dusty unopened boxes in libraries and museums. I would have thought that calling attention to the fact that it is impossible to write with accuracy about our own history was a worthwhile thing. All I got for my trouble was a crank letter accusing me of being unjust to the Victorian Keeper of Public Records. (I did not even know of that gentleman's existence.) What I do know is that immense collections of historical memorabilia have been donated to public bodies in the capital cities, including Canberra, and that shortages of staff prevent the indexation of material appertaining to the arts, which are considered of low priority. What infuriates me is that, until such time as these monumental collections are indexed, they may not be touched by people engaged on major, or even minor research projects, such as this one. It is not surprising under these circumstances, that no comprehensive histories of the arts in Australia exist. What has been written – including these pages – is based on information obtained often at third and fourth hand, often encased in the glove of ignorance. Thus the early history of opera and ballet in Australia will continue to be reported complete with all the mistakes which carry over from work to work. I have done my best to eliminate inconsistencies. Where two or more different interpretations or dates exist I have often left them out.

Perhaps this is a plea for tolerance. If so, so be it. For every verified fact or verifiable opinion in these pages there must be three which have been left out deliberately and three more which may have been verified incorrectly. I only hope that anybody who uses this volume as a source of reference in years to come checks my facts before taking them as gospel. Don't trust the printed word in book or journal form when it comes to the arts in Australia!

opera

How Did It All Begin?

In view of the fact that nobody has been able to establish precisely when opera as an art form began, nobody should complain because there is dispute as to when it first appeared in Australia.

People argue whether, in ancient Greece, Aeschylus and Sophocles wrote the words to music dramas that can be described as operas. Or they speculate as to which of the three Orpheus operas (Peri's, Monteverdi's or Gluck's) was the beginning of the art as we know it today. Immense volumes of musicological speculation have been written on the subject and it is one of the more pleasant aspects of this volume that neither writer nor reader has to wade through even a summary of all the alternatives.

Finding out what happened during the last 150 years in Australia should not present too great a problem then. Or should it? It should be very simple to marshall all the basic facts which can be established about the presentation of opera in this country and to announce with some confidence from these facts that Australia more than held its own during the last hundred years at least. Let me start by trying this exercise in a small way – before demolishing my own argument.

1834: the first opera staged in Australia, *Clari, or The Maid of Milan,* by Sir Henry Bishop, performed in Sydney and featuring Eliza Winstanley, Australia's first star of opera, the first to go overseas and to achieve fame as an expatriate. (Who says Melba was the first?)

1842: The Carandinis bring opera to Hobart.

1847: The first opera actually written in Australia produced in Sydney; Isaac Nathan's *Don John of Austria.*

1861: William Saurin Lyster brought the first visiting opera company to Australia, coincidentally in the same year that saw the first visiting cricket team.

1865: Lyster's repertoire had grown to twenty operas, including *Don Giovanni, The Barber of Seville, The Marriage of Figaro, Faust* (only two years after its London premiere!), *Lucia di Lammermoor,* William Vincent Wallace's *Maritana* and two major works by Meyerbeer, *Les Huguenots* and *Le Prophete.*

It would not be too hard to go on from there, but I see little point in building a house of cards which I propose to demolish myself. A myth is as good as a mile when it comes to Australian operatic history and, until such time as somebody sits down and writes an authoritative work on the subject, unsupported statements in innumerable publications by authors even less qualified than I will continue to be treated as fact. And little wonder, when there is no central source to which one can turn for verification.

Enthusiasts have always been better at keeping records than the people actually engaged in the arts and Australia is no exception to this practice. Programmes and playbills are notoriously inaccurate in their claims; no manager in his right mind will publish bad write-ups, nor will he stress cuts and interpolations, let alone falsification and open fraud in presentation. So, let me correct the 'facts' I presented above.

1834: a work advertised as the celebrated opera of *Clari, or the Maid of Milan* was indeed performed at the 'New Theatre Royal' in Sydney on Friday, 31 October 1834. There is some dispute as to whether *Clari* was an opera at all; Sir Henry Bishop had a nasty habit of putting other people's music into vaudevilles or operas of his own. I do not suggest that *Clari* belonged to the class of Bishop's *The Libertine* (adapted from *Don Giovanni*), *Artaxerxes* ('curtailed' from Arne, whatever that means) or *The Night Before the Wedding* ('from' Boieldieu). I do suggest that *Clari* belonged to those of his many works which were dramatic recitatives with interpolated songs, either serious or comic, works like *Teasing Made Easy, Exit by Mistake* or *Who Wants a Wife?*

If *Clari* was a work of this type, the pattern of presentations by its impresario, publican Barnett Levey, remains unbroken. Had he not been staging, with considerable success, various imported burlesques by less famous authors and composers than Bishop? Had he not, in fact, built his Theatre Royal and then New Theatre Royal on concerts of popular music, rather than fully staged performances? A quick look at Levey's background makes the staging of any kind of serious work that could be called an opera most unlikely.

Barnett Levey ought to be a lot more famous than he is, since he was an early cousin of another upsidedown planner, Joern Utzon. A shopkeeper and auctioneer by profession, he decided to go into the theatre business and formed a company with 200 shareholders on 19 November 1827. Newspaper reports give a fascinating glimpse of what then happened. By January 1828, we are told, 'canvas has been procured for the scenes and an amateur has been employed painting them'. Later that year the scenery has been made and actors have been employed and 'Mr Levey is now looking for plays'! It takes a genius to make scenery and employ actors before knowing what the play is going to be or when the theatre will open.

A year later (no performances yet!) Levey gets a licence to open his theatre, which apparently still does not exist! There follow eighteen months of concerts given in the saloon of the Royal Hotel, which was the building on which Levey had actually been engaged, not a theatre at all. After the said eighteen months, in December 1830, Levey goes bankrupt and the hotel (not theatre) is sold at a heavy loss.

An apparently prosperous interlude as a jeweller and watchmaker ensues until 24 August 1832 when Levey obtains another licence to open a theatre. Only then, on Boxing Day 1832, the first Theatre Royal of Sydney actually opened, the attractions being *Black-eyed Susan* and *Monsieur Tonton*. The theatre appears to have been a temporary annexe to the Royal Hotel and another year was to pass before Levey converted an old store behind his hotel into the New Theatre Royal.

What was it that Levey staged in his new theatre? The titles mean little to us today, but we do know that actors and actresses had to be able to sing and dance. Buckingham, Levey's resident comedian, made history within months of the opening by striking for more pay. Levey actually paid up and was severely chastised by the editor of the *Sydney Gazette* for giving in!

More to the point, Levey's first leading lady, Mrs Taylor, 'possessed a sweet voice which enabled the management to stage such operas as *Don Giovanni*'!

Behold! What have we here? A performance of *Don Giovanni* in 1834? Our poor historians do seem to have a strange set of values. It seems more than strange to bother with Bishop's *Clari* when Mozart's masterpiece was to hand. It is not recorded whether any of Mozart's music was actually used on this occasion, but the presentation was actually en-

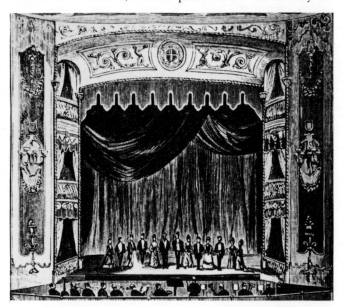

titled *Giovanni in London,* and nobody knows precisely what this 'operatic extravaganza' contained.

Clari however, was the vehicle which launched 'Home Sweet Home' on the world and *Clari* had an Australian leading lady. English-born Eliza Winstanley was all of fifteen years old and appeared more than once in the course of the evening's entertainment. One work was not enough to attract the public and there was a lengthy playbill ending with the classic line: 'The evening to conclude with *AGNES, OR THE BLEEDING NUN* – MISS WINSTANLEY'.

Our first overseas 'star', Miss Winstanley, did actually go

Opera without music? A Sydney paper reported that on 31 October 1834 the first opera produced in Australia, Sir Henry Bishop's *Clari*, was staged 'without any music'! A year earlier Sydney's New Theatre Royal offered entertainment with an orchestra when it opened. Surely they didn't cut *Home, Sweet Home* and twenty-one other numbers from the advertised 'celebrated opera' by Bishop.

overseas, but it is significant that she became famous (well, let us say, known) as an actress and writer in England. Are we still to believe that she made her start in opera as a singer?

Researching Australian operatic history is like reading a detective story. There are plenty of clues, but a much greater number of red herrings. I cannot prove that *Clari* was the first *opera* to be presented in Australia or even that Eliza Winstanley was its first *prima donna*.

Though *Clari* contained no less than twenty-two musical numbers, there is a reference in the *Sydney Herald* of 3 November 1834 which states: 'On Friday evening was produced the dramatic opera (without any music) of *Clari* . . .' If all those musical items were cut, how much sense would the remaining spoken lines have made? The whole work was built by Bishop around 'Home Sweet Home', which appeared throughout in many different guises. Without it the whole *raison d'être* for the piece disappeared.

As for young Eliza, we could even have here a case of mistaken identity! It was customary to refer to artists of all kinds as Mr or Mrs or Miss So-and-so and if the Miss Winstanley who was the *Bleeding Nun* was indeed Eliza, it does not necessarily follow that the Miss Winstanley who played *Clari* was the same person. *The Australian* of 4 November 1834 reported (about the same performance): 'Anne Winstanley sang *Kate Kearney* very prettily'.

Who was Anne Winstanley? Presumably Eliza's sister, though we cannot ignore the possibility that the reporter could have got the name wrong. Yet if Anne (or Eliza) actually sang an Irish song at the New Theatre Royal that night, is it credible that *Clari* would have been performed without 'Home Sweet Home'? It does not seem very likely, specially since *Clari* (complete with music) became a regular item on Australian playbills in the years that followed.

The question still remains: who was the Miss Winstanley who sang extensively in concerts and oratorios between 1834 and 1846 when Eliza (not Anne) set sail for England?

The whole thing is an area of speculation awaiting a musical Sherlock Holmes. Let me summarize the facts as I interpret them: (a) A semi-opera called *Clari* by Bishop was performed in 1834 in Sydney; (b) The evening (though not necessarily *Clari*) did include some music; (c) Two Misses Winstanley probably appeared and, if there were indeed two, both were sopranos, but only Eliza went on to achieve international fame – as a Shakespearean actress and an authoress.

On to 1842 and the Carandinis in Hobart. It takes a little digging, but some of the facts can be unearthed without too much trouble and some of the mystery of *Clari* and Eliza Winstanley also becomes less mysterious in the light of the happenings in Hobart.

In the first place it was not the Carandinis who came to Hobart, but Mrs Michael Clarke and an ensemble of artists who, admittedly, did bring opera to Hobart. But they also brought Shakespeare and ballet to Tasmania, they sang, acted, danced and even painted their own scenery, and they continued to do so for nearly four years, playing in a theatre built in 1837 which still exists today, now called the Theatre Royal.

Good luck to the admirable people who brought culture to our colonial ancestors, but are we really to believe that their performances of Weber's *Der Freischütz,* Bellini's *La Sonnambula* or Auber's *Fra Diavolo* were what we would consider performances of opera today? I doubt it.

The stars of Mrs Clarke's troupe were *prima donna* Theodosia Yates Stirling and 'a successful professional dancer', one Gerome Carandini, said to have been the 10th Marquis of Saranzo or Sargano. (I don't propose to investigate the obscure Italian ancestry of the gentleman; his Australian life is far more interesting. See also the ballet section of this book.) Theodosia was more than a singer, she was a talented musician who had been chorus mistress at Drury Lane in London in her youth. She was to become the mother of Nellie Stewart, whose talents prior to becoming the most famous Australian to shine in comedy until well into the twentieth century included appearances in grand opera, as well as Gilbert and Sullivan, over many years. In 1888 Nellie Stewart sang Marguerite in *Faust* for twenty-four consecutive performances! No wonder she became a comedienne, after inevitably losing her singing voice.

Nellie's mother was partnered by the handsome Italian count, Carandini. Dancer Carandini made his debut in Hobart as a singer! A critic describes him as a counter tenor, though there is some doubt whether the term then meant what it means today. However, vocal achievements in Mrs Clarke's company may even have included a counter tenor, as we understand the term, singing Weber or Bellini. In due course Carandini married seventeen year old Mary Burgess, a contralto, who promptly became a professional singer under the title of Maria Carandini. Her place in later Australian history is secure, (see below) but her initial efforts in Hobart are of curiosity rather than musical value; Maria (not her husband) sang the *tenor* leads in most of the operas presented there!

It must be clear that the twice-weekly performances presented by Mrs Clarke in Hobart in the 1840s bore little resemblance to the titles we find in history books. It is not just that Theodosia Yates Stirling sang Lucy in *Lucia di Lammermoor* (vocal and orchestral parts scored by herself from memory!) one night and played Lady Macbeth in Shakespeare's tragedy the next, but opera and ballet and drama were mixed in the one evening more often than not. To make the picture even more ludicrous to us, the orchestra consisted of the local brass band which would only play on the stage itself, where it could be seen.

Maria Carandini Mary Burgess was all of seventeen years old when she married the glamorous Italian Count Gerome Carandini in Hobart in 1842. As Maria Carandini she sang not only contralto roles in opera, but most of the tenor leads as well. She had a long career as a singer in Australia, but her role as an impresario left a more lasting mark. Like her contemporaries in the nineteenth century, she travelled overseas to recruit her leading singers, but she was at least Australian herself.

We thus have a picture of Boieldieu's *Jean de Paris,* the first proper opera to be presented in Australia, with a woman playing the title role, a male dancer in a singing role, scenery painted by the artists themselves and the band on stage behind the singers. So much for 'The Carandinis bring opera to Hobart'.

1847: the first Australian opera, or rather, the first opera written in Australia, Isaac Nathan's *Don John of Austria.* (The first opera by someone *born* in Australia was probably Stephen Hale Marsh's *The Gentleman in Black,* first performed in 1861, but written in 1847 or 1848. It owed more than a little to Nathan's *Don John*). Isaac Nathan was an ancestor of one of Australia's more illustrious modern musicians, Charles Mackerras. As a result we know a lot more about him than about any of his contemporaries. Equally, we know more about Nathan's music, because Mackerras, not unnaturally, has taken the trouble to unearth some of his ancestor's works. The most accessible item is the overture to *Don John of Austria.* Mackerras orchestrated the only existing score (for piano) and it has been recorded. Enjoyable as a period piece, it is ephemeral at best and it is not surprising that Nathan's descendant did not persevere with his task. Thus the first opera written in Australia (a historic milestone, if a small one) was no better and no more successful

than any of those that have followed since.

Nathan published his own musical magazine, *The Southern Euphrosyne,* and consequently was his own best publicist. We have no reason to doubt Nathan's claim that it was 'the first opera written, composed and produced in Australia'. We are less likely to find in any history book the few critiques with which the work was honoured. Not all were as damning as that of the *Port Phillip Patriot and Melbourne Advertiser,* whose correspondent wrote that it was 'the most pointless, passionless, rechauffe, unartistic production that has ever emanated from any brain'. R.I.P., *Don John!*

As for the Irishman, William Saurin Lyster and his magnificent nineteen years of presenting opera in Australia, it is no discredit to his name to point out that a large part of his extended repertoire was performed when on tour in halls without stages, scenery and sometimes even costumes. Verdi, Wagner and Meyerbeer were offered in this manner in places as far apart as Brisbane and Warrnambool. Let us praise this pioneer of opera on what must have been a grand scale for Australia in the 1860s and 1870s, but let us not delude ourselves that Lyster's *Lohengrin* or *Huguenots* were performances such as the names imply today. Perhaps Lyster never went as far as the Carandinis, who in 1850 offered 'grand opera' performed on a stage made up of billiard tables pushed together, but, curiously enough, the claim that his productions were 'on a scale which could not be bettered outside the great musical centres of the Old World' was not as far off the mark as the foregoing may imply. Still, it would have been more correct to say that things were as bad overseas as they were in Australia in Lyster's time.

There are no detailed histories of opera in nineteenth century Australia, but we do know that some of the stranger happenings were only in line with things as they were in even the best opera houses overseas and I speak now of Europe and America, not Australia. The practice of altering scores, of cutting whole acts, even of adding music from other works had not died out at that time. The haphazardness of operatic life in the 1860s, the years in which Lyster (and with him opera) began in this country, can be read in the memoirs of Colonel J. H. Mapleson, whose career as an impresario covered London and most of the United States from 1858 to 1888.

Mapleson employed the best singers of his time, not casually picked up locals. His memoirs treat as normal what is to us extraordinary and they give a very vivid picture of what was involved in presenting opera to the most discerning public of that time. (Berlioz' memoirs give an equally vivid picture of opera in Paris, but I choose Mapleson because his time coincided exactly with the arrival of Lyster.) Singers like Patti, Jenny Lind, Ilma de Murska, Tietjens, Trebelli, Giuglini, Nordica, Mario, Nilsson (Christine, not Birgit) and Albani sang for Mapleson. They were the Melbas and Carusos of their time. We can thus take it that his opera company was a fair example of what opera in London was like in 1861.

Mapleson's way of dealing with crises was realistic, to say the least. Barnett Levey was faced with one striking comedian and gave in. Mapleson was faced with a striking chorus in a grand opera like Meyerbeer's *Huguenots* and simply proceeded without the chorus! Indisposition hardly fazed Mapleson. When Azucena in *Trovatore* contracted influenza, he managed to get through a whole performance without the substitute, who happened to be a soprano, singing at all. The contralto's two big scenes were omitted entirely and during 'Home to Our Mountains' Azucena conveniently remained asleep, leaving Manrico to sing alone!

On another occasion the tenor, Giuglini, decided not to sing and Mapleson went off by hansom cab to cancel the performance. In the Haymarket his horse knocked down a gentleman, who turned out to be an English tenor, one Walter Bolton. Without hesitation Mapleson asked if he could sing the part of Lionel in *Martha*, which Giuglini was scheduled to sing that night. Bolton replied that he knew the part not, but had sung the aria 'M'appari' in concert at times, in English. Mapleson assembled Tietjens and Trebelli, the co-stars, and arranged for Bolton to go through

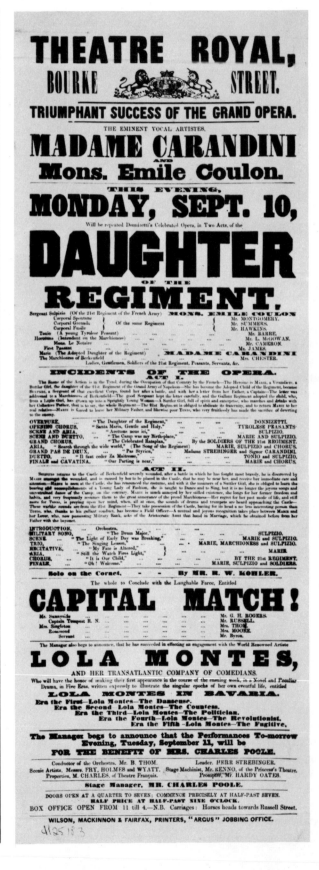

A typical triple bill of the time, featuring an opera (*Norma*, starring the famous Catherine Hayes), a ballet (starring Thérèse Strebinger and Count Carandini) and the usual farce (*My Young Wife! and Old Umbrella* by an uncredited author, though room was found to bill others, including the machinist and the prompter).

When possible, as in the case of *The Bohemian Girl*, the obligatory ballet was performed as part of the opera of the evening. The again uncredited farce in this case (*A.S.S.*) is to be followed by a classic in the next programme. *The Rivals* by Sheridan (uncredited) ranked no higher than *A.S.S.* — as a support for an opera!

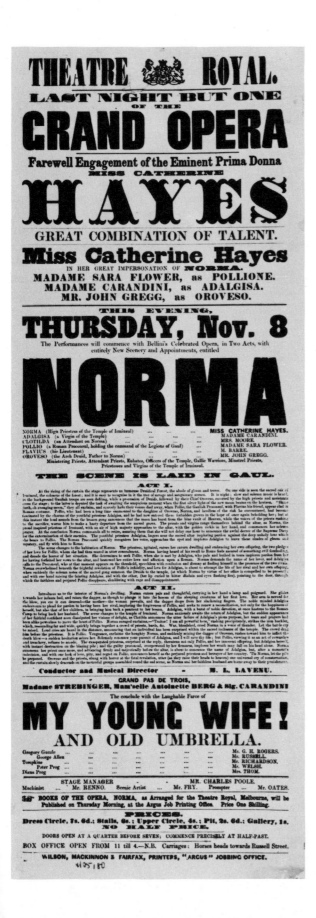

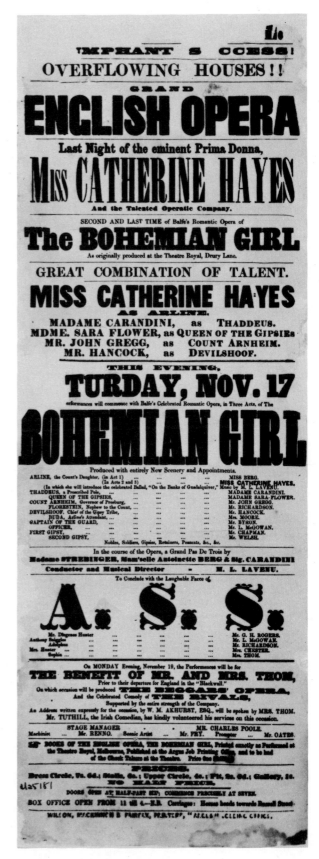

A prima donna of colonial Australia Catherine Hayes, also known as 'The Rose of Erin', appeared extensively throughout Australia in the 1850s *before* bringing opera in costume to San Francisco! (Australia was artistically not as wild as the Wild West.) Sydney publishers Woolcott & Clarke printed the *La Hayes Quadrille* with engravings of her in three favourite roles.

The importance of being Lohengrin A page (*right*) from an 1877 edition of *Australasian Sketches*, which illustrates the news of the day. *Lohengrin* holds the centre of the page and *Aida* the bottom right hand corner, but they have to share their glory with the Poultry Show, H.M.S. *Cerberus* and a revival meeting!

LA HAYES' QUADRILLE.

the motions of Lionel without doing any singing – except for the famous aria. And so the 1862 performance of *Martha* went on that night, the tenor only opening his mouth to sing one aria in Danny Kaye-style Italian, mainly by repeating the word 'M'appari' as often as necessary. The aria was encored twice and the London Press the next morning was unanimous in their praise of the new tenor star!

Singers who had no idea of music or text, who sang parrot fashion, abounded. The tenor Giuseppe Fancelli retired after a long career to undertake an interesting hobby: to find out what the parts he had been singing were all about! 'In *Medea*', he remarked, 'I have played Jason; but what has he to do with *Medea*? Am I her father, her brother, her lover or what?' That Jason was Medea's husband seems not to have occurred to the man who portrayed the part for so many years.

It was, of course, still opera of the singer, by the singer and for the singer. Adelina Patti had the far from abnormal clause in her contract that she was not required to attend rehearsals! So much for London opera in the 1860s.

Let us be clear about this: though Lyster and his successors may have presented a travesty of opera as we understand it, they did no more than follow in the footsteps of their colleagues overseas. They were impresarios in the true sense of the word, people who were out to make money from the presentation of opera and, though they all sooner or later went close to or passed the point of bankruptcy, hope sprang eternal. In the process they brought a great deal of enjoyment to the colonies, for their public was not familiar with the older operas, let alone the novelties of the day.

It is hard for us to comprehend the excitement the production of a new opera created in those days, for in recent times composers have not come up with modern *Fausts* or *Lohengrins,* operas which Lyster staged as rapidly as they came out in Europe.

While history has always concentrated on singers, opera as a medium also flourished without stars in every country, more so in the nineteenth century than in the twentieth, though there are signs of a return to the old ways now. Going to see a new drama, with or without music, was a big event and we must remember that opera in Australia began at a time when the 'grand' in grand opera really was grand. We laugh today at the ridiculous plots of Verdi's *Trovatore* or *Ernani,* let alone the English ballad operas like Wallace's *Maritana* (which was *not* written in Australia) or Meyerbeer's *Les Huguenots.* Our ancestors did not; they had never heard the now immortal lines 'Never darken my doorstep again' or 'Dead, and never called me mother' and when they did, they were enthralled, (all the more so when the words were sung). And when Australians began to write their own operas, their plots were in line with what the public expected. Nathan's *Don John of Austria* was no worse than many a Verdi libretto; come to think of it, it includes a stack of characters from *Don Carlos* and *Ernani.*

Like Schiller's play, on which Verdi's opera *Don Carlos* is based, *Don John* has some foundation in historical fact. Nathan's librettist, Jacob Montefiore, drew on several previous dramatizations of sixteenth century Spanish history including Victor Hugo's *Hernani* to fabricate the plot which, had it been written well and composed by a master, should have had a success similar to the French or Italian operas of that time. It is far from easy to condense, but runs something like this: Don John is the illegitimate son of Charles V and thus the half-brother of Philip II of Spain, only he doesn't know this; he is being raised by Don Quixada (not Quixote) who wants him to enter the Church. John, however, is in love with a Jewess named Agnes (not the Bleeding Nun) who is unfortunately, also loved by King Philip. When the latter calls on her and finds John in her company, he banishes him to a monastery, the same monastery to which Charles V has retired after giving up his throne to Philip. (Remember the monk in Verdi's *Don Carlos?*) Charles, of course, is all for John and gives him his sword. In the meantime Philip, having been spurned by Agnes, sends her off to the Inquisition and confronts John, who draws Charles' sword and thus reveals his real identity. There is a big brotherly recognition scene, all is forgiven and exit poor Agnes into exile, where she is safe from both her suitors, or they from her. Finis. *Don John of Austria's* plot is an improvement on *Ernani,* though its libretto is a mess. Anyway, Isaac Nathan was not a Verdi, more's the pity for Australia.

Mc Varley

Cerberus at Practice

The late T. Wray

Sept. 2nd

Revival Meeting

Lohengrin

Virginius

Masonic Ball

The parting Kick

THE new Helmet

Return Ball

Royal

Poultry Show

Dynamite Experiments

Scene from Aida

9

I have spent some time in rubbishing early Australian performances of opera in an attempt to shock the reader into reassessing history. The tendency to praise the local article excessively and to gloss over failings is a common trait in all small communities. It is easy enough to admit errors in areas in which we excel. Australians can afford to be generous when dealing with cricket, pop music or beer-drinking, but the moment you enter the field of the arts the defences go up. Australia has left no lasting mark yet on the world of opera, music or other performing arts. Only self-delusion tells us otherwise.

The phenomenon of Melba was the stepping stone to the illusion that the numerous Australian singers who have gone overseas make this an operatic country. The facts were quite otherwise. During the nineteenth century opera was treated here, as it was in Europe, as a popular entertainment. The arias of Verdi and Rossini were the pop songs of their day here as elsewhere and the plots of the operas, as much as the music, were the secret of their success. If the staging was somewhat more primitive than overseas, the audiences were also less discerning.

Australia fell behind when musical and artistic standards everywhere started to rise. The public in Europe and America were beginning to see virtues in opera other than novelty and demanded ever greater musical and dramatic perfection. The Australian public was trained to applaud singing alone until long after the age of the producer had dawned. Local military bands provided the music for decades after 'proper' operatic performances became the norm. Singers capable of reading music were the exception, not the rule. Producers did not exist. Sets of any kind of unity were unknown; one garden looked like any other and few managements saw anything abnormal in presenting the Scotland of *Lucia di Lammermoor* with Greek columns as a background. There were no royalties to pay and pirated editions which had been mutilated by previous users were mutilated even further to suit local conditions.

The explanation for this backwardness lies only partly in the handicap of distance. The great majority of our critics to this day are simple reporters, only a few of whom, over the years, have acquired some knowledge of their subject. Most are here today and gone tomorrow, leaving their readers none the wiser. As for reporters, the people who are supposed to report what is new in the world, they aim at the lowest common denominator which, in the case of the arts, is abysmal indeed.

Nowadays this matters not too much, since anyone seriously interested in any particular subject has access to specialized publications or, in the case of opera, direct contact via films, television and the Australian Opera, which has now achieved a standard equal to that of some of the best companies overseas.

At the beginning of this century the situation was different. News from overseas was presented exclusively in the daily press which was interested in only one thing: the glorification of Australia. (Let us not forget that this was the time of the great growth of nationalism throughout the world and news everywhere was aimed at putting the home-grown article first.) In operatic terms this meant the glorification of the native-born singers who went overseas, and a totally false picture was created by the endless flow of new 'Melbas' and reports of their successes.

The time was to come (during the last twenty years) when Australian singers would flood the market, in England at least, and quite a number would make it into the big time. All credit to them, though even now the percentage who are as good as we are told they are by the Press is severely limited.

As recently as 1967 a major book was published about Australian singers which devoted thousands of words to the names that fled across the pages of our newspapers for the first fifty years of this century. Let us be realistic: apart from Joan Sutherland, Australia has not had a singer in the Melba class since its foundation. Among the countless 'stars' between Melba and Sutherland there were, at the most, two or possibly three who can be considered major artists, though none had the box office appeal of their greatest contemporaries.

(I do not include Frances Alda. New Zealand born, and trained by Marchesi in Paris from the age of nineteen, her years in Melbourne as a child hardly qualify her to be classed as an Australian singer.)

I am not speaking of a critical assessment of their art, but purely of their box office appeal, and only Marjorie Lawrence can be said to have had that in any degree. I leave the choice of the other two to the reader, but Florence Austral, to give the most glaring example, was not among them. Austral may have been a great singer, but her career never really got off the ground — and it is no good saying that this was because she contracted multiple sclerosis: 'excuses' don't wash when you are dealing with historical fact. Austral sang with the British National Opera, a company which rates abysmally low in historical terms. She appeared occasionally at Covent Garden and she sang but once with the Berlin State Opera. No matter what critical acclaim was hers at the time, no matter how great the qualities that are apparent from her recordings, the fact remains that in her twenty years abroad her name did not rate among the stars of the time, nor did her records ever sell to any extent in England, let alone on the continent. Austral's fame, if not posthumous, came only after her retirement.

Not that this made Austral any the less newsworthy in Australia. She and Evelyn Scotney, Amy Castles, Gertrude Johnson and dozens of others were never far from the head-

The star who was a star Toti dal Monte, one of the most famous non-Australian singers to visit this country to date as part of a full opera company. Dal Monte ranked among the top stars of the world, was a popular idol and captivated audiences here in 1924 and 1928, specially when she decided to marry her leading man, Enzo de Muro Lomante, in Australia.

The star who wasn't a star Lina Scavizzi, brought to Australia twice by Melba and Williamson's to star as Tosca (*below*) and in other roles. The Australian public adored her, but she never amounted to anything overseas and her name can not be found today in any serious encyclopedia of singers or opera.

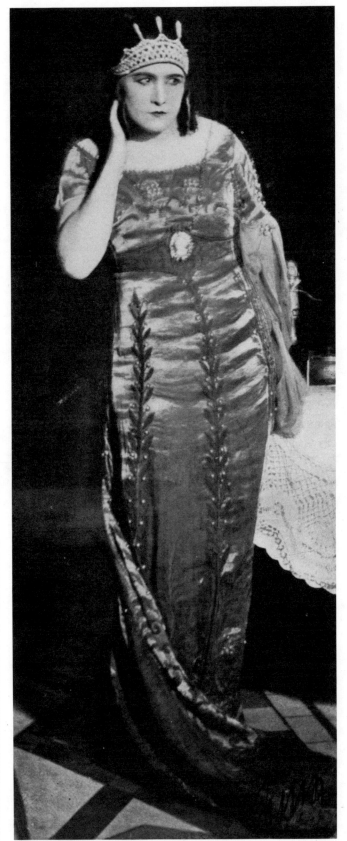

lines. Every young singer leaving for England had her (rarely his) first appearances plastered across the front pages, not just in local papers, but in the national Press. The naivety of the Press was (and still is) incredible. A concert at the Walthamstow Town Hall rated the same space as an appearance at the Albert Hall. The immense local fame of a singer like Amy Castles made news of her every appearance overseas, but it is hard or impossible to find any reference to her today. In spite of claims that she sang leading roles for two years at the Vienna State Opera, she does not rate a mention in Marcel Prawy's comprehensive book about that theatre.

If I seem to be destructive again, I beg the reader's indulgence. I seek to establish the reasons behind the decline of opera in Australia, or at least its failure to improve along with overseas trends. The constant plugging of singing as the only component worthy of mention did the art untold harm. Not only was an illusion of unrealistic vocal standards created, but any reference to musical, dramatic or scenic standards was not considered newsworthy. If Amy Castles was good enough for Vienna, then Amy Castles was good enough to star in opera at home. Nobody wishes to deny this. But if Amy Castles sang *Madame Butterfly* as well in Melbourne as she did in Vienna (if she did indeed sing it

The prima donna who sued Rina Malatrasi, one of the most popular sopranos of the post-war J. C. Williamson Italian Opera Seasons, sued a Melbourne critic for adversely criticizing her performance as Madame Butterfly. Unfortunately Malatrasi's looks were better than her voice, for she failed to leave any mark internationally.

there) her conductor was Slapoffski and not Weingartner and the production facilities and staff of the Vienna State Opera were not those available at the Princess Theatre.

The public had every right to believe that the kind of opera presented in Australia from 1900 to 1950 was first class. Certainly the critics gave it no cause to believe otherwise and, lacking the ability to make comparisons, even singing standards of decidedly inferior quality were accepted. Local singers had to be praised, since they so obviously were a great success overseas, and the snob value of Italian imports seems to have played havoc with artistic values. When Melba brought Toti dal Monte to this country in 1928, the tiny singer was naturally accepted readily. Other sopranos in the same season included the great Giannina Arangi-Lombardi and Hina Spani. Yet the success of the season – for reasons which remain a mystery – was the inferior Lina Scavizzi and to this day I am asked for her recordings. Many years ago I did actually hear one of these. History was right and we were wrong. It is not that dal Monte, Arangi-Lombardi

and Spani were better than Scavizzi, but that the public and the critics could not correctly assess her qualities in line with what was then, and is now, accepted overseas.

In more recent years there was another parallel in the unaccountable popularity of Rina Malatrasi. Why she should have outpolled Gabriella Tucci in 1955 is a mystery which will remain buried in history; at no time did Malatrasi leave any impression on the world operatic scene.

Obviously Australian audiences remained unsophisticated to a degree which is not easy to understand. Some of the greatest singers of the century had been heard in this country, yet it was only the arrival of long-playing records which brought a reaction and set new standards which have, perhaps, gone a little too far the other way. Performances like those heard on records are rarely, if ever, heard at La Scala or the Metropolitan and the fact that our singers today do not measure up to those standards does not mean that they are not the equals of the great majority of artists singing in Europe.

The prima donna who didn't sue Gabriella Tucci outshone Rina Malatrasi during Williamson's 1955 International Grand Opera Season and went on to become a major artist in the world's best opera houses and also record a number of complete opera sets. She is seen here as Violetta in Verdi's *La Traviata* with Danilo Vega.

A Hundred Years of Imported Opera

2

For almost exactly one hundred years, roughly from 1850 to 1950, Australia relied almost totally on imported opera companies, though some of them remained for so long in the country that their personnel quite literally became natives. From the first, the glamour of 'imported stars' carried all before it and, if the number of singers actually imported was often small indeed, none of the companies of any permanence could have come into existence or continued to operate without imported managers and artists.

The very first performances of opera in Australia were admittedly staged by Mrs Clarke, who may well have been Australian-born, though it seems unlikely. But she engaged her artists in England and her leading man was the Italian, Count Carandini. He in turn married a Tasmanian girl, Mary Burgess, who, as Maria Carandini, became a singer and, as Madame Carandini, an impresario. Two Australian ladies started opera in this country in the 1840s, just as two others, Gertrude Johnson and Clarice Lorenz, were to do one hundred years later. The point is that the latter could and did draw solely on local talent, while the former could and did not. Madame Carandini stayed around for many decades, the grand dame of Australian theatre, but her activities also took her overseas and her singers there, as here, were mostly English, Irish or American. It would be pointless to list the huge number of 'stars' of those days here; their names mean nothing to us. But an Irishwoman, Catherine Hayes, was Australia's first great opera star and an Irishman, William Saurin Lyster, was the first impresario to bring some rough equivalent of European opera into existence here.

Catherine Hayes was known as 'The Swan of Erin' and her career in America prior to her tours of Australia throws an interesting light on comparative standards in opera in both countries during the 1850s. Hayes arrived in San Francisco in 1852 and was the first singer there to sing arias during concerts in costume! This was more than a decade after the Carandinis had begun regular performances of opera, however primitive, in Hobart and five years after Nathan wrote the first Australian opera. (San Francisco's first full opera was not staged until 1854 and it starred Catherine Hayes after her return from her first Australian concert tour. The opera was *Norma*.)

Lyster brought his first company here from America and his leading stars were the American tenor Henry Squires and the English soprano Lucy Escott, who for eight years starting in 1861, sang the principal parts in almost all of the 1300 odd performances given by Lyster's company! Six performances a week was nothing unusual in those days and an unbroken fourteen consecutive stagings of *Les Huguenots* in 1862 must surely have been some kind of world record, which will never be broken now. Most of the seasons played in small theatres, but the occasional monster did by then exist and was played; Melbourne's Theatre Royal sat 3300

William Saurin Lyster, the man who came closest to presenting real opera in Australia from 1861 to 1880. His productions had many of the virtues and failings of much which was seen in England or America at the same time. Any lasting popularity of opera as an art in Australia was certainly founded on the work he did here right up to the time of his death.

and singing over the mostly brass orchestra in those conditions needed a voice of some size!

While Squires was ultimately replaced by an Australian-bred, if not Australian-born tenor, Armes Beaumont, Lyster continued to rely on imported artists, ranging from half a dozen members of his own family to guests as internationally famous as Anna Bishop and Ilma de Murska. He paid rather less attention to his productions; local theatres used to carry

their own selection of scenery and costumes from which the visiting artists chose whatever suited them. Lyster's original six months tour turned into a nineteen year season, interrupted only once by an unsuccessful foray into the United States. It ended in 1880 with Lyster's death in Melbourne. There seems to be little doubt that any serious following for opera which existed in Australia before the turn of the century was the result of this admirable gentleman's efforts.

Lyster was followed by Martin and Fanny Simonson, French and Italian respectively. Their company followed the pattern of Lyster, except in as much as they used to go bankrupt more often. Discipline was almost non-existent, since the directors used almost entirely Italian singers, mostly unable to speak English and used to having their own way, to the point of deciding which operas they wanted to sing and with what colleagues. Whenever the tenor and soprano wanted to sing different roles they took the law into their own hands. In 1889 a performance of *Carmen* in Sydney ended in total chaos as the singers on stage abused the conductor, whose side was capably defended by the audience. Simonson cancelled the season and swore never to go back to opera. However, within a week performances were under way again with the same singers, if not the impresario. It didn't last, of course, and neither did Simonson's resolution to forget about opera in Australia.

Meanwhile, the American actor James Cassius Williamson shrewdly acquired the Australian rights to the Gilbert and Sullivan operas and found himself the richest impresario in the land. The stars, naturally enough, were Williamson and his wife, Maggie Moore – American by birth and American by marriage. George Musgrove began to import a series of opera companies from Italy and Germany and things really began to heat up after the turn of the century when Williamson began to bring Italian groups to this country. The then new Puccini operas inevitably led up to the great event, the first of the Melba seasons in 1911. While under the Williamson banner, this first truly complete company to be brought to Australia was under the direction of yet another Irishman, Thomas Quinlan, who imported 200 people including principals, chorus and a full orchestra. The opening on 2 September 1911 offered Melba and McCormack in *La Traviata* and the firm founded by Williamson did not look back for half a century. Quinlan followed up with another company the following year. It was more ambitious than the first and included not only Wagner's *The Mastersingers of Nuremberg,* but the complete *Ring of the Nibelungen* cycle. It may have been over-ambitious, but not all the fault for the losses it incurred lay with Quinlan. Melbourne had a smallpox epidemic, and a general strike in New Zealand forced him to cancel his season there. Then Williamson himself died unexpectedly in Paris and the First World War wrecked plans for a 1915 season. But the demand for grand opera had been created and the successors of Williamson were ready to meet it.

The importance of the many J. C. Williamson grand opera seasons over the years lies not so much in their encouragement of local talent, which was minimal, to say the least, but to the interest in the art which they generated with the public. Just as Pavlova stimulated a thousand and one young girls to take up ballet, so did Melba inspire a thousand and one young girls to follow her example. The problem all of them faced (and Williamson's did nothing to help) was always that there were no local opera companies in which to gain experience; at best, there was a chance of chorus or small parts in some company yet to be imported.

The occasional company launched by independents was more generous to local talent, though need rather than any desire to be constructive was probably the motivation. The Gonsalez Italian Grand Opera Company presented by George Marlow in 1916, for example, had some good male singers, but was decidedly inferior on the distaff side. When it ultimately broke up, it reassembled under various other managers who were only too happy to use local talent to back up the few Italians still remaining. If Gertrude Johnson's name was to go down in history in later years and Amy Castles, Browning Mummery and Fred Collier are still remembered, the same opportunity was offered by managers Frank Rigo and Count Ercole Fillipini to Vera Bedford, Thelma Carter, Elsy Treweek, Patti Russell, Gladys Verona or Nellie Leach. All gained experience, but only those who went overseas got anywhere.

Melba herself, of course, loved to play the great patron and the three seasons she staged with Williamson's in 1911, 1924 and 1928 had their share of Australian singers. But those were all-star companies of a quality that Williamson's never had the courage to bring out on their own and competing with McCormack, Dal Monte, Borgioli or Granforte was hardly a fair test for the local singers. The occasional English-sounding name in the Melba seasons almost invariably turned out to be non-Australian, (Phyllis Archibald), unless she happened to be a Melba protégé (Stella Power).

What makes the Melba seasons historically so important is that they were so very adventurous in their repertoire. The sop to Australian music given via one solitary Fritz Hart one-actor coupled with *Pagliacci* is unimportant in relation to the fact that a Melba season was likely to present fifteen to twenty different operas in the course of a season, all sung by more than proficient artists. The 1928 season featured twenty-four works, including the Australian premieres of Puccini's *Turandot, Manon Lescaut* and the three operas of the *Trittico,* Montemezzi's *L'amore dei tre re,* Cilea's *Adriana Lecouvreur,* Mascagni's *Lodoletta,* Massenet's *Thais* and Hart's *Deirdre in Exile.*

As for the standard of productions, we are told that over 100 people were brought from Europe, that 'scenery has been painted to the right designs and in accordance with tradition. Thousands of costumes have been purchased', etc. etc. Yet among the 245 names listed in the credits there appears not the name of even one producer or designer! One presumes that all the twenty-four operas were staged or arranged by the Stage Director, Carlo Farinetti, who must have been a genius of the highest degree.

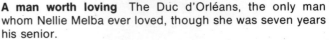
A man worth loving The Duc d'Orléans, the only man whom Nellie Melba ever loved, though she was seven years his senior.

Once again, it should be stressed that Australia was not necessarily backward. Opera seasons in England rarely mentioned producers in those days, though the trend toward improvement had already begun. Opera was no longer pure entertainment, but it still relied on the star syndrome, the imported star syndrome, and we should not be too critical of Melba for following the system which made her name and fortune. That she knew her public is only too clear, because – unlike the 1965 Sutherland-Williamson season –

A La meilleure de mes ami
Madame Mathilde Marche
souvenir de son élève
reconnaissante et affecti
Nellie Melba.

The Williamson spectacle Melba convinced J. C. Williamson's to present grand opera in the grand manner and made money for them, largely by appearing in many productions herself. However, the non-Melba nights were also sold out regularly, because no expense was spared to stage the productions. In 1928 Melba appeared but briefly in the Williamson-Melba (not Melba-Williamson) Grand Opera Season, giving some of her final final farewell performances. But the stars she helped to pick were top stars indeed. This is the Triumphal Scene from *Aida* in 1928. (Front three figures at left: Giannina Arangi-Lombardi as Aida, John Brownlee as Amonasro and Francesco Merli as Radames.)

the non-Melba nights also were regularly sold out. In 1924 the Melbourne season of twelve weeks included sixteen operas and attracted 211,200 paying customers! That is a truly astronomical figure for a city of 885,700 inhabitants.

Of course, it *was* Melba's Farewell Season, or so the public was led to believe. And so was the 1928 season, which took place fully two years after her *final farewell* at Covent Garden and the *final final* farewell at the Old Vic. I am not sticking my neck out by stating which of the many authentic last appearances of Melba was really her last (presumably the one on her death bed, when she is said to have sung a few bars of Gounod's *Ave Maria*), but in 1924 she followed her Farewell Season with a Farewell Concert at His Majesty's Theatre on the 14 October which was broadcast and heard as far away as Sydney, Auckland and, the Press reported, in California. Her fellow artists on that occasion consisted of the principals of the opera company and included not one Australian. The Italians, along with the audience, which had

contributed $36,000 to the Fund for Limbless Soldiers, sang *For She's a Jolly Good Fellow* and world-wide tributes poured in, as they did again, and again, and again. Every available space in the theatre was covered with flowers, festoons of gum leaves sparkled with hidden lights and huge shields with realistic paintings of Australian native birds (not including Melba) covered the front of the dress circle and the balcony. As for what decorated the stage, words can hardly describe it. Fortunately a photographic record exists and this speaks for itself – of the awe in which Melba was held, of the money Melba could draw, of the power Melba held over her public and of her knowledge of publicity gimmicks, though the word may not have been invented at that time.

Many books have been written about Melba, too many perhaps, and her contribution to keeping opera alive through these tours is all that need be said about her in these pages. She succeeded in making opera loved to a point which has

Which farewell? Melba's long series of farewell performances looked, and quite possibly were intended to be, genuine enough. Nevertheless, one wonders what Melbourne audiences who attended this Farewell in 1924 thought when the durable old lady returned to sing again four years later, aged sixty-seven. The decorations seen here were only a small part of Melba's homage in this early example of a typical Melba Farewell. Immense floral displays covered not only the stage, but auditorium and foyers as well. Melba's famous Covent Garden Farewell on 8 June 1926 was not her last London Farewell either; there was another one six months later at the Old Vic!

not yet been equalled today – the qualities of the Australian Opera notwithstanding. Proof of this exists in a letter written to the Manager of His Majesty's Theatre during the 1924 season by an opera lover who begged him to put on a performance of *Bohéme* 'without Melba'! He did so want to see Puccini's opera and all Melba nights were sold out. If only they let somebody else sing Mimi, he might get the chance to enjoy the opera of his dreams! Now, there was a true opera lover, if ever there was one, and one would assume that there were others like him in the Melbourne of 1924.

The imported companies that followed, after Melba retired and finally died, helped to keep the interest alive, but Williamson's without Melba did not have the gift of choosing the right artists or perhaps the peak of interest had been passed in Australia, as it had overseas. The age in which singers alone could fill the house was passing. No doubt Gigli would still have broken all records, but Lina Pagliughi,

Bruna Castagna and Apollo Granforte could do so no longer in 1932. After the war the Firm tried again, twice. In 1949 they toured nine operas, popular potboilers one and all, and turned a small profit, mainly due to the unexpected popularity of Rina Malatrasi, who enchanted the Australian public. Apart from Alvino Misciano and Mario Basiola there was not a singer of even average international standard in the cast. What possessed the company to undertake the 1955 season in the manner in which it did is a mystery. No doubt Nevin Tait, getting on in years, thought he could recreate the magic of the Melba seasons – without Melba, or Dal Monte, or Borgioli, or the many others.

No less than thirteen operas were staged in 1955 with a huge imported cast which did not have a single box office name among them. One, Gabriella Tucci, was to go on to become a star in later years. Another, Umberto Borsò, showed immense promise in 1955, just two years after his debut, and later did manage to get into La Scala, the Metro-

The dangers of over-selling Dame Nellie Melba and Dino Borgioli in the 1924 production of *La Bohéme*. One pitiful letter received by the manager of His Majesty's Theatre in Melbourne asked for a performance of the opera 'without Melba'. He did so want to see *La Bohéme* and all Melba performances were sold out in advance!

politan and Covent Garden, finally returning to Australia during the 1970s. Ken Neate had already made a name on the European circuit and at Covent Garden. Perhaps the aging Afro Poli had something to offer still in artistry, if not in voice. As for the rest, few if any were ever heard of again and their standards of voice and even experience were on the whole no better than that of the contingent of forty Australian singers who supported these 'stars' in the chorus and occasionally in small parts. These Australians included Donald Smith, John Shaw, Clifford Grant, John Young, Kevin Mills, Rosalind Keene, Wilma Whitney and Justine Rettick. Though all the productions used existing costumes and scenery, making the venture a comparatively cheap affair, the steadily reducing public for all but a few operas (Malatrasi still pulled them in for *Butterfly,* the critics notwithstanding) the season made a huge loss and it looked as though Williamson's had wound down the curtain on

their operatic activities. But they had not reckoned on the meteoric rise of Joan Sutherland.

So, ten years later they tried to repeat the Melba success formula with the Sutherland-Williamson International Grand Opera Company. In many respects it was a good try. Apart from Sutherland, they had Pavarotti, who was certainly as good as Borgioli was in Melba's time, though not as solidly established and Elisabeth Harwood had some of the glamour of Dal Monte, though again not the name, and John Alexander to this day does sing regularly at the Metropolitan Opera House in New York. Joseph Rouleau, Richard Cross, Alberto Remedios, Spiro Malas and Monica Sinclair also had, and have, some reputation. They were backed, with some courage on the part of Richard Bonynge, the Artistic Director, by members of the Elizabethan Trust Opera Company, which was disbanded for the duration of the season. Thus a good many local singers were given the chance to sing leading roles in the company of overseas singers and the general benefits to singers and audiences alike were probably good value for Australia, if not for Williamson's, who lost heavily.

Margreta Elkins, Joy Mammen, Robert Allman, Ronald Maconaghie, Clifford Grant and Lauris Elms were fairly billed among the company principals. It really was a pretty reasonable sort of affair with five brand new productions, three built around Sutherland: *Lucia di Lammermoor, Traviata* and *Semiramide*; the others were *Eugene Onegin* and *Elisir d'amore.* Sutherland nights were automatically sold out; other nights were automatically empty, Pavarotti notwithstanding! A small loss would probably have been made had all nights been sold out. Since they were not, it proved to be the swan song for opera staged by the firm responsible for bringing more good opera to Australians than anybody else up to that time. It is doubtful whether Australia will ever again see a fully imported opera company offering seasons on the scale provided by Williamson's.

The 'National' Theatre

3

Gertrude Johnson was a very determined woman, a formidable woman; the kind who is so often attracted to the arts, launches grandiose schemes and usually falls flat on her face. If 'Gertie' never actually fell flat on her face, she nevertheless reached a time when her abilities declined and with them the brain-child she brought into the world. The ambitiously named 'Australian National Theatre' very nearly became all that the name implied, though it failed to realize its creator's dream in the end. Along the way it left a lasting mark on the history of the performing arts in Australia and on opera in particular. No book on theatre in this country can ignore the National Theatre, or the tragedy that, operatically, it came to nothing in the end.

Lest it be thought that someone close to the National Theatre (the author of these lines) has lost his marbles, let me make it clear that what has arisen out of the − literal − ashes of the old National is *not* precisely what Miss Johnson would have wished, though without her it could not have come into being. I refer to it as tragic, because Miss Johnson's plan was a good one, it worked admirably up to a point and it might quite logically and realistically have become a real National Theatre of Australia, if only . . .

It all began in the Victoria Centenary Club in Melbourne. To be precise, it happened at 8 p.m. on the 4 December 1935. Starting with a capital of £8, Miss Johnson managed to enthuse a group of leading citizens to establish 'The National Theatre Movement, Victoria'. It is ironic that the organization which ultimately became a purely Victorian body also started as one. Perhaps success came too quickly and too soon, for within five years it became the 'Australian' National Theatre, which it remains, in spite of its local character, to this day.

Miss Johnson and the National were around so long and the history of both have been written so often that it is time to bring both into perspective. The 'principal soprano at Covent Garden', who returned from London to that fateful meeting in 1935 and was inspired by Lilian Baylis and the work she had done at the Old Vic and Sadler's Wells, was not one of the great singers of Australia. Let us stop fooling ourselves; few of the 'world-famous' Australian singers were what the local Press would have us believe they were or are. Miss Johnson recorded extensively in England (on the dark blue, that is, cheap, Columbia label) and her qualities as a singer are there for all to hear. She had a fine coloratura voice beset by some uncertainties and a style which was outdated even then. She was at her best in the simple art songs of Cyril Smith, which she recorded with the composer himself at the piano. It is significant that none of her records have been included in any of the many anthologies of old recordings.

Miss Johnson gave up her career − some say because of a broken romance, others to realize her dream of a National

Gertrude Johnson The founder of the Australian National Theatre Movement in Melbourne, as she would have liked to be remembered, singing Musetta to Melba's Mimi in the final London farewell performance of Dame Nellie at the Old Vic. The fact that Melba was decidedly unfriendly on that occasion only lent spice to the many retellings of that wonderful occasion.

Theatre – to return to Australia for good. Wealthy in her own right, though by no means rich, she was able to rally groups of prominent citizens to her cause and there were few, if any, in Victoria between 1940 and the mid-1950s who did not have their name on one of her ventures at some time or the other. The original subscribers paid six guineas, a lot of money in those days, but within a year the National Theatre had 2000 members, though literally nothing had been produced beyond speeches full of good intentions.

The one good intention that was there from the beginning, and is all that remains of Miss Johnson's early plans, was the idea to make the National Theatre Movement 'a testing, training and proving ground for the talented enthusiast in drama, opera and ballet'. Like the Elizabethan Theatre Trust, the National's first priority was drama, though its fate was to lie in opera. The training of young artists to professional standards was to be a continuing policy which, like the parent body, had its ups and downs over the years. It is important to remember, though, that this was the first Australian venture to acknowledge that just acting, singing or dancing is not enough. The performing arts in Australia had until then always been on an amateur level, an inspired amateur level quite often, but amateur just the same. It is only in the very recent past that artists have been able to train seriously for a career in the theatre under proper tutors, instead of finding their way through practical experience in amateur or – in the case of the more talented – professional companies. Like Lilian Baylis, Miss Johnson saw the need to create a trained pool of talent out of which young performing companies could be built and she set about the task with a vengeance.

Giving money to subsidise training is not the road to O.B.E.s and knighthoods today, let alone in 1936. The patrons of the arts clustering around Miss Johnson wanted their friends, specially their friends in viceregal circles, to see something of their 'work'. The very first National Theatre production launched strikes us as slightly quaint for a group aiming so high. It was a *'Joyous Pageant of the Holy Nativity'* staged in December 1936 in the Princess Theatre. Six months later this was followed by Shakespeare's *As You Like It,* then *The Barretts of Wimpole Street* and *The Flying Dutchman.* The opera was produced by one Garnett Carroll, later to become a noted impresario and the owner of the Princess Theatre in Melbourne.

The Honorary Director (Miss Johnson accepted no payment for her services during the thirty-eight years of her rule) lost no time in cashing in on the glory these productions brought to her sponsors. A permanent home for the planned schools was found in a charming old church hall at St Peter's, Eastern Hill, and in due course, ballet, opera and drama schools were created, while constant productions kept the name of the National Theatre Movement before the public.

The war proved to be the making of the National. Run by do-gooders (in the best sense), the cause of the war effort, troop entertainment and the like occupied the staff of the National full time and the lack of imported shows created a suddenly larger than ever public for its dramas, ballets and operas. A *Marriage of Figaro* in 1940 was followed by *The Beggar's Opera,* with Beatrice Oakley as Polly Peachum. Musical direction for all these productions was in the now somewhat feeble hands of eighty-three year old Gustave Slapoffski who had been brought to Australia to conduct opera in 1900 (!) having been in charge of the Carl Rosa Company in England before that. Still, the public was grateful for the small mercies his band of singers could provide and nobody noticed when one night the old gentleman was found to be quietly snoozing away, while orchestra and cast continued with unallayed energy.

The fifteen operas staged during the war years at Eastern Hill were an adjunct of the new National Theatre Opera School and, if the singers were young and inexperienced, the repertoire was surprisingly varied. It included four Mozart operas, potboilers like *Rigoletto* and *Martha*, and goodies such as Messager's *Monsieur Beaucaire,* and Gluck's *Iphigenia in Aulis.* Year by year the productions continued and, as the war ended, the need for a permanent opera company became clear. Through the Movement's effort in raising funds for patriotic causes Miss Johnson had added many valuable friends to her clan and when the time came to strike, she struck with amazing swiftness.

Forty-five principal singers, a chorus of 110, no less than forty-five dancers and an unnamed and uncounted orchestra presented a season of 'Grand Opera' at the Princess Theatre in March and April 1948. The five operas were *Rigoletto, Aida, Faust, Carmen* and *The Marriage of Figaro.* If there was ever a more ambitious first-up professional opera season in Australia, I would like to hear of it. Not that the claimed title 'professional' should be taken too seriously. It was indeed the first truly native company in that all the singers emerged from over 600 auditions held in Melbourne. There were no imports on the stage or behind the scenes, but the lack of professionalism was in the pay packets which, in the majority of cases, were empty.

By 1948 Herman Schildberger and his National Theatre Opera School had begun to play a leading role in providing singers for these full-scale opera productions. Miss Johnson's work, not surprisingly, proved to be most effective in the field she knew best. Though ballet and drama actually anticipated opera in the scheme of things – probably for financial reasons – it was opera which brought the National its greatest recognition. That first *Rigoletto* at the Princess Theatre had Miss Johnson's star pupil, Barbara Wilson, as Gilda and Robert Simmons as Rigoletto. (Twenty-eight years later Simmons was still singing with the Australian ·Opera, having had a career overseas in the 1950s and 1960s.)

The talent in the company was versatile indeed. Stefan Haag not only sang Marullo, but was one of the assistant conductors! (The other was Douglas Gamley, one of the best of our musical expatriate composers and conductors of the post-war years.) The administrative cast lists already read like a social and artistic Who's Who, with the Governor, Sir Winston Dugan, as Patron, Sir John Latham and Sir

Thomas Nettlefold among the Trustees, Sir Robert Knox as President and Lady Angliss (later Dame Jacobena) as his deputy. Professor Bernard Heinze and John Rowell were among the Vice Presidents and an Advisory Committee included Florence Austral and Horace Stevens!

I don't propose to start listing name after name, but the fact that, at such an early point in its career, people such as these gave their practical and financial help to the National Theatre may explain its ultimate success, (if not its final decline as a producing company).

The success of that season in 1948, based soundly on purely local talent, much of it from the National Theatre Opera School, proved conclusively that a demand for opera existed at the box office and that it could be satisfied without great star imports. Throughout the coming years the National Theatre proved that native opera could indeed exist. Only the financial realities proved a stumbling block; the days of unpaid and underpaid staff and singers were numbered.

Perhaps the artistic standards of those early years were not of the highest, but the last international opera season had been in 1935 and a new public had grown up during the war. At least Joseph Post was available as musical director and Post had been the most proficient of Australian opera conductors since his debut in 1931 and was to remain so for many years yet. Visually the operas, all produced by William P. Carr, did not live up to the magnificent sound produced by the massed voices, most of them young. The veteran baritone Frederick Collier was the exception, but he lent immense strength through his experience. Among the bit players, singing both Mercedes and Siebel, was Betty (now Elizabeth) Fretwell.

Plans announced for the second season were even more ambitious: *Boris Godounov, The Bartered Bride, La Bohème, Don Giovanni* and a revival of *Carmen.* Getrude Johnson was nothing if not ambitious, and the success of the first season gave her reason to be confident. How haphazard her methods and those of her staff actually were can be gauged from the fact that only one of these five announced works materialized, *The Bartered Bride.* However, the actual season of six weeks in 1949 included six works, not five! *The Tales of Hoffman, Martha, The Magic Flute, Fidelio* and *La Traviata* joined Smetana's opera to produce a season possibly even more successful than the first. Yet this was only one third of the first of many 'Festivals of the Theatre Arts' to be staged by the National Theatre in the Princess Theatre. The opera season was followed by two weeks of the National Theatre Ballet Company and two weeks of Shakespeare's *Twelfth Night* and Tennessee Williams' *The Glass Menagerie!*

Within one year of starting its professional activities the National Theatre Movement had staged ten weeks of ten

Marjorie Lawrence in Australia Her only appearance in opera in Australia, as Amneris in the Melbourne National Theatre's ambitious *Aida* in 1951. Lawrence had by then been paralysed from the waist down for twelve years, but this had not stopped her from singing in opera at the Metropolitan and other famous houses.

different operas, ballets and plays in the 1600 seat Princess Theatre in Melbourne. And the whole thing was planned and executed from its minute offices and studios in Eastern Hill and used a huge number of the students of all three schools, who obtained some excellent experience in the process. Miss Johnson's dream of building an Australian Old Vic–Sadler's Wells looked rosy indeed in 1949. Not only did the public flock to see the productions, but the Victorian Government contributed $10,000 toward the cost of the Three Arts Festival.

Several notable debuts took place during this 1949 season. Miss Johnson recognized the potential of the young Ronald Dowd, who made his operatic debut in *The Tales of Hoffmann* and also appeared as Florestan in *Fidelio*. It was also

through the medium of *Hoffman* that Stefan Haag first tried his hand as a producer, an event which was to have long-lasting repercussions, particularly since his musical background gave the Offenbach work a more cohesive style than the other operas, though their musical values may actually have been higher.

Having established a successful pattern, Miss Johnson saw no reason to change it. A similar festival in 1950 saw productions of *Madame Butterfly, Rigoletto, The Barber of Seville, The Flying Dutchman* and *Hansel and Gretel*. The opera company (meaning the management of the company, for the singers were called together only for the season) had acquired a most efficient repertoire which could be repeated *ad infinitum* and on the occasion of the 100th Anniversary of the

The executive director of the Elizabethan Trust learning the ropes. Stefan Haag (*below*) playing Papageno in *The Magic Flute* with Barbara Wilson as Pamina for the Melbourne National Theatre. Haag not only sang, but was an assistant conductor before going on to produce and act administratively in the years before he began his climb to the top position of the Trust.

Australia's forgotten expatriate Albert Lance (*below*) has been a leading tenor in Paris for twenty years, but few associate the name with Lance Ingram, who sang Hoffmann in the 1954 Royal Command Performance in Melbourne. Nothing has been able to lure the long-ago naturalized Frenchman, seen here as Rodolfo in *La Bohéme* with the National Theatre, back to his native shores.

Founding of Victoria in 1951 the company actually presented a full season without having to include a new production. All the glory that year went to the National Theatre Ballet which not only offered Australia the first ever four-act *Swan Lake,* but what was to be the only genuine Australian ballet for many years to come, *Corroboree.*

The highlight of this Jubilee Season was *Aida,* specially staged for a returning Australian of truly international fame, Marjorie Lawrence, whose remarkable autobiography, *Interrupted Melody,* had just been published. Lawrence's continuance of her career, though paralysed from the waist down, had brought her more fame than her magnificent voice had done. Getting her to sing Amneris in the Melbourne *Aida* was a tremendous scoop, though for some curious reason the company failed to take advantage of it. The programme made no mention of Lawrence's infirmity and many a curious onlooker must have wondered why Amneris remained seated throughout the production, which Lennox Brewer had built around her. Betna Pontin's *Aida* was passable and young John Shaw already sang Amonasro well, but overall vocal standards were hardly worthy of the famous visitor.

The season as a whole was, in fact, well below the standard of the first two, though the Rossini *Barber* had a sparkling trio of Rosinas in Barbara Wilson, Margaret Nisbett and Verona Cappadonna. Others from the local rosters to leave a serious impression were baritones Morris Williams

To the Met via Channel 9 One of the world's best basses, Clifford Grant (*below*), in his first role, as Balthasar in Menotti's *Ahmal and the Night Visitors* with the National Theatre in 1954. After that came a spell in the Channel 9 Chorus, the Sutherland-Williamson Opera Season, immediate acceptance in San Francisco and London in 1966 and finally the Metropolitan in New York.

and Keith Neilson, while Betty Fretwell stepped up to sing the Countess in Mozart's *Figaro*. Nevertheless, the financial success was such that a four week supplementary season was staged, adding *Madame Butterfly* and *Rigoletto* to the repertoire.

As a sidelight on the state of music in Australia in 1951, commercial radio stations were still running their own orchestras and when the National Theatre Festivals began to take on the aspect of truly professional success, the A.B.C.'s Victorian Symphony Orchestra took turns with the 3DB Symphony Orchestra in playing for the season. The thought of an orchestra capable of playing for opera and ballet being attached to a commercial radio station seems strange nowadays. We forget that it is still possible to buy records of music with Arturo Toscanini conducting the orchestra which was created specially for him, the N.B.C. Symphony, (N.B.C. standing for the National Broadcasting Corporation – of New York, not Melbourne, of course).

After three professional seasons Miss Johnson's National Opera Company appeared to be soundly ensconced. Audiences and critics responded to what was being offered and standards, if still low, were not that much worse than what Covent Garden under the Rankl regime (see The Rankl Disaster) was offering in post-war London. With admirable foresight plans were made for the only logical next step: collaboration with another opera company which had recently been formed in Sydney.

The unexpected sensation The opera which set the Melbourne National Theatre on the road to universal acceptance, Stefan Haag's production of Menotti's *The Consul* with designs by Louis Kahan, was a sensational success in 1953, at a time when modern opera had even less box office appeal than today. It was also the ideal vehicle for Marie Collier (Magda), seen here with Robert Simmons (John Sorel).

The Australian Opera
That Never Was

4

What should have been the beginning of the Australian Opera occurred in 1952. Miss Johnson in Melbourne joined Mrs Clarice M. Lorenz and her Sydney-based National Opera to present an Australia-wide tour using the resources of both companies. In the light of subsequent history it is amazing that this one joint venture ever took place; probably the pressure of prominent citizens behind the two ladies in their respective capital cities had something to do with it.

There had been rivalry between the two groups ever since Mrs Lorenz had decided to call her company The New South Wales National Opera during the previous year. Miss Johnson rightly felt that her use of the word 'National' since 1935 gave her some kind of priority, and she had just cause to claim that she was doing a good job under the banner of The Australian National Theatre Movement, covering also ballet and drama. And here was this New South Wales upstart adopting a name which had been her trade-mark for fully sixteen years!

The N.S.W. National Opera had started modestly, but with remarkable public success in an opera-starved Sydney, with *Carmen, A Masked Ball* and *Seraglio* in 1951. Clearly, the successes of Miss Johnson in Melbourne had stirred the Sydney citizens into action. Sydney, like Melbourne, had its fair share of excellent local singers, most of whom had trained in the admirable local Conservatorium directed by Eugene Goossens. The Con. had much better facilities than the National Theatre Opera School in Melbourne. Thus, while Miss Johnson had a longer direct tradition and several years of 'professional' seasons as a head-start, Sydney singers had actually performed in full-size productions of works as large as Wagner's *Mastersingers of Nuremberg*. Goossens and his predecessors were far more progressive in their thoughts and professional in their approach to opera, giving their singers a much sounder background than that available to their Melbourne counterparts. Apart from *The Mastersingers,* the Conservatorium's last season prior to Mrs Lorenz' first appearance on the scene included Debussy's *Pelleas and Melisande* and Verdi's *Falstaff*. Goossens had long ago abandoned the standard repertoire and in 1951 he staged *Otello, Gianni Schicchi* and his own opera, *Judith.* In later years they were followed by even more ambitious productions such as *Boris Godounov* and Wagner's *Die Walküre!*

The more professional approach of the Sydneysiders manifested itself from the very start. They may have been late in the race, but they were not going to be stopped from being the best. The very first season of the N.S.W. National Opera invaded enemy territory by going to Melbourne, playing in the hardly ideal Tivoli Theatre and opening in the middle of Miss Johnson's National Theatre Arts Festival! It *was* an outrageous invasion, particularly since it actually duplicated one of the operas of the Festival, *Carmen,* and used one of Miss Johnson's conductors, Joseph Post, whose duties with the Melbourne company ended four days before the invaders opened at the Tivoli.

For the first, and possibly the last time, Melbourne had two professional opera companies playing at the same time. (Not counting some early companies, whose efforts were hardly comparable.) In the light of operatic history in the coming years it is interesting to compare the singers appearing in Melbourne in both companies in 1951. It would have been hard to predict at the time whether these, rather than Norma Lever, Betna Pontin, Ivan Dixon, Ivor Sheridan, Linda Parker or Phyllis Rogers would make the grade. It can be argued that all made the grade up to a point and the following list should not be taken as an attempt to play off one company against the other, let alone one singer against the other.

Singers appearing in the two 1951 Melbourne seasons:

Melbourne National Opera	Sydney National Opera
Alan Ferris	Valda Bagnall
Elizabeth Fretwell	June Bronhill
Kevin Miller	Geoffrey Chard
Keith Neilson	Ronald Dowd
Margaret Nisbett	Neil Easton
John Shaw	Alan Ferris
Robert Simmons	Alan Light
Barbara Wilson	Eric Michelson

You will see that Alan Ferris (like conductor Post) appeared in both companies, showing that an interchange of artists was already taking place. Also, Ronald Dowd had played his first roles with the Melbourne company at a time before the Sydney one came into being.

Thus Mrs Lorenz had a very sound basic ensemble to add to Miss Johnson's company when the joint season of 1952 was planned. It was the stated ambition to make this 'the forerunner of a truly Australian National Opera'. Each company played host in its own city and productions were identical in each, though local artists were usually given preference and John Brownlee returned to his native land to sing Don Giovanni and Scarpia. There was a further joint season in Brisbane.

1952 was the high point of native opera in Australia until the present Australian Opera began to establish itself. Melburnians will claim that the 1953 and 1954 seasons by Miss Johnson's company were better without the Sydney group and Mrs Lorenz' advocates will claim the same for their team in Sydney. In retrospect even the most biased Sydneysider may have to give the later honours to Melbourne, but the best of the Melbourne company's last two seasons could not compare with the overall excellence of the joint season, which should really have been the foundation stone of the Australian Opera.

Six operas were staged in three cities: *Lucia di Lammermoor, Tosca, Don Giovanni, Lohengrin, Masked Ball* and the double bill *Cavalleria Rusticana* and *Pagliacci* – the first three by the Melbourne group and the last three by Mrs Lorenz' company. The season opened in Melbourne on 15 March 1952 with John Brownlee as Don Giovanni, supported by Phyllis Rogers, Joyce Simmons, Verona Cappadonna, Morris Williams, John Dudley, Alan Eddy and John Shaw (who played Masetto). Understudies included John Young as the Don, Fretwell for Donna Anna and Eric Michelson for Ottavio.

The second performance saw the sensational debut of Marie Collier in *Cavalleria Rusticana*. Collier appeared 'cold', never having sung in opera before, her only professional experience consisting of chorus work in Williamson's short revival of *Oklahoma!* in 1951. The debut of the young chemist's assistant was awaited with interest because at a party prior to the opening of the Arts Festival of 1952 (which included the usual National Theatre ballet and drama seasons) it was announced that Collier would sing in the Triumphal Scene from Verdi's *Aida* and that this would be the National Theatre's contribution to the Royal Command performance before King George VI on 22 March 1953. The king was to die and the performance was cancelled, but in 1952 to announce a completely unknown singer as Aida for that occasion was met with joy, envy, interest, enthusiasm or laughter, according to the person involved. For any country which could produce singers like Austral, Lawrence or Brownlee to field an untried newcomer before the King seemed total folly to most, but Miss Johnson's ear had not failed her. After the premiere of *Cavalleria Rusticana* there were no further dissenting voices. While all other roles, no matter how small, were covered by several singers, Collier had Santuzza to herself. No other singer was listed to sing, or sang the part, during the whole of the tour!

Ronald Dowd sang his first Canio, Alan Light was Tonio and Joseph Post again conducted the Victorian Symphony Orchestra. For the first time all the operas were properly designed and if the production did not quite equal the designing standards, the year certainly saw an approximation of what was considered reasonable operatic presentation overseas. The operas could certainly hold their own against those seen at Covent Garden in 1952, a fact easier to appreciate after looking at the names of the designers: John Rowell, William Constable, Desmonde Downing, Robin Lovejoy, Louis Kahan and Timothy Walton.

This was also Elizabeth Fretwell's debut as Tosca and Robert Allman found his operatic feet for the first time playing the small part of Sciarrone. Lance Ingram (later of international fame as Albert Lance) sang some of the Cavaradossis and Brownlee was the Scarpia.

The Sydney season that followed was as great a success

The faces of young Marie Collier The most flamboyant singer to come out of Australia, Marie Collier died in London in 1971 after a fall from a window. She lived her forty-four years as a series of highs and lows, the highs being artistic and the lows personal. Her name was box office at the Metropolitan, at Covent Garden and in cities from Buenos Aires to Vienna or Palermo. Versatility was her strength even during the first two years of her career, which began in Melbourne.

Collier in her debut role (*top left*) as Santuzza in *Cavalleria Rusticana* during the 1952 joint season of the Melbourne and Sydney National Operas. The young pharmacist's assistant fresh from the chorus of *Oklahoma!* was an instant sensation.

A slight case of mis-casting and Collier's last appearance before going overseas: Helen of Troy (*left*) in Offenbach's *La belle Hélène* in 1954. It was also the only flop in which she appeared in Australia.

The Royal Command Performance (*above*) before H.M. Queen Elizabeth II at the Princess Theatre in Melbourne, 1 March 1954. Collier as the Venetian courtesan Giulietta in *The Tales of Hoffmann*.

The role which established Collier as a major dramatic actress as well as a great singer. The final curtain (*right*) of the 1953 National Theatre production of *The Consul*. Magda Sorel is about to gas herself.

The mature Collier in the role which catapulted her to international fame in 1965 when she replaced Maria Callas in *Tosca* at Covent Garden. The fact that she already had a long string of successes to her credit before that was overlooked. Three years later she repeated the role in Australia, first with Tito Gobbi and then with Raymond Myers (*below*) as Scarpia.

Collier's triumphant return to Australia as a top star for the 1964 Adelaide Festival, as Cressida (*top*) in Walton's *Troilus and Cressida*.

Collier starring at the Metropolitan in New York (*bottom*) in the 1967 world premiere of Marvin David Levy's *Mourning Becomes Electra*, with Sherrill Milnes. It was her debut at the Met and she remained a favourite of New Yorkers until her death four years later.

as the Melbourne one, even though, by an incredible managerial blunder, it was forced to open without Brownlee, the intended star of the opening night. Nobody had bothered to check Brownlee's commitments prior to planning the season and he was scheduled to sing a concert in Melbourne on the evening of his Gala Premiere in Sydney. Not only the first, but the second performance of *Don Giovanni* in Sydney starred a young unknown named John Young, one day to be the Administrator of the company which is now the Australian Opera.

The failure of the two 'National' companies to repeat the unquestioned success of the 1952 joint venture did not, as might be expected, result from a head-on clash between the two leading ladies, or any other great disaster. It seems to have been the individual opinion of both Miss Johnson and of Mrs Lorenz that each company was carrying the other, that each could become the truly national company on its own. Perhaps it was ultimately Mrs Lorenz and her Council who made the fatal move, because after the end of the most successful joint season of 1952, the N.S.W. National Opera changed its name to The National Opera of Australia. Since the *Australian* National Theatre's founder, Gertrude Johnson, had been awarded on O.B.E. for her work with the *National* Theatre Opera Company, this could only be regarded as a slap in the face. There is no record of any serious planning for a joint season in 1953, but Miss Johnson went over to the attack, planning not just a foray into Sydney, but a tour covering Perth and Adelaide and even Broken Hill, with principals identical to those seen in Melbourne. Local musical societies provided chorus and orchestras and local councils gave financial backing.

It really was a bold move by a company which had aimed to be truly 'national' according to its name since its formation nearly twenty years earlier. Subsidized by the Victorian State Government and an astonishingly large number of commercial enterprises and private donors, it obviously had good friends with influence outside Victoria as well. Australian Consolidated Press, the Sydney-based newspaper empire, actually guaranteed the Melbourne company's Sydney season against loss, while Mrs Lorenz' ambitious return season to Melbourne later in 1953 was backed by neither the N.S.W. Government nor sponsors from either city. What both ladies forgot was that opera could not continue on a semi-amateur basis, that singers and staff would ultimately have to be paid a living wage. Miss Johnson's backing was strong, but her plans – possibly as a result of Mrs Lorenz' challenge – were too ambitious and deficits began to escalate alarmingly.

The National Opera of Australia (no mention of N.S.W. or Sydney in the title now) fared even worse. Both companies were heading rapidly toward financial disaster, yet neither could see the writing on the wall. It was war! The fact that in opposition to each other the better woman had

to lose as well, was overlooked by both parties.

Not that the public had anything to worry about. It was suddenly presented with an avalanche of opera of astonishingly good quality. Part of the Elizabethan Trust Opera's problems in years to come can be traced back to the excellence of the last seasons of both the National companies.

The annual Melbourne Arts Festival staged by the National Theatre in 1953 covered nine weeks, including five of opera, during which *La Bohème, Cosi fan tutte, Tosca, The Barber of Seville* and Menotti's *The Consul* were staged. *The Consul* was a runaway sensational success, again because of Marie Collier. It was an enterprising move, the first truly modern opera ever staged in Australia, and succeeded beyond all expectations to become a milestone by which operatic standards were measured for years to come. *The Consul* made Stefan Haag's name as a producer. The designs by Louis Kahan were excellent, though the drabness of the subject allowed for few frills, and modern abstract design techniques were still unknown. But principally it was the superb musical content that held the whole thing together. Menotti's opera is not great music, but it is great theatre and the long background of practical performing experience which the National Theatre had offered its singers via its opera school and its semi-professional seasons was now paying off. The cast backed up Collier's truly international standard Magda Sorel to the last man. Later charges that the Elizabethan Trust Opera Company stole all the National Theatre's artists almost look to be true. In *The Consul* alone could be found Fretwell, Shaw, Allman, Robert Simmons, Joyce Simmons, Wilma Whitney, Dorothea Deegan, Justine Rettick, Stefan Haag and a very young Lauris Elms; ten singers out of the cast of fourteen ended up in the later company, not to mention the conductor, designer and producer!

For its Sydney season, split between the Tivoli and the Theatre Royal, the Melbourne company added *Madame Butterfly* for additional box office appeal, but casts remained mostly as they had been in Melbourne, though John Shaw was promoted from bit parts to Scarpia, the turning point in what was to prove a very lengthy career indeed. What the (Sydney) National Opera of Australia brought to Melbourne in exchange was hardly comparable, though it looked good on paper. It was identical to its Sydney season: *Carmen, The Barber of Seville, Cavalleria Rusticana, Pagliacci, La Bohème, The Flying Dutchman, Endymion* and *The Devil Take Her* looks like an eight opera schedule. In fact, the last two were Australian one-actors by John Antill and Arthur Benjamin, which were presented twice in the three-week season of five programmes. Antill conducted his own youthful and rather insipid work, while Tibor Paul was the principal conductor of the (very much) scratch orchestra. The Sydney company even had to acquire a Melbourne *prima donna*, Glenda Raymond. Its other star was Ronald Dowd and the

The star that never was Barbara Wilson, Elizabeth Fretwell and Marie Collier (in that order) were the first soprano stars of the Melbourne National Theatre. Wilson played all the coloratura roles, Gilda, Violetta, Rosina and Lucia, with a clear voice and considerable dramatic ability. Her early retirement prevented her equalling the success of her colleagues. She is seen, *below*, in *Lucia di Lammermoor* with Eric Michelson.

fact that he had already sung that year with the Melbourne company was, naturally enough, not acknowledged. Others in the casts included Geoffrey Chard and Marjorie Conley, Neil Easton, John Dudley, Tais Taras, Alan Light and Robert Eddie. Compared with previous years it was not a good line-up and bringing a company such as this to Melbourne did not help the balance sheet or the Sydney company's attempt to topple Miss Johnson's operatic empire. Something had to give.

The longer established Melbourne company moved ahead steadily, its next goal clearly in sight: 1954 would see a Royal Command Performance of opera, not the original mish-mash with Collier and the *Aida* Triumphal Scene. The Sydney group had already begun to slip. What finally sealed the fate of both companies was the very thing which seemed to assure the survival of the stronger – Miss Johnson's National Opera: the visit of Queen Elizabeth II and its artistic aftermath, the Australian Elizabethan Theatre Trust.

The indestructibles Robert Allman, baritone, (*below left*) in 1953 as Mr Kofner in *The Consul*, and (*right*) in 1975 as Simon in *Simon Boccanegra* with Gregory Yurisich.

The indestructibles Elizabeth Fretwell, soprano, (*left*) in 1953 as Cio-Cio-San in *Madame Butterfly*, and (*below*) in 1975 as Tosca with Donald Smith.

John Shaw, baritone, (*right*) in 1953 as Schaunard in *La Bohéme*, and (*below right*) in 1976 as Scarpia in *Tosca*.

The indestructibles   Ronald Dowd, tenor, (*below*) in 1952
as Cavaradossi in *Tosca*, and (*right*) in 1976 as Herod in
Salome with Rosina Raisbeck.

It was not politics which caused the Royal Command Performance of Opera to be staged in Melbourne. Not only was that city the theatre capital of Australia, but in 1953 the Melbourne National Theatre had shown beyond doubt its superiority over the Sydney company that had tried to steal its name. Prior to 1952 there might have been an equal battle, if battle there had to be. Together the combatants made a formidable team; divided they fell, and Sydney fell more quickly because Sydney had neither the history nor the political influence of Melbourne. At the same time, it should be accepted that the lack of political – meaning financial – influence may very well have been responsible for the poor showing of the Sydney group in 1953. Suffice to say that Melbourne won the fight for the Royal Command Performance of Opera, while Sydney got the Royal Variety Command Performance. (It never has been very clear why there were no Command Performances of ballet and drama. Neither may have reached the standards of opera, but it is more likely that social 'Command Performances' were so numerous that there was not time for more than one theatrical one in each city.)

The performance itself, which took place at the Princess Theatre on Monday, 1 March 1954 was a new production of Offenbach's *The Tales of Hoffman* which, with its many leading roles, chorus and ballet, gave an opportunity to many to show their paces. Haag's production was excellent and the cast full of the same singers who have assured continuity to opera in Australia ever since. Collier got her chance at the Royal Command showing after all, though as Giulietta instead of Aida. Albert Lance sang Hoffman with excellent volume and tone, but without a trace of the poet, and John Shaw and Lorenzo Nolan played the triple roles Coppelius-Dapertutto-Miracle and Cochenille-Pitichinaccio-Franz admirably. The three female roles were shared by three sopranos – the idea of a single singer for three such diverse parts was as yet unthought of in Australia. Barbara Wilson and Elizabeth Fretwell were Olympia and Antonia and greatly to be preferred to their successors in these parts only three years later. Among the chorus appeared young Nancy, now Nance Grant, Cavell Armstrong, the year's Sun Aria Winner and Jean Brunning. Volunteers to work as extras were not accepted for the special performance, but it should be noted that at all performances they included Mary Hardy, the comedienne-television compere who has not yet to my knowledge made capital out of having appeared in opera before the Queen. (Among the ballet could be found Geoffrey Ingram, ten years later the first Administrator of the Australian Ballet.)

La Traviata (Wilson-Raymond McDonald-Allman), *Butterfly* (Fretwell-Lance-Shaw), *Albert Herring* (Max Worthley-Kathleen Goodall) a revival of *The Consul* and a double bill of *Hansel and Gretel* and *Ahmal and Night Visitors* nearly completed the eight weeks devoted to opera in the 1954 Festival, built around the Royal Command Performance.

The National Theatre Drama Company was represented by a fortnight of Shaw's *Caesar and Cleopatra,* but the ballet was absent, except as the moving spirit behind three weeks of Offenbach's *La Belle Hélène,* which followed the opera season. Produced by Stefan Haag, this had the unlikely coupling of Marie Collier and musical comedy star Max Oldaker in the leads, the year's Mobil Quest Winner, Ron Austron, as the King of Salamis and Clifford Grant, starting a long career now established overseas, as Hector. Everybody else in the opera company mucked in to take, if not play properly, the other roles, be they great or small. As a ballet spectacle it was a fine opera performance, as appropriate as the monumental Collier was to the part of Helen.

It was a somewhat sad wind-down for the National Theatre Opera Company, though nobody knew that this was the beginning of the end. In spite of all the public acclaim, the losses were immense. Miss Johnson was forced to place her hopes in the new Elizabethan Theatre Trust which, ostensibly, was to provide her with the means to regenerate her company's fading fortunes. What actually happened was that the National Theatre went on its own independent way, hoping against hope that the new upstart would fail, as it nearly did. (See the later chapters on the Trust Opera Company.)

In the meantime Moomba, Melbourne's people's festival, was making a slow start and the National played its part by providing opera, ballet and drama in the parks, using its own students, with the occasional outsider in a leading role. Typically adventurous and artistically disastrous ventures were performances of *Aida* and *Norma,* played in howling winds and rain, under-rehearsed, under-sung and under-staged, but still using the full symphony orchestras of the A.B.C.! The goodwill of the golden years was still present and Miss Johnson's board of directors seemed to be able to find backing for the wildest schemes, even the quite incredible 1958 production in the Olympic Swimming Pool of Coleridge Taylor's immense oratorio *Hiawatha* with a chorus of 300 and a huge ballet (all in full costumes, performing amid scenery fifteen metres high, while massed canoes full of Indian warriors failed to complete the simplest manoeuvres). It was a complete return to the unpaid amateurism with which the National Theatre started, though Neil Easton, Alwyn Smith, Victor Franklin and other coped professionally enough with the solo parts.

The Sydney National Opera succumbed to the same financial problems which had beset Miss Johnson, and in the same year. While the latter was playing before the Queen in 1954 Mrs Lorenz sent her troupe to New Zealand with disastrous results. The last of her managers proved no better than his endless predecessors and the point was reached when there

Royal Command Performance, Melbourne 1954 (over) with a cast of then unknowns, who were to make news at home and abroad. Note in the chorus Nancy (now Nance) Grant and, among the Guests (read 'extras'), television personality Mary Hardy. Not listed is understudy for the Mother, Lauris Elms.

was no money to pay the singers. They had actually agreed to continue without pay when Mrs Lorenz heard about it and flew to New Zealand with some ready cash. Rumour has it that she was then forced to pay the return fares with a worthless cheque. True or not, such happenings are not uncommon in operatic history. Unfortunately people like Mrs Lorenz are eternal optimists and she tried to recoup the company's fortunes with a season at Sydney's huge, late and unlamented Palladium Theatre. Its four-and-a-half metre apron stage presented some unusual production problems and even the best singers found themselves floundering. Things were not made any easier by a policy of playing each opera three nights in a row to save a few dollars on stage hands!

Rigoletto, Faust, Trovatore and *Madame Butterfly* were sung more than well, under the baton of English conductor Warwick Braithwaite, by Ronald Dowd, Tais Taras, Alan Light, Neil Easton, Raymond McDonald and the young Margreta Elkins, who alternated as Azucena with another novice, who had followed the company from New Zealand, Heather Begg. Alan Light had no understudy and sang three Rigolettos in a row, while alternating as Mephistopheles, De Luna and Sharpless! The venture was doomed from the start and the company disintegrated very quickly.

When it became obvious that the Trust's lofty initial aim to 'support existing organizations' proved to have unacceptable conditions attached to it (see Trust chapters), Miss Johnson followed Mrs Lorenz into limbo, if a little more slowly. The National Theatre still had its three schools, if not the finances to give students exposure in the full-sized Princess Theatre, as of old.

Miss Johnson's answer to this situation was little short of lunatic, but her backers — unaware of what the future held — fell in with her plan. If Lilian Baylis could raise the money to build Sadler's Wells, Gertrude Johnson could build a National Theatre in Melbourne. So, in 1956, a Building Appeal was launched to build or buy a theatre to become the home for the Australian National Theatre, its schools *and Companies.*

The next eighteen years were unhappy ones. Though money rolled in initially ($119,000 of it), rising building and land costs swallowed up any hopes for ultimate success. A series of fires destroyed any incentive to proceed with the venture, yet the capital invested under the shrewd eyes of Miss Johnson's few remaining backers multiplied and in 1974 The National Theatre in St Kilda was actually completed and opened, though not by the National Theatre's own opera, ballet or drama companies; that honour went to the two budding 'regional' companies, Ballet Victoria and the Victorian Opera Company. Only the schools, which occupy the ground floor of the huge building remain as a lasting memorial to Gertrude Johnson's memory; she died in 1973,

as the finishing touches were being given to the reality of her dream. It was the teaching of the arts which was her primary aim and it is the teaching of the arts which is her final monument. The Opera School in particular (under the direction of Peter Rorke) has remained true to her principles. It does not teach singing, but teaches singers to perform in opera. It is easy to say that the school is not producing a John Shaw, Elizabeth Fretwell or Marie Collier every year as it did twenty-five years ago. I query the premise. Shaw, Fretwell and Collier were not world-famous when they started at the National, and who is to say that young singers like Peter Pianella, John Pickering, Carole Mackenzie, Jonathan Summers or Lynette Kutchewski will not be the Shaws and Colliers of the future? Summers' career in England seems to be heading in this direction already. Only time will tell and at least the students now have the opportunity to appear once or twice a year in a full-size theatre under ideal performing conditions to practise what they are taught. In this way the National Theatre is fulfilling its destiny.

PRINCESS THEATRE

by arrangement with
Garnet H. Carroll, O.B.E.

THE AUSTRALIAN NATIONAL THEATRE MOVEMENT

ROYAL PERFORMANCE

PROGRAMME

8 p.m. ———— PROLOGUE: "TALES OF HOFFMANN"

8.30 p.m. ———— Arrival of Her Majesty the Queen
and His Royal Highness the Duke of Edinburgh.

GOD SAVE THE QUEEN

TALES OF HOFFMANN

OPERA IN THREE ACTS

By
OFFENBACH

Orchestration
VERDON WILLIAMS

Scenery and Costumes by
LOUIS KAHAN

Choreography by
VALRENE TWEEDIE

Stage Director
JAMES CONVERY

Producer—STEFAN HAAG

Conductor—JOSEPH POST

THE NATIONAL THEATRE OPERA CHORUS
Chorus Master—Dr. HERMAN SCHILDBERGER

THE VICTORIAN SYMPHONY ORCHESTRA
by arrangement with the Australian Broadcasting Commission
Leader—BERTHA JORGENSEN

CAST

in order of appearance

Nathaniel	NOEL SPARK
Nicklaus	DOROTHEA DEEGAN
Hoffman	LANCE INGRAM
Herman	LEONARD DELANY
Spalanzani	STEFAN HAAG
Cochenille	LORENZO NOLAN
Coppelius	JOHN SHAW
Olympia	BARBARA WILSON
Giulietta	MARIE COLLIER
Pitichinaccio	LORENZO NOLAN
Schlemil	ROBERT ALLMAN
Dapertutto	JOHN SHAW
Antonia	BETTY FRETWELL
Crespel	KEITH NEILSON
Franz	LORENZO NOLAN
Miracle	JOHN SHAW
Mother	JUSTINE RETTICK

Guests, Dancers, Masqueraders, Servants and Ballet.

CHORUS—LADIES : Cavel Armstrong, Lola Brukner, Jean Brunning, Shirley Dummett, Nancy Grant, Marcia Griffiths, Ruby McBean, Shirley Nicholls, Mary O'Phelan, Lola Wright.

CHORUS—GENTLEMEN : Norman Carbuhn, William Creswell, Robert Gowtey, Frederick Lang, Russell Rowley, Conrad Raff, Benjamin Reilly, Ray Sawyers, Ralph Small, Arthur Thomas, Stanley Weekes.

BALLET—Marion Ward, Gayrie MacSween, Valrene Tweedie, Pauline Jones, Kay Smith, Noelle Aitkin, Janet Keyte, Gwenda Kaires, Judith Cohen, Sandy Brown, Bruce Morrow, William Carse, Vivian Arnold, Geoffrey Ingram, Ronald Reay, Mel. Clifford.

Guests in Act II
June Brown, Peter Norton, Harry Starling, Mary Hardy, Betty Rechtor, John Ludbrooke, Pamela Greenall, Robert Eastgate.

ACT 1 : The Home of Spalanzani about 1780.

ACT II : A Terrace in Venice about 1800.

ACT III : The Home of Crespel about 1820.

SYNOPSIS

Offenbach's masterpiece is based on three separate stories by Hoffmann. It was first produced in Paris in 1881.

The prologue takes place in the taproom of Luther's tavern in Nuremberg. The students are drinking and singing. Hoffmann tells them of the three unfortunate loves in his life. Each of the three acts reveals one of these.

ACT I. is of his love for the beatuiful Olympia, who is really only a wonderful mechanical doll.

Interval

ACT II. tells of his violent passion for the beautiful courtesan Giulietta. She encourages him in order to steal his reflection in a mirror to please Dapertutto, an evil genius. Twice had Hoffmann passed through the fire of passion and been scorched by its flames.

Interval

ACT III. he experiences the deepest, purest, and only real love of his life, but dire misfortune awaited him once more. Antonia, who loves him in return, is afflicted with consumption, unknown to Hoffmann.

— *Finis* —

The Elizabethan Theatre Trust

5

The Australian Opera sprang out of the original Australian Elizabethan Theatre Trust which was created in 1954 to commemorate the first visit of Elizabeth II, Queen of England and Australia, to the Antipodes. The Trust, in spite of a chequered career, continues in existence as an autonomous body, no longer the subject of mud-slinging as in days of old, but still slightly suspect to the old guard who once fought it, but have long run out of ammunition.

The Elizabethan Theatre Trust must reappear periodically in any survey of the theatrical arts in Australia, but a detailed history or assessment of its present role is out of place in these pages. Let us just say that since the arrival of its current General Manager, Jeffry Joynton-Smith, in 1970 it has proceeded carefully on a strictly proscribed course, governed by the one thing it never had in its more turbulent years: sound business management. Whether its existence beside the Australia Council is an anachronism or not, whether it should be disbanded, amalgamated with the Council or whether it should expand in new directions are matters which concern only the functionaries of the immense bureaucracy which has grown up around the arts since the creation of the original Australian Council for the Arts, (now the Australia Council).

Opera and ballet are no longer the concern of the Trust. Suffice to say here that it appears to be fulfilling its functions with a degree of success that should silence all critics. If it does not, it only goes to show that critics are human (a statement often disputed) and subject to failings, among which sour grapes are part of the annual harvest.

What makes the Trust important in this context is the fact that both the Australian Opera and the Australian Ballet were originally part and parcel of the Trust's activities. The Opera was actually the Elizabethan Trust Opera Company, while the Ballet was under the direction of the Trust, though it was an independent body which could have broken away had it wished to do so. The ballet's potential independence resulted in its comparative lack of involvement in the political and artistic crises which followed each other in the opera field.

The Australian Elizabethan Theatre Trust, also known variously as the Elizabethan Theatre Trust, the Elizabethan Trust, the A.E.T.T., or simply The Trust, was born out of the desire to procreate drama, not opera or ballet! Even more surprisingly, it was the procreation of *Shakespearean* drama which was the starting point, yet of all the performing arts, Elizabethan theatre has been least promoted by the body which actually bears its name, (though, as explained earlier, the 'Elizabethan' in the Trust's title was not derived from the Elizabeth of Shakespeare's day).

Yes, it all began with straight drama, even though in time, as the Trust grew, the complaint was universal (and justified) that it treated drama as the Cinderella of the arts.

It was an odd description, because the two Ugly Sisters, opera and ballet, turned out to be beauties who ran off with two Prince Charmings, Fame and Fortune, while Cinders remained for too many years grovelling in the ashes. It is a long story, and at least the beginning must be told.

It was in the fateful year of 1951 that the company led by John Alden, in an Australia-wide tour of Shakespeare plays, sowed the seed which resulted in the Elizabethan Theatre Trust. It was the company manager, one Elsie Beyer, who approached the Arts Committee for the Jubilee Year for a grant of $20,000 to enable the John Alden Company to continue touring in Australia. She didn't succeed, but the Committee's Chairman, one Charles Moses, found his way through the Canberra jungle to the most famous non-medical doctor in Australia, Dr H. C. Coombs, then the Chairman of the Commonwealth Bank.

At this point Elsie Beyer and John Alden disappear from view. Moses, the head of the Australian Broadcasting Commission, knew the benefits that a soundly backed artistic management can bring to the arts and Coombs fell in with his ideas. Not that Moses and Coombs were worried. There was plenty of legitimate theatre around at the time. Repertory companies, both professional and amateur, were playing to good houses and the commercial theatre was in the midst of the great post-war boom. *South Pacific* and *My Fair Lady* were following *Oklahoma!* and *Brigadoon* and it needed a Jeremiah to foresee the impact of television still to come. But there was already need for subsidy in some areas of the performing arts; opera and ballet were beginning to price themselves out of the market. Moses had seen the promised land and if he objected to the take-over of his project by Dr Coombs, he did not show it.

The arrival of the Queen in 1954 gave the Trust its initial impetus. Two hundred and forty thousand dollars was raised, $180,000 from the public and $60,000 from the Federal Government and for the first time a body dedicated to promoting the arts was offered tax-deductibility for donations. It was a revolutionary concept and so was the policy which was outlined at a series of public meetings. The Trust would not create its own companies, but would assist existing bodies to improve their standards and to work together toward a national policy in the arts!

Dr Coombs learnt his lesson very quickly, but not until he tried to implement these initial aims, which were unrealistic to say the least. The ladies and gentlemen (mainly the former) in charge of the many theatrical bodies in Australia clung tenaciously to their hard-won privileges. The successful joint opera season of the Melbourne and Sydney 'National' companies of 1952 had proved one thing: in a joint success there is less personal glory than in separate failure. And personal glory was the name of the game!

In 1954 Dr Coombs blithely waved away any thought that Mesdames Johnson and Lorenz would not collaborate if offered assistance at Federal level. After all, they were both heavily in debt and could not fail to follow lofty ideals backed with hard cash. The man known as 'Nugget' still had his head stuck in the golden sands. He believed he could create great Australian opera and ballet companies, perhaps even a national drama company. Elizabeth II would be honoured by the creation of a cultural heritage as great as that present in the day of Elizabeth I.

When the Elizabethan Trust Opera Company was brought into being it was a birth too close to the birth of a typical Australian pioneer child in the 1800s for comfort. Threatened miscarriage was as real as the possibility of abortion. Fathering the infant was easy – isn't it always! – but bringing it into the world was another matter. A nine year gestation period, with another four years in labour, was due not to any lack of innate robustness in either mother or child, but the lack of any kind of operatic gynaecologist. A series of doctors attended the confinement, each learning his craft at the expense of the child, but the Trust in its pains to bring forth the Australian Opera stubbornly refused to call in experts to assist it.

Great credit may be due to the various novices in opera management in charge during the opera company's formative years, particularly to John Young and Stephen Hall, but they and their predecessors learnt on the job. If they learnt well, they did so at the expense of the company they were building. It is staggering that they achieved as much as they did and their failings were the failings of the theatrical community in this country, not their own. Expecting young singers to make up for poor planning, inefficient management, artistic inexperience and a basic lack of know-how in all departments was to court disaster. One top-rank administrator at the very start would have repaid his own salary in financial returns in no time at all and the unending traumas of the first ten years would have been avoided.

The fault lay not with the ever-changing administrators, but with the Trust's Board of Directors, for refusing to face the reality that Australia has never yet bred its own opera managers. They hired boys to do a man's job and forgot that the boys in the backroom are more important to the success of an opera company than the best of singers. The history of opera in Australia since 1954 must be read in the light of the success or failure of its administrators.

The creation of the A.E.T.T. in 1954 initially had the opposite effect to its intentions in the field of opera. One of the main considerations of the new body had been the fact that the two 'National' opera companies in Melbourne and Sydney were heavily in debt and unlikely to survive without some form of financial assistance. To put the record straight, the assistance was in fact offered and rejected, because the Trust asked for a say in the two companies' affairs.

This was not an unexpected reaction – except perhaps to the as yet artistically innocent Dr Coombs.

Miss Johnson in Melbourne and Mrs Lorenz in Sydney, not unreasonably, pointed to the excellent work their companies had done and feared that their life-work would be destroyed through outside interference. Less reasonably, they expected money to be handed to them regardless of results. It proved ultimately to be one of the great ironies of the Trust venture into opera that its own financial forays in the field proved to be, if anything, even less successful than those of the two ladies to whom it refused to hand its funds with no strings attached.

It was a strange impasse and one, considering the people involved, which may have been unavoidable. The money man, Coombs, felt the need for tight financial accounting, as accountants have done since time immemorial. He did not know that trying to run any kind of theatrical venture, let alone an opera company, on strict business practice lines is an impossibility.

In 1955 Hugh Hunt, the first Executive Director of the Elizabethan Theatre Trust actually created a Board of Directors to head what was to be called 'The Australian Opera Company', with power to create an Opera Advisory Committee, a Finance Committee, an Itinerary Committee, to hire executive staff and to do a thousand and one other things needed to start an operation many times the size of the Trust itself. At that early stage the creation of a huge bureaucracy was planned down to the last detail!

Gertrude Johnson and Mrs Lorenz were members of the original board and then of the Opera Advisory Committee which was to do the actual planning. Their colleagues on the latter included a set of reasonably independent and responsible people from whom the two ladies had very little to fear.

Sir Charles Moses, as head of the A.B.C., had the power to give the A.B.C. Symphony Orchestra in each state to the company, something he had done for past Melbourne and Sydney seasons and would do in future for the Trust operas. Frank Tait controlled the Williamson theatres in which all opera companies had to play. Sir Bernard Heinze was a senior musician whose ability in programming would have been of value (though many thought Joseph Post might have been a better choice). The only other member of the Opera Board was the ubiquitous Colonel Aubrey Gibson, whose efforts in the fund-raising field were to be a great asset to the future company.

All in all the proposed Opera Board, if the two ladies had played ball, could have been a very sound proposition for them. They were the only two members who really knew what was involved and should have got their way without too much difficulty. Unfortunately their way was not one but two ways: mine and mine. Not even the success of their

1952 joint venture had been able to iron out the fact that here were two inflexible heads, neither of which would accept second billing, let alone billing *en bloc,* which is what the Opera Board would have meant. It is more than likely that their ultimate refusal to sit on the Board was caused in each case by the presence of the other.

There was talk of the Trust offering management services, to allow each company to remain independent, with a possible interchange of artists and eventual joint seasons, but management from outside was quite unacceptable and it is not necessary to quote the exact terms of rejection on each side; they amounted to the same thing: we did all right without the Trust and we don't need it now. Famous last words!

With the Chairman of the Commonwealth Bank at its head, the Trust could hardly be expected to bow to two stubborn old ladies and it finally began to plan an initial independent season for 1956.* It was a notable year for Australia because it saw the introduction of television, and for Melbourne, because it was the year of the Olympic Games. It also happened to be the bicentenary of Mozart's birth, resulting in a rash of new Mozart recordings and immense coverage being given to his works throughout the world. Perhaps fortunately, this fact finally swung the Trust to choosing an initial season of four Mozart operas, rejecting the first over-ambitious idea to programme Wagner's *Mastersingers* and Strauss' *Rosenkavalier;* the mind boggles at tours of those two productions by a raw new company.

The decision was a wise one but it would hardly have been made by the opera company's first General Manager, Robert Quentin, a man widely experienced in drama, but with no experience whatever in the field of opera. Fortunately the prospect of regular pay and exposure in all states had resulted in mass desertions from the camps of both Miss Johnson and Mrs Lorenz. Stefan Haag had been responsible for the Melbourne National Theatre's most successful productions and Joseph Post had conducted the companies in both capital cities for many years. As Production Manager and Musical Director they did an admirable job in countering Quentin's inexperience. The repertoire for the 1956 season consisted of *The Marriage of Figaro, Don Giovanni, The Magic Flute* and *Cosi fan tutte.* On the assumption that the Olympic Games would bring immense international audiences to Melbourne, two world famous guest stars, Sena Jurinac and Sesto Bruscantini, were engaged for the Melbourne season only, replacing local singers who sang their parts in Adelaide, Perth, Brisbane, Hobart and Sydney.

---

* It should be noted that the last full-scale seasons by the two older companies were those of 1954, fully two years earlier, and that the Trust did not therefore madly rush into competition without giving them the opportunity to become a part of the Greater Australian company.

The start of the present The programme of the very first production of the Elizabethan Trust's as yet untitled opera company in 1956. The present Australian Opera is a direct continuation of this. Neil Warren-Smith is the only singer in this cast who has sung with the company without interruption. (John Shaw had many years overseas before returning on a regular basis.)

THE AUSTRALIAN ELIZABETHAN THEATRE TRUST
by arrangement with J. C. WILLIAMSON THEATRES LTD.

present

The Marriage of Figaro

by WOLFGANG AMADEUS MOZART

Book by Lorenzo da Ponte, after Beaumarchais, Translated by E. J. Dent

with

THE WEST AUSTRALIAN SYMPHONY ORCHESTRA
by courtesy of The Australian Broadcasting Commission.

Musical Director: JOSEPH POST
Associate Conductor: ERIC CLAPHAM

Production by DENNIS ARUNDELL

Scenery and Costumes designed by KENNETH ROWELL

The action takes place during one day in and about the country residence of Count Almaviva

ACT   I   AN ANTICHAMBER
ACT II   THE COUNTESS' BOUDOIR
ACT III   THE GREAT HALL
ACT IV   A SECLUDED PART OF THE GARDEN

There will be three intervals   ten minutes each

General Manager for Opera — ROBERT QUENTIN

CHARACTERS IN ORDER OF APPEARANCE

Figaro, valet to Count Almaviva .... JOHN CAMERON

Susanna, maid to the Countess, fiancee of Figaro ... ... VALDA BAGNALL

Doctor Bartolo ... ... KEITH NEILSON

Marcellina, his housekeeper ... ... WILMA WHITNEY

Cherubino, a page-boy ... ... BETTINA BENFIELD

Barbarina, a village girl ... ... JAN ROSS

Count Almaviva ... ... JOHN SHAW

Don Basilio, a music master ... ... EREACH RILEY

Rosina, Countess Almaviva ... ... NITA MAUGHAN

Antonio, a gardener, father of Barbarina, uncle of Susanna NEIL WARREN-SMITH

Don Curzio, Counsellor at law RAYMOND McDONALD

Servants and Villagers JEAN BRUNNING, ELAINE SIBRETT, JANICE GOLDMAN, JOAN LEVECKE, -JOY MAMMEN, BETTY WEST, JOHN COCKERILL, GREG DEMPSEY, NORMAN HODGKINSON, NOEL McCABE, PHILIP SHALVEY.

Footmen   I. DONALDSON, T. GUY, L. OWENS, C. SMITH, C. WILSON.

OPERA STAFF

Production Director ... ... STEFAN HAAG
Stage Manager ... ... COLLEEN GOUGH
Stage Manager ... ... WILL THOMPSON
Business Manager ... ... JOHN ROHDE
Music Assistant ... ... GEORGE HUMPHREY
Press Officer ... ... BETTY BATEMAN
Assist. Stage Manager ... ... JOHN COCKERILL
Assist. Stage Manager ... ... ANGUS KIDSTON
Opera Secretary ... ... JOAN LEVECKE
Electrician ... ... ERNIE LIETCH
Wardrobe Mistress ... ... MARY POXON

Scenery and properties made by Joe White and assistants in the workshops of J. C. Williamson Theatres Ltd., and at the Princess Theatre, Melbourne. Scenery painted by George Kenyan, Dres Hardingham and Rupert Browne.

Costumes made under the supervision of Phyll Foulkes in the wardrobe of the National Theatre, Melbourne.

Headwear by Marjorie Head. Wigs by Barnetts and Mei Picci, Melbourne. Footwear by Maloney and by Imbesi, Melbourne.

Special jewellery by Lustre Jewellery Co.

Handpainted costumes by the Art School of the Melbourne Technical College.

Electrical Equipment by Strand Electrics. Special effects for "The Magic Flute" by Pani, Vienna.

Publicity: Ron Patton Ltd.

The Opera Company wishes to state its indebtedness and to express special thanks to Miss Gertrude Johnson of the National Theatre Movement, Melbourne.

Jurinac and Bruscantini were indeed fine singers to feature in an all-Mozart season in Mozart's Year. Unfortunately nobody thought to inform them that the operas would be performed in English and only weeks before their arrival desperate telegrams flew back and forth begging them to at least learn the recitatives in English, but to no avail, and who could blame them? By default, the leading local singers had to learn most of the set pieces in Italian so that the ensembles at least would be sung in one language.

In the end, the Melbourne season was the least successful. Melburnians were glued to brand new television sets, or present in person at the various sporting fixtures, and takings at the opera failed to equal the 80 per cent capacity which was reached in all other cities.

Melbourne notwithstanding, the initial season of the as yet unnamed opera company ('The Mozart Opera Season 1956') was unquestionably a success, a much bigger success than any season for a good many years thereafter. It gave the company a flying start, and the inevitable deficit which must accompany any tour of opera involving roughly 8500 miles, was less than $40,000. Box office takings of nearly a quarter of a million dollars were $50,000 more than the company took in 1966, ten years later!

It is not too hard to find the reasons for that first season's success. The creation of the A.E.T.T. had received extensive coverage. While not only the company's General Manager, but also its Press Officer, Betty Bateman, were ignorant of matters operatic, each in his or her own way did an excellent job, the latter not least in promoting opera as family entertainment. The grand dames in their jewels came anyway, but Bateman managed to bring in the mums and dads, and what they saw was to their taste; and this last fact — too quickly forgotten — was in the end to bring the whole venture to fruition, though more than a dozen years were to pass before the instinctive correctness of this way of promoting opera was to be exploited deliberately.

The producers of this first season were Stefan Haag and Dennis Arundell, one Australian and one English, both experienced not only in making opera work, but in making it entertaining. Haag is often accused of being unsubtle, but subtlety was the last thing the Australian public wanted in 1956. Subtlety involves the grasping of finer points which can only be appreciated after long familiarity with a work. A very small proportion of the original audiences would have been familiar with these four Mozart operas and, if Haag brought many a point home with a sledge hammer, that suited them fine. As for Arundell, his productions of *Figaro* and *Don Giovanni* bore the imprint of Sadler's Wells, the home of opera aimed at the people, rather than at the snobs. No better two producers could have been chosen to launch those particular works at that particular time.

Yet ultimately the success belonged, as always in Australia, to the singers. While many of the best had wandered off overseas while waiting for the new company to become

The first of the first *The Marriage of Figaro* which launched the Elizabethan Theatre Trust Opera Company, which became the Australian Opera. Valda Bagnall as Susanna, John Shaw as Count Almaviva and Bettine Benfield as Cherubino led an ensemble of singers which the company was not to equal for many years to come.

a reality (we had lost Marie Collier, Elizabeth Fretwell, Robert Allman, Albert Lance and John Lanigan, to name but a few) the pool of singers built up in Melbourne and Sydney still held enough fish to produce standards which were vocally substantially better than those at Sadler's Wells, though histrionically still lagged behind.

A local Don, John Shaw, grasped with both hands the opportunity to out-sing Bruscantini's Leporello in *Don Giovanni* and as Count Almaviva also stole *The Marriage of Figaro* from smooth-voiced John Cameron's Figaro (or Bruscantini's, when that master was singing the title role).

Max Worthley, still in his prime, was a superb Ottavio and Tamino, while Marjorie Conley amply demonstrated what a great loss to opera her early death three years later was to be. Her husband, Geoffrey Chard, already well on the way to the fine career he has had (and is still having) in England, was Papageno, Keith Neilson, Jenifer Eddy and Valda Bagnall more than held their own and the appearance in small parts of singers like Neil Warren-Smith, Gregory Dempsey and Raymond McDonald showed that the company was already building from strength.

There were actually four guests during that first season. Jurinac and Bruscantini, who amply justified their presence by singing superbly, were joined by expatriate Stanley Clark-son who, unlike his fellow-guests, played Sarastro in all states and made a deep impression (pun intended). Finally, another Australian, Kevin Miller, returned for some performances of Ferrando in *Cosi fan tutte*.

Though scenery and costumes were meagre by modern standards, they were entrusted to experienced designers who made much out of the little which was at their disposal. Kenneth Rowell, Desmonde Downing, Tim Walton and Louis Kahan are all still very much in the business today; the last three had designs in the 1975 Australian Opera Season, though the first left us many years ago to meet the demands for his services overseas. He is now one of the highest-priced, in both cash and estimation, designers in the world.

Lest it be thought that the whole thing just happened overnight and happened without problems, the vagaries of travel in 1956 should be remembered. Moving a company of singers by air was financially unthinkable and the thought of flying at all as recently as twenty years ago was still anathema to many people. Theatrical companies went by train and principals were envied the 'luxury' of their claustrophobic sleeping cupboards by choristers forced to sit upright all night in the coaches.

The Theatre Royal in Adelaide saw the birth of the com-

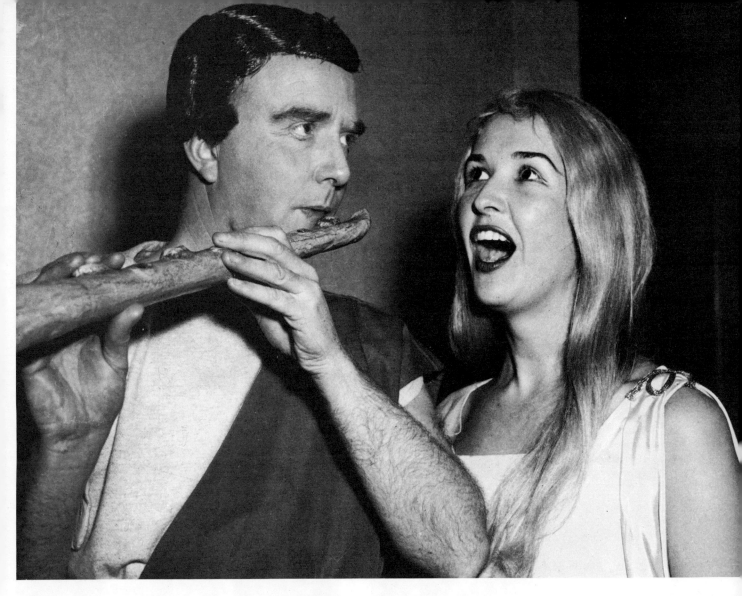

Marjorie Conley, one of Australia's best young singers, who died tragically in 1959 before her great promise could be fulfilled. In *The Magic Flute* during the Elizabethan Trust Opera Company's first season in 1956, with Adelaide tenor Max Worthley as Tamino.

pany on 21 July 1956, but its season there was followed not by Melbourne or Sydney, but by Perth a short four weeks later. And almost immediately management and artists were plunged into their first crisis; a crisis not of their own making. Train services in those days were no better than they are now and, almost inevitably, the Opera Special struck trouble in the midst of the Nullabor Plain. While the train was not involved in any spectacular wreck, a twelve-hour delay played havoc with pre-planned rehearsals for the 23 August opening at Her Majesty's Theatre in Perth.

It is strange what priorities people adopt in emergencies. The final dress rehearsal was to take place on the 22nd, the day the company was stuck at Kalgoorlie. A special aircraft was chartered and brought eight of the principals to Perth by 11.30 a.m., leaving Neil Warren-Smith, Jan Ross and Raymond McDonald to follow on with the chorus. Perhaps Antonio, Barbarina and Don Curzio are not the most important members of *The Marriage of Figaro* cast, but a full dress rehearsal without them (or the chorus) must have been a farce. Perhaps the formidable Betty Bateman arranged the whole thing as one of her superb publicity stunts? It would have been quite in keeping and certainly made the headlines, as did her promotion ideas which worked wonders, though they may make us smile today.

'Love's Amusing Round-About' (echoes of *La Ronde*) advertised *Figaro,* and *Cosi fan tutte* was billed as 'The humorous tale of a woman's flirtations'! Presumably Marjorie Conley's Fiordiligi was the flirt, though Eunice McGowan's Dorabella could have sued for defamation. 'The intriguing story of a Don Juan' made it clear that John Shaw in *Don Giovanni* was an operatic personification of Errol Flynn, while erudite scholars pointed out that Giovanni was Italian for Juan and that the opera was in fact about Don Juan himself. As for Stefan Haag's *Magic Flute,* complete with his daring young girls on their flying machine (the three 'Boys'), it was billed in simple pantomimic language as 'Enchantment – Fantasy – Comedy'.

It was a time of happy-go-lucky improvisation, aimed at an unsophisticated audience. There were protests at the 'cheapening' of Mozart, but musical and production standards were way ahead of those of J. C. Williamson's Italian Grand Opera Season of the year before. No doubt the growing Italian migrant population stayed away in their hundreds, but this was opera for the people starting at a level which Lilian Baylis' Sadler's Wells Opera reached only after two decades of continuous operation. And it was the people rather than the musical snobs who came to that first season. If they came for all the wrong reasons, if they were

51

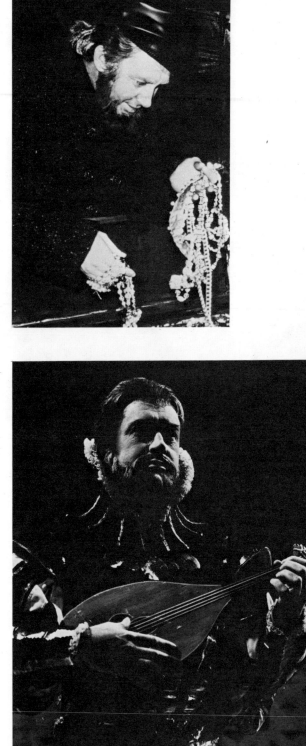

The many faces of Neil Warren-Smith The 'oldest inhabi-
tant' in terms of service with the Australian Opera. Warren-
Smith is the only singer who has sung continuously with
the company since the first Trust season in 1956 and has
provided many historic landmarks with roles like Boris
Godounov and Baron Ochs.

Above, as Tommaso in d'Albert's *Tiefland*, 1955; *above
right*, as Daland in *The Flying Dutchman*, 1967; *right*, as Don
Giovanni in *Don Giovanni*, 1967; *far right*, as Bartolo in *The
Barber of Seville*, 1958.

The many face of Neil Warren-Smith As Kečal (*above*) in *The Bartered Bride*, 1957; and as Boris (*right*), in *Boris Godounov* with Allan Ferris, 1966.

perhaps disappointed and bored when the *Magic Flute* did not include the Great Levante, the important thing was that Quentin and Bateman put bums on seats and Haag, Arundell and Post at least offered value for money, though the $2.10 top price was considered just a little steep. At a price three times as high ten years later the company's overall takings were 20 per cent less! Let us not underestimate the worth of that first season or the value of the team that started it.

There appears to have been an idea in the minds of the Trust and/or Robert Quentin that the loss made in 1956 was somehow a disgrace. The fact that J. C. Williamson's had lost a lot more during their international season the previous year was immaterial. The day had not yet dawned when operatic deficits were accepted as inevitable. Singers were, after all, only engaged by the season. Admittedly, they were paid, which is more than could be said of most of those appearing in the pre-Trust local companies, but the expense of rehearsals was minimal; no pay or half-pay was the rule and not the exception. And with salaries in the $50 per week range for principals it should have been easy to break even on 'small' operas like those of Mozart, always remembering that orchestral costs were nil, thanks to the benevolence of Moses high on Mount A.B.C., or so the reasoning went.

It was determined therefore to improve the performance in 1957, to eliminate all that wastefulness, to play more popular operas, to attract a larger public, to import more principals, to limit the season and to enlarge the repertoire. It was a foolproof method of going bankrupt. By some miracle the company survived 1957 with a deficit of only $53,000 after reducing its season from twenty-seven weeks to seventeen. Not that the year did not see some excellent performances of opera, but ambition began to rear an early and ugly head; everybody wanted to have his or her genius recognized and the multi-headed artistic management was the worst offender.

Nevertheless, certain patterns emerged in 1957 which ultimately proved to have such merit that they returned in later years, just as the aiming at non-operatic audiences in the first season was forgotten, only to be resuscitated by Harry M. Miller and Tony Frewin in later years. The best of these ideas was the principle of importing singers of Australian origin who had made good overseas (and God knows there were enough of those even then) and to star them in roles in which they had already proved themselves. Nothing helps a young company more than to work alongside artists who know exactly what they are doing. The brief visit of Jurinac and Bruscantini during the Melbourne Olympic Season had proved the point already, though the language problem prevented it being fully effective. Now the company concentrated on people who had sung their parts in English with success.

Working his way up   The man who turned the fortunes of the Australian Opera in 1966, John Young, sang and produced his way up to the top before becoming the company's Administrator. As Mr Peacham in James Mills' 1957 production of Gay's *The Beggar's Opera* with Jenifer Eddy and Wilma Whitney. Young specialized in character roles after experience in musicals like *Kismet*. He played Spalanzani in *The Tales of Hoffmann* on opening night 1957 when the revolving stage stuck and he was forced to ad lib for eight and a half minutes, concluding with a rendition of 'I'm Walking Backwards for Christmas', without music by Offenbach.

Much has been written about Joan Hammond's great contribution to opera in England as well as in Australia. (Let me leave her title to her post-opera life; Joan Hammond was the grand dame of opera long before she was damed with great praise.) In 1957 she reigned supreme in the great *prima donna* roles wherever they were performed in English. Her Tosca was universally admired in better company than Australia could provide and it was as Tosca she was brought back to her homeland by the Trust.

This was a Tosca in the grand manner, in the grand old manner perhaps, but *Tosca* defies modernization and Tosca is, after all, a *prima donna* playing a *prima donna* and Hammond had always had that strange quality of stars known simply as 'presence'. Her first act entrance may have been corny and old-fashioned, but the moment she appeared there was unmistakably Somebody up there. If ever a singer had the ability to draw applause with an entrance, that singer was Joan Hammond and Tosca was the role to bring out that quality. The fact that she sang the part superbly throughout her career is almost incidental.

In a totally different field Elsie Morison had similar presence. Hers was more ethereal in a role like Mimi and more earthy as the country lass, Mařenka, in *The Bartered Bride*. *La Bohème, Tosca* and *The Bartered Bride* were built around their soprano leads and proved to be the big successes of 1957. *Otello* and *The Tales of Hoffmann* were of a lesser stature and the between-season *Beggar's Opera* was more notable for the appearance of John Young as Mr Peachum, Shaw's McHeath and young Jenifer Eddy's Polly, than as the popular entertainment it should have been, but wasn't.

But, Hammond and Morrison notwithstanding, local singers were still the backbone of the company. No other country has produced innately adaptable singers in such quantities. The Trust may well have gained from the previous training and experience of young singers in companies such as Melbourne's and Sydney's competing National Operas, but its producers were still dealing with raw material which had instinctive artistry rather than any degree of professionalism. They carried off their performances with tremendous panache, but also with enough improvisation to give a professional producer heart attacks. It was just as well that people like Stefan Haag were used to working in the chaos which surrounded the Melbourne National Theatre Opera seasons; he thought little of it when his singers made wrong entries, as long as they were alert enough to make the audience believe that that was where they were supposed to put in an appearance. And Australian singers are nothing if not enterprising in an emergency.

Any success the company had in 1957, apart from the contribution of Hammond and Morison, came from the sheer *joie de vivre* of the enlarged company. None of the works required the ensemble discipline of the Mozart operas, all gave opportunities for belting out their best notes for the most effect and there was ample space for high jinks, although not in the two major serious works, *Tosca* and *Otello,* both produced by the veteran baritone Arnold Matters. The former relies almost totally on its three leading singers and, apart from Hammond's imposing Tosca, both Ronald Dowd and John Shaw had sung Cavaradossi and Scarpia many times before.

With Dowd and Hammond at the peak of their form and Shaw well into his best years, though still rather young, Puccini's 'cheap little shocker' was cheap only in that the Trust's economy-packaged season used Tim Walton's old Melbourne National Theatre sets. (They were still good enough to bring applause ten years later, when they were resurrected for the Gobbi-Collier-Smith Adelaide Festival restaging!) If anything was needed to prove the quality of Gertrude Johnson original seasons, one has only to compare Walton's set for the last act of *Tosca,* with its immense statue atop the Castel Sant'Angelo, with the feeble 1974 Australian Opera setting which would have cost many times more than its brilliant ancestor.

The 1957 *Tosca* on one fateful occasion turned into more blood than thunder. John Shaw is a powerful gentleman and a powerful Scarpia. One night, as Tosca stabbed him, he grabbed her knife, which jumped from his hand and hit Joan Hammond near the eye, causing it to bleed profusely. Since Scarpia was supposed to be dead, Shaw could do nothing to help his wounded colleague who, in true old trooper fashion, determinedly completed the act while wiping the blood off her face with the table napkin she still had in her hand. Cries of 'Miss Hammond has been stabbed' echoed backstage, only to be met by her inseparable companion Lolita Marriot's reply: 'It can't be Miss Hammond! It must be John Shaw. It wouldn't make sense if he stabbed her!' True enough, but surely that was the only case in operatic history of Scarpia turning the tables on Tosca.

The *Bohème* sets also came from the National Theatre, (as did *The Beggar's Opera*) but here Robin Lovejoy took over his first professional opera production, apart from a trial run with the N.S.W. National Opera. His *Bohème* was not as stereotyped and traditionally fussy as Stefan Haag's and it was largely carried by Elsie Morison and her playful colleagues. Perhaps Max Worthley was too light a Rudolfo, perhaps Joy Mammen too shrill a Musetta; with Neil Easton, Alan Light and Neil Warren-Smith they produced a suitably undisciplined lot of Bohemians among whom Morison's Mimi shone in delightful contrast. Her death produced rather more than the usual flood of tears.

The logic behind this second Trust season was hard to follow. More productions spread over a shorter season were unlikely to produce a greater return, or less of a loss. Yet ambition knew no bounds and the company actually en-

gaged dancers, who were used indiscriminately to obtain maximum value from their services. Their contribution to *The Bartered Bride* was minimal, but at least that opera does call for dancers and some of its most familiar music would have gone by the board if the 'ballet' had not been available. Smetana's immortal opera was fortunate indeed in its execution – in fact, none of the offerings fell below a pretty substantial standard, whatever the blindness of the financial planning. Elsie Morison repeated her world-famous Mařenka with pathos, fine voice and a Czech-ness surprising in an Australian. This was no *Verkaufte Braut*, but a *Prodaná Nevěsta*. She was partnered by Max Worthley, a tenor then at his lyric best. Neil Warren-Smith reached major status as the marriage broker, Kečal, and a surprise hit was made by Raymond McDonald as the stuttering Vašek. The production by Stefan Haag was 'assisted by John Young' who also played the Ringmaster. Using his own text and principals he still appeared in the chorus, which included names like Joy Mammen, Gregory Dempsey, John Germain and Madge Stephens.

This was the year of the infamous revolving stage (hand-operated) and its vicissitudes; not only did it enable *The Bride* to change scenes without stopping the action, but it relied rather too heavily on casual scene shifters who had some difficulty in distinguishing left from right. One wheeled Kečal off stage just as he was supposed to start

his aria. Regrettably, both noticed the mistake simultaneously, both reversed the procedure and two negatives continued to make a positive – in the wrong direction! Finally Neil Warren-Smith began his aria off stage and nonchalantly wandered back onto the set which had by then miraculously found its way into the right position. It was to be a long time before stage management and lighting were to be considered worthy of skilled or experienced staff.

That ever-present opera bogey, laryngitis, made itself felt for the first time in the company's history when it hit Ronald Dowd during the Brisbane season. Trying to sing Cavaradossi while rehearsing *Otello* proved to be too much and by the time Verdi's masterpiece opened in Sydney, Dowd was in serious trouble. At the second performance his place was taken with spectacular and unexpected success by Raymond McDonald at five hours' notice. McDonald, the brilliantly weak Vašek of *The Bartered Bride*, was neither physically nor vocally equipped to sing Otello, one of the heaviest tenor roles in the repertoire. Cast as Cassio, he did not even get a full run-through, had to be prompted from the wings, had to appear cold, not only before a live audience, but before A.B.C. microphones broadcasting the performance, and still gave the performance of his life. McDonald actually completed all the Sydney performances before Dowd was well enough to take over the role in Melbourne.

(As a result of this one indisposition Ronald Dowd was to be cruelly downgraded seventeen years later! A second-rate import played the first *Tannhauser* in the opening season of the Sydney Opera House because it was 'too risky' to cast the by then fifty-eight year old Dowd in the premiere. Dowd had his revenge later by giving a world-class performance in the part for weeks on end, while his reliable overstudy retired ignominiously to European obscurity.)

When Dowd finally tackled *Otello* in full voice in Melbourne he gave an impressive performance, as did Joan Hammond and John Shaw as Desdemona and Iago. If there were failings in the performance, they were to be found in Arnold Matters' stolid production, for which Robin Lovejoy had to assist with the crowd scenes. It was a much too ambitious project for such a young company. *Otello* needs supreme singers and, whatever its virtues, *Otello's* second coming in the 1970s proved once again that it is an opera best left to international opera houses, if only because it is unrealistic to ask any singer to appear more than half a dozen times in one season as Otello.

Joseph Post conducted all the operas in 1957 as he had during the Mozart season. His musicianship in opera was unequalled in Australia and nobody who ever sang with him had anything but the highest praise for him. There were certainly no musical failings during his two year tenure as musical director. Whatever the reasons, and there were many, he chose to return to the bosom of the A.B.C. and year-round employment with a safe future. His loss was to be felt keenly, though Eric Clapham more than adequately took over the balance of his performances.

Staging a *Hoffmann* within three years of the National Theatre one, which had featured a vastly superior cast, a much better production (by the same producer, Stefan Haag) and the glamour of a Royal Command Performance was sheer lunacy. Even the most elementary opera buff will recognize at least some of the names in the following comparisons:

	1954	1957
Hoffmann	Albert Lance	Victor Franklin
Olympia	Barbara Wilson	Florence Pong
Giulietta	Marie Collier	Joyce Simmons
Antonia	Elizabeth Fretwell	Madge Stephens
Coppelius Dapertutto Miracle	John Shaw	Alan Light

No doubt audiences enjoyed *Hoffmann* as they always will, but in artistic terms it was a gamble which should not have been taken and did little more than stir up the Trust's Melbourne enemies, who quite rightly pointed out that Miss Johnson not only could do better, but had done better. It was a bad case of 'anything you can do I can do better' backfiring without much sympathy for the Trust from any quarter.

The man who saved the bacon Raymond McDonald (*below*) with Joan Hammond in the 1957 *Otello*. The small-voiced small-figured player of small-sized roles took over one of the heaviest tenor roles at a moment's notice when Ronald Dowd was suddenly taken ill. McDonald sang all but one of the Sydney performances with great success, though his long consequent career showed him to be a finely musical lyric tenor alone.

Right: McDonald in his properly allocated role as the stuttering Vašek in *The Bartered Bride* with the returning expatriate, Elsie Morison.

The Rankl Disaster

6

The departure of Joseph Post from the Trust Opera left the door open for Karl Rankl, who was appointed Musical Director, (a term which to him meant Artistic Director) in 1958 at the magnificent salary of $160 per week. Rankl appeared to be a major catch, because he was the man who had been in charge at Covent Garden for five years! The salary the unfortunate man was prepared to accept should have warned the Trust that it was a fish too easily caught, but its ignorance in matters operatic was abysmal. English migrants with operatic tastes threw their hands up in horror; the man who had been responsible for those dreadful nights at the Garden could not possibly do anything but wreck the new Australian company! In fact, Rankl was not the only reason for the failures to come, though he did bulldoze the administration into overspending to the extent that the season of the second year of his three year term had to be cancelled.

Rankl's term at Covent Garden was from 1946 to 1951, a period when things in England were admittedly bad. Nevertheless, the singers at his disposal included Flagstad, Schwarzkopf, Hotter, Welitsch, Silveri and just about every major English singer you could mention, plus Australians like Joan Hammond, Sylvia Fisher and Ken Neate. Rankl himself conducted twenty-four of the thirty operas produced during his five years in London, including Wagner's *Ring, Tristan, Mastersingers, Boris Godounov* and a scandal-producing *Salome* starring Ljuba Welitsch and designs by Salvador Dali. Yet the best that his obituaries could say of Rankl· was that he was 'building for the future', meaning that possibly the great days at Covent Garden under Kubelik and Solti would not have come as quickly as they did but for Rankl's groundwork.

Was Australia really looking for more 'ground work'? The 1956 and 1957 seasons were musically and vocally better than much produced by Rankl in London during those years. His departure from that scene was greeted with relief and I have been unable to discover anything of any value achieved by Rankl during the intervening years 1951–58. This was the man to whom the Elizabethan Trust Opera was presented on a platter, to do with as he wished. And he did and he wished; did he ever!

During that first year he wished on his unsuspecting public the travesty of an un-pretty gawky Mary Poppins, Constance Shacklock, as Carmen, of all roles. He elevated the no doubt worthy, but completely outclassed chorister Elizabeth West, to Elsa in *Lohengrin,* and appointed an experienced drama producer like John Sumner, without allowing him a say in casting!

The season was not an unmitigated disaster; there was too much talent in the company and, despite his tendency to act the tin-pot dictator, Rankl was an efficient conductor and the good orchestras of the A.B.C. were still at his disposal. It would have been almost impossible to fail completely and Rankl did not fail, he only ruined the company financially. God knows why his contract was renewed on the eve of 1959 when his direction had forced the abandonment of the next season. His contract had a get-out clause, but the Trust obviously believed that Australia must be wrong and the great Rankl must be right. The man behaved like God, so he must be God and if Moses was not his prophet, neither he nor Coombs showed any inclination to interfere in Rankl's re-appointment.

As for the Trust itself – busy as it was with looking after Hugh Hunt's abortive national drama company and entering the ballet field – its financial wizards either slept or looked the other way, even before Rankl's arrival. Four of the five operas in the 1958 season required big choruses. All demanded new sets. Singers had to be imported for several key roles and it was surely no coincidence that they included Covent Garden stock from the Rankl era. Sylvia Fisher and Raymond Nilsson were at least Australians being brought back, but the choice of Shacklock to sing Carmen and Ortrud was the type of thing which in years to come would drive opera lovers to distraction: 'Why import at all when better local talent is available', was the most common cry. Alternatively, if local talent is not available, why schedule an opera which demands a leading role that cannot be filled within a set budget?

Only sheer economics or personal favouritism can explain Shacklock's Carmen, yet this, the worst opera production up to that time, was the greatest box office success. The aiming of publicity at the masses for two years was still paying dividends and packed houses clearly were unaware that this under-sung travesty of Bizet's masterpiece was anything but what grand opera was all about. There was a magnificent orchestra conducted superbly by Rankl or most acceptably by Georg Tintner, making his first appearances here. Nilsson's José cut a dashing figure in his uniform, and his voice was quite acceptable, but Shacklock was prim and unexciting. The Escamillo of Robert Simmons was a sad case of miscasting and John Sumner's production amounted to little more than stage direction. According to him, 'I was asked to come and direct some traffic on a pre-ordained journey'. Sumner has never returned to opera production. His magnificent creation of the Melbourne Theatre Company has been his life's work, and working under Rankl's thumb on this one production of opera was obviously enough for him.

Carmen succeeded in spite of herself and so did *The Barber of Seville,* aimed at the same audience. The rest of the repertoire did not. With a man like Rankl, a 'world-class' conductor, in charge, the artistic pretensions of culture began to rear their ugly heads. The fact that the public accepted Mozart served up as popular entertainment was forgotten.

Too many highbrows, critics included, were clamouring for a greater degree of seriousness in programming and at this point the company fell well and truly between the traditional two stools. *Carmen* and the *Barber* were offered as a sop to popular taste. *Fidelio* and *Peter Grimes* were the offerings to higher standards and *Lohengrin* the bridge between the two – a curious bridge when it was presented in the dullest imitation-Bayreuth culture-down-your-throat manner. The *Carmen* public stayed away from *Peter Grimes* and the *Peter Grimes* public stayed away from *Carmen*. In the meantime Rankl was busy raising his own banner of excellence by demanding more and more rehearsals and more and more singers.

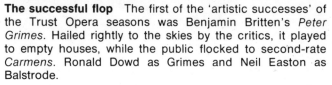

The successful flop The first of the 'artistic successes' of the Trust Opera seasons was Benjamin Britten's *Peter Grimes*. Hailed rightly to the skies by the critics, it played to empty houses, while the public flocked to second-rate *Carmens*. Ronald Dowd as Grimes and Neil Easton as Balstrode.

What once had been a band of happy-go-lucky talented young artists suddenly became a hard-working disciplined batch of imitation-European singers. Whatever they may have learnt from Rankl, they forgot to enjoy their work and it showed. The chorus sang out magnificently, the orchestras were better than ever, the ensembles came in exactly on the beat, but something was missing. Joy Mammen managed to achieve considerable success by singing Micaela's foolproof aria to herself. Ronald Dowd achieved a tremendous personal triumph as Peter Grimes, a role he was to repeat with equal success in England and Germany. It is difficult to find much else to pick out among the dozens of major performances of the season, though more shall be said about the production of Rossini's immortal *Barber*.

Robin Lovejoy alone achieved any kind of glory as a producer with his precisely paced *Peter Grimes*. Britten's opera

The first multi-purpose set Stefan Haag designed his own set for the 1958 production of Beethoven's *Fidelio*. The five squares in various elevations doubled as jailer's room, prison yard, dungeon and the world at large in the grand joyous choral finale seen here in all its glory. The orchestra outnumbered the chorus by three to one and conductor Karl Rankl made sure that everybody knew it.

Fidelio twelve years later   The 1970 *Fidelio* belonged to the era of visual splendour; Alan Lees' designs were a long way from Haag's economy set in 1958. The fact that the chorus still numbered only thirty-six was overlooked in the brilliance of John Copley's first production for the Australian Opera.

suited Rankl's pedantry admirably. Music and production demanded the kind of discipline Rankl was trying to instil in the company, while nobody expected vocal splendours from anybody except Dowd, who obliged magnificently. Sylvia Fisher, sadly out of voice throughout her months in Australia was a convincing Ellen Orford and the small part of the Methodist fisherman, Bob Boles, was tailor-made for the awkwardly moving young Donald Smith. Lovejoy even provided his own designs, giving the whole thing a unity of purpose which would not be equalled by the company for many years to come. Unhappily, *Grimes* was not box office with either of the publics at whom the season was aimed. *Fidelio* and *Lohengrin* were known to the *cognoscenti*, but Britten was still beyond the pale. Excellent write-ups managed to increase audiences in most cities, but it was not enough.

There are some who actually liked Stefan Haag's *Fidelio* of 1958 which was revived five years later. And why not? Didn't the whole cost of all costumes and scenery add up to no more than $1600? Wasn't this exactly the kind of economy the company needed? Actually, it is doubtful whether necessity was the father of this invention, though the management surely embraced it with open arms. Haag until then had been strictly a traditional producer and when he decided to go the other way he went, like the girl from Kansas City, just about as 'fur as fur can go'! A single square rostrum with four identically sized squares attached to each side was used for Rocco's room, the prison, the dungeon and the Halleluia finale, which can take place anywhere except in a dungeon, prison or Rocco's room. The four side panels were raised and lowered to create different patterns, all of which had only one thing in common, the necessity for the singers to climb steep inclines and to do their singing struggling to keep a foothold. Talk about leaving things to the audience's imagination!

Haag admittedly had a model from which he took his revolutionary simplification of a traditional production. Wieland Wagner, a grandson of Wagner himself, had started the vogue of replacing the very detailed realism demanded by his grandfather's scores with wide open stages lit cunningly to make much of very simple impressionistic props. There is no harm in experimentation – unless you fail, and Haag failed. His only justification was to be found among those who considered that the simplification of the stage picture allowed greater concentration on the music; in other words they welcomed a good performance in concert form. The trouble was that even at the best of times, apart from the orchestral sounds drawn by Rankl from the various A.B.C. orchestras, the performance failed to reach musical standards acceptable to the average listener and a poor concert performance of *Fidelio* is no replacement for a traditional production.

Sylvia Fisher, as Leonora, was a shadow of her former self. Looking ill and ungainly, she sang without control and all the sincerity in the world could not mask her inability to cope with the music. Neither Raymond McDonald nor Serge Baigildin, arising from the chorus to take over occasional performances, could carry off the deceptively negative role of Florestan. The only strength of this *Fidelio* came from two singers who continue to be mainstays of the company to the present time, who sang the same roles again as recently as the 1970s. Neil Warren-Smith's Rocco remains one of the great performances in opera and Alan Light's Pizarro is possibly the most successful role in the repertoire of the man who has probably more parts behind him than any other singer in the company. Between them they could hardly save the evening, not could young Clifford Grant, vocally superb, but visually awkward, as Don Ferrando.

Lohengrin is a work of great dramatic potential with some of Wagner's most easily assimilated music to back up what any average producer can make work with a little thought and a great deal of money. Stefan Haag again tried to copy Bayreuth, but the production looked like provincial ostentation done on a shoestring. Anybody delighting in the lushness of the music, admirably realized by Rankl in the pit, was distracted by the visual cheapness of it all. As for dramatic tension, there was none. The one redeeming feature was Dowd's dignified and well-sung Swan Knight. Neil Easton was a strong Telramund and Constance Shacklock oozed villainy and chest tones, not always at the same time, but often enough to make a substantially better impression than she did in *Carmen*.

The failure of *Lohengrin* had to be laid squarely on Haag's self-indulgent production, designed – like *Fidelio* – by himself. Stefan Haag always was a talented producer, if not an inspired one, but as he grew in administrative stature his natural talents were to fade. It was a case of the old, old story: an artist cannot judge his own work and even producers need the discipline of collaboration, preferably from above, in making decisions. To a lesser degree Stephen Hall was to follow the same path in later years, but in 1958 it seems remarkable that the supposed dictator Rankl was satisfied to throw his considerable muscle into productions which were an eyesore. Again, a knowledge of his background explains the seemingly inexplicable: at Covent Garden Rankl worked for years with dreary pre-war sets brought out of mothballs to be stuck together with tin-tacks and sticky tape. Most probably he didn't notice the stage picture anyway.

Ignoring the 'artistic success' (read: box office flop) of *Peter Grimes,* the production which was the only link with the traditions set in the first two seasons was the unjustly maligned *Barber of Seville* produced by Haag in top comic form (prior to Rankl's arrival) in Hobart, admirably conducted by Eric Clapham and with bright practical sets by John

Northcote. If the Trust burnt its financial fingers in 1958, it was not the fault of this *Barber* which quite possibly prevented the whole company from going up in smoke. Not only was it launched before the rest of the season, not only did it make its unspectacular way throughout the year, but it continued unstoppably for a long country tour after the season was over, its cast the sole survivors of a company which, officially, ceased to exist at the end of 1958.

It is worth spending a little time on this 'worthless' *Barber*. Its values were those of opera as staged in Australia to that time and if they were not the values of today, they were one heck of a lot better than the pretensions of the Rankl epics.

Stating the obvious, that Rossini's *Barber of Seville* is an almost foolproof bit of stage tomfoolery, it nevertheless requires two very powerful ingredients that are too often missing: good voices and singers who can act. Donald Smith, finding his professional feet for the first time, was not the most polished Almaviva, but the beauty of his voice made up for histrionic shortcomings. On the other hand Glenda Raymond and Robert Simmons were impeccably right for their parts. The career of Glenda Raymond never quite overcame her appearance as Melba in an early endless radio biography, but there can have been few more delightful interpretations of Rosina in the history of opera, for here were looks, true comedy style and a voice which, if small,

67

was pure and well placed. However, as Lanza was penalized for playing Caruso on film, so was Miss Raymond penalized for not being another Melba. As for Robert Simmons, this excellent artist sang flexibly and acted with immense gusto. Smith, Raymond and Simmons produced a small-voiced *Barber* in a small set which toured in small theatres and they did full justice to an old war-horse in a typically Australian way; and the term is meant as a form of praise.

It was this Australian improvisatory quality which carried early Trust operas like the *Barber*. There was none of the discipline which made *Peter Grimes* a prestige product, but there was showmanship galore and really very little to which musical purists could object. The cast was completed by Neil Warren-Smith as Basilio and Alan Light as Bartolo – with Gregory Dempsey as the Notary! He has come a long way since then and so has Bruce Clarke, who played the guitar for Donald Smith's serenade.

When this *Barber* went on tour Rosalind Keene took over from Glenda Raymond and John Germain claims that for two years he sang nothing but Figaros. Georg Tintner played the piano (where was Rankl when he was needed then?) and the cast not only sang, but loaded and unloaded scenery, travelled all day by bus, sang at night, re-loaded scenery, slept briefly and enjoyed life upon the wicked stage in temperatures well over 40°C, in a 9 a.m. to 1 a.m. routine which is fondly remembered by the artists today, but must have been hell at the time. In one country town Neil Warren-Smith's Basilio blithely sang 'thank you, thank you' while Donald Smith's Don Alonso was loudly proclaiming: 'Peace and joy be yours forever, hey, the bloody joint's on fire'. And it was. Exit the singers, the audience acted as firemen, and then everybody went back to Rosina's singing lesson as though nothing had happened!

In the meantime, back at the farm, the management decided that the artistic triumphs of 1958 could not be afforded in 1959 and cancelled the next season. Apart from the few singers running around the outback with the *Barber,* the whole company suddenly found itself out of work. Some went overseas, some retired, some adopted the old wartime motto: they also fight who sit and wait. Among those who waited was Joan Sutherland back in England, promised Gilda in *Rigoletto,* and Gertrude Johnson in Melbourne, promised a joint production of *Lucia di Lammermoor.* To Sutherland, as yet undiscovered, it would have meant a lot, but the contract never materialized. (And just as well, or Sutherland might never have sung that Covent Garden *Lucia* in February 1959 which made her an overnight star.) Miss Johnson, no doubt, saw her lost *Lucia* as a sign that all her predictions were coming true, that the Trust would fold and that her National Opera would be reborn. Unlike Sutherland, she did not get a consolation prize.

The Birth of a Dinosaur

7

From 1960 onward the Adelaide Festival was to play a large part in the development of opera in Australia. In 1959, the year in which the whole future of the Elizabethan Trust Opera was in doubt, Adelaide was still looking indulgently at its own little opera company, the appropriately titled Intimate Opera Group. Opera has been described as a dinosaur doomed to extinction, but the capital of South Australia nursed its own baby reptilian so carefully that it may prove opera's critics wrong one day.

No record of any artistic endeavour of continuing value is ever complete at the time of writing, hence this chapter may be proved ephemeral before publication day. It is impossible to judge history in the making, only retrospect can tell us whether the walls of the castle fell before or after completion. Opera or ballet as 'oncers' may ultimately lead to more lasting things, but it is opera *companies* and ballet *companies* which make the kind of history with which this book is concerned. From the start the regional companies have come and gone, some to disappear, some to reappear, none to date having established a tradition even remotely as continuous as that of the Australian Opera.

The word 'crisis' is part of the daily vocabulary of opera companies and where once upon a time the invariable blow-up was caused by clashes of temperament, in our time it is the clash of unbalanced budgets which gets unhappy administrators in every country of the world climbing one obstacle (or wall) after another in the vain hope that once this problem is solved, the next will solve itself. It never does and then the game of musical chairs begins again: this one resigns, that one is appointed and somebody or other foots the bill because: 'The same mistakes will not be made again'. There is no logic of any kind in the continuing existence of opera as a performing art. Only a lunatic argues the pros and cons with inflexible accountants and only a lunatic accountant would agree with even the best administrator of opera, because their battleground is a barren field on which neither contestant can win.

In 1975 the Australian Industries Assistance Commission was instructed by Mr Gough Whitlam, Prime Minister of Australia, to undertake an Inquiry into Assistance to the Performing Arts which included the following term of reference: 'Whether assistance should be accorded the performing arts in Australia and if so what should be the nature and extent of such assistance'. The chairman of the Inquiry, Mr R. Boyer, took the Prime Minister's instructions literally. The question he asked for many days, of many witnesses was: 'What benefit does the public obtain from the arts?' — And answer there was none.

How does one measure enjoyment or edification, depending on whether you consider art pleasurable or educational? How do you relate this abstract astral ectoplasm which flows between performer and audience in money terms? Again and again, Boyer, saddled with an impossible task, was brought back to opera by witnesses in all walks of art, not only the opera men. This art has become so expensive to produce that seat prices would have to rise to undreamed heights to balance the budget. Would people really pay half a week's wages to spend one evening at the opera? There is no way that the existence of opera can be justified at the box office or in the accounting room. The fact that it continues to flourish in a country such as Australia can only be attributed to the existence of the most illogical animal on the face of the earth: man.

Is opera really the dinosaur nearing the natural end of its evolution with which the Chairman of the I.A.C. Inquiry equated it time and again? By all the rules in the book it should be, but the darn thing won't lie down; the moment it shows the slightest sign of collapse somebody manages to slip another crutch under its weakening joints, though for every surviving specimen there are three who perish, or so it would appear. The whole thing belongs in Alice's world of Wonderland; these dinosaurs are only ever seen to die, and nobody pays any attention to when or where their eggs are hatched. And the eggs must exist, for the news-making collapsing monsters do not appear spontaneously.

Let me briefly analyse the growth of what is only a baby dinosaur in Mr Boyer's book and hope that in years to come it will grow into a long-lived monster capable of avoiding the suicidal tendencies of its species.

Adelaide is a city of culture, a city of comparative peace next to the flesh pots of Sydney and Melbourne. They hasten slowly in Adelaide and if I hear a murmur of 'Thank God!', my sympathy lies with the murmurer. Not for Adelaide the short-lived operatic dinosaurs that collapsed over the years in the two larger cities. It is significant that in one of the smallest operatic fields in a musically underdeveloped country, Adelaide, meaning South Australia, was the last to acquire a regional professional opera company. Throughout the years of royal battles fought not *with*, but *by* battleaxes, in Sydney and Melbourne, Adelaide was content to welcome visiting companies that fought for survival elsewhere, where the stench could not affect the delicate noses of its worthy citizens.

Melba was heard in Adelaide; J. C. Williamson's took their companies to play there, first at the Theatre Royal, later at Her Majesty's. The Elizabethan Theatre Trust and the Australian Opera brought prestige productions to grace the Adelaide Festivals. Were the citizens downhearted? They were not. They waited their turn and when it came, it came at leisure, like everything else in Adelaide, and it came without trouble – like everything else in Adelaide? Well, perhaps that is stretching things too far, though the citizens of Sydney and Melbourne would consider it so; again comparatively speaking.

The birth of New Opera South Australia is a model of how a well-behaved young dinosaur should be brought into the world. There is nothing terribly exciting about its creation and perhaps there are some budding dinosaurs elsewhere who can learn a lesson or two from their South Australian brother or sister. (What is the sex of Opera?)

The amateur companies of South Australia never had the pretensions of the 'professionals' in the other states. At best they toured operettas in the Barossa Valley before the turn of the century, or the large German community and its Liedertafels put on single 'operas' in costume. Occasionally 'philharmonic' groups provided the only other local attempts at opera. There were, of course, parallels to the operatic activities at the music conservatoriums in capital cities elsewhere. Clive Carey's appointment to the Adelaide Conservatorium in 1924 produced the first South Australian opera performances recorded as 'proper' staged operas. It may well have been Carey fifty odd years ago who set the pattern which is the reason for New Opera's success today. The Conservatorium provided the only tradition of opera in Adelaide and its first work was Purcell's *Dido and Aeneas*. If Gluck and Mozart followed and retained their place over the years, a leavening of more popular works also crept in, including the inevitable *Maritana*.

By 1957 the continuing student productions at the Con began to pall a little. Nobody can quite say today what started the ball rolling, but the presence of Anthony Hopkins as composer in residence at the University of Adelaide must have been felt. He had formed the Intimate Opera Group in England and it was another Intimate Opera Group in Adelaide which staged what is indeed an intimate opera, *Three's Company,* by none other than Anthony Hopkins, in that year.

This was no attempt to start an opera company. The most incredible thing in operatic terms was that for some years Intimate Opera programmes listed no administrative staff other than people who actually worked on staging the operas; stage managers, set designers, and so on. There was no manager, administrator, committee, nor even patron; just a small group of professionals who were doing their own thing strictly within the budget their own pockets allowed. For some years the repertoire of the irregularly spaced productions was restricted to small cast operas with piano accompaniment, mainly falling back on English works like Hopkins' admirable three singer opener.

Three's Company has a delightful libretto by Michael Flanders (later of Flanders and Swann of *At the Drop of a Hat* fame) and could be sung easily by John Worthley, William Harrison and Jacqueline Talbot, who became the key singers of the group for some years to come. The set was designed by Stan Ostoja-Kotkowski and the producer was the chief vocal coach at the Conservatorium, Barbara Howard. Her name did appear on the programme, but that of Kathleen Steele Scott did not. These were the two ladies who started the stone rolling, though they obviously didn't know how much moss it would gather.

The Intimate Opera Group continued in fits and starts over fifteen years and, incredibly in such a volatile field, it seems to have had none of the storms and crises of similar companies elsewhere. Around the time of the 1960 Adelaide Festival, Lady Bonython became its Patroness. Whether her contribution was financial or prestigious, or both, is immaterial, but her name does not appear to have been used as a fund-raising source.

The company led by Mrs Steele Scott set sights realistically. There were no *Aidas, Carmens* or *Maritanas*. The repertoire was solidly restricted to works that were easy to stage without making great vocal demands on its roster of local singers; Mesdames Steele Scott and Barbara Howard took turns with Rae Cocking, Marie Bates, Thomas Edmonds, Margaret McPherson and the original *Three's Company* trio.

Programmes were often shared with ballets staged by Elizabeth Dalman's ballet school which in years to come was to turn into the Australian Dance Theatre.

There is no great glamour to be found in operas like Ravel's *L'heure espagnole*, Falla's *Master Peter's Puppet Show*, Menotti's *The Telephone* or Mozart's *Bastien and Bastienne* and, significantly, the company continued to stage English works: Hopkins' *Hands Across the Sky*, Lennox Berkeley's *A Dinner Engagement* and Arthur Benjamin's *Prima Donna*. (I know that Arthur Benjamin was born in Australia, but his music is English in every sense of the word.) Adelaide was the only Australian city to parallel the development of opera in England, though the city did not produce Australian native operas in its early years. And, perhaps because Adelaide is the most English of the Australian cities, audiences accepted works which supposedly more sophisticated cosmopolitans dismissed as wishy-washy playthings.

The first steps into bigger works by the Intimate Opera Group also remained in the English sphere; in fact, it continued as an exact replica of the mother country's musical development. Benjamin Britten, unable to obtain backing for operas on the *Peter Grimes* scale, refused to leave music drama alone and wrote smaller works which could be staged more cheaply. This was exactly what Mrs Steele Scott's group needed. *Albert Herring* and *The Turn of the Screw*, small by grand opera standards, were large by intimate opera scales of values at a time when subsidies were still in the distant future at federal, as well as state level.

Albert Herring was given three performances at Union Hall in October 1958 with the full orchestra demanded by Britten – all of thirteen players. Though there was no continuity of employment, no backer, no official management, the team at the core of the venture remained intact, suitably amplified for this 'major' venture. Barbara Howard played Lady Billows and Kathleen Scott, who sang Florence Pike, also produced, thinly disguised as K. Steele Scott.

In the end it was another Britten work which produced the first official subsidy for the company. In 1960 the Elizabethan Theatre Trust handed over $1000 to pay for an orchestra for *The Turn of the Screw*, because it was the Australian premiere of a Britten opera. If the thinking was hazy, as it so often is with subsidies, it proved an important encouragement to the Intimate Opera Group.

The Adelaide Festivals were well under way by the early 1960s and Intimate Opera was invariably a participant. In case the festivals should be interpreted as a financial strengthening of this incredibly self-supporting group, it should be noted that the Festival itself was struggling in those days. Companies taking part not only were not subsidized by it, but actually contributed to its financing by having to pay for inclusion in the official programme! For the Intimate Opera Group, mainly engaged in lunch-hour presentations of small cast one-acters, this was a severe burden to carry. The Elizabethan Trust Opera and the Australian Ballet used the Festival simply as the occasion for the annual Adelaide stop in their touring programme. Local companies, without continuous existence, had to create something out of nothing for the Festival and creating a small thing where nothing exists is much harder than continuing a large thing already operating.

Fund-raising from private sources began to become a necessity if the Intimate Opera Group was to continue in existence and 1970 saw the beginning of some support from the newly-created Australian Council for the Arts. Slowly but surely the company's administrative structure began to develop. The two leading ladies, who anywhere else would have insisted on being prominently displayed, discreetly withdrew into functions where they could do more good than on the stage. The late Barbara Howard, a professional singer, retreated to costume design, while Steele Scott and Powell Harrison ran the administration from their homes in Clarence Park and Lockleys.

The 1970 Festival season was a model of building up what was by then visibly a company of future potential. The temptation to aim for greater glories must have been immense after thirteen years of existence without serious problems. It was resisted. Adelaide and its visitors saw instead an example of sensible planning for a company which was in fact, as well as name, still an intimate opera group. Five evening performances of a double bill of Ravel's *L'heure espagnole* and Menotti's *The Old Maid and the Thief* were backed by nine lunchtime stagings of each work as a single entity. With prices at 80 cents for the latter and $1.50 for the double bill at nights, both in the tiny A.M.P. Theatre, the possibility of profit was non-existent, yet the impact on the future of the company was immense. It led to the swan song of the Intimate Opera Group two years later, a swan song which turned out to be rebirth without complications. The swan which had never been an ugly duckling turned into the most beautiful and efficient dinosaur Mr Boyer could ever have expected.

The last efforts of the group under its original management (still led by Steele Scott and still including Barbara Howard) came in 1972 and followed the trend toward contemporary Australian opera without losing its intimate nature. An ideally balanced trilogy of works repeated the lunchtime and evening pattern of performances of the 1970 Festival. Pergolesi's *La Serva Padrona* for the classicists; Gustav Holst's *The Wandering Scholar* to continue the English tradition which hallmarked the company's career; Peggy Glanville-Hicks' *The Glittering Gate,* to introduce an Australian work at last. Premiering an opera by an expatriate was a bold experiment. Glanville-Hicks, like Malcolm Williamson, is shunned by the establishment, which is happy to claim both as Australians, but fails to stage their works in Australia.

John Milson was the producer and the singers were Robert Dawe, Janet Lasscock, Dean Patterson, Daphne Harris, Anthony Clark and Michael Lewis, with William Harrison the sole survivor from the first production in 1957.

The Adelaide Festival operas of 1972 were not the most important productions of that year, nor were they the last of the Intimate Opera Group. Both honours belong to the remarkable success which grew out of two performances in The Olde King's Music Hall theatre-restaurant in November of that year. It appears an unlikely venue in which to stage an Australian opera with success and it says a lot for the reputation of the company in Adelaide that a modern Australian work could attract a dining public at $6.00 a person, but it did.

Nobody seems to know exactly whose idea it was, nor are the economics of the thing terribly clear, though the enthusiasm of Harry Eggington, the manager of the Olde King's Music Hall, must have helped swing the deal. The occasion was the celebration of the seventy-fifth birthday of Margaret Sutherland, the doyen of Australian composers. The opera presented, *The Young Kabbarli,* had been premiered in Hobart in 1965. Its new look in such an inauspicious setting was to make it known Australia-wide.

The Young Kabbarli is the story of Daisy Bates, who spent fifty-two years of her life caring for Aborigines in the outback. Though it only has four singing roles, it is a complicated work to stage, involving, as it does, Aboriginal dancers, the use of a didgeridoo and a complicated score for ten players. Patrick Thomas, seconded from the A.B.C., conducted, and visiting Israeli guest producer Moshe Kedem was also responsible for the designs. Mezzo soprano Genty Stevens

Festival fare The Adelaide Festival generally manages to get some special production for its main venue, the new Festival Theatre. In 1976 it saw the Australian Opera stage the first Australian performance of Alban Berg's modern masterpiece, *Wozzeck*, in superbly visual designs by Timothy O'Brien and Tazeena Firth. Conductor Edward Downes and the Adelaide Symphony Orchestra were the stars, but the sheer visual impact of the sets stole the show. Not satisfied with spectacular scenery, the designers provided brilliantly costumed extras, such as the lady on the left and the group on the right, to act as living props. Centre, left to right: Gerald English as the Captain, Raymond Myers as Wozzeck and Grant Dickson as the Doctor.

The young Kabbarli The Adelaide production of Margaret Sutherland's opera on the life of Daisy Bates among the Aborigines was first staged in a theatre restaurant and then transferred to Melbourne's National Gallery Great Hall in 1972. The only Australian opera to be recorded to date was produced on a shoe-string, as this picture shows quite clearly. Genty Stevens as Daisy Bates.

made a deep impression as Daisy Bates and the other parts were sung by Dean Patterson, John McKenzie and Carol Kohler. Although David Gumpilil in a key role was described as 'guest dancer and Aborigine Singer' his excellent contribution in the latter capacity is better described as chanting; real singing by an Aboriginal in the most authentic-sounding primitive music sequences would have been somewhat out of place.

Plans to extend the exposure of *The Young Kabbarli* outside Adelaide were laid along before its premiere. Not only was the whole production transferred to Melbourne for another tribute to Margaret Sutherland in the Great Hall of the National Gallery, but E.M.I. recorded the work in full, giving it, and Intimate Opera, the honour of being the first Australian opera ever to be recorded. It was also the first recording in quadrophonic sound ever made in this country.

The fact that Intimate Opera is given no credit on the

recording of *The Young Kabbarli,* while there is a mention of 'New Opera (S.A.)' inconspicuously hidden after credits for financial assistance, hides the metamorphosis of Intimate Opera into 'New Opera South Australia' in 1973. Once again the changeover was gradual. There was little evidence of anything radical having happened beyond a policy statement, and even that clearly stated that the new body 'Would NOT (their capitals) be a Grand Opera Company, but a Music Theatre Ensemble presenting the best works of today with a sprinkling of the classics.'

A full-time administration and board of management was formed. Funds were made available by the South Australian Government as well as the Australia Council. Kathleen Steele Scott became the chairman of the Artistic Committee which laid down policy, providing continuity to the present day. The first season was totally in keeping with all that went before – except that suddenly the money was there for a full orchestra, chorus and scope for larger works, though far from 'grand' ones. *Dido and Aeneas* and Ibert's *Angélique* started the new regime and if I seem to stress the development rather than change, let me remind you that the purpose of this detailed dissection of what happened in Adelaide is meant to show how things should happen in opera, but so very rarely do.

The first season at the new Adelaide Festival Theatre saw productions of that old faithful *Albert Herring* and later Rossini's *Count Ory*. Guest conductors Georg Tintner and Richard Divall were brought in from other states and new singers were added to cope with the larger theatre, while regulars developed the broader style they might never have achieved without having had such long training in actual productions over the years. Eric Maddison emerged as Albert with Daphne Harris, Norene Lower, Rae Cocking and David Brennan in support. For the more difficult *Count Ory*, Norma Hunter was loaned by the A.B.C. with Paul Ferris as the Count, Norma Knight as Isolier and Dean Patterson from the early days as Raimbaud. John Milson and Stefan Haag were the producers.

Reverting to stated policies – which the Festival Theatre productions had not really interrupted – December 1973 saw the company in Theatre 62 with smaller operas, smaller casts and a smaller orchestra. *Down the Greenwood Side* by Harrison Birtwistle and Melanie Daiken's *Mayakovsky and the Sun* both continued the tradition of modern English operas, though these belong to the *avant garde* of today instead of the yesterday of Britten and Hopkins.

In 1974 New Opera's activities positively exploded, yet artistic standards remained higher than anywhere in Australia, only possibly excluding the Australian Opera. Almost overnight New Opera was on the lips of opera lovers in every state and envious glances were cast toward Adelaide. Where did this sudden unity of artistic and financial management suddenly appear from? Why were the constant crises of other states not repeated in this one city alone? Perhaps the fact that management and artists were busy working hard instead of blowing unnecessary trumpets had something to do with it. Perhaps working under ideal conditions in the Festival Theatre helped. More probably, the fact that the company produced good results encouraged the subsidizing bodies to put up rather than shut up in disgust, as happened more often than not in other states.

South Australia had the only Premier with a theatrical background at this time. Not that Don Dunstan was likely to take an active part in the running of New Opera, but results speak for themselves, and when the head of a government is able to judge for himself whether his financial advisers are correctly evaluating something as ephemeral as artistic standards, then the arts are likely to get all the help they need, or the budget can stand. This has obviously happened in Adelaide and it would be as well if the rest of Australia learnt the lesson being taught down there.

The emergence of Leoš Janáček as a box office attraction in Australia did not start with the Australian Opera's *Jenůfa*, but with the far more complex and difficult *The Excursions of Mr Brouček* staged at the 1974 Adelaide Festival by New Opera. At the time Janáček was still considered far too experimental for Australian audiences; none of his operas had ever been performed in this country. The logic of choosing *Brouček* rather than the much more famous *Jenůfa* or *The Cunning Little Vixen* was obscure, but it proved to substantiate the judgement of the company's directors.

What was required first and foremost was something that could be made into a major production spectacle. The fact that singers like Gregory Dempsey, Marilyn Richardson and Thomas Edmonds were available was hardly enough to fill the immense new Festival Theatre. Something sensational was required and, whatever the opera's musical worth, it was the production which turned a respected regional body into a company worthy of national recognition.

The Excursions of Mr Brouček involves a journey to the Moon and time travel, combined with period comedy ideally suited to visual effects. Adelaide happened to be the home of Ostoja-Kotkowski, whose electronic light experiments had been prominent for years. (He had also designed the company's first production in 1957!) Dealing with the eight scenes of *Brouček,* ranging from the hidden treasury of King Wenceslaus, and various scenes of Prague in 1888 and 1420, to a very inhabited surface of the Moon, Ostoja-Kotkowski was given his head and delivered the goods. Producer John Tasker admirably used the magnificent raw materials at his disposal and Patrick Thomas took firm charge of the musical content. *Brouček* was a triumph which was only dampened by the failure of the national subsidizing bodies to make provision for this kind of success to be seen in the other states as well. Those four performances of Janáček's opera will remain a legend in Australian operatic history. They also remain the largest venture of New Opera to date, one which is unlikely to be equalled except under festival conditions, unless some very drastic changes take place in terms of funding.

Any thought that the company's worth was enlarged by presenting its work under ideal conditions in one venue alone was dissipated in the same year when its four seasons were each staged in different locations. After the major exertion of *Brouček* at the Festival Theatre, productions were staged in the three months September to December in, respectively, the Royalty Theatre, the so-called Space in the Festival Theatre complex, an experimental theatre-in-the-round, and Theatre 62.

Stravinsky's *Renard* was coupled with Larry Sitsky's Australian classic *The Fall of the House of Usher* and Monteverdi's *Combattimento di Tancredi e Clorinda* with Kurt Weill's *Seven*

Cheap but not nasty Maximum effect with minimum resource in Adelaide's 1973 production (*left*) of Birtwistle's *Down the Greenwood Side*, a typical mini-opera obtaining visual impact by means of masks. Shaun Gurton as Dr. Blood.

Right, new name, but no change in policy. In 1976 New Opera South Australia became the State Opera of South Australia, but its productions remained realistically within small budgets, while retaining a high artistic standard. Patsy Hemingway and Denis O'Neill in Cimarosa's *The Secret Marriage*.

Below right, the ABC of stage production, or how to make much of very little and still to do it tastefully. Bizet's *Dr Miracle* produced by New Opera South Australia in 1975. John Wood, Norma Knight and Judith Henley.

Deadly Sins. The latter pair proved to be a near sensational coupling when presented as the opening production in the Space at the Festival Theatre.

Justin McDonnell, who had been working quietly in the background as Administrator since before the changeover (that is exactly what a good administrator should do: work quietly in the background), suddenly emerged as an original designer-producer in the Monteverdi. It was an ultra-modern presentation of a very old masterpiece, played 'in-the-round' with complete success. Wal Cherry's production of the *Seven Deadly Sins* was, if anything, even more successful, capturing the Brecht style to perfection. Robin Archer and Avis Smith played the singing and dancing sides of sinful Annie, while Tessa Bremner and Roger Pahl mimed the original conceptions for the singers, David Galliver, Margaret MacPherson and Eric Maddison.

The success of the Weill-Brecht *Deadly Sins* could not have influenced the choice of their *Little Mahagonny* four weeks later; the company's planning is too good to allow quite such quick substitutions. Nevertheless, it was an inspired juxtaposition. *The Little Mahagonny* is the original on which *The Rise and Fall of the City of Mahagonny* was built. The Australian Opera's production of the latter, which followed in Sydney a month after the Adelaide staging of the earlier, smaller work, lacked the bite provided by the local boys, Chris Winzar (director) and Axel Bartz (designer). It was dangerous to court direct comparison with the national company, but New Opera succeeded in upstaging it.

1975, which did not have an Adelaide Festival, may well turn out to have been a key year for New Opera; it is almost too much to hope that the raising of the company's sights will continue at the present rate. The initial two productions followed the pattern of the modest double bills which the Adelaide audiences have come to expect and appreciate. *The Soldier's Tale* of Stravinsky and Bizet's youthful four-character *Dr Miracle* were followed by Janáček's *Diary of a Man Who Vanished* and a baroque *Madrigal Show* based on Banchieri. Ronald Dowd and Gwenyth Annear appeared as guests.

The danger of a loss of individuality was there in the company's first production in Her Majesty's Theatre – the venue for really grand opera in years gone by. The choice of opera was in the true tradition of the company; Britten's *Turn of the Screw* returned to the scene of past triumphs. Nevertheless the production's virtues lay in the three leading singers, 'guests' Dowd, Annear and Ailene Fischer. For the first time New Opera followed the pattern of other regional companies, which are inclined to ignore the building of a local ensemble in favour of getting 'the best'. But since 'the best' can be heard anywhere else in Australia, some of the company's individualism was lost.

The next production offered a better balance, with Marilyn Richardson, a true guest star, as Fiordiligi, while Rae Cocking, Norma Knight, James Christianson, Dennis O'Neill and John Wood backed her to create a new *Cosi fan tutte,* brilliantly designed by John Stoddart and produced by Anthony Besch. This opera also toured the country as part of a new scheme to keep singers employed full-time. Though it was a different cast which went outside Adelaide, the inclusion of Gwenyth Annear ensured a high standard, specially since Myer Fredman, who conducted all five 1975 productions, went on the road as well.

I cannot attempt to bring in all operas produced prior to this book's production date, but it may be appropriate to end the history of New Opera by reporting the staging of two specially commissioned operas for the 1976 Adelaide Festival. Larry Sitzky's *Fiery Tales* and George Dreyfus' *The Lamentable Reign of King Charles the Last* had the common virtue of being excellent, if somewhat bawdy, entertainment – which is as it should be, since Sitzky's *Tales* came from Chaucer and Boccaccio and *King Charles* straight out of Canberra's most turbulent years. Perhaps the Dreyfus opera was too close to intimate revue and its subject will prevent it from gaining a permanent place in the repertoire, but it served its purpose as music entertainment pure and simple. Chris Winzar's production of *Fiery Tales* stressed the sexuality of its subjects, but Sitzky's music was good 'modern antique' and the large cast was given music that really needed singing, instead of the usual *Sprechgesang*. An excellent cast was led by Norma Knight, Dennis O'Neill, John Wood, Patsy Hemingway and, believe it or not, a member of that first *Three's Company* cast, William Harrison!

If I have made the creation of New Opera sound like a glamorous undramatic evolution of an opera company built upon a rock of good will and hard work, I have been close to the truth. Of course there were bad times and good times and things happened which should not have happened. Life is like that. But compare what happened in the sleepy South Australian Capital with the paroxisms of operatic life anywhere else and New Opera really does become an unreal Disneyland, which exists for the enrichment of life in Adelaide.* It has acquired an admirable permanent musical director in the form of Myer Fredman and Mrs Kathleen Steele Scott is still on the Board of Management; and if that isn't a remarkable achievement in the most volatile theatrical art there is, then nothing can astonish any more. One can only hope that the course of true love (for opera) for once will forever run smooth.

---

* In 1976 New Opera South Australia changed its name to The State Opera of South Australia. At the same time Justin McDonnell left to create a Music Theatre department at the Sydney Conservatorium. The new Administrator is Ian Campbell.

The man in the moon Matej Brouček (Gregory Dempsey) with Etherea, the moon maiden (Marilyn Richardson) in Janáček's *The Excursions of Mr Broucek*, the production which catapulted opera in South Australia into the national limelight at the 1974 Adelaide Festival.

Hammond to the Rescue

8

The creation of the Adelaide Festival in 1960 was to become a major factor in boosting the cause of opera. Not only did it create an artificial market for the art in a city not exactly lavish in its past demands, but it was to provide an artistic and financial incentive which the national company used to the full. In future years major stars were imported, major productions staged and major audiences created through the Festival. Initially there was little more than goodwill — and not too much of that. All right, so Adelaide had a bright idea that it would become the Edinburgh of Australia, but what actually did it offer to any company willing to participate? Precious little in relation to the costs involved in staging opera. Nevertheless, the Elizabethan Trust Opera Company was clutching at straws in the year after its first unwilling sabbatical and the publicity alone which the Festival could bring might kick off a revival of public interest and lift fast sinking hopes for the future. Alas, it was not to be.

During the four years 1959–62 the Trust Opera Company disbanded twice and was reassembled twice, in each case to start seasons at the Adelaide Festival. There is every reason to believe that the Festival rescued the Elizabethan Trust Opera from oblivion, if not financially, then at least by encouraging it to survive for the glory of Australia — meaning the internationally promoted Adelaide Festival.

If it did survive, the credit does not belong to the Executive Director of the Trust, Hugh Hunt, the Director of the Opera, Robert Quentin, or its Musical Director, Karl Rankl. The sport of Trust-bashing was well under way and, in spite of mounting criticism, bringing in top-level experts was considered unnecessary. Who could afford good management while there was a shortage of singers? And why was there a shortage of singers? Because the annual close-down of the company caused anybody with any sense to desert the sinking ship. Fortunately a few of the best had more loyalty than sense and hung around to save the company once it started moving again.

In an attempt to replace *prime donne* with cultural pretensions plans were made for the 1960 Festival to stage the first Australian Opera in living memory, Arthur Benjamin's *A Tale of Two Cities* — without first establishing where the additional $27,000 required was to be found! Not surprisingly, the Adelaide Festival Committee, which had raised an original $2000 with difficulty, declined to help and any hope of native opera vanished into the mists of the future — 1974 to be precise.

To save his bacon Rankl went back to Joan Hammond and Ken Neate, old friends from his days at Covent Garden. The mind boggles to think what would have happened in 1960 without Hammond. She was the be-all and end-all of the season in all states, though the lack of direction in matters artistic sadly let her down again and again. A somewhat subdued Rankl was forced to curtail his demands – unfortunately only after his management agreed to stage Richard Strauss' *Salome*. In view of the huge A.B.C. orchestras at his disposal it seemed a good idea; Hammond had the voice for the part and Rankl knew the work well from the notorious 1949 Dali-Brook production at Covent Garden. Unfortunately (that word seems to dog most of the years of Trust Opera seasons) Stefan Haag in his new position as Assistant Director picked this production plum for himself. With due respect to Haag, who is a respectable producer of repertoire operas, the sensuous sexuality of *Salome* simply passed him by. Unfortunately (there is that word again) the same can be said of Joan Hammond's lascivious teenager. Teenager!

I have praised Miss Hammond effusively as a true *prima donna* and she certainly sang Salome with a magnificent opulent sound. If only it had been a broadcast or recording! Nothing is less likely to convince visually than a *prima donna* Salome. Hammond in 1960 produced voice and voice alone. Rankl produced sound and sound alone. Haag produced a traditional grand opera to suit his *prima donna,* who worked valiantly, but in vain, to change her traditional spots – and who would want her to? Certainly not the public who came to hear another Tosca and went away bewildered, and far from scandalized. Whatever had been said about Rankl's Covent Garden *Salome,* it was no better musically than this Australian one, but its producer Peter Brook did make his public sit up; he continued the principle that *Salome* should shock, and shock it did. The only shocking thing about the Trust *Salome* was its inclusion in the repertoire when the company's fortunes and policies were near their nadir.

Lest it be thought that *Salome* was a disaster, it was not. Perhaps being simply dull is a worse condemnation, but the designs of Raymond Boyce, though badly executed, had their virtues and the singing of Hammond and Neil Easton (later Robert Allman) was virile and commanding. On the acting side Justine Rettick and Alan Ferris made much of Herodias and Herod. The original plan to sing the opera in German was abandoned, but in vain. For all the understanding the audience got of the English text, it might just as well have been sung in the original language. Playing in theatres as large as Melbourne's Palais did not exactly help either.

Unrealistic planning (*Salome* replaced an abandoned *Traviata* which was to star Gabriella Tucci, Elsie Morison and Una Hale in rotation!) produced a very strange season. Joan Hammond practically produced *Madame Butterfly,* though company manager Tom Brown was given the programme credit. The result was vocally acceptable (Hammond, Neate, Allman) but looked what it probably was: a replica of the production toured by the Carl Rosa Company in the British provinces during the war. There was a sort of *Rigoletto* with 183 cm Ronal Jackson as a monstrously lanky jester. Ken Neate, even taller, was at least a romantic

figure and so was Glenda Raymond, still singing her best as Gilda. Robin Lovejoy produced what he could under impossible conditions, but the popularity of Verdi's music won the day, as Puccini's did for *Madame Butterfly*.

And for the first time the company brought back an existing production; Haag's *Magic Flute* from the opening season was chosen to star Ken Neate, who had been a fine Tamino in years gone by, but whose voice was darkening dangerously for Mozart. The teamwork of 1957 was missing. Ronal Jackson was again hampered by his height, which made his Papageno look like a gigantic plucked chicken in his well-worn costume. Bagnall and Warren-Smith were excellent as Pamina and Sarastro, but Glenda Raymond's voice was too fine and pure for the evil Queen of the Night.

As in the case of *Peter Grimes* two years earlier, the odd man out turned out to be the artistic sleeper of the season. Stefan Haag's believable collection of Puccini operas masquerading under the then unfamiliar *Trittico* label were a model of traditional opera with exactly the three faces which Puccini had demanded. The *grand guignol* of *Il Tabarro,* the sugar sweet *Suor Angelica* and the Rabelaisian *Gianni Schicchi* made an ideal evening for those who bothered to investigate. While they grew in numbers, they did not grow fast enough in each city before the time came to move on. Louis Kahan's utilitarian sets were suitably appropriate and the casts shone with immense vigour. Neil Easton and Robert Allman vied for honours, alternating as the unhappy Michele, and Gregory Dempsey sang his first heroic voice lead in *Il Tabarro*. The much under-rated Valda Bagnall did the impossible and brought *Suor Angelica* to life both vocally and histrionically. This performance, thanks to Bagnall, Rettick's excellent Princess and Haag's underplayed staging, was a revelation to local audiences, small as they were. *Suor Angelica* is said to have been Puccini's favourite opera, an opinion which few critics share! The later production by the Australian Opera (in 1973), with its Christmas card miracle at the end, proved them so right that the *Trittico* was quickly turned into a *Dittico* when the two outer operas, *Tabarro* and *Gianni Schicchi,* were performed on their own. No such thing would have happened to Haag's 1960 staging. It backed Puccini up to the hilt. *Gianni Schicchi* was another of the endless milestones for Neil Warren-Smith, who was in his element in Haag's expert comedy routines.

Local singers carried the main weight of the season and the occasional non-appearance of Hammond or Neate was resented, though one understudy made headlines which would have been much larger had Hammond dropped out of *Salome* ten years later. Ex-opera singer Maria Wolkowsky was called at a few hours' notice from her faithful typewriter to save a Sydney performance of Richard Strauss' opera from cancellation. Without ever having sung Salome before (and

Simplicity which worked The 1960 setting (*top*) of Puccini's *Suor Angelica*, the middle of three one-act operas making the *Trittico*. Painted columns and simple effects were more successful than the expensive, but tasteless 1973 production which was promptly dropped, making the *Trittico* a *Dittico*. Valda Bagnall as Angelica and Justine Rettick as the Princess.

Musetta/Marietta at the receiving end On 31 May 1960 Sydney singers missed their chance to get back at acid-penned critic Maria Prerauer when she sang one performance of *Salome* (*bottom*), replacing Joan Hammond without a rehearsal. After the performance Maria Wolkowsky-Prerauer is congratulated by Alan Ferris and Justine Rettick.

having to improvise her *Dance of the Seven Veils*), she satisfied an audience which probably welcomed some excitement in the midst of a dreary season. No reports have come down to me of the prowess on stage of the lady variously known as Maria Prerauer, Musetta or Marietta, but I have no reason to believe that our fiercest music critic in any way disgraced herself. (Do I hear cries of 'Pity'!?) As Wolkowsky she had had quite a substantial career in Europe and England, but that Salome proved to be her last appearance as a singer.

No, 1960 could hardly be called a successful year for the Trust Opera Company. One winner out of five, and that one box office poison! (The *Trittico* was billed without mention of Puccini or the names of the operas and by the time the good word got around, it was too late.) No wonder the company collapsed again. Rankl departed into renewed obscurity and a remarkable reason was found for not having a season in 1961: none of the A.B.C. orchestras could fit Trust seasons into their schedules! Whatever the real reasons (apart from lack of funds), the Trust did not use the year of rest to put its administrative house in order and 1962 was to be another step on the apparently inevitable road to perdition.

Der Rosenkavalier versus The Student Prince

9

During the second year of rest, the first and only attempt was made to implement the Trust's original policy of helping regional companies instead of competing with them. The failure of that solitary experiment can be laid on the doorstep of both parties. It is a sad little tale, but one which needs to be told.

In 1961 Gertrude Johnson in Melbourne gloated at the failure of the Trust Opera to equal her own earlier successes. Due to good financial management the National Theatre Movement in Melbourne had succeeded in wiping out the debts made during its last pre-Trust years, it had collected substantial funds to buy the Toorak Village Cinema and was preparing to convert it into the National Theatre which would make the company's fortune yet! But, most of all, Miss Johnson was itching to show that miserable upstart, the Trust, what a mistake it had made in leaving her out in the cold.

Negotiations began for the National Theatre to stage a season in 1961, while the Trust Opera was disbanded, with financial and other assistance from the Trust, but without any interference in artistic matters. Miss Johnson actually obtained the rights to stage Richard Strauss' *Der Rosenkavalier,* which had never been seen in Australia, at a time when the famous film starring Elisabeth Schwarzkopf was packing the public in. Staging a *Rosenkavalier* takes a lot of money, but the Victorian Symphony Orchestra (which had been unavailable for the Trust Opera!) was suddenly free again, the Victorian Government of Henry Bolte was offering a subsidy and the Trust was at last coming to the party. It all looked too good to be true – and was!

With considerable shrewdness it was decided to couple the locally unknown *Rosenkavalier* with *La Bohème.* Less logically, and possibly without the knowledge of the Trust, it was decided to stage *The Student Prince* as a sure-fire way of raising money to pay for any possible losses on the Strauss opera. Then came the crunch: the sum offered by the Trust to the National Theatre to stage a Melbourne season of grand opera in 1961 was a princely $10,000!

Miss Johnson took the $10,000 without batting an eyelid, dropped the two operas and produced *The Student Prince* alone, realizing a cool profit of $60,000 in three months! The fact that this included the Trust's $10,000 was never forgiven and the whole exercise was held up as the example why the Trust needed artistic control over ventures it helped to finance. Dr Coombs was a very angry man!

Regrettably, the unexpected financial windfall for the National Theatre was more than off-set when the theatre, being rebuilt in Toorak, burnt to the ground before it had been properly insured. In the eyes of the Trust it was poetic justice, though it is interesting to speculate what would have happened if the original plans had been implemented with proper backing. When *Der Rosenkavalier* was finally staged by the Australian Opera in 1972 (at a production cost of $100,000) it was an enormous success. Could it have saved the National in 1961? In the light of its later policies, perhaps not.

By then, of course, the Sydney Opera House loomed larger than the burnt National Theatre in Melbourne ever had, if anything not yet visible above ground level can be said to loom. On the eve of 1962 the management of the opera company still believed that the magnificent edifice would open in 1964! Planning, therefore, was aimed at presenting bigger and better seasons to lead up to the big event. The logical way to start this was to cut back! The reasoning appeared to be that the money saved by reducing the 1962 season would enable a bigger one to be staged in 1963 and that this would then convince one and all that the company was ready for the big event. What actually happened was that standards slipped even further. Fortunately the opening of the Opera House also receded into the distance.

The years leading to the abyss, out of which the Elizabethan Trust Opera might well have failed to climb, were not happy ones. There was no lack of critics inside and outside the company and backstage politics waxed fast and furious. Opportunities were given and lost through prevarication or timidity. For every opera staged, two were planned and abandoned.

The age of the inferior guest 'star' rising gloomily above eclipsed local talent was at hand and the best that can be said for the last years under Haag is that the losses, which were so severely criticized at the time, were really pretty reasonable compared with subsidies being given in other parts of the world. Against that, it had to be admitted that there was very little to show for the money. *Traviata, Bohème* and *Carmen* continued to attract the masses in inferior productions, but the attempts to repeat artistic credits in esoteric items like *Peter Grimes* and the *Trittico* continued to fail. Nothing seemed to go right and only the high-and low-lights are worthy of being chronicled here.

Among the opportunities missed were two great ones indeed. Charles Mackerras was appointed Musical Director and Anthony Besch almost became multi-media director for the Trust by proposing to mix drama production elsewhere with the artistic direction of the opera company. Mackerras, in his then inexperience, restricted himself to some admirable, if unspectacular, conducting, but Besch backed out hastily.

The incredible Ana Raquel Sartre, however, made enough publicity for herself to more than compensate for Mackerras busily hiding in the pit. Her Australian exploits are certainly worthy of a closer look. In true *prima donna* style Sartre first kept the Press waiting, then tried to prove that she was one of those fabled stars, whose temperaments are an essential part of a performance off, as well as on, stage. She capped the lot by slapping a critic's face in public – a care-

fully staged event which made headlines throughout Australia and (supposedly) operatic centres throughout the world.

Sartre was one of the best-looking singers around. She even possessed a voice of reasonable size and beauty. The great mystery, which escaped the notice of the management and most of the critics, is that Sartre, *a mezzo soprano,* was engaged to sing Violetta in *La Traviata,* the greatest *soprano* showpiece role in the repertoire. By eliminating the standard high note interpolations, Sartre actually managed to sing all the notes, though not always in the correct pitch. She looked superb and made enough appearances in the Press to make the non-opera buff believe that she was indeed a star – after all, even Callas had her off days by 1962! She also had, like Callas, a wealthy husband who in turn helped to keep the presses rolling by maligning the Sydney Opera House. The fact that Martin Carr happened to be right long before the big storms broke, unfortunately did not improve his wife's singing. There is no truth in the report that a vain attempt to try for a top C one night at the Palais in St Kilda dislodged a huge batten and caused it to crash to the stage from above. Fall it did, spectacularly. If its fall was not caused by her singing, it is to her credit that Sartre's voice and composure were not affected in the slightest by the commotion it caused.

International Incident The Brazilian bombshell who slapped a critic's face. Ana Raquel Sartre with Ronal Jackson in the 1962 *Traviata*. Sartre was a beautiful woman, but fireworks off-stage did not make up for their absence in the music.

It is regrettable that reports such as the above should be the biggest contribution to Australian operatic history in 1962, but facts are facts. Peter Baillie, a handsome young tenor from New Zealand, used Sartre's *Traviata* as a useful stepping-stone to a successful career in Europe. Ronal Jackson was far more at home as the older Germont than when

Hats when still in fashion The disastrous *Ariadne auf Naxos* failed in 1962 even after three producers had taken her in hand. Neither Geoffrey Chard's hat nor Rosalind Keene's fine singing could save the show.

he had been starred and feathered in *The Magic Flute*. Jackson was never given the opportunity to show his best side in this country. The day when the repertoire would be tailored to the singers available was still in the distant future. Ambition rather than sense governed the selection of works to be presented. It was: We shall do *Ariadne auf Naxos*! And only then: Who can we find to sing it? Or produce it? Or design it? It was thus that a travesty of Richard Strauss' opera came to be the dubious highlight of the 1962 Adelaide Festival.

Ariadne is one of the most difficult operas to stage successfully – it was to prove so again in 1975 when the Australian Opera made a more valiant stab at it. It requires at least three major singers and a producer of genius, since the whole thing really doesn't hang together. The second half was originally part of a multi-media production of Molière's play, *Le Bourgeois Gentilhomme*. Strauss and Hofmannsthal

reworked it into a full-length opera by replacing the play with a lengthy prologue involving the supposed composer of the opera proper and the singers appearing in it. It needs a delicacy of touch rarely found among producers of opera, it needs a designer of genius and, above all, it needs a production organization which can do justice to all that is involved in such a hazardous endeavour. This was to be the *Peter Grimes* of 1962, or did that honour belong to *Falstaff,* an almost equally difficult opera?

It may not matter very much today, but a passé producer of plays was imported from London to stage *Ariadne;* his first and his last attempt at opera production, I believe. Charles Hickman was experienced enough in the theatre to have bumbled his way through the whole thing had he had a first-class team to work with, but he did not. So great was the disaster in Adelaide that for the first (and last) time (to date) a production was restaged by another producer in mid-season; by two producers actually, for Stephan Beinl had to call Stefan Haag to his aid, since he was more than fully occupied getting *Falstaff* and *Don Giovanni* on the boards. Thus the triple-headed *Ariadne* wended her unhappy way from state to state playing to empty houses. What vocal virtues there were (Una Hale's big-voiced Ariadne, Althea Bridges' touching composer, Rosalind Keene's brilliantly brittle Zerbinetta) went for nought and no attempt to blame the public for ignoring the staging of Strauss' 'masterpiece' (masterpiece?) could hide the ineptness of the programming.

Falstaff was little better, once again planned without any thought of possible casting. It was Falstaff without the fat knight! In desperation veteran retired baritone Arnold Matters was brought forth as the local hero for the Festival. Since fruity Falstaff is hardly a golden-haired youth, Matters produced a more than adequate swan song to a long career, but other states had to make do with a light-weight young man imported from America, via Vienna, one Norman Foster, who was an admirable artist in every way but one – he didn't have a clue what Falstaff was about, vocally or histrionically.

In the end it was Alan Light's magnificent Ford who stole the show wherever it was seen. Nobody noticed that for the third time out of three tries the local talent outshone the imports. *Falstaff* was saved by Beinl's practical staging, the first of many such productions which were to serve the Australian company well over the years to come. Beinl was no Zeffirelli or Visconti, but he knew what was wanted and almost always brought it off – when he had the right singers at his disposal.

Beinl's practical *Don Giovanni* rounded off the season with Jackson as the Don, Warren-Smith as Leporello, Peter Baillie, and the two *prime donne*, Hale and Sartre, sharing the soprano honours, though the success of the evening was undoubtedly Cynthia Johnson's sparkling Zerlina.

The name Edward Downes appeared on the scene fully ten years before his appointment as Musical Director of the Australian Opera in 1972. Prolonged negotiations in 1962 had Downes ready, willing and able to come to Australia to plan and institute a new regime. Oh, the dreams which were spun and the glories ahead! But they came to nothing because, after six years in existence, the Trust and its opera company were still run by amateurs planning without the foresight Downes had then, and proved to still have much later. Money crises are the staple diet of opera administrators and the future may have appeared bleak in 1962. Nevertheless, the failure to grasp Downes when he was there for the asking was to have more lasting effects than Haag imagined.

In 1963 Stefan Haag was appointed Executive Director of the Elizabethan Theatre Trust. This should have severed his connection with the opera to some extent; in fact, it did not. Having rejected Downes, Haag was forced, perhaps against his will, to continue as the moving force in the company, though from a higher level. Charges that he was neglecting other aspects of the Trust's activities in favour of opera were justified that first year, but circumstances caused him to make a virtue out of necessity. (An almost exact parallel occurred when Stephen Hall succeeded Haag as Executive Director of the Trust five years later. Both men were already committed to production and other duties with the opera company after their elevation and both insisted on continuing the work they loved not wisely but too well.)

Basically the situation at the end of 1962 looked promising. Haag had been moved up into a position in which his penchant for opera could only help the company. Federal and state governments greatly increased their grants in the hope that the Trust would one day fill the once more delayed Sydney Opera House after completion. John Young, well experienced in administration by now, became Production Director and all that was really needed was a good artistic director.

The appointment ultimately made was basically sound, though based on the same faulty premise which applied in the case of Rankl. Wilhelm Loibner was another in the German GMD (Generalmusikdirektor) tradition. He was prepared to come to Australia full time, to be present throughout the season and to take charge of all matters artistic. Unfortunately (there is that word again) he was not a top man in his field and was burdened with a soprano wife who was not in the class of a later administrator's spouse, Lone Koppel-Winther, who was to raise some controversy in the mid-1970s. Ruthilde Boesch was a somewhat mature German *prima donna* of the old school, useful enough here and there, but no 'star' to overshadow resident singers. She caused considerable trouble directly and indirectly, finally refusing to sing at all when Walter Stiasny, the conductor of *Die Fledermaus*, chose to give the premiere to a pretty young New Zealand soprano, Mary O'Brien. It is an indication of Loibner's ineffectiveness as a Musical Director (and/or husband) that one of his three assistant conductors was able to go against his wishes in this manner. His lack of authority was not replaced by a firm hand elsewhere and 1963 turned out to be, if anything, a greater disaster than 1962. Only the introduction of the foolproof *Fledermaus* kept the company together during the summer of 1963–64 and managed to stave off total financial disaster.

The choice of *Die Fledermaus* was prompted by the undoubted successes in the field of a commercial management's import, the Sadler's Wells production of *Orpheus in the Underworld*, starring June Bronhill, and the Melbourne National Theatre's *The Student Prince*, which was followed by *The Desert Song* and *Show Boat*. The American musical was dying, but the public wanted musical theatre and *Die Fledermaus* was a good choice; in fact, with one exception,

it was even the best production of the year, thanks to Stefan Beinl's staging and Desmond Digby's commercial designs. Unfortunately this high rating was due more to the dismal standards elsewhere than to any particular brilliance of *Die Fledermaus*. Be it recorded that Stiasny conducted stylishly, Mary O'Brien showed voice, looks and charm, as Rosalinda, and Robert Gard made an excellent impression as Alfred in his first role with the company, straight from the National Theatre *Show Boat* tour. Beinl was also responsible for the one acceptable opera of the year, *The Marriage of Figaro,* with designs by Kenneth Rowell. The vocal standards were not as high as during the first season, in spite of Elizabeth Fretwell's return after nine years overseas. Ronal Jackson was a good Count, Cynthia Johnson superb as Susanna and Figaro marked the debut of another New Zealander, Ronald Maconaghie, who immediately caught the public's fancy and hasn't disappointed it since. *Faust, Fidelio* and *Bohème* completed the repertoire.

John Young produced *Faust* with some incredible back-projections, anticipating in a less erotic manner the idiocies of the 1973 *Tannhäuser.* In his own words: 'It was the worst production anybody ever staged'. Haag repeated his bare-stage *Fidelio* and New Zealand provided an imported *Bohème* designed by Raymond Boyce. It was quite a year for New Zealand/Australia operatic trading. Mary O'Brien, Peter Baillie, Ronald Maconaghie and *La Bohème* proved a pretty good exchange for the Trust's *Magic Flute* which had toured New Zealand the previous year.

Vocal standards were generally poor. Another 'star' import, Edward Byles, had a notably large voice, but also a notable lack of musical and dramatic abilities. His Rodolfo was acceptable in a full-throated Italian provincial style, but his Faust was an abomination. Fretwell starred as Fidelio, Light and Warren-Smith repeated their fine Pizarro and Rocco, and Raymond Myers made an early debut as a resonant Ferrando. Light also stole the *Faust* honours as Mephisto, with Mary O'Brien overtaxed as Marguerite.

Attendances in 1963 fell to an all-time low, principally because the general public was beginning to wake up to the fact that popular operas also need to be sung well. Neither *Bohème* nor *Faust* packed them in. The company itself was in disarray with internal faction fighting and an almost total loss of team spirit – and it showed.

Incredibly, worse was to come.

Regional Opera
10

In a country as large as Australia the establishment of local groups, be they in the field of opera, ballet, drama or any other art form, is far more important than in more thickly populated areas like Europe or the United States. Not only do they have literally hundreds of minor opera companies of varying importance, but their citizens are within easy reach of many major centres of the art; it is not inconceivable for a Londoner interested in opera to spend a few days in Milan or Bayreuth or, if the bug bites hard enough and the bank account permits, even New York. Similarly, the influx of Americans into Europe each year is on a scale which enables opera buffs to see and hear the work of the majority of the world's companies almost at will.

Considering that Australia is immensely proud of its singers, the popularity of opera and operatic music here is not surprising. On the other hand, the snobbery element, which places anything imported above the local article, has been ruinous to indigenous opera until the comparatively recent past. Even now, the true worth of the Australian Opera is definitely not recognized by the vast majority of audiences. Living on an illusion of excellence created through recordings of complete operas by casts which are rarely, if ever, assembled by even the best overseas houses, expectations are much too high. Unfortunately the traveller who can be bothered to visit the opera in Europe or America looks almost always for all-star casts, goes to the best available or simply does without. Anybody who has seen Domingo or Nilsson or Ghiaurov returns to Australia starry-eyed, remembering only the greatness of each singer. Naturally, he cannot find their like in the Sydney Opera House. (It is very curious the way those who have seen inferior opera overseas conveniently forget about it very quickly.)

There is an abundance of operatic weeds which grow alongside some admittedly magnificent blooms overseas. The standards in 90 per cent of European opera houses are no better than those of the Australian Opera and those of the majority are decidedly inferior. The balance includes the great showcases in the capital cities which admittedly can outclass even the best we produce in this country by sheer weight of budgets available. It is easy to forget that a small-scale production of high quality, say the Australian Opera's *Jenůfa,* can be a lot more enjoyable than, say, *Simon Boccanegra* played at the Metropolitan with an international cast, or a scandalously inferior *Trovatore* in Munich. It so happens that I saw all three within one twelve month's span and I can assure you that the local audiences in Munich and New York on those nights would have looked with envy toward our national company. Of course, we can't equal the best the world has to offer, but we can more than hold our own against the *average* standards of opera houses overseas.

The popularity of opera as a medium of entertainment is hardly appreciated in this country, where it is considered

Too much too soon The Victorian Opera Company's 1975
Mary Stuart, magnificently sung by an all-star cast, nearly
bankrupted the company. The limited budget simply could
not afford such excellence. (Centre left to right: John Wood,
David Parker, June Bronhill as Mary Stuart, Barry Clarke and
Nance Grant as Queen Elizabeth.)

an esoteric taste. That a family of father, mother, children
and miscellaneous relatives should regularly visit the local
theatre year in year out is almost inconceivable in our island
nation, but it is the norm in almost any city elsewhere which
has regular seasons of opera. Add to that the (unjustified)
belief that what is shown here is inferior and the most expensive art form in the world becomes a luxury we cannot
afford. It can be claimed that devoting 80 per cent of the
annual budget of the Music Board of the Australia Council
to opera is grossly unfair to music in general. Unfortunately,
the expense of producing opera is such that its survival is
dependent on the spending of these astronomical sums, while
ordinary music making can exist on a much smaller budget.

Accepting that the public considers even the Australian
Opera inferior, the disdain with which it greets minor companies becomes more easily understood. Until fairly recently
all opera outside the national company was amateur in
character. Dozens of small opera companies had their little
life spans, changing as their patrons and/or participants ran
out of money or into artistic crises. The introduction of
subsidies at federal and state levels has begun to change
the picture, but many years will pass before the ideal of
permanent opera companies in all capital cities becomes a
reality. That the Australian Opera will one day become the
Sydney Opera Company is inevitable, but the sheer costs
involved with trying to create only one parallel company
for Melbourne stagger the imagination. Just as audience potential in Sydney in 1966, when the large hall in the Opera
House was taken away from the national company, gave no
indication of the immense present demand, so is there no
sign at present even in Adelaide, the most successful regional
opera centre, that the city can support a full-time company
in the forseeable future.

The arts are full of quicksilver temperaments devoid of
business sense. Like all truisms, the statement is a simple
one of fact. Artists want to 'do their own thing', administrators want to run things efficiently and if the twain ever
do meet, it is the exception rather than the rule; a quick
look through the pages of this book will prove the point.
Opera companies are invariably formed by singers and musicians, who then find backers, who then in turn try and
put in some kind of administration. The only known alternative is the company run by government decree, and that
works only in countries in which the bureaucrats have been
opera lovers for generations. What happens then is the lesson
of Vienna, or any Italian city you may care to name; crisis
follows crisis and the government foots the bill. In a minor
fashion Australia is following the pattern right now.

There is little point in trying to cover every little opera
company in the country. It is no reflection on Tasmania
or Western Australia or the Capital Territory to say that
their officially accredited 'regional' opera companies are not
yet developed enough to stand historical scrutiny. The initial

success of the rejovenated Queensland Opera, in 1975, under
the guidance of John Thompson, will hopefully lead to bigger things. 'Unofficial' local groups like Sydney's long-
established Rockdale Opera and the more recent Sydney
Opera Company are in the same position. Good, bad or indifferent, their work has not been continuous long enough,
nor are their annual grants large enough to ensure a sound
future. The remarkable exception of South Australia is dealt
with in the chapter on opera in Adelaide.

Let me deal briefly with Victoria as a pattern which is
closer to the reality of local opera groups as they exist at
the time of writing. I do not say that any one other group
has followed the same path or will follow it; only that the
case of the Victorian Opera Company in Melbourne is fairly
typical. There is a very good chance that it will make the
grade, that in time it will grow and improve, that its support
locally and at federal level will continue and that audiences
will ultimately justify its existence on a permanent full-time
basis. I add, hastily, that there is no guarantee that my optim-
ism will be justified. In an art which has the Metropolitan
Opera House and Covent Garden threatening retrenchment
and even closure at regular intervals, nothing is sure but
uncertainty.

The V.O.C. grew out of amateurism and its growth was
gradual. For a solid twenty-five years it grew and developed.
1943's Mont Albert Choral Society became the Youth Operatic Society, the Hawthorn Operatic Society, the Victorian
Light Opera Company and, finally, the Victorian Opera
Company. All productions were financed by the participants,
costumes were made by the singers, the board of directors
elected by the artists themselves. One man, Leonard Spira,
finally turned an amateurish plaything into a serious musical
body when, in 1962, the constant diet of Gilbert and Sullivan grew tiresome. Playing in venues as varied as the tiny
Russell Street Theatre, the huge Palais in St Kilda or some
local church hall in Toorak, Spira produced results which
made both critics and the public sit up.

Spira started with excellence in a most unlikely area for
an amateur company: orchestras created for each short season,
whose standards were miraculous at a time when the Trust
orchestras did not yet exist. (For all I know, Spira's miracle
players all went into those orchestras in the end.) My first
experience of the V.O.C. was a performance of *The Merry
Wives of Windsor* at Russell Street, when thirty musicians
crammed underneath a microscopic stage apron produced a
magical overture – and that is not an easy piece to play!
On this solid foundation were placed singers in the making,
who gave performances no worse than those they produced
in their later professional careers. John Pringle in his early
twenties may not have been a *basso profundo,* but he played
parts like Osmin and Falstaff with a gusto and artistry which
carried all before it. A young Janice Taylor sang with sweetness and charm. Margaret Haggart already produced that

shattering top register which has by now made her a permanent member of the English National Opera at the Coliseum in London. Graeme Ewer sang and clowned with *élan* and even genuine amateurs, like tenor Ian Stapleton, gave performances of professional standards.

For six years Spira, the inspired amateur, an architect-turned-hornplayer-turned-conductor, went from strength to strength. For the first time an amateur company was treated with respect rather than condescension by the critics. Then the man at the helm decided to go to study overseas and the inevitable happened: in one year standards disappeared and the debts doubled. After one short burst of renewed activity in 1969, when the season included Lauris Elms in Gluck's *Orpheus and Euridice* there was a return to amateurism of the worst kind. The new Australian Council for the Arts tried to keep the ailing infant alive, but it was a struggle until a new key man appeared on the scene in 1973 – Richard Divall, another conductor.

Divall had been a brief *enfant terrible* on the Australian music scene, doing excellent work and promptly undoing it again by an uncontrolled exuberance which sat ill with administrations trying to control him. The V.O.C. gave him the responsibility he needed and the Council backed his plans, as did the state government. A policy of esoteric works catering for a minority audience, until then neglected, quickly brought back the packed houses of 1969. Monteverdi, Purcell and young Mozart left their marks. Production standards, which had been the weak point of the company even in Spira's day, began to improve. If Divall imported rather too many Sydney artists to please Victorian nationalists, at least musical standards were good and the repertoire adventurous enough to make people sit up. Lack of business management, always the weak point in young companies, made for heavy losses, but those were the days of ever-increasing subsidies.

Joan Hammond, recently-made a Dame for services to music, became a board member and then Artistic Director.

In a brief flourish, or flash, of grand operatic fireworks, 1975 saw a production of Donizetti's *Mary Stuart* with June Bronhill, Nance Grant and David Parker, which showed promise of a future Melbourne Opera that could one day compete with the future Sydney (present Australian) Opera. Alas, over-ambition nearly killed the cat, for good opera also means money-losing opera and *Mary Stuart* was no exception. Unbelievably, the company tried to cash in on the apparent bonanza: box office operas with box office stars. *Hansel and Gretel* was staged at the Comedy Theatre with two guest stars from the Australian Opera. Guest stars in *Hansel and Gretel?* The deficit sky-rocketed. *Don Pasquale* with June Bronhill? Well, yes, but Donizetti after Donizetti? The company's new home at the National Theatre was nearly full, but three performances with expensive stars in an 800 seat theatre cannot but produce further losses. The Victorian Ministry for the Arts complained about this, that and the other. Dame Joan Hammond resigned amid a lot of publicity about changes of policy. A deficit of $84,000 was announced for 1975.

The Victorian Opera Company* met a duplication of the kind of troubles which beset the best companies overseas. Financial and artistic crises while standards and audiences are rising are the norm, not the exception in opera. They were not the end of the V.O.C., but another step on the way up. It may only be a small company as yet. It still has a long way to go, but its troubles in recent years have been administrative rather than artistic. (Changes of repertoire or policy are a part of normal growth and the resignations of artistic directors seldom kill a company.)

At the time of writing new plans have not yet been announced. But a viable regional opera company exists and the subsidizing bodies will not lightly let it die. Companies in other states please note.

---

* In 1976 the Victorian Opera Company changed its name to The Victoria State Opera.

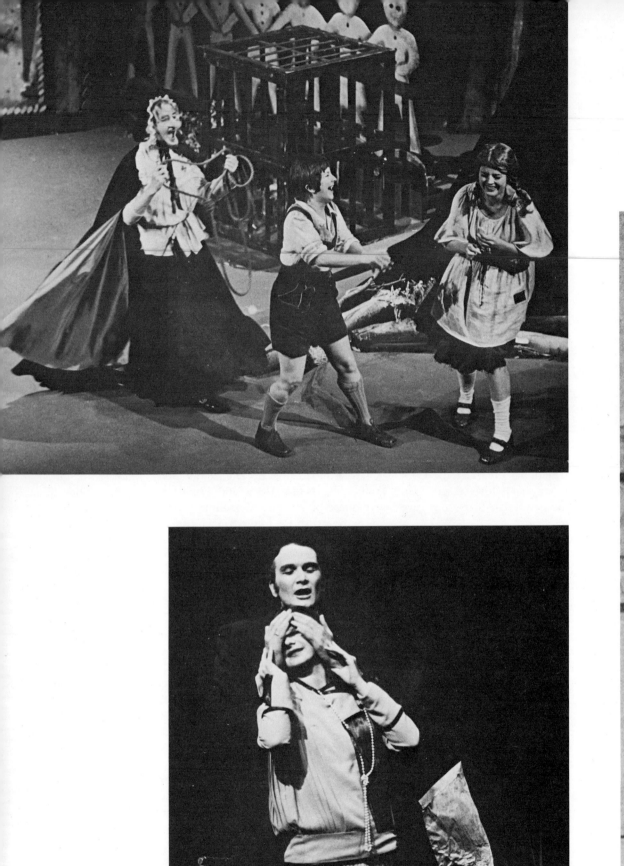

Regional opera at the cross-roads The Victorian Opera Company's attempts to build a public were a little uncertain in the mid-1970s. For the family there was a pantomime-style *Hansel and Gretel (left)*, staged at the Comedy Theatre with guest stars (!) and all (Joan Thomas as the Witch, Jennifer Bermingham as Hansel and Eilene Hannan as Gretel); for esoteric tastes there was Hindemith's *Hin und zurück* (*below left*, with Ian Dickson and Halina Nieckarz); and January 1976 saw Donizetti's *Don Pasquale* (*below*) with June Bronhill backed by local singers as her foils (Russell Smith's outrageously funny Pasquale listens to the smooth advice of Ian Cousins' Malatesta).

Australian Operas

11

National pride demands that Australia should have a national school of music and that this should include opera. Fair enough, but no way has yet been found of guaranteeing quality high enough to attract present or future audiences. Since the concept of subsidizing the arts became reality, there has been much greater exposure of music written by Australians than in the past, but the sheer cost of staging opera has left it trailing far behind other contemporary music.

Current controversy is being kept alive, not unnaturally, by the composers who want to see their operas performed. Music can be judged by academics from the written page. Librettos can be read. Designs can be seen. Singers can be heard. Operas must be performed. It is as simple as that! Opera is the most complicated hybrid to be found in the arts and the sum total of its components does not necessarily make a whole of equal quality. It is all very well for the Australia Council or the Australian Opera to hand out commissions to composers to write operas; they will produce scores, and have produced scores, which must then be judged by various people with a view to possible performance.

The argument has been put forward that the commissioning of an opera must include its staging. This is hardly valid. In the arts, as much as in commerce, there is a point at which one must cut one's losses and, unfortunately, in this case the factors affecting the final decision involve not only financial risk, but personal opinions. You cannot measure the practicability of a stage work as you can the working of an engine, or the design of a household article.

Writing about Australian operas is not easy. The theory that any work written by anybody loosely associated with this country automatically becomes Australian is a tenuous one, even though the Broadcasting Act has laid down guidelines which are almost ludicrously open to manipulation. A man who was born in Australia, but who left it as a child and never returned, can write Australian music, and a man born in Europe, who comes to Australia in middle or even old age, has his European compositions accepted as Australian music. The whole thing is an exercise in self-deceit.

The most famous 'Australian' composer of operas today is Malcolm Williamson, born in Sydney in 1931. He left Australia in 1953 and not one of his published works, opera or otherwise, was created in this country. His ten operas range from chamber works aimed at children, like *The Happy Prince,* to full-blown romantic works, like *The Violins of Saint-Jacques.* All have been performed in England, most with success, and his reputation internationally is impeccable; Williamson is one of the most successful composers of opera in the world today. Yet what is there Australian about his operas, beyond the accident of birth? None have Australian subjects and none have been performed in Australia, unless you count the presentation of some of the chamber works staged in the course of seminars run by Williamson himself during visits to Australia, or an A.B.C. television production of *The Violins of Saint-Jacques*.

The question whether the Australian Opera should present Australian operas is a particularly sensitive one. The principle has been the subject of lip-service by every musical director and administrator the company has had, yet the results have been a sum total of two performances of one double bill of one-actors in 1974. (I do not include Peter Sculthorpe's *Rites of Passage,* which cannot by any stretch of the imagination be called an opera in the conventional sense, whatever its virtues; and I will grant it has many.) The reasons why promises and good intentions have not materialized into anything solid are almost exclusively financial.

The relationship between modern works (operas included) and low box office is not exclusive to Australia. Managements overseas have long ago given away contemporary works as box office attractions. In the case of music, works can be slipped into concert programmes containing other, financially more viable, titles. Opera is a different matter entirely. The change in the fortunes of opera during this century came about because the public refused to accept twentieth century music. I know that much of the music rejected half a century ago has by now entered the repertoire but basically you cannot deny that after Puccini and Richard Strauss the public eagerly awaiting the production of new operas ceased to exist. Controversy and scandal, rather than popular musical acceptance, became the only forms of box office attraction and neither ingredient can sustain interest in a new work for very long. The few operas written in this century that have gained continued support represent a minute part of what has actually been written for the operatic stage in all this time.

But creativity must go on and, particularly in an age when the future of music itself, let alone opera, is uncertain, composers must be encouraged to experiment. In one respect they are, of course, perfectly right: there is no way in which progress can be made unless their operas are performed. But a fiendishly expensive exercise, which has no hope of covering its costs at the box office, should not be a part of the budget of the Australian Opera. If funds are to be made available to encourage the writing *and production* of new Australian operas, then they must be provided as a separate project undertaken by the Australian Opera or some regional company. No organization hanging on the brink of financial disaster from year to year can be expected to budget for this kind of thing and the Australian Opera's failure to do so must be taken in the context that the company has created a large market for a product by using its resources wisely. It could not have done so if the propagation of operas with in-built losses had been a part of the programme. Artistic or nationalistic considerations simply do not come into it.

The number of Australian works that have been staged within living memory is limited indeed and it is more than doubtful whether any one person would have seen them all. The number that have actually been written is much larger; the ratio is probably somewhere in the region of six or seven to one and this has been going on since the beginning of the century. Were this an academic chronological record, time could be spent in assembling all the information available (which would still fall short of completeness) but that is not the purpose of this exercise.

Starting with Isaac Nathan's *Don John of Austria,* which is the first locally written work described as an opera, whether it was or not, (see 'How did it all begin?') there were composers and writers galore who tried to cash in on the magic word 'opera' in the Australia of the middle nineteenth century. The craving for entertainment was great indeed and there was no shortage of cash. Every form of theatrical entertainment flourished. If much of it was substandard, the public was not aware of it. What went on on those stages, or what passed for stages, gave pleasure to a people whose life still resembled that of the early pioneers. To write operas to compete with what passed for Weber, Wallace, Meyerbeer or Verdi seemed easy, and even was easy. Nobody will ever know how many Australian operas were written in the nineteenth century, for most only existed in manuscript and, at best, the names survive in some dusty newspaper files.

In a day when novelty was still the key word to operatic success, William Saurin Lyster made capital out of presenting 'the first original opera ever brought upon the board of an Australian theatre'. Stephen Hale Marsh's *The Gentleman in Black* was performed in Melbourne in 1861, but Nathan's *Don John* had already been staged in Sydney in 1847. The claims of both are open to doubt, but at least they had a degree of originality in plot. Earlier, concurrent and later works were almost without exception straight adaptations of plays which had been seen in Australia, with music added. Those were the days when references to the classics of ancient, middle and recent ages lent an aura of learning to an author or a composer. As in America about the same time, acquiring an education the easy way, by attending plays, readings, exhibitions and the like, was considered uplifting and the more entertaining the event, the greater its success. Thus, when Isaac Nathan launched his own music magazine, an amazing venture for a city like Sydney, in the 1840s, he called it the *Southern Euphrosyne.* I am sure more Sydneysiders in 1842 knew who or what a Euphrosyne is than would in 1976. (She was one of the three Graces, the daughters of Venus.) Similarly, when Charles Nagel bastardized Moncrieff's English burlesque, *Shakespeare Festival, or The New Comedy of Errors,* he called it, believe it or not, *Shakesperi Conglommerofunidoginammoniae!* It was as good a way as any of disguising the piece's origins, lent the needed aura of respectability and duly filled the house.

Others tried to cash in on scenes set in the new colony by transplanting English plots into local settings suitably embroidered with the author's own and, presumably, his audience's morality. Nobody today wants to remember that racial discrimination against the Aborigines extended to their inclusion in plays and operas as Australian equivalents of the American Negro as portrayed during the slavery years. Not that *Life in Sydney* or *The Currency Lass* were operas, but then I ask again, was *Don John of Austria*?

During the following years numerous original (or near original) Australian operas were written and quite a few produced. Since they were usually staged, and written to be staged, for single performances by amateurs, they had a great deal of improvisation about them. It was spectacle rather than drama, which would have needed extensive rehearsal, that provided the attraction; in 1866 Charles Horsley's *The South Sea Sisters* featured a full-scale corroboree danced by real Aborigines, which was the sensation of this – opera?

The various German communities throughout Australia, specially around Adelaide, provided regular productions of Australian operas in German. These, even when performed in proper theatres, were little more than static concerts in costume. The occasional composer who managed to have his works performed by full-size opera companies did not always have the greatest of faith in his own talents. When Luscombe Searelle went to South Africa in 1889 after having had no less than three of his operas performed by the Montague-Turner Company in Sydney, he took with him a complete pre-fabricated theatre to Johannesburg, where his own opera company played not his *Estrella* or *Bobadil* or *Isidore*, but Wallace's *Maritana*!

It may be as well to mention at this point that William Vincent Wallace, whose two years in Australia brought immense benefits to the musical life of this country, did not start composing operas until seven years after he left Australia. The myth that *Maritana* was wholly or partly composed here was probably started by Wallace's most influential friend, John Philip Deane, the man who kept him hidden from his creditors in an attic in Rowe Street in Sydney for weeks, and who called his house 'Waldemar', a name made up of the first syllables of Wallace, Deane and *Maritana*. Young Wallace, who was only twenty-two at the time, left Australia owing £2000; like most musicians arriving in or departing from Australia in the early years, there was an unmusical cloud over his private life.

There is little point in trying to survey the many other Australian works produced in the second half of the last century. Even the operas written in the early 1900s, though their manuscripts are being kept with great care, offer little reward to the student, and the prospect of any revival is remote indeed. What does arise out of, for example, the

life of G. W. L. Marshall Hall (George William Louis, to satisfy those who, like myself, have always wondered what the initials stand for) is that the problems facing Australian composers were as great then as they are now.

Marshall Hall was a very major figure in Melbourne's musical life from 1890 until his death in 1915, though his activities were mostly restricted to the orchestral field and teaching. As for all composers of the time, opera held a fascination for him, though not even he could obtain a performance of *Aristodemus,* a twenty-five scene Greek tragedy, though a German translation was actually printed for the Melbourne Liedertafel. His *Romeo and Juliet* showed the continued influence of the classical-scholar syndrome which so attracted audiences, but it also failed to get performed. It was taken by the composer to Germany and translated for production, but without avail. In London he fared a little better; his *Stella* was performed at the Palladium as part of a variety bill in 1914. It is claimed that this was responsible for *Stella's* failure. The fact is that London variety bills in those days presented variety indeed. Mascagni himself conducted *Cavalleria Rusticana* (with Alessandro Valente as Turiddu) as part of just such a bill at the Hippodrome, just as Diaghilev's Ballet Russe was at the Coliseum. They did not fail. Do we have to ask why Marshall Hall did?

Most Australian operas of the past have their failure blamed on outside factors, usually because they were performed by students or amateurs. Arundel Orchard wrote what was for many years the only comprehensive book on music in Australia (and thereby perpetuated any number of fallacies and errors) but his operas did not have the exposure his book received. *Coquette* (1905) was reasonably successful in spite of its amateur cast. *The Emperor* (1906) was a flop. *The Man in the Moon* failed to survive one rehearsal. His opus magnum, *Dorian Gray,* took ten years to write. Two years later one act was performed by the students of the N.S.W. Conservatorium, who were promptly blamed for the failure of the opera, which has not been heard from since.

Alfred Hill, the one composer who can be classed as major among resident Australians (who were born here and worked here) was a little more lucky with his ventures into opera, just as his symphonies stand head and shoulders above those of his contemporaries. Arguments that they belong to an earlier, romantic, period are neither here nor there; Hill did produce the goods, and people are not only listening to his music still, but paying hard cash for it. His operas have not lasted so well, but at least two of them, *Tapu* and *A Moorish Maid,* obtained professional performances in 1904 and 1906 respectively. Royalties amounted to $200 and $120, sums not quite as small as they may appear to us today, but his *Giovanni* (what another one?) brought him nothing, because it was staged by a grand 'Australian Opera League' formed by himself and Fritz Hart with great hopes and the promise of Marshall Hall that all the expected proceeds of overseas performances of *Stella* and *Romeo and Juliet* would be made available to this new body. I suppose it can be said that Hall kept his promise, since he made nothing out of either.

The appearance of Fritz Hart, the most prolific of all opera composers in this country, brings a touch of sadness into the action. Hart, in spite of the Fritz, was an Englishman whose Cornish family tree went back as far as 1100. Unlike Hill, who had studied extensively in Germany, Hart was educated solely in England before coming to Australia in 1909. His fellow students included Vaughan Williams and Holst, but his music is closer to Debussy and the French impressionists. He wrote fourteen operas in all and seven of them have been staged at one time or the other. Only one gained the professional performance they all should have had, *Deirdre in Exile,* which appeared in the 1928 Williamson–Melba Grand Opera Season in a double bill with *Pagliacci.* Quite possibly Melba's friendship for Hart, the owner of the Melba Conservatorium, had a bearing on the choice of *Deirdre.*

The problem with Hart's operas lies less in the music than in the libretti, which he wrote himself. They are mostly concerned with Celtic legends and are inclined to be twee in a manner which today makes them decidedly old-fashioned. Unfortunately words and music, as usually happens in the case of composer-librettists, are completely integrated and it would be impossible to separate them. The occasional work, like *Even Unto Bethlehem,* can still be heard.

There is an outside factor which has held back not only recognition, but even inspection of Hart's operas. Due to difficulties with the 'establishment' in Melbourne, Hart accepted the post of musical director of the Honolulu Symphony as a full-time position in 1937, and all his scores went with him. One result was that until fairly recently Hart was no more than a name to the Australian musical community and he often did not even appear in books in which he should have played a major role. His works have now been donated to the State Library in Melbourne by his widow, and much of his music, if not his operas, is at present being recorded by the A.B.C. Time alone will tell whether the accessibility of the scores will produce any hidden masterpieces.

As head of the Melba Conservatorium, Fritz Hart was responsible for the performance of Australian operas other than his own. He played perhaps the major role in staging Australian works, which need not be listed in detail, in amateur or student performances, and revived some of the forty odd operas which have been written in Australia during the present century. This number compares unfavourably with the forty-six listed nineteenth century operas, nearly all of which were produced in their own time, if with varying, and certainly not lasting, success. But then, things were a little different in those early days and no attempt has ever been made to revive even one of those period pieces to enable us to judge its worth.

I do not really feel inclined to play along with the theory that operas written by expatriates should appear in a volume entitled 'Opera in Australia'. The A.B.C. offered Malcolm Williamson's *Violins of Saint-Jacques* in a new television production recently, proving only that the Australian Opera was probably right not to stage it. The music is certainly lush enough and the sensationalism of the voodoo-dominated story has some attraction, but by no stretch of the imagination can it be described as Australian and, if we are to have unknown works included in the local repertoire, there is a huge reservoir of local operas of greater importance than *The Violins.* On the other hand, it can be stipulated with some justification that, if money is to be spent on the production of an Australian work under the terms of the Act as it now stands, we might as well be offered something tried and proved, like Williamson's opera, or Arthur Benjamin's *A Tale of Two Cities.*

The odd man out among expatriates is a woman, Peggy Glanville-Hicks, who has a following in *avant garde* circles which brought about a staging of her opera, *The Transposed Head,* when she returned briefly in 1970. Nevertheless, she has been an American citizen for thirty years and now lives in Greece. 1972 saw her short curtain-raiser, *The Glittering Gate,* performed at the Adelaide Festival and the acceptability of her music, electronics and all, and her logically dramatic libretti, may yet bring her greater local exposure. She still has two major works up her sleeve, *Sappho* and *Nausicaa,* the latter to a text by Robert Graves based on Homer. With a cast of 150 and an audience of 4800 it had an enormous success at the 1961 Athens Festival, since when all has been silence.

The number of composers resident in Australia who are fighting for representation is really very limited in relation to the amount of noise they make. Two of the most likely contenders appear to have dropped out of the race already! Peter Sculthorpe, arguably the major musical talent in Australia today, was supposed to produce the great Australian epic to launch the Sydney Opera House. For whatever reason, his work was not staged until a year after the great event and *Rites of Passage* proved to be a vital piece of total theatre, but hardly an opera. Opera is music drama, *Rites of Passage* has no action, no principals and the chorus sings in several different languages. As a one-work non-opera creator Sculthorpe is not in the race for the moment.

Colin Brumby many years ago led the performing field with a whole series of home-grown and home-performed mini-operas which he and his wife staged in Queensland with considerable success. Most were children's operas, but

his *Seven Deadly Sins* was in a more serious vein and parts of it were recorded. I don't know what made Brumby throw in the sponge, but he has not produced an opera for some time. Children's operas (or operas for schools) seem to be the medium in which Australian composers excel. Apart from Brumby's run of works, which toured the East coast for years, Geoff Carroll's are probably the most successful. His *Professor Kobolt and the Krimson Krumpet* is constantly revived, as is Peter Narroway's *Ticka Tocka Linga*.

That leaves only three serious contenders for Australian operatic honours, in alphabetical order: George Dreyfus, Larry Sitzky and Felix Werder. Dreyfus is the most vocal of the three, casting unending stones into the operatic millpond, refusing to take 'No' for an answer. The man must be admired for his perseverance. In 1973 he (or rather his wife, Kay Dreyfus) actually arranged a major opera symposium in Melbourne, which only thinly disguised its pur-

pose of promoting the composer. If this sounds derogatory, it is not meant to be.

Dreyfus quite possibly stands the best chance of ultimate success, whether the Australian Opera ever stages his rejected *Gilt-Edged Kid* or not. Of the three, Dreyfus is the most commercial, the most likely to produce something the general public will accept and his kind of aggressive showmanship will certainly sell his works – if they are good enough. Not unnaturally, he has been pressing the virtues of his first opera, *Garni Sands* (1965) and has managed to have it staged not only throughout Australia, but even in New York. *Garni Sands* is not as good as Dreyfus believes or believed; its confused libretto alone will prevent it from becoming a lasting success. However, its successors have the kind of theatricality which has brought fame to some recent overseas works. Hans Werner Henze and Gottfried von Einem have made careers out of writing facile music of no great intrinsic value to librettos which have considerable merit as sheer entertainment. *The Young Lord* or *The Visit of the Old Lady* are being produced because people enjoy the initial impact of plot and action; their success has the same basis as Britten's *Albert Herring*. None of the three works will ever have its 'arias' sung or its melodies medlified. Once the novelty wears off (as in the case of *Herring*) productions will have prestige rather than a large box office. But they will be produced and that is, after all, what composers like Dreyfus want and need. His ventures in the operatic field and outside it show the right kind of feeling for words to impress the listener. The early *Galgenlieder* (Gallows Songs) showed the way. Had he stuck to this path, his first opera might have been more quickly accepted. The very title of his contribution to the 1976 Adelaide Festival, *The Lamentable Reign of King Charles the Last,* was funny enough to create an audience. If 'sold out' notices are a criterion, *King Charles* was a success, but Tim Robertson's topical political intimate revue material will make the work very quickly outdated. As for the, by now, famous *Gilt-Edged Kid,* its rejection by the Australian Opera in favour of two other one-acters, after commissioning all three, may well have been a political one – Canberra-political rather than opera political. (Dreyfus has been staging it as a freelance ever since.)

The Australian Opera double bill, which was actually performed (twice!) in 1974, really contained only one opera which needed doing, Sitzky's *Lenz.* The management has resolutely refused to explain the choice of Werder's *The Affair* in preference to Dreyfus' *Gilt-Edged Kid,* but an outsider can perhaps guess at what lawyers may have advised the Australian Opera not to say: Werder's opera was set in the Australian political sphere, it satirized politicans at a time of great political changes and it could well have seen the light of day for no better reason than that it gave the producer, Stephen Hall, the chance to open the curtain on a huge picture of the then Prime Minister, Gough Whitlam. Dreyfus' opera would have had to be a masterpiece to beat the publicity value of Werder's work, which appealed to no critic and few of the public, but did keep the audience amused in a bewildered sort of way. If Werder was a Henze, *The Affair* might have been another *Young Lord,* but he is not and it was not.

Larry Sitzky falls into a different class. He has written what could be described as the most successful modern Australian Opera, *The Fall of the House of Usher,* based solidly on the original Edgar Allan Poe story, which is an ideal vehicle for visual drama supplementing a music score of some body. *The House of Usher* has been produced in most Australian states and by A.B.C. television. It is hardly a fad, nor have there been enough performances in each instance to say that it is a popular success; but the announcement of a performance is invariably greeted with respect in a field

A grand opera Prime Minister The famous, or infamous, painting of 1974's Prime Minister Gough Whitlam dominated Felix Werder's one-act opera *The Affair*, which was set in an Australian embassy somewhere overseas. Etela Piha and Robert Eddie sending themselves — and the opera? — up.

where groans are more commonly heard.

Sitzky's second work, *Lenz,* was a *succès d'estime* when staged by the Australian Opera. It is one of the few modern works which gets better as it goes along; most such operas start with a good idea and then peter out. Anybody not taken with *Lenz* at the start is completely committed when the final curtain comes down; no mean achievement. It is too early to know whether Sitzky can become the Tippett of Australia, but he is musically the most successful contender to date.

His *Fiery Tales* was the 1976 Adelaide Festival coupling for Dreyfus' *King Charles.* Based on two stories from Chaucer and Boccaccio, it should be a roaring success if ever it is again staged in Chris Winzar's production, which maximized the sexual goings-on to the most. Musically most acceptable in its context, *Fiery Tales* is only a transitory work, but one of which Sitzky need not be ashamed.

I regret that Felix Werder must tail the field, and not only alphabetically. He is the most prolific of opera composers and has, I believe, ten or eleven in manuscript. They vary from small trifles to very major works indeed and hope for him springs eternal. He writes with an incredible facility, but *The Affair, Private,* and *Kisses for a Quid,* as far as I know the only of his operas to have been performed publicly, show a disregard for the human voice which, if it exists in the unperformed works, makes their neglect understandable. Werder is extraordinary in that he does not demand that his singers correctly pitch the notes he writes. How he expects the results to reflect his intentions is not clear.

James Penberthy in Perth, is another composer who has a large number of unperformed works, several on Aboriginal themes. Until they are given a hearing, their worth cannot be evaluated. Only *Dalgerie,* with lyrics by Mary Durack, was performed in 1959, Gregory Dempsey singing the Aboriginal lead, Mundit.

This leaves a solitary work by the oldest-living Australian composer, Margaret Sutherland. The undoubted success of *The Young Kabbarli* (which has been recorded by H.M.V.) in Hobart, Adelaide and Melbourne is all the more gratifying because the subject is genuinely Australian – the story of Daisy Bates, a pioneer lady whose care for Aborigines was her whole life. It is far from being a lasting masterpiece, but then there has never yet been an opera written in Australia which can be so described.

Even without going into the detail which some may have expected in this chapter, I have devoted considerable space to something which really does not exist, native Australian opera. It is a fragile plant with which we must persevere and which must be encouraged. At the same time it is foolish to pretend that this is not the musical field in which Australia lags furthest behind the rest of the world.

Australian opera by the Australian Opera The first native work which can truthfully be described as a proper opera was performed by the national company in 1974. Larry Sitzky's *Lenz* was based on a German subject, but it was an Australian opera. Ron Stevens as Lenz unsuccessfully trying to raise the dead.

More Canterbury Tales Not the regrettable sequel to the famous musical, but an Australian opera, Larry Sitzky's *Fiery Tales*, which adds Boccaccio to Chaucer for good measure. New Opera South Australia showed none of the prudishness which marred its commercial cousin's watered down *Canterbury Tales*. A few minutes before the happy scene shown *below*, all the characters, except the gentleman on the extreme left, were engaged in amorous combat, with three totally naked bottoms in full and active view of the audience. The audience's smiles at the 1976 Adelaide Festival were as broad as those of the singers seen here. Left to right: Keith Hempton, Daphne Harris, Patsy Hemingway, Lyndon Piddington, Howard Spicer, Dennis O'Neill and Norma Knight.

Australian lese-majesty George Dreyfus and his librettist, Tim Robertson, opted for verbal rather than visual wit in *The Lamentable Reign of King Charles the Last*, played in a double bill with Sitzky's *Fiery Tales* by New Opera South Australia. King (Prince) Charles plays the lead in an intimate revue-style opera involving Queen Elizabeth, Princess Anne, Winston Churchill, a dog named Hamlet and various thinly disguised political figures, including King Gosh (Whitlam), Prince Don (Dunstan) and Sir Blow Joh, the Hoon of Petersen. The lady playing King Charles (Patsy Hemingway) does a strip-tease and a standard lamp named Australia Felix Mendelsong tries to keep out of Hamlet's way for obvious reasons. (Left to right: Patsy Hemingway, David Brennan and John Wood.)

The Mixture, Not as Before

12

Opera and ballet don't mix — or do they? Most German opera houses and Covent Garden in England run opera and ballet companies simultaneously. The economics are fearful, but there are certain advantages which cannot be ignored, mainly the fact that opera principals cannot sing on consecutive nights without endangering their voices; it is much easier to train muscles for continued exertion than vocal cords. In fact, muscles must be exercised constantly, while excessive strain on the fine membranes of the throat is positively dangerous to their continued wellbeing. Thus the ability to alternate ballet with opera reduces a company's needs in the star singer field, and that can be of vital concern to the artistic, if not the financial success of a season. The monetary counter-productiveness lies in the fact that the ensemble must be paid by the week, whether singers are used nightly or not, and the same applies to the ballet company, which usually ends up as a very secondary step-child when it comes to numbers of performances scheduled.

Nobody has yet invented a 'ballet house' in opposition, or parallel, to the opera house which can be found throughout the world. The exceptions which prove the rule, Covent Garden or Stuttgart, to name but two, are rare indeed. More commonly the ballet company is used as a filler to take the pressure off the singers and fillers rarely are blessed with generous budgets. In its early days at Sadler's Wells the Vic-Wells Ballet played only two out of each week's seven performances and one of those was the Saturday matinee! To what extent the arrangement held back the company's emergence as a major force cannot be established at this late stage. It could even be argued that it was a good thing because it prevented a limited amount of talent from being over extended.

The continued drubbing which the Trust received from all quarters in 1963 was far from encouraging, but the policies implemented by it under the leadership of Stefan Haag became almost masochistic in nature. There was an almost visible death wish in the air. Lack of money was the universal complaint at whose door all blame was laid, but the real villain was ambition. Too much too soon was the motto and when too much failed, the logical (?) thing was to try something even bigger. Thus the concept of the joint opera/ballet season of 1964 was created. If there was thought in the planning, it defies indentification. When original ideas were aborted through outside influences, through unexpected disasters or through the inevitable cash shortages, the management was not prepared. Only one thing is certain: the season began with the Adelaide Festival and proceeded from there according to schedule. No changes were made beyond what would normally occur in the course of any theatrical tour; in other words, plans were laid and executed regardless of the consequences. The best that can be said is that the year enabled the opera company to stay together a little longer. Ironically, or perhaps consequentially, there was to be no season in 1965!

It is easy to be wise after the event, but all logical indications pointed to a pulling in of horns in 1964. The undiscriminating public had ceased following the standard box office works like *Bohème* and the discriminating public had long ago lost interest. Only a drastic raising of standards could pull the company out of the doldrums. Operatically, the sum total of 1964 proved to be an acceptable esoteric showpiece for the Adelaide Festival in Walton's *Troilus and Cressida,* an experimental staging of Verdi's *Macbeth* (hardly box office at the best of times), an un-Mozartean *Cosi fan tutte,* another shockingly bad *Carmen,* a revival of *Die Fledermaus* of the previous year and the Carl Orff double bill *The Wise Woman/Catulli Carmina,* which was the only literal collaboration between the opera and ballet companies. All of this was staged throughout Australia alternating with performances of ballet which, perhaps in silent protest, proved to be dispirited and uninspired, though on a higher level than the opera since the Australian ballet was a continuing body which had created its own standards.

A side effect of the season, which was to have lasting results, was the howls of protests from the players of the A.B.C. orchestras. The reluctance of A.B.C. musicians to exchange their white tie and tails image for obscurity in the pits of Her Majesty's in Adelaide, the Palais Theatre in Melbourne or the despised Tivoli in Sydney was understandable. Doubling their duties by adding ballet to their chores in 1964 made matters worse and also cut into planned concert schedules. It speaks highly for the A.B.C. that it agreed to the ambitious new schedules. If anything precipitated the creation of the first Trust orchestra it was the experience of this year.

The third of the Adelaide Festivals began to attract international attention. Britain's grand old man of music, Sir William Walton, was the star attraction and the Australian premiere of his only opera, *Troilus and Cressida,* was a logical centrepiece, though it is hardly a popular work. The idea to extend *Troilus* to form the nucleus of an all-Shakespeare Festival was put forward and prompted the addition of Verdi's *Macbeth.* When it was found that the scheme was unworkable, and *Carmen* was added to cater for the masses, *Macbeth* unaccountably was retained. Probably John Shaw had been engaged to sing the title role before the impracticability of the scheme had been discovered: it was the kind of thing which happened regularly in those days, as was the non-appearance or late appearance of overseas artists. Raymond Boyce's new production of *Carmen,* using his own designs, was rehearsed in Sydney and also in Adelaide without a Carmen. Jean Madeira graciously turned up for the final dress rehearsal! Marie Collier was more generous, putting in an appearance fully five days before *Troilus and*

Cressida was premiered!

The performances of Walton's opera were probably the last, as well as the first, to be staged in Australia. It is a static work at the best of times and really suitable only for festivals. No attempt was made to tour *Troilus,* though the Adelaide production by Robin Lovejoy (with designs by Frank Hinder) with two imported leads, Richard Lewis and Marie Collier, was more than acceptable. Peter Baillie, Allan Light, Ronald Maconaghie and Norman Yemm (not yet of TV *Homicide* and *The Sullivans* fame) carried the local banner very much to Sir William's satisfaction and Joseph Post miraculously resurfaced to conduct later performances.

The company had no musical director, only conductors. John Hopkins and Walter Stiasny did their best with the South Australian Symphony Orchestra to save *Carmen* and *Macbeth,* but to no avail; the goings-on (or lack of) on stage and backstage proved an insuperable barrier. It is ironical that throughout those early years of the Trust Opera Company its strength lay always in its orchestras and conductors, which were unable to make up for the lack of artistic standards, while in later years, when the A.B.C. orchestras were replaced by the Trust's own musicians, the stage action improved to the point that critics throughout Australia were firing off at the pit. The protesting A.B.C. musicians in 1964 certainly had a point: their excellent efforts to save poor productions went for nought, yet the good productions of later years received their full due, in spite of poor orchestral playing.

Macbeth, the other part of the ill-conceived Shakespearean season, was entrusted to designer Stan Ostoja-Kotkowski. This Polish-born lighting genius has carved quite a groove for himself in Australian arts, but *Macbeth* was more a grave than a groove. Resident producer Stefan Beinl, who carried the major burden of Trust productions until his untimely death in 1970, tried to build a brooding modern shadow-play around his imported expatriate protagonist, John Shaw. Ostoja-Kotkowski provided a multi-purpose set which served as both battle field and banquet hall. What an enormous steel bridge had to do with either was never clear and the monstrous structure was sold for scrap at the end of the season on the sound principle that $24 in hand is worth many hundreds in storage costs. With it went any hope of ever restaging one of Beinl's few outright failures. Ukrainian-born migrant Tais Taras was a sweet-voiced Lady Macbeth, making nonsense of Verdi's desire that her voice should be hard, stifled and dark, 'the voice of a devil'. Serge Baigildin sang Macduff's aria very well.

Macbeth was sung in Italian and *Carmen* in French, the latter presumably because Jean Madeira was a reasonably well-known exponent of the role in French. The fact that she was born in Illinois was neither here nor there. Why *Macbeth* was produced in Italian is not clear either, unless there was a sudden thought that international visitors should hear opera as they would hear it overseas. It is not known what they thought of a French *Carmen* sung by American, Italian and Australian singers or an Italian *Macbeth* with Australian, Ukrainian and Russian soloists. It was certainly not the start of an original language policy, but just another of the haphazardly-made decisions of a company without an artistic policy.

Nicola Filacuridi was the Don José to Madeira's *Carmen*. Boyce's production was so bad that it followed *Ariadne,* in having to be doctored by another, production director John Young, who (quite rightly) makes no claim to having improved it. Madeira left after Adelaide to have her place taken by Gloria Lane, a much better singer if not as realistically earthy as Madeira. Miss Lane, best-known previously as the excellent Secretary in the original production of Menotti's *Consul,* arrived in Australia primly respectable until greeted by Edward Downes (here to inspect his supposedly imminent new realm) with: 'What are you doing here, Tits?' Thereafter Miss Lane did her best to live up to her nickname, in the process somewhat distracting public and critics alike from her undoubted vocal abilities. That she had a magnificent voice, apart from a magnificent figure, was considered of less import than that she 'cheapened' *Carmen* by showing too much of both ends of her anatomy. (And at a recent critics convention it was claimed that opera critics are music critics!)

Robert Allman took over *Macbeth* from John Shaw and also sang Escamillo, both with great verve and volume, though his voice then was rougher than it is today.

The Australian Ballet staged the world premiere of Helpmann's *The Display* for the Adelaide Festival and a gigantic tent production of Shakespeare's *Henry V* starred John Bell, later to appear with the Australian Opera as a producer. Less noticed was a young actor playing the Earl of Cambridge and the Duke of Orleans, Dennis Olsen, not dreaming that within a few years he would sing the lead in five operas for the national company – Gilbert and Sullivan comic leads, but leads just the same – and any success they had was certainly Olsen's.

The fact that both the ballet and the opera played simultaneously at the Adelaide Festival was not of tremendous significance. Each played on its own nights and few people, apart from the harassed stage staff, thought any more about it. Having brought the two companies together, one of the most curious non-happenings was the fact that their only joint production was not staged for the Festival. And yet the coupling of Carl Orff's opera *Die Kluge* (under the title *The Wise Woman*) with the ballet-pantomime-oratorio *Catulli Carmina* would have been an ideal presentation for any Festival, while having small audience potential elsewhere.

Oddly enough, the opera came off best in this double bill when seen in non-Festival cities. *The Wise Woman* was played for laughs by producer Stefan Beinl. The political and humanistic purposes of Orff's morality play were lost in slapstick, just as in Haag's *Cosi fan tutte* Mozart's satire on love and marriage disappeared. Nevertheless, *The Wise Woman* was well sung and brilliantly acted by its three Rogues, Robert Gard, Ronald Maconaghie and Alan Light, while Cynthia Johnson sang beautifully in the title role and the miniature set of Ronald Sinclair served its purpose admirably.

Catulli Carmina, in total contrast, was a disaster. Orff used an antique Latin text to tell some ribald tales, which would have created a sensation in 1964 had they been staged in their true colours. Producer-choreographer Joanne Priest either was a prude or assumed (perhaps rightly) that the time for sexual liberation was not yet at hand. It is a mystery how a production based on a major erotic work was allowed to proceed in a Sunday School atmosphere of delicate posturing by the ballet, while the opera chorus lustily sang about the pleasures of the flesh – in Latin! The academics attending might have got some kicks out of the lyrics. The general public did not.

Haag's *Cosi fan tutte* met some degree of success as a musical farce, but his production in modernistic period style built around a single bandstand-like set (by Desmond Digby), with young Patrick Thomas conducting, failed to please most critics and Mozart lovers. The cast was more than adequate. Neil Warren-Smith as Don Alfonso and Cynthia Johnson's Despina were closest to the ideal not reached by the production.

It was also Neil Warren-Smith who produced the only worthwhile contribution to the Gala Performance staged at the Elizabethan Theatre in Sydney on 29 September 1964 to celebrate the tenth anniversary of the foundation of the Elizabethan Theatre Trust. Warren-Smith conducted and sang, with the Sydney Symphony Orchestra fully dressed in period costumes, complete with wigs, Cimarosa's delightful one-man opera *Il Maestro di Capella*. As for the rest, Stravinsky's *The Soldier's Tale* represented all aspects of the Trust's activities – opera, drama and ballet. Helpmann produced and appeared as the Devil with Kathleen Gorham, Norman Yemm and John Bell. The rest of the programme was made up of ballet *divertissements*. The whole thing was typical of the Trust at that time, a multitude of talent all rushing off in different directions at once.

When it was announced that J. C. Williamson's were proposing to stage an international opera season in 1965 starring Joan Sutherland everybody heaved a sigh of relief. Here was a way to continue operatic life without risk to the Trust, while the opera company could be completely overhauled. It was thought that with a full year's planning a new start could be made in 1966. The singers would be used by

Williamson's in the interim.

The usual grandiose plans were afoot. Edward Downes was about to have his dreams for putting opera in Australia on its feet realized after some years of haggling. 1966 would be the turning point in the company's fortunes, as every past year had been the turning point. That the forecast happened to be true this time was not thanks to the plans made in 1964. None of those materialized, but the management structure of the Trust Opera was altered. John Young of-

ficially became its Administrator and, in the course of discussions with Downes in London, was introduced to Stephen Hall. The stage was set for the hard climb to success, even though Dr Coombs never did raise enough cash to meet the artistic demands Downes made as a condition of coming to Australia.

It was back to square one in 1966, and to a most unlikely character, who was to produce the impetus which would start the ball rolling.

The Young Years

13

The title of this chapter wrote itself. Not only were 1966 to 1969 the years of John Young's administration, but they were the youth of the present Australian Opera. Before dealing with John Young – the unlikely character of the last chapter's ending – the role of Stefan Haag must be examined. Haag was a product of Gertrude Johnson's National Theatre, a young singer of character roles who had shown an early flair for production and gone through the mill of pre-Trust opera in many states, learning his craft the amateur way, through experience. It is a pity that events were to highlight his activities during those years in which he was the subject of criticism, because Haag was to a very large extent responsible for the early successes of the Trust Opera. One dreads to think what Robert Quentin would have done in 1956 without Haag's experience to back him. Unfortunately, the very fact that he was the most experienced Trust executive – the most experienced amateur, perhaps, but the most experienced just the same – caused successive administrators of the Trust to leave matters operatic to Haag.

The Australian Ballet was always a separate entity. The drama activities of the Trust never really got off the ground and, in line with previous theatrical history in Australia, opera was the great hope for the Trust's future. The man who knew most about opera had to be a key person and Stefan Haag was that man.

With hindsight it would, of course, have been better to back up Haag with somebody who had professional experience in running an opera company. Perhaps the ubiquitous Karl Rankl was thought to be the answer, perhaps not. The point is that everybody from Dr Coombs downward knew even less than Haag about it. Nobody has suggested that Haag was not sincere, that he did not do his best, that he ruled with a hand of iron or even that he engaged in the kind of power politics which were to beset the company after his departure. He was a sincere man doing a job to the best of his ability and as time went on it became more and more obvious that it was not within his compass to develop further. There is a close parallel between Haag and his mentor, Gertrude Johnson, who also started an opera company, brought it considerable success and then did not know how to go on from there.

It may not matter now exactly what went wrong, but Haag's complete control of the opera must be stressed in any history of the company as 1966 approaches. He was by then Executive Director of the whole Trust. Will Thompson was the 'Manager' of the opera company and John Young was 'Production Director'. Theoretically Thompson and Young were in charge. In practical terms Haag ran the opera company and its artistic policies. He also continued to produce at least one opera each year. A man who loves opera doesn't let go easily, as history has shown, and Haag was no exception.

There are many parallels between the careers of Haag and Young. Both were Australians, both started as singers, went into production and ended up running the Trust Opera. In fact, it was Haag who first brought Young into the company, just as Young was to bring in his own successor, Stephan Hall. Young started with Eugene Goossens at the Sydney Conservatorium, singing in those incredible productions Goossens and his daughter Jean managed to put together. During the 1952 combined National Operas season Young went to Melbourne to understudy John Brownlee's Don Giovanni and ended up opening the Sydney season singing the Don. That, I am afraid, was the high point of John Young's career as a singer, though he was to play many parts over the years, curiously enough many of the same parts in which Haag specialized – the comprimario roles in *La Bohème,* for example.

Young's adventures after that initial start to his career read like something out of a novel. One day he should write a book about his travels around Africa, of singing Faust to an ex-Paris bass' Mephistopheles in a nightclub in the Chad, of being stranded without petrol in the Algerian revolution and having to sell not only his truck, but his wife's harp (!) to get out. Unlike Haag, Young had no continuity in opera because he lost his voice too many times, didn't work with any one company for long and started his producing piecemeal in odd places. Among other things, he sang the Wazir in the Australian production of *Kismet* and was the compere of the floorshow at Checkers night club. You could say that he had a checkered career. (Pun intended.) Finally, John Young sang Sparafucile in Hobart in 1959, directed *Oklahoma!* (also singing Judd) and ended up as Manager of the Theatre Royal because he was the only theatre man around, a sequence of events not unnatural in the operatic history of this country.

That Young was a good artist of natural ability is unquestioned. He proved it when singing Mr Peachum in the Trust's *Beggar's Opera* back in 1957. He had his first try at producing professionals when he 'took over' the circus scene in the Trust's *Bartered Bride* in which he played the Ringmaster. Young is nothing if not realistic about his abilities and disabilities as a producer. He freely admits to having been responsible for two of the worst productions ever seen anywhere, a *Hansel and Gretel* in Perth in 1959 and the infamous Trust *Faust* in 1963. Disarming as such candour may be, it does make one wonder on what basis he was chosen to become Production Director of the opera company.

At the end of 1964 John Young was sent overseas to learn all about the job he had been doing since 1962, production director of an opera company. When he returned, he found himself in the midst of a lengthy game of unmusical chairs, involving yearly changes of titles, and a most convoluted power-play worthy of any soap opera on television. Rather than recount the details of these vital years, which would only confuse, let me sum them up in the pecking order in which they began in 1966. It was then Haag, Hall, Young. It became Haag, Young, Hall. Then Haag was knocked out and Hall became Young's boss as Executive Director of the Trust. Finally, four years later, Young departed and only Hall remained as the head of the opera company, which became the independent Australian Opera. Any attempt to clarify further would simply confuse the reader, but the background should be kept in mind when assessing the work done by Young and Hall to build a major force out of the shambles which existed following the Sutherland-Williamson's year (1965).

It would be foolish to underestimate the part John Young played in the three short years after he became the Administrator of the company under Haag in 1966. The company was at its lowest point, it had just missed a full year of activities for the third time in the ten years of its existence. Young was not qualified for the job he took and he did not set the world on fire. It can even be argued that his departure came at the right moment. The fact remains that after three years in office he left a company well on the way to becoming what the Australian Opera is today, a world-class company.

There had actually never been a continuous Trust Opera Company, but only a series of seasons which drew on singers who, by luck or perseverence, had managed to remain available in Australia. Jobs between seasons were hard to get and not all were in the singing field. Some kind of continuity of employment was essential if a permanent company was to be formed, but it would take more than one year in which to make this a reality. Perhaps it was the threat of having the Sydney Opera House large hall taken away from opera which was the final straw, but solid forward planning began in 1965, for 1967!

On paper, 1966 was a step backward compared with the season prior to the Sutherland-Williamson Tour. There were only three productions compared with six in 1964 (not counting two operas produced in Perth alone) and seasons in each state were cut back severely. Yet suddenly there was quality rather than quantity. The repertoire was chosen to suit the singers available locally, except for one who returned on a permanent basis. Donald Smith, who had gone overseas some years before and had done well in England, answered the call to sing Manrico in Verdi's *Trovatore* with alacrity; this was another production which was imported, complete, from New Zealand. *Boris Godounov* was staged as a vehicle for Neil Warren-Smith and *The Barber of Seville* used the small pool of established local favourites in minimal settings by Ronald Sinclair.

The whole thing was an economy package which worked. The operas were well balanced, the singing was good enough to satisfy people who had the previous year been hearing Sutherland and Pavarotti, and the general climate for opera was looking up, even though the double disappointments of the Sydney Opera House and the non-arrival of Downes must have depressed the management no end. Nothing could be done about the Sydney Opera House which, in any case, was clearly not going to be completed for many years yet. A replacement for Downes was found more easily.

The availability of Denis Vaughan to become Musical Director of the company was a stroke of good fortune badly needed. Vaughan was an Australian in the news, because he had been making waves in musical circles by extensive research into the authenticity of published operatic scores, principally those of Puccini. None of the conglomorate of guest conductors used in 1964 were available and strong musical leadership, for what was basically a new company, was needed. Vaughan was a pedagogue first, a conductor second and a musical director last, but Verdi's *Trovatore* was right up his street and John Young's conception of *Boris Godounov,* in its original Mussorgsky version, undoubtedly challenged Vaughan's musical taste buds. This *Boris* remained Young's one outstanding achievement as a producer. He had seen the opera in Russia in 1965 and came to the conclusion, well before the general overseas trend, that Mussorgsky's own scoring suits the psychological drama of the tragic Russian tsar much better than the lush re-orchestration of Rimsky-Korsakoff which was, and still is, commonly used in place of the original. By adopting it for his Australian production he immediately lent an aura of adventurousness to the occasion, which went well with Vaughan's notoriety as a musicologist revolting against the establishment. It is doubtful whether Vaughan made any revolutionary returns to original Verdi in the score of *Il Trovatore* ('Di quella pira' retained its unwritten top Cs) but in terms of giving the season appeal for serious opera lovers, the Young–Vaughan enterprises succeeded admirably.

A further indication of the new serious-mindedness was the decision to announce a policy of playing operas in the original langauge wherever possible. In 1966 this meant compromise as practised in most European capitals, that is, standard works which are well-known to the public and do not rely on verbal drama are sung in the language of origin, while comedies and works involving spoken dialogue are produced in the language of the audience. Only one work, *Trovatore,* in 1966 was affected; not even Covent Garden was game to produce *Boris* sung in Russian at the time and *The Barber of Seville* obviously fell into the second category anyway. The point is that the Italian *Trovatore* established once and for all that Australians would accept original language productions, making the engagement of guest artists in future years easier, and generally lending a sense of international quality to the works so produced.

The ubiquitous Barber Rossini's *Barber of Seville*, constantly revived and extensively toured over the years in innumerable thrown-together productions, which never failed to please. This typical cast, from 1966 included, left to right, Robert Gard, Doreen Morrow, Ronald Maconaghie and Norman Yemm (before his rise to fame in television drama series).

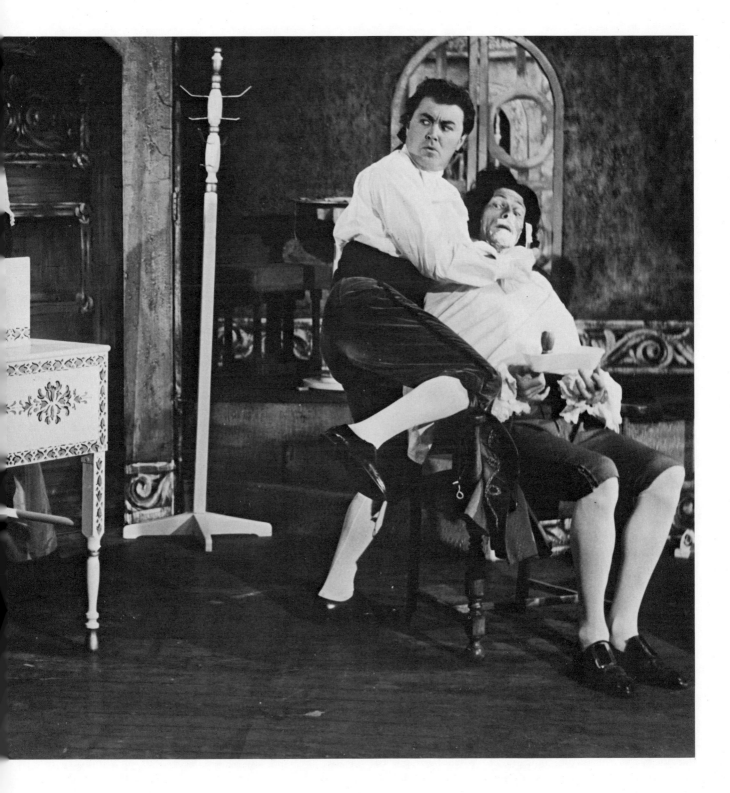

The thought is inescapable that the snob appeal of 'foreign' opera can make the singing sound better than it actually is. Fortunately the decision coincided with a general raising of artistic and vocal standards and it was certainly not imagination or snobbishness which caused public and critics alike to take to the new system.

The success of the 1966 season, in spite of the severely trimmed budget, proved that sensible planning can pay. With only three operas in the repertoire, there was still something for everybody; the *Barber* for the family, *Il Trovatore* for the lover of singing and *Boris* for the man seeking the unusual. Coincidentally anyone going to a work outside his own field of interest was not disappointed, though the usual charge that *The Barber of Seville* was played for slapstick was levelled. It is true that Rossini's masterpiece can be made into a work of art, but nobody seeing the work can doubt that it is intended to be farce, and interpreting it as such is as common in the European theatre as it is in Australia. The fact remains that it was well sung and well acted by Robert Gard's highly professional Almaviva, Maconaghie's Figaro and actor-singers like Norman Yemm and Alan Light as Bartolo and Basilio. Rosalind Keene finally graduated from small parts to official principal as Rosina. Gerald Krug conducted.

Clearly *Boris* and *Trovatore* were the more important musical events of the season and it is hard to say which was more successful. That the public actually flocked to *Boris Godounov* is remarkable in itself and Neil Warren-Smith's powerful interpretation must be given the major credit. It was an astonishing achievement for an Australian artist without a long international career behind him and totally justified the staging of a difficult and far from popular work. Not only did he act with deep conviction but he coped with the music in a quite astonishing manner, cutting with ease through the large A.B.C. orchestras, even in theatres like the cavernous Palais in Melbourne. It was an achievement which would have convinced any sensible singer to aim for a career overseas without delay. It has been Australia's good fortune that Warren-Smith decided not to be sensible, and in the years which followed he has produced a regular series of great performances.

The other star of *Boris* was, of course, the chorus. Russian operas are always chorus happy and *Boris* is no exception. Not since 1958 had the Trust tackled a chorus opera with any seriousness, but Young's idea was to use the chorus as the nucleus of the future company and when *Boris* proved that such a nucleus could be as good as this one he set out to implement his plan as quickly as possible. Within a year being a chorister was the only sure way to obtain full-time employment with the Trust.

Rosina Raisbeck joined the company to sing Marina in the Polish Scene, which Young had added to his arrangement of the 'original' *Boris*. (There is no actual original, because Mussorgsky's first thoughts were never performed and what passed for a first performance in 1874 was dictated by political rather than musical considerations.) Serge Baigildin was a fine, if small-scaled Dimitri, Light a boisterous Varlaam and Donald Shanks, singing Pimen and still in his early twenties, already looked like a Boris of the future. The admirable Robert Gard left a deep impression as the Simpleton, a very minor part which represents Mussorgsky's bridge to the political thoughts he was not supposed to have about Mother Russia's problems. I have actually seen *Boris Godounov* performed without the Simpleton and few would miss him. To create a central character out of his few lines needs artistry of a high degree and this was one of the first instances in which Gard showed what a great asset the company had acquired when he joined it. (His Almaviva may have been more important to the general public, but Rossini's high jinks are in a different class.)

Enforced economies meant basic sets for *Boris Godounov* and William Constable's painted cloths were not the most successful. Producer Young insisted on realistic costumes, however, and the distribution of funds was indeed a wise one. You cannot crown a tsar of Russia without splendour and, by concentrating attention on the central character, the background came to be of secondary importance. William Patterson created a coronation robe covered with 2208 beads, pearls and glass pendants which was worthy of the Bolshoi itself. The rest of his costumes were equally authentic. Props used throughout were solidly realistic and when, in the Clock Scene, Doreen Morrow looked, acted and sang convincingly like the boy the Tsarevitch is supposed to be, the illusion was perfectly realized. *Boris* can only be staged as a realistic opera and the staging was, within the limitations of the background, a complete success.

However successful *Boris* may have been (and it was a great success) it was *Il Trovatore* which was to decide the future policies of the company. Both its virtues and its failings were to reappear again and again in the coming years and, fortunately, its virtues far outweighed its failings, which were totally scenic. Stefan Beinl produced and Raymond Boyce designed this *Trovatore* for the New Zealand Opera Company. It was imported lock, stock and barrels for Di Luna's soldiers to sit on. (Customs men two years later solemnly watched as the huge sets were formally burnt. Had they remained in existence, or been broken up for future use, the company would have been up for heavy import duties!) There were those who liked the sets, there were those who did not. I count myself among the latter because I feel for singers who are forced to clamber over a continuing expanse of steep slopes reminiscent of the sails of the Sydney Opera House. How the season concluded without a few broken bones is a mystery. Singers are not mountain goats

(though they may on occasion sing like them) and the settings for which Verdi calls include private chambers and prison cells which look pretty ridiculous when the floor angles up *and* down at something like 45 degrees. Admittedly, there were a few spectacular effects, notably the Monastery Scene, but any multi-purpose set which remains in position through a performance must relate to all the scenes, not just a few.

Fortunately for the history of opera in Australia what was projected from the slopes of Biscay and Aragon was Italian opera at its best. The singing was close to the best heard during the Sutherland season and the orchestra was vastly superior. The language was Italian, the conventions were Italian, even the flaws were Italian, but they were small indeed. Any public with a desire for Italian opera was completely satisfied by this production and the Trust was certainly justified in repeating the formula in years to come. It was logical to stick to a good thing, faults and all, after ten years of continuous disaster.

Young's desire to add a Manrico voice to the company's roster was understandable. There has never been a dearth of lyric tenors in Australia, but the despised top C remains the audience's darling. Raymond Macdonald, who sang Manrico in the original New Zealand production, never realized the potential shown during his impromptu Otellos in 1957 and had returned to lighter roles. Ronald Dowd was having a successful career overseas, which he was unlikely to break on any kind of permanent basis. For personal reasons Donald Smith wanted to return to Australia and, if the gamble paid off, the company could afford to offer him permanent employment. The gamble did come off and Smith himself played no small part in it. His success was immediate. His was no longer the lyric tenor of old. He had been singing Calaf in *Turandot* opposite Amy Shuard at Covent Garden and the voice that filled that huge theatre with ease could hardly fail in the much smaller ones in Australia.

It is no reflection on Donald Smith's Manrico to say that in the end his was not the greatest success of the production. That honour went to Lauris Elms, appearing for the first time with the Trust. Elms had gone overseas after early work with the Melbourne National Opera, had been successful in England, but had returned to Australia for family reasons. Her appearances in the Sutherland-Williamson season no doubt brought her to the attention of the Australian public, but her success as Azucena was much more spectacular. The combination of Smith and Elms was exciting in the best way that opera should be exciting and it was their joint effort which was the springboard from which native opera really took off.

Their colleagues were competent enough, but not in the same class. Rosemary Gordon, a New Zealander of German birth, was the only member of the original production to come to Australia. Leonora was not really her part, but she was beautiful and sang with intelligence and musicianship, carefully avoiding the part's fireworks which were outside her range. It was not an exciting performance, but one which complemented the others very well. Alexander Major as Di Luna was a different proposition. He was a Hungarian migrant who appeared one day as the last singer in a day-long audition and left his audience stunned.

Major had a superbly controlled high baritone of excellent quality which should have been a great asset to any company. Unfortunately it was not matched by musical or dramatic intelligence of the same standard. His bearing was stiff and unyielding and he had a notable gift of always finding the right spotlight and standing just outside it when he had to be seen. In the already dark sets of *Trovatore* this tendency served to hide his awkward carriage and dull acting; his contribution was a largely invisible voice singing some very difficult music superbly. It was some time before the public would realize that Major was not a potentially great new star, but that he was Major at the first performance of *Trovatore* and would stay Major in exactly that manner for the rest of his stay with the company, a useful singer capable of coping with almost any role efficiently, but without creating much excitement. Although a Hungarian, Alexander Major was the very model of an Italian opera singer. It also happened that that was the kind of singer the company needed at that moment and his contribution in the years to come should not be underestimated.

Denis Vaughan's tenure as Musical Director was restricted to 1966. He was the last to have the A.B.C. orchestras at his disposal. Gerald Krug, a young musician of undoubted ability was his assistant and for a few performances Romanian Robert Rosen took over all three operas with great efficiency. Why Rosen, an operatic conductor of extensive experience, did not continue with the company is one of those mysteries which will never be solved. It may have been a communication problem; his English was very far from perfect.

1966 was the turning point for opera in Australia. After ten years of steadily declining standards, the jump in quality was quite spectacular. The spectre of the Sydney Opera House appeared to haunt Haag, Young and Hall again and again. The exterior of the building was complete, but opera had, in this first year of success, been relegated to the smaller hall. What went on in that building, which looked like turning into the whitest elephant in history, was of vital importance to the future of the opera company.

The Sydney Opera House

14

Paris has its Eiffel Tower, New York has its Empire State Building and Sydney has its Opera House. The fame of no building in history has spread more quickly than that of the monumental sculpture erected by Joern Utzon on Bennelong Point in the middle of Sydney's harbour and in the shadow of the bridge which, until 1973, was the most notable man-made landmark in Australia.

Sydney is indeed fortunate in having the Opera House. It has caused the usual surge in theatrical activity which appears in the wake of new centres of the performing arts, but it has also put Sydney and opera in Australia on the map internationally. On the face of it, all is lovely in the garden but, to coin a phrase, the flowers that bloom at Bennelong Point (tra la) have nothing to do with the case; meaning, that the standard of opera presented in this most extraordinary building is high in spite of, not because of, its facilities.

The charge is commonly laid that the Opera Theatre of the complex is unsuitable for the presentation of opera. The resident company has already used the Concert Hall for experiments with those works that are too big for the smaller theatre and there was even talk of building a new opera house in Sydney or of converting an old cinema to provide the extra space which cannot be found at Bennelong Point. But, if faults there are in the design (and there are!), the ingenuity of the Australian Opera's technical staff has overcome them.

The theatre is as unusual as its exterior looks. It is not possible to move productions into it which have been designed for more conventional buildings and vice versa. Facilities backstage are cramped and artists have trouble getting to their allocated positions and even in finding their ways onto and off the sets, which must be specially designed to cope with the limitations of vertical as well as horizontal space. The opera theatre is a mess, but its tenants have overcome the difficulties to such an extent that to any but the most knowledgeable in the audience there is no visible evidence of the handicaps imposed on the performers.

How is it possible that a building costing over $100 million could fail to provide the basic necessities for the very needs implied in its name? It is a long and well-documented story and it must be told here, if in abbreviated form.

Once upon a time some long-forgotten N.S.W. politicians decided to make sure that they would *not* be forgotten by tricking their fellow citizens into starting a monumental building which they well knew would cost far more than the seven millions mentioned in Parliament. The state of opera in Australia in 1956 certainly did not warrant the construction of an opera house in Sydney or any other city. On the other hand, the very name OPERA HOUSE has always loomed large in the histories of cities and there must be hundreds all over the world which sport a building so named without ever having had a resident opera company. In the nineteenth century opera was the ultimate in theatrical entertainment and any building which implied by its name that it could be used to present grand opera immediately became the focus of attention.

There are almost too many things about the creation of the Sydney Opera House which run completely counter to any kind of logic. No matter how successful the end result, the project should have collapsed and could have collapsed again and again. It was the money spent, not the money needed, which kept it alive. Building was commenced almost immediately and once hard cash had been put into concrete, nobody had the courage to see it thrown down the drain; more and more was invested to save the project and, as the expenditure grew, the reasons for pouring ever more into the growing monster became still stronger. It was a snowball that could not be stopped. In the end, it played more than a large part in the 1965 elections that threw out the government which set it rolling, but its successor could no more destroy what had been built than its creator. The Sydney Opera House was as self-perpetuating as the bureaucracy which brought it into being, and just as extravagant.

Nobody will seriously suggest today that the building should be dismantled. Human ingenuity has managed to make it work, though the costs involved in staging opera in the building are vastly greater than they would be anywhere else. The original concept was of a monument to the New South Wales 'visionaries', rather than a practical theatre complex like the one built sensibly and without fuss in Adelaide. The monument has indeed come into being and its problems may not concern the general public too much. But since this is a book on opera and ballet, the phenomenon must be explored. There are 102 million reasons why we are entitled to know the 'whys' and the 'wherefores' of the whole thing.

The building, which from the start was called the *Opera House*, came into being only because the late Sir Eugene Goossens demanded a better home for the Sydney Symphony Orchestra than the antiquated Town Hall. The original design specifications clearly gave concerts priority over opera.

The Sydney Opera House was intended as a home for the local symphony orchestra and facilities for presenting opera were to be made available as a secondary feature! Some opera house! Most curiously of all, the priorities remained unchanged throughout the construction of the building, though the coincidental renaissance in opera has brought public attention to that part of its operation rather than to its primary purpose as a concert hall. To this day opera only plays a minority role in the many activities which take place in this building!

In 1956 the N.S.W. Government offered $10,000 to the winner of an international competition for the design of the Opera House. Seven hundred and thirty-three entries were received and entry fees alone more than covered the value of the prize! It was the only financially sound deal made throughout the whole sordid mess; getting enough competitors to actually pay for the competition was a stroke of genius. The fact that the whole thing was illegal was of secondary importance, but the act authorizing the holding of the competition was not passed until 1960, three years after the winner had been declared and one year after work had actually commenced! It was but the first step toward the incredible bungling which was to follow.

The Danish architect Joern Utzon was declared the winner on the basis of an idealistic drawing, not the fully detailed plans which were stipulated, reasonably expected and supplied by the other competitors. Utzon had no idea how the building he had drawn (not designed) could be built. In fact, he was a very far from experienced architect. At thirty-eight years of age he had had little practical experience; his total credits were two small housing projects and prizes in various competitions. (Later the designs for his Sydney home were rejected by the local council and Utzon never did manage to overcome the surveyor's objections; the building was left incomplete when he departed from the scene.) This was the man placed in sole charge of the whole venture!

The estimate of seven million dollars to complete the building appears to have been picked out of the air. Any larger figure would have caused Parliament to reject the whole thing and, before anybody could query the whole idea, authority to commence building was given, though no proper plans had been drawn up, even for the foundations. Work commenced on 2 March 1959. By then budgeting of a sort had begun and within a year a 'firm' price of $9,760,000 was accepted by the N.S.W. Parliament – 'such cost shall not under any circumstances be exceeded by more than ten percentum'. Famous last words! Five hundred and fifty piers were driven up to thirty metres into the ground until bedrock was struck, while drawings were still being prepared for the foundations which would be supported by them. In fact, throughout Utzon's period as chief architect plans were always completed after work actually started. The podium on which the building rests was begun fully three years before the design for the massive roof shells was completed. As a result, much of this costly work had to be dynamited to accommodate the final structure, which differed very substantially from the original drafts.

Utzon initially worked in Denmark, at the other end of the world. Nobody could understand why the boss of the project should hide himself so far away, but it soon became obvious that the answers to the problems Utzon had set himself were not within his capacity to solve. Instead of seeking outside help, Utzon blithely announced that he had

A healthy white elephant The Sydney Opera House (*over*) has achieved worldwide fame for its unique design and much abuse for the shortcomings of its interior. Seventeen years of dramas and scandals over designer Joern Utzon and the $102 million spent have been all but forgotten. Yet, though operas are being produced simultaneously in both halls of the building, some still claim it is unworkable.

made an ingenious discovery which would make the building better than ever. This meant changing not only the whole shape of the building to what it is now (a remote cousin of the drawing which won the competition) but it meant starting all over again from scratch. Work then commenced on the shells – again, before the drawings were complete. When the Labour Government fell in 1965, the last of the 1,055,941 tiles had actually been placed into position. Yet no finality had been reached about the interior of the building. In other words, the shells were constructed before the use of the space they sheltered had been determined and all the later building problems and present inadequacies of the project can be traced to the limitations which Utzon had unintentionally set, by creating a building from the outside in.

The new Liberal Government, which had forced the issue of the escalating costs of the building mercilessly during the election, now had to deal with a recalcitrant Utzon, who refused to reveal his non-existent plans for the interiors and seating of the halls. Amid some cloak-and-dagger operations worthy of any James Bond thriller, Joern Utzon finally resigned from the project on 28 February 1966, because his new bosses would not allow him to continue as before, the sole master of a financially uncontrollable monster. The case for Utzon's retention is finally beginning to die down, but at the time there were street demonstrations which treated the threat to Utzon like a threat to the environment. It was sheer emotionalism, for nobody (not even Utzon) knew what it was that was being defended, other than the magic name Utzon itself.

(The situation in 1966 bore a strong resemblance to the state of London's British National Opera House, which was rising in Whitehall nearly a century ago; and there must have been a temptation to follow the British model to the end – the London building was razed to ground level and New Scotland Yard built on its foundation.)

Dane Utzon's international team of workers, which included Scandinavians, English, Americans, South Africans and even a solitary Chinese, had been disbanded. An all-Australian team led by Peter Hall (at thirty-four even younger than Utzon had been when he started work) sat down to take stock of the architectural problems, while the government took another look at the occupancy of the building, if and when it was ever to be finished.

Opera in Australia was at its lowest ebb in 1966. The Elizabethan Trust Opera Company offered only three works during one four week season in Sydney that year and attracted less than 30,000 paying customers. Nobody dreamt that ten years later there would be three seasons in the new building totalling over seven months, with no less than eight premieres to add to a huge existing repertoire, and more than a quarter of a million people happy to pay prices four times those of 1966. In 1966 the original plans of a concert hall capable of being used occasionally for opera, backed by a smaller theatre for drama, were still on the drawing board, although stage machinery costing some millions of dollars had already been installed. The trouble was that Utzon had not yet solved the problem of how to seat enough people to pay for it all.

At this point it not only became apparent that Utzon had to go, but that the completed work would make the large hall a doubtful proposition for what was still the primary purpose of the building, the staging of the A.B.C.'s annual concert seasons. The A.B.C. threatened to pull out unless the large hall was completed as a proper concert hall; the concept of a multi-purpose hall, convertible into an opera theatre, had long been criticized in any case. It is easy to be wise after the event, but in 1966 the decision to transfer the opera theatre from the large to the small hall, and to move drama from the latter to the even smaller theatre in which it now finds itself, was the only sensible solution.

The way Peter Hall and his colleagues solved the various problems left by Utzon really cannot be criticized, and that the end result cannot compare with a building properly planned from the beginning was inevitable. Quite apart from the impossible costs of demolishing the famous sails already dominating Sydney Harbour, nobody can deny their monumental splendour. Their retention was inevitable and credit for their creation will always lie with Utzon. But the difficulties which were engendered by their shape are the burden which opera in Sydney will have to continue to bear, except in the unlikely event that a second and real opera house is ever built in that city.

The ingenuity with which the Australian Opera has managed to stage truly grand operas in the Concert Hall during the off-season has made up for some of the shortcomings of the Opera Theatre. From the time the Sydney Opera House opened its doors to opera, on 28 September 1973 with Prokofiev's *War and Peace,* the name of the building has to some extent justified itself. It is *opera* in the Sydney Opera House that makes the news, no matter how much else may be going on in that complex monument to one man's folly. Utzon's vision of this building was always external and that vision, if not in the original conformation, has become one of the seventy wonders of the world.

The Way Up
15

The total staff of the Elizabethan Theatre Trust Opera Company at the end of 1966 was three! John Young, Administrator, his secretary, Evelyn Klopfer (later to be boss of the Sydney Opera Company) and the newly appointed Stephen Hall, who bore by then the ambiguous title 'Co-ordinator'. The total complement of singers was two: Neil Warren-Smith and John Germain, key people who had sung with the company since its inception and had been suitably rewarded with full-time contracts. Nevertheless, an opera company consisting solely of one bass and one baritone with an administration of three was hardly an auspicious start for 1967. The Sydney Opera House, being rebuilt as a concert hall and a smaller opera theatre, was still in the dim distance, well outside any planning programme. But appearances were deceptive. 1966 had been a year of very active planning and the enormous jump of the following year proved that the planning was sound.

Nobody knows how John Young and his board talked the N.S.W. Government into coming to the party at this particular moment, but in 1967 it began a series of annual grants to the company to prepare it for the glories of the new Opera House, if and when it would be finished. The first grant was used to place a nucleus of chorus singers under permanent contract and 1967 thus saw the beginning of a *continuous* company, as opposed to one which was re-assembled every year, or every second year. The basis of starting with the chorus was sound; it was felt that principals had a better chance of finding casual work between seasons. As it turned out, 1967 was successful enough to enable some principals to be continued under holding contracts, but it was the chorus which began the long, and happily steep, climb to the company's present position. At the same time the Trust created its first orchestra, to be used by both opera and ballet companies, and there was thus an immediate continuity both on and below stage.

One part of the planning of Young and Haag (who was still very much involved, though in 1966 he had risen to greater aloofness as the Trust's own structure grew) was the engagement of that extraordinary showman Harry M. Miller as 'Commercial and Promotion Consultant'. One wonders whether there was somebody just busy thinking up new titles for the staff in those days, but whatever the nomenclature, Harry Miller was worth his weight in gold and so was the new publicity director, Tony Frewin. Between them, Miller and Frewin completely revolutionized the whole principle of ticket selling in Australia. The 'subscription' arrived belatedly, but most successfully. Not only did the purchase of tickets *en bloc* for the whole season become common practice, but the old forgotten promotion of opera as a pop-culture thing was suddenly revived and – surprise! – it still worked. The wording may have been a little more up-to-date, but basically the billing of Wagner's *Flying Dutchman* as 'A tempest-tossed romance of wild and sombre beauty' was no better and no worse than the old 'Love's amusing round-about' which sold *The Marriage of Figaro* during the first season eleven years previously. The introduction of Youth Nights on the normally dead Mondays of the season not only filled the theatre, but created new audiences who greeted opera with open arms. Nobody worried very much if the under twenty-six youths often had some rather thirtyish bags under their eyes, the important thing was to create audiences and – full credit to Harry M. – audiences were created in that historic year. The repertoire jumped from three to five operas, plus a revival of the successful *Trovatore*. Seasons were played in Sydney, Brisbane, Melbourne, Canberra and Adelaide and, miracle of miracles, capacity audiences were the rule rather than the exception. For the first time in the company's history there were even overnight queues, though admittedly only for the Youth Nights. Six operas for $5.00 was too good a chance to pass up and a full house at 82 cents a seat produced a fair return in cash, quite apart from invaluable mouth-to-mouth advertising; it was mouth-to-mouth resuscitation for an art close to death in this country.

The fact that Harry Miller's revolutionary promotion schemes filled the theatres in 1967 can be explained in many ways, not least by the age-old theory that people want to be fooled by good packaging. You can dress up an opera season just as you can make a cake of soap attractive through the right kind of wrapping. Yet ultimately the proof of the pudding is in the eating, or rather the hearing and seeing. Had 1967 not seen reasonably good presentations, audiences would not have returned in 1968 and the years that followed. The fact that they did is interesting in more ways than one, because 1967 was not really an artistically outstanding year. In many ways it resembled the very first season of the company. There were gaucheries, mistakes, even disasters, but a completely new spirit surrounded artists and audiences. 'Nothing succeeds like success' is one of the great truisms of this world and people who sat in packed houses enjoyed even an inferior opera more than a better one amid the echoes of empty seats. As for the singers, the response across the footlights spurred them on to give their best and their best was often very good indeed.

The most notable advance was the improvement in the visual aspects of productions. The most negative aspect was the new Trust orchestra, which was a far cry from the excellence of the A.B.C. orchestras of years gone by. There was actually nothing as good as the previous year's *Boris Godounov* and *Trovatore* except the latter itself, which was staged outside the subscription series to full houses. 1967 must be judged as the first year which was fully planned, and executed as planned, without financial waste to speak of. What artistic waste there was occurred in a good cause and added to the history on which the future of the company

was built. It was Harry Miller who set the ball rolling and it was John Young who produced a rollable ball.

The five completely new productions were a mixed bag, the most notable coming from Stephen Hall making a first attempt at opera production in a manner so ambitious as to be almost foolhardy. Surely no producer has ever started a career with Puccini's *Turandot*, but Hall did and succeeded, in spite of all odds. Not that Hall proved to be a master producer in this or any future opera he staged, but he had come recently from Covent Garden where he had worked (as one of many stage managers) with producers like Visconti, Zeffirelli and Hartmann. He had absorbed the then current trend of the new realism, which is diametrically opposed to the blank stage represented in Australia by Haag's *Fidelio,* for example. That a fine stage picture can smooth over musical deficiencies is a reality, however unpalatable it may be to purists, and the impressive set by Friedrich Bliem and costumes by Mel Clifford and Robert Potter looked (and were) fantastically expensive. They were certainly the most ambitious venture in visual splendour of the company to date. With Donald Smith to sing Puccini's music, a superb chorus and a fine ensemble for the minor roles the opera only needed a strong central singer to be a runaway success.

I do not regret having described Morag Beaton's Turandot as 'the mouse that roared', because I have always had an immense respect for her as one of the greatest voices I have heard in my time. She was roundly condemned by many critics, but the criticism was only partly justified. 1967 was the year in which the local ensemble was created and expensive guest artists were an impossible extravagance. Perhaps it was unwise to put a small, unimpressive Scotswoman without any experience to speak of straight into *Turandot*. If so, the same criticism should be made of Stephen Hall for tackling an opera of such size first time up. In his case the gamble came off completely, in her case only partially. Morag Beaton's Turandot was definitely not a failure, because she coped mangificently with the music and it is a role which not many sopranos can encompass with ease. She was indeed a mouse that roared and her roaring was in perfect pitch and rolled across the admittedly under-manned orchestra with the greatest of ease. Rosemary Gordon was a sympathetic Liu and Donald Shanks a far too powerful old Timor. Robin Gordon, on the other hand, was an admirably feeble Emperor. The American, Robert Feist, acted as though he was musical director of the company, which he was not, yet his conducting of *Turandot* and *Rigoletto* was highly professional; probably better than the word implies, for he was working with a completely new ensemble whose weaknesses had yet to be discovered and weeded out.

For all its failings, the orchestra from the first year was to work in much closer harmony with the company than

The mouse that roared Morag Beaton making her debut in the title role of Puccini's *Turandot* in 1967. It was Stephen Hall's first production and the second of the company's Italian grand operas. Diminutive Morag Beaton sang the difficult music with ease.

the full symphony orchestras the A.B.C. had supplied in years gone by. The magnificent sound the latter had provided may have been an asset, but in retrospect it is quite clear that there was a degree of competition between stage and pit which disappeared as soon as the first Trust Orchestra was formed. This was an ensemble that knew its place and many years were to pass before it was to tackle operas in which the orchestra had to carry a burden as important as that of the singers. When the time came it was up to it. In 1967 it was still playing second fiddle, but from the start it was but rarely out of tune. (There was a grave shortage of second fiddlers that year, anyway!)

The Flying Dutchman, in its own way, equalled the success of *Turandot*. Oddly enough, it had the same principal failing, a leading lady short of perfection, but in this case there was less excuse. It may have been asking for trouble to stage two operas needing Turandot/Senta voices, but a first-class Dutchman was available in Raymond Myers, returning with renewed vigour and some very necessary experience to these shores. Neil Warren-Smith was a world-class Daland and the chorus both here and in *Turandot* amply justified its being made first choice when continuity became a financial reality. Kurt Hommel produced traditionally, but well, and Wendy Dickson's costumes and sets, including some spectacular projections of the Dutchman's ship, worked well. The fly in the ointment was another American, Marcella Reale, accepted without audition on the recommendation of Robert Feist. Miss Reale was a good-looking singer, but the voice, while beautiful in itself and of suitable power, developed a disturbing wobble under pressure. Ultimately Reale was to make some contribution to the company's musical fortunes, but in the *Dutchman* she failed to justify importation at great expense.

It is easier to forgive the shortcomings of local singers who place smaller financial strain on the management. The practice of importing second-raters proved to be the only serious flaw in the policies of those years. Inevitably, they acted like prima donnas (male as well as female), inevitably, they got all the publicity that Tony Frewin could throw their way and, inevitably, they failed to live up to the false image which was created. It would have been better to have them absorbed quietly into the ensemble, as happened in later years with singers like Umberto Borsò or Elizabeth Vaughan.

One new production was so bad as to be almost good; good for all the wrong reasons. Putting a producer of pop musicals, aged twenty-one, in charge of *Don Giovanni* was a risk and John Young took it with his eyes open. He claims that the exercise was worthwhile and I will go along with him to the point of admitting that almost anything can be tried. I make only one proviso: that the end result must work. Jim Sharman's attempt to stage *Don Giovanni* as a

The mouse that should have roared – in protest! Morag Beaton alternating the soprano role of Turandot with the contralto part of Maddalena in *Rigoletto*, here with Donald Smith. Singing in two registers during the same season, at times in the same week, seriously injured one of the great voices in the ranks of the company.

game of chess on a bare stage of black and white squares did not succeed, in fact, could not succeed, if only because Mozart's opera does not contain the right combination of characters to produce any kind of chess situation. You can have Donna Anna as the White Queen and Elvira as the Black (or vice versa) but what do you do with Zerlina? And if the Don is the Black King (or the White) who is the White King (or the Black)? Sharman actually attempted to make his 'pieces' move according to the rules of chess, but it was a half-hearted attempt and the singers ignored their squares of operation almost from the first performance.

Never has there been a production in which so many tried so much to do so little to improve the original. What was a badly conceived mistake rapidly became a shambles, and singers, who had attended rehearsals and enthusiastically backed this bold experiment, suddenly complained at the impossible things they had to do and how they affected their voices. As it happened, there were few, if any complaints about the singing, which was generally of a high standard. It was probably this which saved the production because – like Haag's *Fidelio* – sooner or later somebody spoke up in defence of the indefensible and controversy is the lifeblood of the theatre. Youth Nights in particular split into noisy factions and it can be said quite truthfully that demonstrations against productions also serve a useful purpose in raising interest in audiences and self-criticism in management.

Sharman's *Don Giovanni* will remain a memorable production, however much it may have failed, while others of really quite substantial excellence have already been forgotten. In the context of creating a new image to go with full houses and lively debate about the future of the company, this *Giovanni* may even have been a good thing. Complaints there were many, but they queued up for their seats in the following year just the same. This is the stuff that opera is made of.

Musically *Don Giovanni* lacked support in the pit, where Thomas Mayer had trouble getting Mozartian precision from the new orchestra. On stage Robert Gard's Ottavio was the only one of the singers to retain the style of the music completely. Neil Warren-Smith, with the task of trying to hold the whole thing together dramatically, gave up a little too easily, but sang with his usual assurance. Marcella Reale (Anna) might have been singing Puccini, while Maureen Howard was an admirable Zerlina. Rosemary Gordon sang Elvira and Maconaghie a light-weight Leporello.

With a new *Don Pasquale,* Stefan Haag once again proved how good (or backward) he remained in staging comic opera as slapstick. His team of singers supported him to the hilt and though George Molnar's witty sets were not as beautifully executed as a bigger budget might have allowed, the ensemble built around June Bronhill, for once an ideally

suited guest star, ensured a happy evening for all.

Two productions were staged 'on the cheap'. The first of these proved to be an unexpected hit. *Rigoletto,* as restaged by Stefan Beinl in cramped sets and costumes by Ron Reid, was sung so excellently that there was no room left for criticism. Following on the excellent *Trovatore,* this modest production raised operatic temperatures to such a level that future seasons seemed assured. After all, when you can stage two Verdi operas with completely local casts of such quality in one year, then one has to be onto a winner. Audiences, state governments and the Trust certainly believed it and they were right.

Raymond Myers sang his first Rigoletto brilliantly, Donald Smith was dead right as the Duke and any criticism of Janice Taylor's Gilda was purely academic. It may be fashionable to say that Verdi wanted a bigger voice for the role. The fact remains that the likes of Galli-Curci and Dal Monte had been the most popular Gildas of the century and Taylor was completely in their spirit. Her efforts five years later to sing the role with her 'new' heavier voice were unsatisfactory, but in 1967 she made a perfect foil for her two partners. Shanks' Sparafucile was an imposing figure and poor Morag Beaton was forced to sing the contralto Maddalena during the same weeks as her Turandots.

It may be as well to examine for a moment the problems of any opera company to find voices of the rarer type and none is rarer than a true contralto. Many contraltos push themselves up into the mezzo-soprano field under the impression that being a mezzo is more glamorous. Perhaps so, but the tendency to push voices up has resulted in a range of roles which it is very difficult to cast effectively and a company like the then Trust Opera had nothing beyond Lauris Elms in the field. Elms was and is world-class, but she either could not or would not sing Maddalena, a bit part, but an important one. The freak range of Morag Beaton's voice encompassed a strong lower register, but no singer can sing Turandot one night and Maddalena or Ulrica (*A Masked Ball*) the next, without developing vocal problems. Her downfall began in that first season, with those Turandots alternating with Maddalenas. I doubt whether any singer in history was ever asked to cover both roles, let alone sing them at the same time for months on end. No doubt John Young will claim that it was a necessary evil at the time. He should have known that it would end in disaster, as it unfortunately did.

Once again *Die Fledermaus* returned for an extended run to bridge the gap between seasons and *Tosca* was given a dry run for the 1968 revival with Gobbi and Collier. Maureen Howard sang Tosca and started her path down the road to heavier roles for which her voice was ill-equipped. Reginald Byers made his company debut as Cavaradossi and Alexander Major was a sonorous Scarpia. Johann Strauss'

A nice enough young man Reginald Byers as Cavaradossi in *Tosca* in 1968. Launched cold into the lead in Verdi's *Don Carlos*, Byers took time to find his feet, but ultimately came through with flying colours. Good tenors are hard to find and he is very far from that raw recruit of his early days by now.

delightful *Fledermaus* was titivated up to include a Gala Performance in the Ball Scene, featuring stars like Donald Smith belting out the old favourites Regnd June Bronhill played second fiddle as a maid from Broken Hill, rather than the Austrian provinces, to Maureen Howard's excellent Rosalinda and Gard's admirable Eisenstein. The revival marked John Pringle's first appearance with the company as Falke himself. Pringle's ill-conceived attempts to become a bass had at last given way to better counsel and this was the beginning of his real career as a baritone. From the first his ability as a natural actor marked him as outstanding raw material.

Gobbi and Collier

16

The third of John Young's years as Administrator of the Trust Opera was a further step in the right direction. Having missed the 1966 Adelaide Festival, the company returned in 1968 in a glory which could not have been anticipated four years before. For the first time in years there was a major conductor, Carlo Felice Cillario, as principal conductor. For the first time there were some real star imports: Tito Gobbi, Marie Collier, the latter having risen very considerably on the international horizon since her visit in 1964, and also Antonietta Stella, who took Collier's place in Sydney. Marcella Reale returned again (to better effect), as did Ken Neate for the last time. With three productions scheduled for the Festival, a spectacle to surpass all previous spectacles was clearly the aim. The fact that Gobbi and Collier had to star in the old Melbourne National Theatre Tim Walton sets of *Tosca* once more was mitigated by the undoubted fact that they still looked mighty good – from a distance; they went to the tip after this, their last tour. Compensation was offered by a new *Tannhäuser* and *Don Carlos,* none of the three operas being sung in English.

Tito Gobbi's association with the company was to prove fruitful until two years later the tax man ended the goodwill he found out here. Stefan Haag restaged *Tosca* with Gobbi as Scarpia, Collier as Tosca and Donald Smith as Cavaradossi. The combination of three major singers, each a personality as well, was irresistible. Donald Smith proved once and for all, for the benefit of his own countrymen, that he is indeed capable of holding his own in the best company. Gobbi's presence on stage also showed up the fact that singers in the local company have a degree of professionalism which is not shamed by a master craftsman like Gobbi. It is all very well to hear of these things at second hand, but when it is shown that the best in his field, Gobbi, is not that far ahead of our own boys, then that is really something to crow about.

Tannhäuser and *Don Carlos* repeated the pattern of *Turandot* of the year before, presenting a scenic spectacle with professionalism and imperfections. Nevertheless, there was progress, not only in steadily increasing attendances caused by the value for money visible in these productions, but actual improvement in quality of presentation and, more importantly, musical standards. Critics necessarily must pick out negative as well as positive qualities when reviewing a performance. As far as the general public is concerned, it is the overall enjoyment to be gained which counts and that was an undoubted advancement over 1967, though the plum of the year's productions was not staged at the Festival; once again it was a 'sleeper' that stole the honours, Puccini's *Girl of the Golden West.*

The traditional production of *Tannhäuser* (Beinl) with rather magnificent designs by Kenneth Rowell was an almost unqualified success, largely due to the conducting of Cillario.

He conducted with such verve and energy that on the opening night he knocked his score to the ground and nearly lost his trousers, when his braces gave way while he was trying to recover it. (The brand new Head of Music Staff, conductor William Reid, who stood by as prompter, was observed backstage, via closed circuit television, attempting to hold up Cillario's vital garment and was promptly dubbed 'the Perv'.) Meanwhile the cast waited immobile in the midst of the most complicated Songfest ensemble wondering what had happened. Unperturbed (in spite of Reid's continuing first-aid) Cillario, orchestra and cast restarted after a long pause, a model of the team work which had taken hold of the whole ensemble since the change of direction two years ago.

Marcella Reale had blessedly lost the *tremolo* in her voice and was an appealing Elisabeth. Unfortunately Ken Neate, looking absolutely splendid and acting with great conviction, had imported a *tremolo* of his own which marred his performance. Raymond Myers was a strong Wolfram and Morag Beaton a full-voiced Venus, but the mirrors of the Venusberg and the improvised ballet rather let the side down. On the whole it was a *Tannhäuser* worthy of a festival such as Adelaide's and by far the most impressive production, overall that the company had staged to date.

John Young himself produced the first ever performance of Verdi's *Don Carlos* in Australia. Desmond Digby's costumes were admirable, but Raymond Boyce's multi-purpose set, consisting of prison-like bars surrounding the stage at all times, regardless of the scene being set indoors or outdoors, became monotonous. *Don Carlos* is a French grand opera (though sung here in Italian) and the spectacle of a whole *auto-da-fé* on stage was simply beyond the capacity of the company at the time. Yes, it was a 'grand' production, which kept faith with the new policy and whether the public liked it or not, it was not disappointed. Musically the performance conducted by Robert Feist was not in the Cillario class, nor were the singers on the whole up to their task either. The notable exception was Neil Warren-Smith as King Philip, a nobly sung and acted interpretation. Rosemary Gordon was a sympathetic Elisabetta and Alexander Major a well-sung dull-stick Rodrigo. For once Lauris Elms, wearing an historically accurate, but unnecessarily unflattering eye-patch, was out of her depth quite literally, the high tessitura of Eboli lay, possibly temporarily, out of her range, and John Young's production made her character completely unsympathetic. It was not one of Elms' best parts. Reginald Byers made his official debut as Don Carlos, a role at the time right out of his reach, though the potential of the voice was already present.

The 1968 Festival was also the first occasion on which the company trotted out major singers in *comprimario* roles for special occasions. Maureen Howard's Page in *Don Carlos*

The man from Bundaberg, California Donald Smith in Stephen Hall's best production, the 1968 *Girl of the Golden West*. Queensland-born Smith revelled in the Wild West goldrush setting. His brawling proved too realistic for him in Melbourne when an injury to his knee put him out of action for several weeks.

and Janice Taylor's Shepherd's Voice in *Tosca* were very worthwhile contributions to the overall effect and a welcome change from the usual dreary small part players which can be found in even the best company. Furthermore the existing one-singer-one-part policy, which had resulted in occasional spectacular last-minute appearances of understudies, went by the board. Suddenly there was advance planning for 'covers', singers who where scheduled to play parts after the original cast had had its run. Audiences will always grumble at this kind of thing, but it is standard practice in all countries and abused much more overseas than in Australia. International opera seasons begin their premieres with several major stars, who then drop off one by one after the first few performances – after the critics have had their say. If Placido Domingo sang all the performances of all the operas in which he sings the first night, he would be faced with singing just about every night of the year!

From 1968 onwards, double casts became the rule wherever possible. On many an occasion it even happened that the major singer sang the role after a minor one had premiered it, a custom which still occurs when programming demands it. Clearly Raymond Myers could not sing both Wolfram in *Tannhäuser* and Rodrigo in *Don Carlos*. The parts were shared by Myers and Major, with John Pringle covering both and singing his first major role in Sydney not as an understudy, but as a principal. Ronald Maconaghie did the same for Wolfram and outshone both his forerunners with the most pure Fischer-Dieskau-like lyricism. Rosemary Gordon and Marcella Reale shared Elisabeth, and Tosca was farmed out between Collier, the specially imported replacement, Antonietta Stella, and the already tried Maureen Howard. Smith and Byers shared Cavaradossi and Myers replaced Gobbi when the time came.

The new policy came not a day too late, but the best laid plans of mice and men don't always work out and disaster struck on opening night in Sydney. The audience for the Gala Premiere *Tosca* was ready to assemble. Donald Smith was indisposed, but Byers was ready to step in. Then, in the car on the way to the theatre, Antonietta Stella collapsed. Though Howard could have gone on, John Young decided that a special Gala could not proceed with two understudies out of three and the 'audience was forced to go home, or rather to surrounding restaurants which had not done such a roaring trade or seen a better-dressed clientele in their history. Under the subscription system the gala audience got its *Tosca* some weeks later and, though they went home in good spirits on 11 June, they returned in a murderous mood. There is no evidence that that performance was any worse than the premiere would have been, but the audience wouldn't admit it.

The hit of the season came from an unexpected quarter, and was created largely by yet another of the new policies of the Young regime; *The Girl of the Golden West,* Puccini's ridiculous horse opera, became a sound success, through being sung in Italian. In spite of its American Wild West setting, it was as well that audiences could not understand the text of Belasco's outdated play. Minnie, the not-so-tough bar-owner in a Californian gold field, was made to measure for the American Marcella Reale. She sang and acted the part well and to say that she looked too young for a tough bar-room boss is not a valid criticism, since we are told by Puccini that she is a girl who has never been kissed. Donald Smith also was completely at home. There was just no difference between the ten gallon hat worn by Smith's bandit, Dick Johnson, and the traditional digger's hat; somehow the hat managed to turn up at one side without any help from anyone. More to the point, Smith's voice slipped around the Puccini melodies with the greatest of ease.

The Girl was to be Stephen Hall's best work as a producer, though it was only his second effort. The designs by Friedrich Bliem were most appropriate and worked to perfection. The ensemble of singers after nearly two years of continuous work was perfect. This Puccini opera is really an ensemble opera rather than a star vehicle, though it did have Caruso in its first production in 1910. Alan Light's villainous Sheriff was vocally and dramatically the black-hearted and black-voiced villain supreme and apart from the fine contributions from expected quarters (Gard, Maconaghie, Major, Germain) a whole row of choristers turned in excellent cameo roles. Joseph Powell, John Heffernan, Paul Rutenis, Joseph Grunfelder, Diane Holmes and others have taken their place in the chorus before and since, while sometimes stepping into the limelight as they did in this Puccini opera in 1968. Their occasional appearances in minor roles have been vastly better than those of any Italian or American opera chorus members. Much has been written about their collective brilliance in operas like *Tannhäuser* or *Boris Godounov,* too little about their playing of parts, though it must be admitted that responsible casting, as in *The Girl of the Golden West,* has shown them to greater effect than their occasional emergence as understudies in the really big roles.

The one economy of the season proved to be a minor success – against all odds. Stefan Haag reproduced his 1960 *Magic Flute*, craftily hiding the old sets in deepest shadows. Deliberately, or accidentally, this forced a playing down of the comic aspects of Schikaneder's idiotic plot and the result was an admirable exercise in straight Mozart; quite a change after the comic excesses of years gone by. Gard was the strong Tamino, backed by Maconaghie's sympathetic Papageno and Rosemary Gordon's idiomatic Pamina. Warren-Smith and John Pringle did well in the weightier roles and only the poor Queen of the Night provided the stumbling block to overall excellence. Helen Kerby was a young

High drama in Adelaide The premiere of Verdi's *Don Carlos* at the 1968 Adelaide Festival. Rosemary Gordon being comforted by the black-hearted (and black eye-patched) Lauris Elms as Princess Eboli.

American soprano about whom even Harry M. Miller could find nothing more startling to say than: 'She was offered the opportunity to audition for the Detmold Opera House but decided instead to accompany her husband to Australia.' It is admittedly hard to find good singers for this most difficult role and Miss Kerby had a pleasant enough voice, which might well have been of considerable use to the company. But casting her as the evil Queen of the Night was a mistake.

In the meantime it looked as though John Young's undoubted success in his third year as Administrator of the Opera Company of the Trust would lead to even better things in 1969. In 1968, 160,800 seats had been sold and box office receipts exceeded half a million dollars, a 150 per cent increase over the previous year. Harry Miller had produced no less than 33,000 subscribers, all of whom were potential customers for the next season and few would have argued with the fare which had been provided for them. The financial picture for the next year is not clear because the records overlap, offering a 1969/70 eighteen months to compare with the preceding twelve months. The season was planned to provide a five months tour to the usual centres and this was followed by the first of the Gilbert and Sullivan seasons. Figures conveniently link the two, making an accurate financial assessment of the 1969 *grand* opera season difficult. On the other hand the growing number of subscribers and the generally high standard of the five productions – only slightly below those of the previous year, possibly because there was no Adelaide Festival – indicated a satisfactory state of affairs.

John Young's last year was historically a further step in the right direction, though another palace revolution should have been a warning of changes to come. The end of 1968 finally saw the departure of both Dr Coombs as Chairman of the Trust and of his protégé, Stefan Haag, as its Executive Director. Stephen Hall leap-frogged from being John Young's assistant in the opera company to the post of 'Secretary and Co-ordinator' of the Trust. In plain language he took the place of Haag and became Young's boss. Sir Ian Potter replaced Dr Coombs.

In 1969 Tito Gobbi returned to star only in Melbourne in Stefan Beinl's *Falstaff*. It was a distinct improvement on his earlier production using the same sets and costumes, but really no more than a vehicle for Gobbi. The public still did not take to Verdi's last opera, in spite of Carlo Felice Cillario's admirable musical direction. As it happened, it was a subdued Gobbi who returned – perhaps his tax worries affected his performance. Even so, Ronald Maconaghie's assumption of the title role in Sydney was not in the same class and the rest of the singers did not distinguish themselves greatly. Pringle was a fine Ford and Elizabeth (formerly Betty) Fretwell returned to sing Alice. The usual lack

of mezzos resulted in the promotion of chorister, Diane Holmes, to principal status; her Mistress Page was acceptable, if on the light side. Justine Rettick's Quickly showed the onset of a decline only too rapid, a great pity in view of the excellent work she had done over the years. Only the young lovers, Robert Gard and Janice Taylor were in top form, but youth does not a *Falstaff* make.

The most remarkable event of this production was the sudden appearance of veteran Adelio Zagonara, a five-foot-nothing Bardolph to the six-foot-six Pistol of Donald Shanks. Zagonara, in his sixties, brought out of retirement in Australia, proved to be a joy and his clowning at no time interfered with proper reverence for the music which his voice encompassed with surprising ease. Zagonara was one of the great *comprimarios* of all time. Though bit parts were his lot because of his diminutive size, he belonged to the old tradition and he added immensely to the production.

The new *Masked Ball*, again led by now Principal Conductor Cillario, was a roaring success, though it was based solidly on local singers and not on any imported star. Money was beginning to come in from sources other than the public; $193,000 from the new Australian Council for the Arts and $175,000 from various other subsidies. *A Masked Ball* was the first production designed for the new Sydney Opera House stage, the dimensions of which were now known, though the completion date was still in the dim future. It was indeed a splendid affair and one worthy of any opera company. Desmond Digby's designs were brilliant

134

The first of the spectacles Verdi's *A Masked Ball* was designed in 1969 for the stage of the Sydney Opera House, fully four years before the opening. It remains the spectacle it was intended to be. *Over*, the 1975 revival with John Shaw as Anckerstrom (left); Eilene Hannan as Oscar with Donald Smith as the dying King Gustav (centre); and Eilene Fischer as Amelia (right).

Rosemary Gordon, a much admired singer, upstaging (visually only) the most popular star in the history of the Australian Opera, tenor Donald Smith, in the last act of *A Masked Ball* in 1969.

and so was their execution. (They were commissioned by the Australian Elizabethan Theatre Trust's Ladies Committee, one of the earliest examples of such sponsorship in Australia. Until then we had completely missed out on one of the mainstays of overseas opera companies, obtaining private donations for productions, or parts of productions.) The producer was Tom Brown, another ex-executive of the company and, beyond inconsistently returning to the Swedish historical names of the characters for an authentically Italian production, he made a thoroughly professional job of it in a traditional manner which was welcomed by the public with open arms.

Donald Smith was the undoubted star as the ill-fated King of Sweden, or Governor of Boston, as Verdi had it. Smith was by now at the very peak of his form and that was truly international in quality. He moved easily and with assurance, overcoming a far from romantic presence with considerable dignity completely in keeping with the character of the unfortunate monarch. His queen was Rosemary Gordon at her not inconsiderable best and Robert Allman rejoined the company on a permanent basis, making his debut as a strong, if rough, Anckerstrom-cum-Renato. An unexpected hit came from Glenys Fowles, a young West Australian soprano making her debut, as the transvestite page, Oscar. Fowles was to become a star very quickly and perhaps too readily left us for greater glories abroad, though credit must be given that she returned, when possible, to the company that helped her to make the grade so quickly. Casting from strength to make maximum impact, the initial production had no less than Neil Warren-Smith and Donald Shanks as the two conspirators, surely the best singers the parts have ever had anywhere in the world!

For all the money which suddenly appeared to be available, the 1969 repertoire was not really so very lavish. The revival of *Boris Godounov* was indeed welcome, specially since the scenery had quietly been replaced with a new set by Friedrich Bliem, and what a difference it made! Warren-Smith was better than ever, as was his partner, Donald Shanks as Pimen. The rest was much as before, the Polish Scene still being the weakest in spite of a change of protagonists. Marina and Dimitri liked Fretwell and Byers no better than they did Raisbeck and Baigildin in 1966. Harry Miller, who had departed along with Stefan Haag, had built an entirely new audience and, with the new scenery, they found *Boris* an imposing spectacle indeed. The chorus, under its newly acquired chorus master, Geoffrey Arnold (imported from England at the same time as resident conductor William Reid), carried all before it. The planning did not seem to be good, but it worked, and that, after all, is all that matters.

The other two productions of 1969 are less happily remembered. There was still that tendency to unearth the esoteric. Every year there were rumours of Menotti's *The Saint of Bleecker Street* or Pizetti's *Murder in the Cathedral.* Happily these came to nothing. (Asked the reason for planning such a dismally unsuccessful work as the former at one point, John Young replied that it contained an excellent role for Nicola Filacuridi, a tenor who happened to be available. Designs were actually prepared before better sense prevailed! Menotti as a vehicle for a tenor is unheard of, even in Australia.)

The choice of Wolf-Ferrari's *School for Fathers* seemed almost as contrary, except that the work is a pleasant enough lark, a modern Donizetti-cum-Rossini bit of pottiness. It is tuneful and everlastingly cheerful and few would have been offended by its inclusion in the repertoire, though it could be, and was, argued that the money spent on Beinl's production could have been better used elsewhere. Perhaps so, but Bliem and Digby produced pleasant sets and costumes, William Reid made the most of the music and the resident singers sang well – unfortunately swallowing the fine Dent translation so that hardly a word could be understood. The heroes, musically, and villains philologically, were led by Donald Shanks, Maureen Howard and the two Gordons, Rosemary and Robin. (The last-named being a notable exception as far as the bad diction went.)

And then there was *Madame Butterfly,* a long way from the kind of production seen in 1960. This time the Japanese opera from the pen of Puccini was going to be authentic; it was designed by one Yoshi Tosa, produced by one Yoshie Fujiwara assisted by one Hidetaka Kiyomya, and in Sydney Cio-Cio San was sung by one Michiko Sunahara, Japanese one and all. It was authentic Japanese all right, down to the standards prevailing in opera in Japan, which were bright, clean and decidedly old-fashioned, no matter how authentic Butterfly's ugly wedding hat may have been. Fujiwara had not up to that time set any operatic world on fire and he did not do so here. There was more justification for liking the new Butterfly than the old one and it lost no audiences for the company, but it was hardly a world-beater. David Parker made a good company debut as Pinkerton. Outside Sydney Maureen Howard took over from the vocally indifferent Japanese leading lady, only to prove again that Puccini is too heavy for her voice. Cillario in the pit at least assured everyone that Nagasaki was not worthy of the fate which befell it thirty-five years after Butterfly's act of hara kiri.

The retitling of the company as The Australian Opera was announced during 1969 and at the end of the season John Young presided over its inauguration – two weeks before being given the sack by the newly independent body's Chairman of Directors, Claude Alcorso. An official announcement that Young had become the Director of Orchestras for the Trust was actually made before he was

Gimmicks in vain Wolf-Ferrari's *School for Fathers* was a lost cause in spite of Stephan Beinl's imaginative production Donald Shanks and Alan Light are fishing with varying success, while John Pringle has his eye on a bird. The action moves fast and furious over the canals of Venice, whose pollution may account for the small size of the fish.

asked to accept it. Young, not unnaturally, took offence and resigned on the spot. Whether it was time for him to go or not, it was one of the less glorious moments in the history of the company. Young had been a popular administrator, too popular perhaps in that he was too ready to make promises he could not always fulfil. The fact remains that he took over an abysmal failure and he left a healthy singing infant. For that alone the company should have thanked him. His

place was taken by the duo which had run the Trust after the departure of Stefan Haag. Stephen Hall became Administrator and Donald McDonald Director of Finance of the new Australian Opera. The reign of Hall was not to be entirely smooth, and in the case of McDonald it was also to be short. Yet to them belongs the credit for bringing the company into the Sydney Opera House and into the critical eye of world opinion; no mean feat under the circumstances.

Stephen Hall

17

Stephen Hall is the model of a self-made man. In America he would no doubt have made his financial as well as artistic fortune, if given the opportunities he was in Australia. To him belongs the credit of bringing the Australian Opera to full maturity, ready to move into the Sydney Opera House, and it was during his reign that overseas magazines began to take note of the company's activities as a valid contribution to the international scene. It is not easy to see why he failed to hold his position, unless it be the fact that Hall overestimated his capacity for work and tried to do too many things at once.

Like his predecessors, he learnt on the job, starting with six years in London during which he turned from his early acting career to stage management, including a spell at Covent Garden. He returned in 1965 to act in the same capacity for the New Zealand production of Gershwin's *Porgy and Bess* when it toured Australia. It was an enormous success, the huge Maori cast led by the late Inia Te Wiata as Porgy convincingly replacing the usual Negro cast. Hall's management of the complex production impressed the Trust and Hall became the assistant of Stefan Haag, whom he was ultimately to replace.

The appointment was made just before Christmas 1966 at a time when planning for the next year was well under way and while John Young happened to be away ill. As a result Hall was catapulted into becoming Acting Administrator of the opera company at a time when it was just beginning its upward climb. The first Elizabethan Trust Orchestra was being formed to cater for both the opera and ballet companies and John Young's plans for grand operas like *Trovatore* and *Boris Godounov* were being implemented. And the need for someone like Hall was great.

In line with the practice established over the years, the new member of the administration immediately began to double as a producer of opera and Stephen Hall's first up effort (*Turandot*) certainly made people sit up. Furthermore, his contacts overseas were a great deal of help in assembling Young's fast increasing staff. Moffatt Oxenbould, then a stage manager at Sadlers Wells, returned, and Douglas Abbott, company manager for the London Festival Ballet, arrived. Hall, as a key man in the Trust, certainly helped John Young to build the opera company and in due course he transferred from the Trust administration to become 'Co-ordinator' for the opera company under Young.

Stefan Haag was the architect of the opera company who failed to realize his ambitions through inexperience; he could be said to be the Utzon of the venture. John Young pulled the baby out of the fire for Haag and put it firmly on its two feet. Stephen Hall acted as graduating professor, bringing it to the point of professionalism. All three had one thing in common, they learnt their trade as they went along and were found wanting in the end by people who were

not exactly the greatest professionals themselves.

From 1970, Hall, McDonald and the new Chairman of the Board, Claude Alcorso, ruled the new Australian Opera between them. During the next years first McDonald and then Hall departed in Young's footsteps and finally an imported General Manager, John Winther, was engaged for the rapidly growing company. Whatever the rights and the wrongs of the administrative juggles, Stephen Hall oversaw the artistic growth of the company from 1970 to 1973 and he cannot be denied the credit for the quality of production offered to the public, whatever may have been going wrong behind the scenes.

Negotiations recommenced for the services of Edward Downes and this time they did not fall through; he was to succeed Carlo Felice Cillario in 1972. Resident producers and resident designers became the norm and gradually the Australian Opera changed from a part-time company working six to seven months of the year to something resembling the permanent companies of Europe, though touring still remained the major activity.

As late as 1972 the Australian Opera's Sydney season totalled no more than three months, not counting a short season of *The Merry Widow*. The latter was an attempt to follow the move, which Young planned and Hall implemented, to close the gap between seasons in 1969 and again in 1971 by presenting Gilbert and Sullivan operas using most of the company's principals and chorus between regular seasons. It worked too, though it might have been wise to drop the original plan of having Stephen Hall produce all the operas after he was appointed Administrator of the company. Not that there was anything wrong with his productions, which succeeded only too well through a freshness in presentation that was a delightful change from the fossilization of tradition, but because it took up much time which Hall needed on more important administrative matters. It may be argued that Hall's ultimate departure from the scene was due to his ego-tripping as a producer instead of concentrating full-time on what is most certainly a full-time job, managing a large opera company.

Gilbert and Sullivan productions form a permanent part of the repertoire of the English National Opera at the Coliseum in London, but as a part of the regular repertoire. The Australian Opera presented them as separate seasons, hoping to catch new audiences for grand opera. The misleading 1969/70 attendance figures of 451,363 (covering eighteen months against all previous twelve monthly figures) indicate an enormous rise over 1968 and a large part of this was due to the addition of the four G. & S. operas presented. Three, *H.M.S. Pinafore, Iolanthe* and *The Pirates of Penzance,* were built around a local discovery, Dennis Olsen, a prominent actor at the time under contract to John Sumner's Melbourne Theatre Company, who had wanted to play those

A magnificent filler In 1969 the Australian Opera staged its first season of Gilbert and Sullivan to keep the company together between seasons. Stephen Hall's untraditional productions brought pleasure to many. *H.M.S. Pinafore* with Donald Shanks towering over the other principals; to his right: Maureen Howard, David Parker, Diane Holmes and Dennis Olsen.

The acting star of the opera Dennis Olsen as the very model of a major-general in *The Pirates of Penzance* in 1969. Olsen has been the keystone to all the Australian Opera's G. & S. successes. He is a magnificent actor-comedian who sings (?) the patter songs with immense clarity and gusto.

'**As idle as a painted ship . . .**' It is the ship which is lying down on the job, not the hard-working painter. Australia cannot afford proper paint frames for scenery and so backcloths must still be executed on the floor. This is the ship for *The Pirates of Penzance* which has sailed successfully over so many stages since 1969.

roles all his life. Hall must be given the credit for ideal casting, but Olsen did the work and proved his worth a thousand-fold. Good as Ronald Maconaghie is as a singer and artist, the comparative failure of *The Yeomen of the Guard,* in which he played Jack Point, only served to prove the essential need for Olsen to hold the productions together. Two years later *The Mikado* and *The Gondoliers* were added to the repertoire and once again the success was immense, in this case abetted by Tom Lingwood's superb designs.

The balance of the casting of the Sullivan operas and their universally fine designs by Quentin Hole, Friedrich Bliem and Vicki Feitscher made Hall's productions an automatic success wherever they played. The company had a lot of natural talent and voices unspoilt by experience in the J. C. Williamson Theatres' G. & S. seasons which (as in England) were more concerned with tradition than excellence; a perfect example of Mahler's dictum that 'tradition is sloppiness'. Robert Gard, Janice Taylor, John Pringle, Glenys Fowles, Maureen Howard, Alan Light and Neil Warren-Smith offered both youth and experience to bring enjoyment to their audiences.

The accent on productions of quality became even more obvious from 1970 onwards, for the importation of producers began in that year. Not counting the misconceived Japanese *Madame Butterfly* of the previous year, there had not been a professional imported producer since the inaugural year of 1956. The company had not perhaps gone back to the good (?) old days when singers invented their own movements, but producers had been recruited at the cheapest

The best Bohème   The Australian Opera achieved truly international production standards with Renzo Frusca's *La Bohème* in 1970. It also marked the debut of Tom Lingwood as a designer for the company. The small-voiced cast did not make the rafters ring, but the ensemble combined to produce pure magic.

Below, in the attic. Left to right: Robert Eddie, Ronald Maconaghie, Donald Shanks, Robert Simmons and Anson Austin. *Right*, in the snow: Anson Austin and Glenys Fowles. *Below right*, in the Café Momus. Left to right: Suzanne Steele, John Pringle, Anson Austin, Maureen Howard and Grant Dickson.

They wanted to set the world on fire – and did. Umberto Borsò and Rosemary Gordon (*below*) in Verdi's *Otello*. It was not a match-less performance, because during the night of 30/31 July 1970 Her Majesty's Theatre in Sydney burnt down and with it most of the season's productions. The Otello sets and costumes were re-made within eight months and *Otello* went on in the other states.

possible price, more often than not from the ranks of the resident staff, which meant that they came cheaply indeed, usually free! Four of 1970's five productions were staged by overseas producers and if only one of them proved to be a major acquisition in the long run, all improved substantially on their predecessors. It is not clear whether it was the producers' professionalism or intuition on Stephen Hall's part that caused fine collaboration with designers as well, but the end results spoke for themselves, though the most lasting example was governed by fate.

Stephan Beinl's sudden death caused the importation of John Copley to stage the new *Fidelio* on which Beinl had worked with designer Alan Lees. Copley in England was forced to accept Lees' work, if not unseen, at least without being able to influence it, as he would have wished to. Copley is one of the world's great producers and Australia has been fortunate in obtaining his services repeatedly since that first *Fidelio*. The results he has produced have been what

should be expected from an overseas producer:– world-class. No doubt Hall, by allowing Lees a generous budget, had a share in making the immense sets a success, but it needs a producer and a conductor to direct a first-class cast in even the best sets to make Beethoven's imperfect opera a success. Copley and Warwick Braithwaite met the requirements, though Braithwaite, already mortally ill, did not equal Copley's *tour de force*. Rosemary Gordon, singing and speaking in her native German with complete authority, looked and acted Leonora to a tee, while Alan Light was a superbly villainous Pizarro, the peak of a long and remarkably well-balanced career.

An even more astonishing case of mind over matter occurred with the new staging of *La Bohème*. This stand-by of all run-of-the-mill opera companies, Australian not excepted, was produced by an Italian, Renzo Frusca. Designs were by Tom Lingwood who, like Copley, was to have a long association with the company, proving his immense

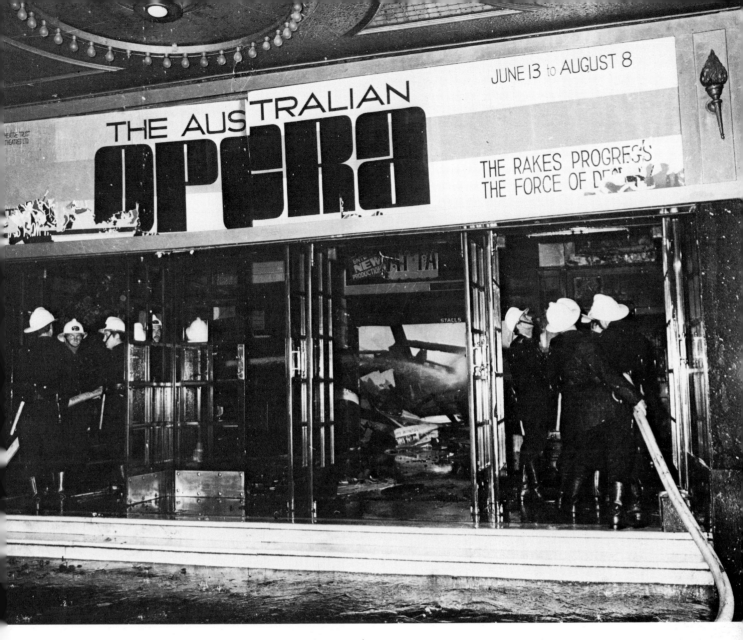

worth. Frusca was little more than a hack, certainly basically no better than the kind of producer Australia had had until then. The cast he was given was deliberately low-key; this was to be a 'young' *Bohème*, a small *Bohème*; the company could not afford the stars to give Puccini his full due, could not even equal local casts of years gone by, when singers like Albert Lance or Marie Collier could ring the rafters. They therefore threw everything behind the designer (as in *Fidelio*) and the producer. Why Frusca was inspired to produce something quite so extraordinary will always remain a mystery; his following productions certainly showed no great genius at work. (What is an even greater mystery is why Stephen Hall three years later chose to 'recreate' the production, deliberately destroying the delicate texture of Frusca's original.)

The *Bohème* of 1970 must remain a milestone in the company's history and, happily, Tom Lingwood's designs remain the same to this day, saving at least the visual charms of the original. John Serge (Sydney-born, but now Italy-based), Glenys Fowles, Ronald Maconaghie, Robert Eddie, Donald Shanks and Maureen Howard led the cast. Later alternatives, Anson Austin and John Pringle, as Rodolfo and Marcello, also fitted the picture of the young, under-voiced, but most authentic bohemians. It was indeed a memorable production, one which has survived some brutal mutilations, which were at least in part corrected by David Neal for the 1976 performances presented as a vehicle for New Zealand soprano Kiri Te Kanawa, making her Australian debut after conquering the world's stages.

As a backwash of Tito Gobbi's troubles to get his fees out of Australia, the company acquired a fine resident producer in the person of Bernd Benthaak from Hamburg. Gobbi was supposed to produce Verdi's *Otello* and to sing Iago in 1970. He had chosen his own Otello, Umberto Borsò, an Italian with an Australian wife, who had been immensely successful here during the 1955 Williamson Opera Season, when he was at the beginning of his career. Suddenly Stephen Hall was faced with an Otello without an Iago, and the need to find a new producer. Ronald Dowd, a fine Otello in his own right, suggested Bernd Benthaak and Hall engaged him on the spot, not just for *Otello*, but as resident producer. John Shaw was talked into returning to Australia to play Iago and Douglas Smith produced some bold, if not exactly inspired, designs.

Otello was a success because, like *Bohème*, it was prepared and conducted by Carlo Felice Cillario, the company's Musical Director. It is hard to go wrong with Verdi's masterpiece if you have the right conductor and the right singers. While Borsò was no Martinelli, he had an excellent voice and was no mean actor. Similarly Shaw was vocally and physically

151

imposing as Iago. The problem was that Borsò and Gobbi would have been matched much better vocally as well as physically. Shaw's towering figure dwarfed Borsò and the drama suffered accordingly. Rosemary Gordon was a most touching Desdemona.

While the production did not set the world on fire, it did manage to leave more than a spark of interest on Sydney's Her Majesty's Theatre, which burnt down during the night following the performance on 30 July 1970, destroying the sets and costumes for all of the season's productions except *Fidelio*. With eight of the season's performances still to go, all completely sold out on subscription, alternative arrangements had to be made in a hurry. Not only were subscribers not disappointed, though they saw only concert versions for their money, but the presentations in the huge Capitol Theatre were so successful that the last night of Verdi's *The Force of Destiny* was attended by an extra 1400 casual opera-goers, doubling the capacity of the burnt theatre.

The success of that concert *Force of Destiny* was somewhat surprising, since the original production had been the one weak link of the season. Produced in a pedestrian manner by Frusca in sets hardly worthy of Tom Lingwood's usual standards, it featured an imported guest 'star' as inept as any which the company had ever had. The reasons why one Franca Como was considered worthy of being imported from Italy are obscure. Her only noteworthy appearance on the international scene since then occurred at the opening of the San Carlo in Naples in 1972 when she took over the part of Turandot from Amy Shuard in the last act, whereupon the artistic director of theatre resigned because the company held him responsible 'for what was happening'. Any success there was belonged to Cillario and to Donald Smith, who was simply superb in one of Verdi's most difficult roles. Robert Allman was the strong Carlo, a role which was later sung by John Pringle. He was highly praised, but has wisely retired to lighter roles in recent years; the kind of controlled belting this role demands would not do his excellent voice much good in the long run.

The last opera of the year was the usual experiment considered so necessary to the public's 'education' at the time, Stravinsky's *The Rake's Progress*. Beautifully designed by Francesca Crespi (her first designs for the theatre) after Hogarth's original engravings, this was notable mainly for the fine work of Robert Gard (the Rake), John Pringle (Nick Shadow) and Janice Taylor (Anne). John Tasker's production suffered inhibitions for which he is not usually noted; the realistic orgy scene featured simulated sex scenes in which the gentlemen kept every button carefully done up!

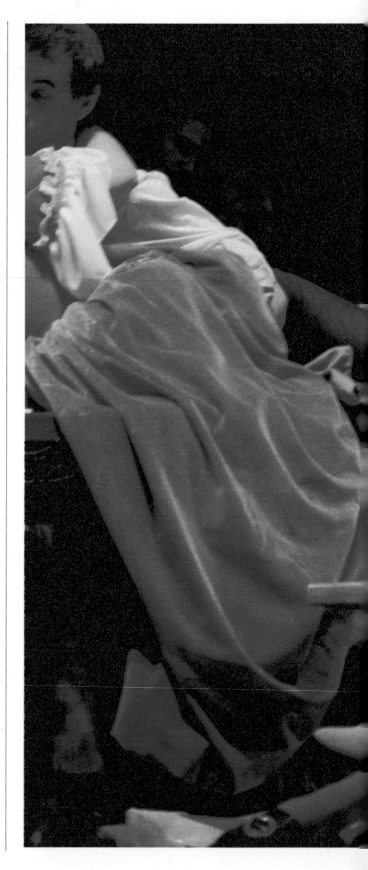

The modest orgy Stravinsky's *The Rake's Progress* gave ample scope for a full-blooded orgy, using Hogarth's paintings as a model. Francesca Crespi's authentic designs and the choristers almost produced the real thing. Unfortunately the management got cold feet; while the ladies were suitably orgiastic, the gentlemen kept their breeches tightly buttoned at all times!

The Opera Explosion Begins

18

The years leading up to the opening of the Sydney Opera House were artistically the most productive of the company and the public response was suitably enthusiastic. The imbalance created by seasons aimed at recruiting audiences for the new Sydney venue's opening left other states complaining that New South Wales was being favoured, and so it was and so it continues to be. It was an inevitable pattern dictated by history and Australia would not have the place in the annals of opera that it has today if Hall and his very active Chairman, Claude Alcorso, had not proceeded as they did.

Listing the operas of recent years in detail would produce a book on its own. I have devoted considerable space to the earlier history of the Australian Opera, because its years in the wilderness are largely unrecorded. The Australian Opera's archives do not contain basic items like programmes of the early Trust productions and the chronicles of this book may form the starting point for the detail which should be poured into some future definitive book on the subject. I will take the view that the productions of the 1970s are still fresh in the minds of most readers interested in opera and try to present a more general picture.

What I would describe as the opera explosion began in 1971 when the Australian Opera staged no less than ten operas, of which only three were revivals. (I do not count the *Otello* which was rebuilt after the previous year's fire and staged only in cities which had not previously seen it.) *Bohème, Turandot* and *A Masked Ball* were restaged, some with the assistance of other than their original producers, but almost entirely with similar casts as before. The fact that the public flocked to hear the same again, reflects the enjoyment it received from them. The exception was Amy Shuard, a great international Turandot, who shared the performances with Morag Beaton. (Shuard died tragically young in 1975.)

The great success of 1971 was John Copley's first production which he completely planned and executed for the company (with sets by Henry Bardon and costumes by Michael Stennett), Mozart's *The Marriage of Figaro*. This, more than anything that had been seen during the past fifteen years, pointed up the immense changes which had taken place since the first Trust Opera season. The first *Figaro*, which started the ball rolling in 1956, belonged to a different era, good as it was at the time. Copley showed Australia what opera in the 1970s was really about. Realism without excess, characters able to survive as dramatic entities regardless of the music and, finally, complete integration of what was happening on stage with the music itself. The *Bohème* of 1970 could have been a fortunate accident, the *Figaro* of 1971 was planned excellence, which worked exactly as its creators intended. This production has been the yardstick by which all subsequent productions have been judged and

Mozart to the life John Copley's superb Marriage of Figaro of 1971. A black-wigged Rosemary Gordon is serenaded by Jennifer Bermingham's Cherubino. Glenys Fowles provides the accompaniment.

Turandot's peacock feather train The splendour of Puccini's Chinese court was captured by concentrating costs in a single costume; the rest was done by clever lighting. Back to front: Ian Campbell as the Emperor, Morag Beaton as Turandot, Umberto Borsò as Calaf in 1971.

The start of the super-spectacular The 1971 production of Verdi's first great success, *Nabucco*, was an instant hit in Australia also. English soprano Elizabeth Vaughan as Abigaille (centre) and Robert Allman as Nabucco (front centre).

157

The unglamorous reality The 1972 *Rosenkavalier* in rehearsal (*top*). Bernd Benthaak directing Rosemary Gordon and Yvonne Minton.

The glamorous unreality The same scene in performance (*bottom*). Yvonne Minton, as Octavian, the girl playing a boy disguised as a girl, on the knee of Neil Warren-Smith's Baron Ochs. With Gordon's Marschallin.

An unsuccessful Rape Not even the provocative title could bring the crowds to see Benjamin Britten's *The Rape of Lucretia* in 1971. This picture of Lucretia (Lauris Elms) and Tarquinius (John Pringle) has more drama than the pussyfooting which passed for rape in the economy packaged production.

it is to the immense credit of Stephen Hall that so many in the following years equalled its success, though none surpassed it.

The singers in *The Marriage of Figaro* entered the spirit of Copley and Mozart most admirably and the decision to revert to English to point up the comedy worked, since Copley managed to obtain a much greater clarity of diction from Ronald Maconaghie, John Pringle, Rosemary Gordon, Glenys Fowles and the rest, than others had done before him. Copley also staged a fine *Rigoletto* which the public loved, and some critics hated, for its realistic court orgy in Act 1.

Nabucco by Verdi was an unknown quantity in Australia, but Verdi's first great success has the needed tunes to appeal to the masses and the production by Renzo Frusca with Tom Lingwood's designs was spectacular indeed, though the Sydney opening was almost ruined by the indisposition of the apparently indestructible Donald Shanks who, after years of rock-like steadiness, succumbed to laryngitis. No understudy was available and Shanks went on, miming the important role of Zaccaria, while a chorister sight-read the music in the pit! The inability to provide an alternative singer was greatly and justly criticized, but the occurrence is not that unusual even in more important houses. Elizabeth Vaughan, a rather prim and unevil English soprano, was imported for the key role of Abigaille and acquitted herself well vocally, if not dramatically. Robert Allman was a fine Nabucco.

Apart from two successors to the Gilbert and Sullivan series, *The Gondoliers* (excellent) and *The Mikado* (not quite up to scratch), the balance of the new productions paled into insignificance next to the high standards now being set. A new *Faust* produced by Bernd Benthaak was mediocre, except for the most promising debut of Joan Carden as Marguerite and Shank's larger-than-life Mephisto. Reginald Byers continued to improve as Faust, but the whole thing did not jell. Moffatt Oxenbould's debut as a producer for Benjamin Britten's *The Rape of Lucretia* was even less successful, in spite of Lauris Elm's Lucretia and Pringle's excellent Tarquinius. It was an economy package and showed it, but presumably was intended to mollify the artier elements in the Australia Council, which was by now pouring hundreds of thousands a year into the company's coffers. The revival of *Otello* was as good or as bad as the burnt original had been; good enough to show what Verdi intended, bad enough to prove that it needs either a better producer than Benthaak or world-class singers to make up for his deficiencies.

There were immense cries of outrage when it was revealed in 1972 that $100,000 had been spent on a new production of Richard Strauss' *Der Rosenkavalier*. It seemed an astronomical figure at the time, but the end result more than justified this apparent extravagance to launch the company's new Musical Director, Edward Downes. *Der Rosenkavalier* was to producer Benthaak what *Bohème* had been to Frusca, one great achievement from an average craftsman and, like Frusca, he was backed by the superlative designs of Tom Lingwood, which really looked like $100,000 – or more. With Downes conducting a specially enlarged Trust Orchestra in each state, the effect of this *Rosenkavalier* – its first ever performance in Australia! – was simply stunning. Copley's *Figaro* may have been just as good, but here was spectacle as well as a brilliant result of operatic team-work.

Much of the effect was due to the cast, only one of which

The magic of Tom Lingwood, whose designs were to dazzle audiences for years to come, demonstrated in the 1972 *Rosenkavalier.* The Presentation of the Silver Rose, with Yvonne Minton as Octavian and Glenys Fowles as Sophie. At left, Mary Hayman as the Duenna.

was imported! Neil Warren-Smith's Baron Ochs was as good as any to be seen overseas. Yvonne Minton, an Australian who had achieved international acceptance, returned to repeat the Octavian she had already recorded for Decca three years earlier. Minton was probably the best imported artist the Australian Opera has ever had in this context, Sutherland not excepted. Rosemary Gordon was a beautiful Marschallin. Glenys Fowles completed the top cast with a Sophie so good that it foreshadowed her quick departure overseas. It was a quartet worthy of being heard anywhere in the world.

A new staging of *Cavalleria Rusticana* and *Pagliacci* was the only other novelty in a year devoted to preparing for the big event of the opening of the Sydney Opera House in 1973. Produced by Stephen Hall, both operas were sturdy standard productions which served their purpose well. Donald Smith and Umberto Borsò alternated in the leads of the two operas and Suzanne Steele, recruited from the operetta stage, proved that she could make a strong point in opera when she sang Santuzza. Maureen Howard was equally good as Nedda in *Pagliacci* and Robert Allman was a fine Tonio. Revivals of *Figaro, Bohème, Fidelio* and *The Force of Destiny* completed the season.

While everything was working toward the great moment when the Opera House in Sydney would open, palace revolutions continued to make headlines. Stephen Hall had, on succeeding John Young in 1969, brought in a young financial wizard, Donald McDonald, to act as General Manager, meaning business manager. The curious billing at the time always listed Hall first, Downes (as Musical Director) second and McDonald last; a strange position for anyone with the title General Manager. McDonald became the most popular key person in the administration, but this did not stop the management from accepting his resignation in 1972, when it was offered for reasons which appeared dubious then and appear dubious now. It was a traumatic experience for the company and brought credit to nobody. McDonald quickly moved to Musica Viva which, at the time of writing, he is still managing. Chairman Alcorso personally took over McDonald's work, pending the appointment of a new 'General Manager'. The position was advertised internationally and finally filled by (echoes of Joern Utzon, if only in terms of nationality) another Dane, John Winther. Winther's idea of what constitutes a General Manager are more in line with the generally understood interpretation of the title, not the third-in-line which had been accepted by the inexperienced McDonald. The acceptance of Winther meant the ultimate departure not only of Stephen Hall, but also of Claude Alcorso. But first those two gentlemen still had their hands full to launch the first season at the Sydney Opera House and, whatever John Winther's subsequent excellent work, the glory of that opening season belongs first to Hall and second to Alcorso.

Verismo reality *Cavalleria Rusticana* and *Pagliacci* 1972. A genuine Italian Turiddu, Umberto Borsò (*top*) and a genuine Australian Italian, Donald Smith (*bottom left*) provided a feast of *verismo* singing which brought the house down every night. Suzanne Steele's talents were rarely used, though she gave fine performances, here (*bottom right*) as Santuzza.

The man from the chorus It is rare indeed for a regular chorus member to be promoted to leading roles. Lamberto Furlan (*opposite*) did so first in 1973 as Turiddu in *Cavalleria Rusticana* opposite Elizabeth Connell. Later he regularly appeared in *Tosca*, *La Bohème* and *Madame Butterfly*.

The Opera House Opens

19

The Sydney Opera House finally opened on 28 September 1973 with a new production of Prokofiev's *War and Peace.* The bridge from the preceding year had been a dreadful *Merry Widow,* capitalizing cheaply on the presence of Suzanne Steele in the company, and a Melbourne season which included a new production of Puccini's three opera evening, the *Trittico.* But the big news was *War and Peace* and how the Opera House could cope with such a production. The American, Sam Wanamaker, was imported to produce, Tom Lingwood designed and Edward Downes not only conducted, but provided the English translation. It was a venture almost too large in conception, but it succeeded brilliantly. Unfortunately the work itself is hardly world-shattering and it seems unlikely that it will ever be revived. To show off the new building it was, however, an ideal choice.

The stage of the Opera Theatre is a curious thing, duplicated nowhere else in the world, having been designed to obtain maximum acting area in a space not only limited, but shaped by the strange roof shell which surmounts it. Wanamaker used the enormous revolving stage to create a, quite literally, round production which, unlike the conventional theatre-in-the-round, had an audience fronting one third of the circle only, instead of surrounding it. The enormous crowds, demanded by Prokofiev and provided by the Australian Opera, entered and exited in circles converging toward the back. The whole thing was stylized to a degree and the twelve scenes followed each other without a single curtain or blackout, an effect similar to what is known as *montage* in films. The star of the show here, as before and again in following years, was Tom Lingwood and his scenic designs, which worked so well, though they aroused comparatively little comment, because the building itself inevitably overshadowed the spectacle of the production.

Nevertheless, what took place on the stage of the Opera Theatre in *War and Peace* has not been repeated and is unlikely to be repeated there, because the company (meaning Lingwood) in 1975 found ways of using the Concert Hall for truly grand opera, which is what *War and Peace* is in effect. Downes and the orchestra outdid themselves, naturally enough, though few in the audience had a great deal of time for what they were playing. The enormous cast was dominated by Neil Warren-Smith as Field Marshall Kutuzov. While Warren-Smith never ceases to amaze, his Boris should have prepared audiences for his performance. The leading lady, Natasha, was, surprisingly enough, the most recent graduate of the company's soprano ranks, Eilene Hannan. She acquitted herself more than well and continued to justify the faith placed in her in the years which followed. Practically the whole of the company made up the rest of the twenty-seven roles with individual lines to sing.

Since statistics are the most impressive thing about *War*

WAR AND PEACE

Opera in 12 Scenes by Sergei Prokofiev
(by arrangement with Boosey & Hawkes Music Publishers Ltd.)

Libretto: Sergei Prokofiev and Myra Mendelssohn-Prokofieva after the novel by Leo Tolstoy
English text: Edward Downes

Conductor: Edward Downes; Producer: Sam Wanamaker; Designer: Tom Lingwood; Lighting Design: Robert Ornbo

Choreographer: Boris Romanoff; Production Assistant: Warner Whiteford; Stage Manager: Freda Chapple

THE ELIZABETHAN TRUST SYDNEY ORCHESTRA
Concertmaster: Robert Ingram

THE AUSTRALIAN OPERA CHORUS
Chorusmaster: Geoffrey Arnold

Characters in order of appearance:

Prince Andrei Bolkonsky	*Tom McDonnell*	Tikhon Shcherbaty	*John Durham*
Countess Natasha Rostova	*Eilene Hannan*	1st German General	*John Germain*
Sonya	*Jennifer Bermingham*	2nd German General	*Robert Simmons*
An elderly nobleman, the host	*John Germain*	An orderly from Prince Andrei's regiment	*Lamberto Furlan*
Footman	*Trevor Brown*	Field Marshall Michael Ilarionovich Kutuzov	*Neil Warren-Smith*
Count Ilya Rostov	*Grant Dickson*	Aide de Camp to Kutuzov	*Trevor Brown*
Maria Dmitryevna Akhrossimova	*Rosina Raisbeck*	1st Staff Officer	*Graeme Ewer*
Madame Peronskaya	*Mary Hayman*	2nd Staff Officer	*John Germain*
Countess Hélène Bezukhova	*Suzanne Steele*	Napoleon	*Raymond Myers*
Count Pierre Bezukhov	*Ronald Dowd*	Aide de Camp to General Compans	*Anson Austin*
Prince Anatole Kuragin	*Robert Gard*	Aide de Camp to Murat	*Virginia Lloyd-Owen*
Dolokhov	*John Shaw*	Marshall Berthier	*Alan Light*
Chambermaid / Old footman / Valet } Servants to Prince Nicholas Bolkonsky	*Dolores Cambridge* / *John McKenna* / *Donald Solomon*	Marshall Caulincourt	*Gregory Marinos*
		Monsieur de Beausset	*Robert Gard*
Princess Marie Bolkonskaya	*Elizabeth Connell*	General Belliard	*Robert Simmons*
Old Prince Nicholas Bolkonsky	*Alan Light*	Aide de Camp to Prince Eugene	*Ian Campbell*
Balaga, Dolokhov's coachman	*Joseph Grunfelder*	Aide de Camp to Napoleon	*Wallace Carroll*
Joseph, Dolokhov's footman	*Gregory Marinos*	General Barclay de Tolly	*Graeme Ewer*
Matryosha, a gypsy girl	*Jacqueline Kensett-Smith*	General Bennigsen	*John Germain*
Dunyasha, young maid to the Rostov family	*Beryl Furlan*	General Rayevsky	*Robert Eddie*
Gavrila, footman to Akhrossimova	*John Durham*	General Yermolov	*Joseph Grunfelder*
Denisov	*Ronald Maconaghie*	General Konovnitsyn	*William Bamford*
Fyodor	*Barry Culhane*	Chorus leader	*John Durham*

There will be one interval of approximately 30 minutes after Scene 6.

First Performance (first 8 scenes only): June 12, 1946—Maly Theatre, Leningrad. First complete performance (in Italian): Florence Maggic Musicale, 1953.

First complete performance in Russia: Bolshoi Theatre, Moscow, 1959. First performance by The Australian Opera: Sydney Opera House, September 28, 1973.

The Australian Opera is indebted to Benson and Hedges for its sponsorship of War and Peace. It gratefully acknowledges this as a major contribution to the development of opera in Australia.

and Peace, this may be the moment to produce a roll-call of the company which only seven years earlier had consisted of two singers and a staff of three. In September 1973 the Australian Opera consisted of fifty principals, fifty chorus, twenty-nine administrative staff, twenty-five production staff, plus Winther, Downes and Hall (in that order) and a Board of Directors of twenty-two. The Elizabethan Trust Sydney Orchestra had seventy members, not all of whom could fit into the tiny orchestra pit of the Sydney Opera House at the same time. A grand total of 246 people being gainfully employed by one Australian opera company!

Stephen Hall's plans for the rest of that first season in-cluded a fair proportion of successes in line with recent standards, but also one major dud which, unfortunately, followed the opening attraction. Apart from its novelty value, it was hardly a notable event. Bernd Benthaak's *Tannhäuser* in its initial staging was something of a *fiasco de scandale*. Musically just acceptable (only Downes' conducting was up to scratch), the idea of replacing the ballet Wagner unwillingly added to the Venusberg with colour slides of the intimate female anatomy was unerotic and totally boring. The rest of Ralph Koltai's sets looked nice, but his costumes left a lot to be desired. To top the lot, Hall had imported a Finnish tenor of total mediocrity to sing the

The war is over The battles of the Sydney Opera House ended on 28 September 1973 when a new war broke out, Prokofiev's *War and Peace*. It was hardly an inspiring work for a non-communist audience, but it did show what the theatre could do, in spite of all reports that the interior was unworkable. The three scenes (out of twelve!) shown here are typical of the spectacle which followed spectacle — and any musical failings were of Prokofiev's making.

War and Peace is unlikely to be staged again in a hurry, but it was a memorable opening attraction for a world-famous building. *Below*, the Russian army ready to fight Napoleon (Neil Warren-Smith as General Kutuzov); *right*, the peace which the army tried to protect (the ball scene); *below right*, the battle won by the people, as well as the army.

title role, Rosemary Gordon looked fine, but found Elisabeth's music a little rich, expatriate Australian Tom McDonnell was a rough Wolfram and only Elizabeth Connell's Venus, made up to look hideous instead of seductive, sang brilliantly. Matters improved musically later when Ronald Dowd sang Tannhauser to Nance Grant's Elisabeth. Dowd had been rejected as 'unreliable' for the opening by Hall, but proved in a long series of performances that he could outsing the imported replacement by a mile. He has since then proved to be one of the most consistently good performers the company has ever had.

On the credit side, John Copley repeated his *Figaro* success with a magnificent *Magic Flute* using just his resident singers (Maconaghie, Carden, Austin, Shanks, etc.) and John Stoddart's sets worked magnificently in the Opera House with all its lifts, if not so well on tour in other states. The *Trittico* produced by Moffatt Oxenbould in Melbourne was on a level with Hall's *Cav. and Pag.*, routine Italian opera, handsomely mounted and well sung. Donald Smith and Elizabeth Fretwell appeared in *Il Tabarro*, Nance Grant in *Suor Angelica* and Raymond Myers sang the title role in *Gianni Schicchi*. Rosina Raisbeck brilliantly appeared in all three works.

The Australian opera, which had been commissioned from Peter Sculthorpe for the opening of the Sydney Opera House did not materialize until 1974. His *Rites of Passage* and two of the seven one-act operas, commissioned by the Australian Opera two years earlier, from other Australian composers, Werder's *The Affair* and Sitzky's *Lenz*, were performed in that year. Sculthorpe's *Rites* was really a ballet-cum-chorus oratorio. It had no soloists and used dancers of the Australian Dance Theatre from Adelaide under the direction of Jaap Flier and Geoffrey Arnold's well-trained Australian Opera Chorus. The Werder-Sitzky double bill had its share of soloists, who could do little with the Werder opus, but Ron Stevens was an effective Lenz, a difficult tenor role which needed an actor with a strong voice. American-born Stevens does not have a beautiful voice, but he has plenty of power, a good presence and considerable acting ability.

By some strange magic each year had produced at least one outstanding production since the tide of the company's fortunes turned in the late sixties: 1974's highlight was

The superlative production 1975's *Jenufa* by Janáček, produced by John Copley with costumes by Michael Stennett and scenery by Allan Lees combined all the best opera can offer (*left*). It established South African Elizabeth Connell as a major star. Lone Koppel-Winther was the fine Jenufa (front right). *Below left*: Robert Gard (front right) was superbly right as Steva.

An actress in the Callas class Lone Koppel-Winther as Tosca (*below*) with Raymond Myers (Scarpia) and Graeme Ewer (Spoleta). Koppel-Winther's ability as an actress in this role even eclipsed Marie Collier.

Janáček's *Jenůfa*, another Copley triumph in which he was greatly assisted by the decor of Allan Lees. It was an outstanding event by any standards, highlighted by an astonishing performance from Elizabeth Connell, a young South African mezzo soprano who came to Australia on a two year contract, only to be lost to us again – if not unexpectedly – when this expired in 1975. Connell's Kostelnička was a totally absorbing study of peasant maternalism and sung quite stunningly. The title role fitted the company's controversial new soprano, Lone Koppel-Winther, like a glove and Robert Gard and Ron Stevens completed a superb set of principals.

When it was found that John Winther, the new General Manager, had a soprano wife, hackles rose very quickly. Charges of favouritism flew fast and furious, but were hardly supported by her performances during her first three years with the company. Mrs Winther is a major actress with a very fine voice, lacking only in clarity of diction, a handicap she shares with Joan Sutherland! Her initial appearance in Stephen Hall's new *Tosca* in 1974 was a major event because of her, not because of Hall, whose production was no more than acceptable on the whole and in parts ludicrous. (No dawn in Act 3!) Koppel-Winther's performance as Jenůfa should have set all minds at ease; it also was outstanding. After that she took her turn with other artists and her performances, like theirs, varied: not all were good. When she was good she was very, very good and when she was bad she was not horrid. What more could anyone ask?

There was a new *Barber of Seville* in 1974 produced by Glyndbourne's John Cox, small-scale in design and in singing, however good. John Pringle's Figaro and Elizabeth Connell's Rosina stood out. A new *Don Giovanni* produced by John Bell (again starring Pringle) was not as revolutionary as Jim Sharman's in 1967, but failed to please the public.

What could not fail to please anyone was the return of Joan Sutherland to Australia in 1974 when she sang the four leading roles in Offenbach's *The Tales of Hoffmann* in Sydney

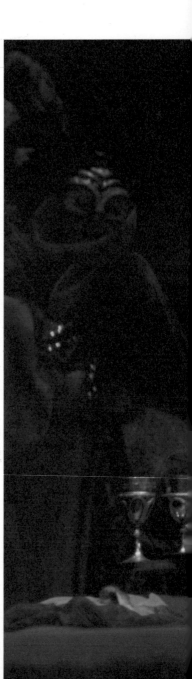

Sutherland returns *The Tales of Hoffmann* brought Joan Sutherland into the ranks of the Australian Opera for the first time in 1974. Playing the four leading roles in Offenbach's only grand opera, she made a deep impression in a most beautifully staged production.

Stella, the opera singer, appears only briefly, but the other three roles normally command three singers. Sutherland sang them all, along with Stella. *Left*, Olympia, the mechanical doll; *below*, Giulietta, the Ventian courtesan; *right*, Antonia, the consumptive singer, with Raymond Myers as Dr Miracle.

The Tales of Hoffmann Henri Wilden as Hoffmann, with French-Canadian mezzo-soprano Huguette Tourangeau as Nicklausse at right. This was Wilden's big chance, his first role in his native French and singing opposite Joan Sutherland, and he acquitted himself with great distinction. (Wilden was born in Mauritius.)

The Wizard of Op Bringing opera to children is the best way to create new audiences for the future. The Australian Opera's *Opera Through the Time Machine* (1974) was a fine example, using standard repertory works introduced by fun characters (*right*). Left to right: Jennifer Bermingham, Graham Ewer, Caroline Lill, Robert Gard as the Wizard of Op and Rosina Raisbeck as Mistress Boomhilda. The artists not only presented, but conceived and wrote this epic success.

with Richard Bonynge conducting. The production was by the Argentinian producer-designer team of Tito Capobianco and José Varona. Apparently the budgets of productions are being carefully played down since the controversy about the 1972 *Rosenkavalier,* but the cost of this *Hoffmann* must have been astronomical. And, once again, it fully justified itself. The Sydney performances with Sutherland and Henri Wilden (Hoffmann), Raymond Myers (as all three of the villains) and Graeme Ewer (in the three far-from-small minor roles) were outstanding in every respect. Mezzo soprano Huguette Tourangeau, who had sung in the same opera with Sutherland under Bonynge in New York at the Metropolitan earlier in the year, was brought out to play Nicklausse again. As someone who saw both productions, I can only state that the Sydney article won hands down on every count. Later performances in other states, with Joan Carden singing exceptionally well in the Sutherland roles, failed to keep up the standard because the sets were not half as effective in theatres for which they were not designed and Bonynge's

guidance in the pit was sorely missed. Full credit, though, to Jennifer Bermingham for taking over Nicklausse with distinction.

The Tales of Hoffmann also played its (or their) part in the success of a remarkable experiment which began in January 1975. The institution of a Summer Season in Sydney brought a completely new dimension to the activities of the Australian Opera. After many successful years of subscription seasons during the colder months in theatres which were not air-conditioned, the gamble that people would go to the Sydney Opera House in mid-summer succeeded brilliantly, not least because operas like *The Tales of Hoffmann* and *The Magic Flute* were suitable for family audiences. Not only that, but the availability of the Concert Hall of the Opera House enabled the company to experiment with a box office opera which was too large to be staged in the Opera Theatre, Verdi's *Aida.*

Once again the credit belongs almost entirely to that remarkable Englishman, now (we hope) Australian, Tom

The Aida miracle In 1975 designer Tom Lingwood proved that grand opera can be staged in the Concert Hall of the Sydney Opera. He incorporated large parts of the hall's own architecture in the Egyptian setting (*right*). Public response to the resulting spectacle has been tremendous. Front right: Marilyn Richardson as Aida. At back: Donald Smith, as Radames, arriving in his chariot.

Lingwood. Though Stephen Hall and Tom Lingwood were credited with the production of *Aida* in the Concert Hall, Lingwood alone was responsible for the scenic designs of *Aida* and for solving the problems of staging opera in a venue which was not designed for the purpose. The difficulties the Opera Theatre presents to productions are as nothing to those Lingwood had to overcome in the Concert Hall. There was no fly tower, no proscenium, no orchestra pit, no lighting, no dressing rooms; almost nothing. On the other hand there was an immensely decorative *modern* ceiling, which could hardly be hidden, right over the proposed acting area. Lingwood cleverly incorporated the hall's own features in his designs and built a huge Egyptian Temple of incredible versatility. The effect is somewhat like staging an open-air opera in a modern Baths of Caracalla under cover, if such a thing can be imagined.

The success of the *Aida* was instantaneous and all performances in 1975 (and again in 1976) were instantly sold

Whatever happened to canvas? Realism in opera production today demands solid sets. Here eleven scene shifters move one small part of the *Simon Boccanegra* set.

out. Musically, the opera was under the direction of Carlo Felice Cillario, who returned to Australia for the purpose. Donald Smith, Marilyn Richardson, John Shaw and Elizabeth Connell made a fine singing team, though the human drama in such a huge space was somewhat lost. Much to everybody's surprise, a second cast of Reginald Byers, Elizabeth Fretwell, Raymond Myers and Lauris Elms sang as well, or, in the case of Elms, even better. A somewhat tame production of the Weill-Brecht *Rise and Fall of the City of Mahagonny* completed the programme for the first Summer Season.

The other 1975 seasons in Sydney and elsewhere began to show weaknesses in repertoire, since operas suitable to local conditions were beginning to run out. The economy of the country was in recession, costs were climbing astronomically and smaller works were sought and produced, whether resources were suitable or not. Who thought of the idea to engage Stefan Haag and his old-time collaborator, designer Tim Walton, to produce Donizetti's *L'elisir d'amore*? Was it this which broke the camel's back and finally caused Stephen Hall to relinquish his post as Artistic Director? Perhaps not, but few will want to remember this backlash to the bad old days of the Trust.

Tito Capobianco and John Copley, not unexpectedly, did better than Stefan Haag. The former staged a spectacular *Simon Boccanegra* by Verdi, which suffered more from Verdi than the performance; it is an opera which needs superlative stars to come to life, not a fine ensemble such as the Australian Opera provided. Robert Allman was a most impressive Doge, alternating with John Shaw. Joan Carden, Reginald Byers and Shanks, alternating with Warren-Smith, made up the rest of the cast, with Cillario in the pit. In Sydney illness struck again, necessitating the importation at a moment's notice of Joseph Rouleau to cover the part of Fiesco. A similar mishap occurred when Myers dropped out of *Rigoletto* and Peter Glossop was brought from London to sing the jester at a few days' notice. The fact that singers of this calibre were considered necessary to replace local artists is an indication of how standards in the company had risen.

Richard Strauss' *Ariadne auf Naxos* returned under Copley's direction in 1975 in a 'mod' interpretation, with John Stoddart's designs transposing it into the 1920s. It worked up to a point, though seeing the *commedia dell'arte* characters as the Marx Brothers, Rogers and Astaire and Marlene Dietrich was a bit startling. Nance Grant was a truly outstanding Ariadne, Ron Stevens a good-looking Bacchus, while Lone Koppel-Winther again proved her value as the Composer. A newcomer to the company, Rhonda Bruce sang a good Zerbinetta.

The importation of Stella Axarlis, a Melbourne-born soprano, to star in *Tosca* only proved that standards in Australia are higher than they are in Dusseldorf, her home base. (And so one would hope!)

Top, the Prologue. Monsieur Jourdain's house has been transposed from the eighteenth century to the 1920s. Left to right: Ronald Maconaghie, Ron Stevens, Nance Grant, Robert Eddie, Robert Gard, Rhonda Bruce, Grant Dickson and Graham Ewer.

Bottom, the Opera. The *commedia dell'arte* characters become modern comedians, including the Marx Brothers, Marlene Dietrich and Astaire and Rogers. Zerbinetta (Rhonda Bruce) as Dietrich with male tap-dancing ensemble.

How to make a dull opera fun The *Ariadne auf Naxos* of 1975 may not have pleased everybody, but John Copley's production and John Stoddart's designs certainly kept things moving.

The Opera: the only characters staying in period for the play-within-the-play are Ariadne and Bacchus (Nance Grant and Ron Stevens, *below*) singing to the gloriously voluptuous heaven.

The decadence of light Richard Strauss' *Salome*, as designed by Tom Lingwood for the Concert Hall of the Sydney Opera House in 1976, makes much of the blood-red moon as it sets over the decaying court of Herod. Left to right: Ron Stevens as Herod, Margreta Elkins as Herodias, Angela Giblin as the Page and Lone Koppel-Winther as Salome.

A designed and designing comic Graeme Ewer (*right*) as Franz, one of three comedy roles he played in *The Tales of Hoffmann*. Assisted by the designs of José Varona (Franz is deaf!), Ewer brought the house down nightly with his solitary *arietta*.

The second Summer Season in Sydney (1976) repeated the successful *Aida* in the Concert Hall and added a fine Lingwood production of Strauss' *Salome* with Marilyn Richardson and Lone Koppel-Winther alternating. Richardson is probably the greatest Australian singer resident in this country at present, but it was generally agreed that Koppel-Winther made more of the part. (She headed the second cast, so what was that about favouritism again?) *The Magic Flute* was repeated and new productions of *Cosi fan tutte* (Copley-Barden-Stennett) and *Albert Herring* (Cox-Butlin) were added. Copley's *Cosi* was as good as his other ventures into Mozart and mostly notable for the emergence of Henri Wilden as a Mozart singer. *Albert Herring* featured an excellent Graeme Ewer in the title role and Nance Grant as Lady Billows. In *Cosi* and *The Magic Flute* a new young South African soprano, Isobel Buchanan made a deep impression.

The balance of 1975/76 saw new productions of Delibes' *Lakmé* with Joan Sutherland, a new *Carmen* with Tourangeau, Mozart's *Seraglio* and Janáček's *Cunning Little Vixen*. Richard Bonynge succeeded Edward Downes as Musical Director in 1976 and this may account for the number of guest stars in the Sydney season. Kiri Te Kanawa, Marilyn Richardson, Clifford Grant, and June Bronhill were scheduled to appear in productions which included *Der Rosenkavalier*, *La Bohème*, *Simon Boccanegra*, *Jenůfa*, *Rigoletto* and *The Marriage of Figaro*. It was a line-up of which any company can be proud and it seemed that the Australian Opera had a somewhat more hopeful future ahead of it than would have been thought not so many years ago. It all depended on one man, though – John Winther.

Twenty years of Cosi fan tutte

Left, 1956, the first Trust production with, left to right, Eunice McGowan, Kevin Miller, Jenifer Eddy, Geoffrey Chard, John Cameron and Marjorie Conley.

Below left; 1965, Stefan Haag's second production: (left to right) Ronald Maconaghie, Peter Baillie and Neil Warren-Smith.

Below; 1976, John Copley's new production: (left to right) Anson Austin, Joan Carden, Jennifer Bermingham and John Pringle.

Cosi fan tutte continued   Producer John Copley recreates real people, not stereotypes. The maid, Despina, in *Cosi fan tutte* (*over*) is hardly likely to be as well-dressed or as clean as her two mistresses. As portrayed by Cynthia Johnson, she is extremely funny and totally believable, no matter how unbelievable her doings. Left to right: Joan Carden, Jennifer Bermingham and Cynthia Johnson.

The Winther of
Our Discontent
20

In all fairness to the gentleman in question, let me complete Shakespeare's quotation: The Winther of our discontent made glorious summer ... There are those who would decry the contribution John Winther made to the history of opera in this country. I am not among them. Some regretted that the job of General Manager of the Australian Opera did not go to an Australian in 1973. The answer to that is that if the Elizabethan Trust Opera had *not* been headed by Australians, the company would probably have reached its present standards ten years earlier.

It will take a great many years before anybody trained in Australia will be able to follow in the footsteps of John Winther or of his successor, Peter Hemmings. Winther had an excellent production team, including Moffat Oxenbould, who came up through the ranks and now carries a title which sounds regrettably like the only one the old Trust failed to invent: he is the Artistic Administrator. Anthony Everingham, the most efficient Stage Director, also started at the bottom and worked his way up to a position which makes him responsible for the whole apparatus of putting operas onto the many-sized stages on which the company still plays. There are others, Douglas Abbot, the imperturbable Company Manager, for example. It is a team in which each member is an expert because he or she is led by an expert.

John Winther came from Denmark, where he worked his way up through the ranks in the Royal Opera House in Copenhagen, starting as a repetiteur and ending as General Manager for ten years. Winther is also a talented pianist and accompanist, as singers and audiences involved in many concerts in this country can attest. It was a rare combination of artistic temperament and business acumen which the Australian Opera obtained when it accepted John Winther on his own terms. 'There must be one person as the final arbiter in an opera company', he said, and he was that person.

There was a becoming modesty about the man and at first he got what he wanted without upsetting people which, in this particular company, was a rare quality indeed. He admitted that he inherited a group of executives who did a good job and simply continued as before. He defended their policies and even their financial budgets, which he was forced to take over. Winther was obviously a diplomat, because the facts added up to a different total.

John Winther was engaged for a three year term in February 1973, six months before the Sydney Opera House opened its doors. The Australian Opera had ended the previous year with a deficit of $150,000, something which was too readily blamed on the departed Donald McDonald and his staff. The projected deficit to the end of the first Opera House season was an additional $300,000 but, according to Winther, that was an over-estimate made in good faith because of the anticipated costs of running a theatre in a building with a disastrous history of inefficiency. Over-estimating a deficit is better than under-estimating one. The point is that 1973 produced a deficit of only $125,000, but this had to be added to the outstanding $150,000-odd.

1974 was the first full Winther year and it concluded with a *surplus* of $400,000, wiping out the deficits of the previous two years and leaving the company with over $100,000 in hand! (All these sums are, of course, book entries, not actual dollars available for spending.) The main consideration is that 1974 was also one of the best years the company had ever had artistically; that is, Winther achieved the economic miracle without lowering standards, cutting seasons or avoiding the immense increases in wages which the year imposed on the whole community in Australia. Quite possibly these spectacular results were due to Winther's ability to raise cash in many different quarters. I don't care. It was his job to be the General Manager, and to produce good opera without over-spending was something quite unheard of in the previous history of the company and its executives.

Partly it was due to a hard-headedness which upset some people in the artistic community, particularly Australian composers, whose works were not performed. Winther's attitude sounds ironical in the light of his ultimate stated reasons for resigning: 'Every night we don't play *Bohème*, we lose money', he said. Australian operas are hard to find, costly to stage and a total disaster at the box office. The pattern of *Rites of Passage*, which Peter Sculthorpe did not finish in time for the Opera House opening, is typical of what still happens. Three operas were commissioned in 1974, but only one was completed on time and that, the rock opera *Hero* by Craig McGregor, was an unmitigated disaster artistically and financially. There was too much reason in Winther's madness to offer comfort to operatic nationalists.

John Winther, his wife and children were naturalized in 1976. His contract was extended, but the battle he initially won cost him the war in the end. The Winther/Downes partnership was musically adventurous and the novelty of the Sydney Opera House made novelties such as *War and Peace* or *Jenůfa* acceptable for some years. Perhaps Downes saw the writing on the wall, perhaps his growing international reputation caused him to leave a company thriving under his hand after only three years. In June 1976 Richard Bonynge succeeded him as Musical Director of the Australian Opera.

Bonynge's arrival coincided with a major financial crisis predicted accurately enough by the shrewd planner who was still General Manager. John Winther was not prepared to wait until it was too late. He blandly announced that the company would have to disband for five months in 1977 unless an extra $970,000 in funds could be obtained in that year. To continue the company's existing work the million and a half expected at the box office simply was not enough! The crisis was ultimately averted, partly through the generosity of Utah Development Company and Foundation, which gave a solid quarter of a million, but the unwillingness of Winther to sacrifice standards at any price produced the expected repercussions.

Suddenly the importance of the box office, which the Australian Ballet had long acknowledged, took on a new meaning. Filling the house became all-important and discontent with Winther's determination to mix the esoteric with the popular repertoire became an obsession with some members of the company's board.

These lines, belatedly added long after the completion of the book, were written too close to the event to see beyond the bland announcement of John Winther's resignation made in March 1977. Animosity to Winther from some singers and staff members was probably no worse than it is in any other case of an iron hand, no matter how velvet the glove, leading a large company. There were no public demonstrations of support for him, nor was there open glee at his fate.

It is to the credit of the board of directors that, having agreed to disagree with Winther, they did not accept his resignation before they had obtained the services of a man with all the qualifications needed to replace him, Peter Hemmings, who had been the Administrator of Scottish Opera since its foundation in 1962.

If Winther's regime was short, it was certainly effective and he left behind a company which had been welded into a first-class ensemble in the European tradition, though it still has a long way to go before a direct parallel can be drawn. Whether a closer approximation is desirable is a moot point. There are virtues to be copied, but there are also handicaps which, one hopes, will never be imposed in Australia: the immense bureaucracy which surrounds opera in Europe, for example. The Australian Opera has all the benefits of the European system – including, since 1974, superannuation for its staff and singers – without being directed from above by king-makers and king-breakers, though history may one day prove otherwise. For the first time a totally home-grown opera company has the respect of its colleagues in other countries. Let us hope that it remains respectable for ever.

ballet

Preamble

What came first, the chicken or the egg? A decision had to be made, when it was decided to produce a book on the history of two arts in Australia, as to which was to take precedence. Was it to be ballet and opera or opera and ballet? Which was the chicken and which the egg? One part had to be written before the other and I am afraid that I chose to tackle the harder task first. (The sword of Damocles, a publisher's deadline, hangs less threateningly when you have finished the major part of a book.)

Come to think of it, the chicken and egg simile is not that inappropriate; ballet as we know it today largely evolved from the ballet insert at the Paris Opera in the nineteenth century and it is almost possible to say that opera was the chicken which laid the golden egg of ballet, and should thus come first. No matter; opera is certainly not more important, let alone better, if you can use such a term about two totally different things. I say some harsh things about opera elsewhere in this book and I will, no doubt, say some harsh things about ballet in the pages to come. Let me, therefore, establish my credentials as a sincere lover of the art.

I was a founder member of the original Balletomanes Club in London back in 1937. (I have no idea whether it still exists; if it does, I am sure it is no longer the same club and that it most certainly is a better club – it could hardly be worse, since balletomanes at the time had only recently been invented by Arnold Haskell.) Being a balletomane does not mean being a balletomaniac. My attitude is that just because I like something does not mean that it is necessarily perfect. The only way we will ever approach perfection in anything is to realize the imperfectness of our idols in whatever area of life or art they may move. One-eyed hero worship does more harm to the worshipped object than harsh criticism. Let me do a little reminiscing about ballet to prove my point.

When I was sweet sixteen I was sixteen but not exactly sweet. Sweetness was for girls or ballet dancers and I had no intention of becoming either. Not wanting to be a girl was soundly based on personal experience, but ballet dancing was something known only through the inevitable caricatures in the comedy classics of the time.

Today things are somewhat different. Many a genuine Ocker sixteen year old may well have been enraptured by the pace and glamour of the Australian Ballet's *The Fool on the Hill* when it was staged for A.B.C. television in 1976. He would have had ample incentive to tune in after experiencing all forms of dance, including ballet, on the small screen. Things were different forty years ago.

I was not aware that I was living ballet history when I became a balletomane in 1936. I saw no special significance in the enchantment of my first *Giselle,* I merely thought it was something just too beautiful. It was quite a while before I discovered that I had witnessed the first appearance

To ballet through Beatlemania   Australian youth was given a painless introduction to ballet via *The Fool on the Hill* when it was televised in 1976. Music and story by the Beatles made it universally acceptable, Tim Goodchild's designs provided a feast of colour and the Australian Ballet reaped the benefits. Unfortunately the *Fool* did not transfer successfully to the stage medium, but there is hope of repeats on television in the future.

Kelvin Coe (left) as The Fool and Paul Saliba (right) as his Alter Ego.

Lucy in the sky without diamonds — and without Lucy, who was danced by Lucette Aldous. The green ladies are the plants from the Land of Lucy (*below*) and the men are Goodchild's brilliant interpretation of the song's lyrics: 'Picture yourself on a train in a station, with plasticine porters with looking-glass ties'.

in the ballet of a sixteen year old dancer (later they said she was seventeen), one Margot Fonteyn. Candidly, I did not become a Fonteyn fan until she was into her forties; the young Margot had faults which people are prepared to admit today, but were not then. I had a lot more respect for Fonteyn's partner, Robert Helpmann. (I think Pearl Argyle was the Queen of the Wilis and I know Frederick Ashton was the villainous Hilarion.) In view of the fact that fate has catapulted me into the position of a ballet critic (and, after this, a ballet author) I suppose there could be some interest in the reasoning behind my young, and certainly inexperienced, judgement of what has become an historic occasion.

In those days casts in the Vic-Wells Ballet playing at Sadler's Wells never changed and, as I almost immediately began to attend both performances the company gave each week every week for years, I saw Fonteyn and Helpmann dance in *Giselle* many, many times. (It seems like hundreds, but it was probably only about forty or fifty before the war interrupted us so rudely.) It would be foolish to say that I remember every detail of that first performance, but it is very vivid in my mind and the following years strengthened my opinions of it; in fact, I think I have total recall mainly because I was so busy fighting for my opinions tooth and nail; Fonteyn very quickly became the gallery's darling and I was the odd man out. Let me use Fonteyn and Helpmann as the yardsticks of the opinions with which the reader who goes past this point will be saddled. And if any of you happen to differ, good luck to you! I'll stick to my way and you stick to your way, and if either of us ever gets to Scotland, it'll be *La Sylphide* he'll see and not *Giselle*.

The young Margot Fonteyn was not only very young, but her technique left a great deal to be desired. She was not strong, had balancing problems which prevented her from holding an *arabesque* or *attitude* and she generally covered sloppiness in technique with charm. For several years even the latter was absent whenever she was involved in classical ballets like *Swan Lake,* or that first *Sleeping Princess* in 1939; her fairly mobile features set into grim determination in every preparation for difficult *enchaînements* and lapsed into a dreadful artificial grin on their completion. At that time Fonteyn was a delight in character ballets like *Wedding Bouquet, Nocturne* or *Façade* (she danced the Polka then, not the Tango), but in classical roles I was not prepared to overlook her weaknesses through starry-eyed adulation, as others did.

Helpmann was a different proposition. His technique never even reached Fonteyn's basic one. He was a flawed dancer, if ever there was one – and he will be the first to admit it. But Helpmann was an artist who could make you forget his faults in any role at all. I saw him dance all the great classical ballets with those ridiculous *entrechats*

and one-and-a-half *double tours*. I quickly caught on to the fact that he was not doing what I thought he was doing; that his *double tours* began a quarter of the way around and ended a quarter of the way before facing front. But every movement began and ended precisely on the music, there was not the slightest sign of effort, there was not an ungraceful moment and there was an intensity of characterization in even the most negative role that swept all before it. He was an artist!

Can a critic be a fan? Can a fan be a critic? I say the answer to both questions is yes, though I know examples of both who are quite beyond reconciling the two. I was always a fan as far as Helpmann was concerned, but I accepted his faults for what they were – limitations beyond which he could never go, no matter how hard he tried (and Helpmann was and is a worker!). He used artifice to create a world of make-believe and that is what theatre is all about. To the fans of Fonteyn, among whom I was not, she could do no wrong; hers was the right way, no matter what the text books may have said. An *arabesque* was a movement in which she moved slowly onto point until she overbalanced and slid into the next step. That is the way Fonteyn did it and that is the way the screaming hordes wanted it. She was too young to hide her faults with artistry, as the older Helpmann could. (But, I suspect that he did it instinctively before he ever joined the Vic-Wells Ballet.)

What happened at Sadler's Wells was, of course, totally insignificant compared with what went on at Covent Garden, and later Drury Lane. The Ballet Russe was playing there and people who went to the Ballet Russe never, but never, went to Sadler's Wells. Fonteyn was not in the same class as Toumanova, Baronova or Riaboushinska, who were no older than she! I fear that in this particular area of fan worship I had to agree, but I could not accept that the miserable Russian seasons, for all their occasional brilliances, were artistically better than the polished performances of the Vic-Wells Ballet. Most were pathetic attempts to stick together ill-rehearsed dancers of no very great worth in costumes which often had actually been used in the original Diaghilev Ballet. The Bakst *Schéhérazade,* which created a sensational impact with its colours in 1910, looked pretty washed out in 1938, the aging Tchernicheva was no oriental sex-pot and Shabelevsky gave no hint of what we had read about Nijinsky's performance as the Golden Slave.

All of this sounds like carping about an era which people envy me for having witnessed. Well, envy in peace! I gloried in it. I starved to attend eight performances a week for one six-week season at Covent Garden and would have gone back for more, but I gloried in it because I saw the faults as well as the beauty and when the faults grew less, when a performance approached faultlessness, it was an experience to be treasured. The glory of ballet – and of opera – is to see and hear people overcome the hurdles which choreographers and composers have set for them. It is instant pleasure, not the kind of artificial perfection which recordings or films can create these days.

Australians have been fortunate in that they have seen a great deal of good ballet, but until fairly recently the exposure has been severely limited and, even today, comparative standards are not easy to obtain in this country. It is hard to be a balletomane when you have to see the same company year in, year out. Half the fun of being enthusiastic about dancing is fighting with others about your own favourites and when the number of dancers and ballets at your disposal is limited, it becomes very hard to find something new to fight about. In this age of rising costs you can't even, as I did, form a ballet company if you are a frustrated dancer. It has been done in this country, many times, but (a) how many people are willing to enter such a lunatic profession on the managerial side, and (b) how the devil do you finance it in an age when dancers expect to be paid a living wage? (Half the secret of the rise in dancing standards today can be found in the square meals dancers get every day.) Being a balletomane in Australia can be pretty frustrating.

Being a ballet historian in Australia can be pretty frustrating too. Ballet has always lived in the creativeness of choreographers. The number of 'classics' is severely limited. You can play and replay famous operas for years on end, but ballet is a much more consuming art and neither the dancers nor their directors could live without a regular supply of new works to perform. It has been that way since ballet first started and, by the look of it, will continue that way for as long as ballet is around. And that brings me back to the difference between dancing and ballet or, to be even more precise: dancing, ballet dancing and ballet.

Let me dismiss dancing as such from our calculations. You can do an excellent Irish Jig or Scottish reel or tap dance or frug (remember frugging?) but that doesn't qualify you to take up ballet. You can learn how to pass your Cecchetti examinations, do the *Aurora pas de deux* and get a diploma to teach ballet, but that doesn't qualify you to take up ballet either.

Ballet in its true sense is much more than just dancing, it is a combination of many arts: music, drama, painting, yes, and also dancing. Perhaps dancing is the heart of the whole thing, but half the things wrong with what is vaguely described as 'modern ballet' is the fact that it mostly consists of dancing without many of the other components. It is pure movement without dramatic feeling; something which happens, begins and then stops, sometimes even without music! There must be a place for experimentation in ballet, or dance if you like, but 'modern ballet' remains modern for only as long as the current run of the current fad. How

many 'modern ballets' have become classics? Name one! And don't tell me that they haven't been round for long enough – I saw modern ballets of pretty high standards forty years ago and what were considered modern classics ten years later have long been forgotten. What happened to Nijinska's *The Blue Train*, Lifar's *Icare* or Massine's *Choreartium?* Yet the *Swan Lakes* and *Petrouchkas* and *Pineapple Polls* go on for ever.

When it comes to the early history of ballet in Australia, the field is even more barren than that of opera. At least one can report the performance of the great Verdi or Puccini works, but Australian operas of the past are no more than names on a piece of paper and the same applies to ballets, only more so. The ephemerality of choreography prior to the invention of film and video tape meant it had to rely on the memory of man to survive. We know that even the great classics of the past have not passed unscathed through the fires of reconstruction by many hands. How then, can we expect to gain an insight into ballets performed, say, a hundred years ago in Australia? There was nobody here to record them, even if methods of writing them down had been invented.

The manuscripts of forgotten operas can be found and studied, but the ballets have vanished into the shadows of time. One result is that the history of ballet in this country, as retold in these pages, will be inordinately short, until we come to living memory. What is the point of listing here all the ballets and dancers of the nineteenth century when we know so little of them? Names alone do not mean very much. The academic record of all that has happened in this field must one day be written and will one day be written, probably by Edward H. Pask, the Archivist of the Australian Ballet. The first volume of his labours, *Enter the Colonies, Dancing!* has been completed. It takes him up to the First World War. Dare I hope that interest aroused by this volume will produce a demand that the chronology be completed and published?

What I offer you here is but a way of discovering – painlessly, I hope – enough to interest the average person in ballet. The ballet lover and balletomane will need no urging to read this first attempt to cover the history however superficially, of ballet in Australia. The same applies in the case of opera lovers and the other half of this volume. The purpose of the exercise is to cross-fertilize (if you will forgive such an invasion of your privacy) the two. If you are a ballet lover, do at least glance at the opera section. You may (I hope) find it interesting. And if you do, there is hope that some opera buff may read your half of the book and you'll meet him at the ballet. Here's hoping.

Keeping our Distance

1

Regardless of modern technology, Australia still suffers from time lag in everything from trade to politics to art. Direct communication via satellite can bring a live performance of ballet from anywhere in the world into our sitting-room in full colour as clearly as if it emanated from a studio in the next suburb. The fact that the only such telecast at the time of writing presented only celebrity interviews before and during a performance of the Australian Ballet in Washington is an indication of our priorities; political figures and pop stars took precedence over ballet on the night of our own company's gala opening in the American capital. We have as yet to see any live production of a theatrical event via television, yet there is no limit to the coverage of tennis or cricket, no matter where in the world it may be taking place. It makes you think, doesn't it?

To keep up with current trends it is necessary to experience some part at least of what everybody is doing in a particular field. The time when interstate, let alone intercontinental communications will cater to minorities, such as ballet lovers, is still in the distant future. With the best will in the world our ballet administrators, who can and do visit other world centres at regular intervals, cannot bring to the Australian public what London audiences can see at home or by travelling to other centres of dance activity. Distance, the barrier between Australia and the world, becomes greater according to the relative importance of the subject of interest; it is very easy to keep up with world politics, less easy to be up-to-date in business and pretty hard to find out what's what in ballet.

Second-hand art is not considered art by many, but it can bring an understanding of trends. Colour reproductions of new artist's paintings can bring a far greater appreciation of the art scene than photographs of new ballets can for the ballet scene. Even filmed ballet, which has been tried extensively, is no more convincing than reproductions of paintings. In any case, costs alone make it totally impossible to bring all that is happening in dance throughout the world to Australia. If, one day, the projected nightmare of no more live theatre actually does come true, if we are only to see ballet and opera and drama via closed-circuit television, then Australia will be in the mainstream of the world scene. Whether anybody will still want to be there is a different matter, of course, but for the moment the reality is that we, the audiences in Australia, cannot be *au fait* with all that is going on in dance elsewhere.

Let nobody deny the claims of the Australian Ballet that it is a world-class company, it is certainly that. But the life-blood of dance and ballet lies in the multiplicity of styles being created and recreated by many, not a few. One great company doesn't make a ballet spring and the smaller groups in Australia most definitely do not have the kind of exposure to world trends that are essential if they are to be creative in the true sense of the word.

Perhaps the meaning of the word 'creativity', as I shall be using it, should be spelt out. There is more than one way of looking at anything which involves individuals being creative. This book, like all books on the arts, must necessarily be biased in more ways than one. No author, no matter how hard he tries, can be completely non-partisan. At best he can make sure that his prejudices, if such they be, are understood by the reader, so that he or she can make up her or his mind whether he or she agrees with any specific premise or opinion.

There is no such thing as spontaneous creation in ballet. Like all art, ballet has been undergoing a gradual process of evolution over many centuries. Individuals have added and subtracted at will, but the claims of 'originality' are invariably false. As Schoenberg rejected harmony, as Picasso rejected realism, so did Isadora Duncan, Mary Wigman, Rudolf von Laban, Kurt Jooss, Martha Graham and dozens of others reject classical ballet. Like Schoenberg in music, they one and all discovered that rejection of one thing does not necessarily mean the substitution of something else. Their theories invariably meant not the creation of something new, but the elimination of something old – and modern ballet to this day follows the same principles. Works may be 'different' in some way, but the basic components are the same as they have always been, reshuffled, restated, re-what-have-you.

The day has already dawned in which music is being written by computers and the new notation methods of dance and ballet will, no doubt, produce a computer choreographed ballet in the near future. The key to the whole problem can be summarized in one statement, which is no more original than anything else in the art world: given enough time, any monkey (or computer) could write the works of Shakespeare; the words are all there for anyone to use, it is only a matter of arranging them in a certain fashion. So also with ballet, using movements instead of words.

For the sake of the argument (otherwise this book will never get started) let us accept that all dance is an extension of movements previously created by others. If so, it is essential that a country as far away from the core of activities in the Northern hemisphere as Australia is should have access to all that is happening at all times, and that is an impossibility now and in the forseeable future; ergo: ballet and dance in Australia lag behind the rest of the world, although not as much as some people may claim.

Return now to the beginnings of this country and the decades which followed it, when it took three months to travel from London to Botany Bay, when no ballet, native or imported, had ever been seen by the greater part of the population, when artists performed before audiences and critics who had no standards of any kind by which they could

A guest star of 1855 Aurelia Dimier in the Spanish Dance from *Paquita*, which she led in Paris together with one Mlle Caroline. In 1855 as in 1955 Australia's guest stars were not out of the top drawer, though Dimier was a pretty good catch at that time. The roles she danced in the ballets she reconstructed herself in Australia were not those she danced in Paris.

assess what was being presented to them. Can we really accept as genuine, for example, the press reports of the 1850s and their technical jargon?

When *La fille mal gardée* was premiered in Sydney in 1855 with the French dancer, Aurelia Dimier in the title role, she enchanted the critics. '... she showed much united elegance and power, the poses, *pas de fascination*, balancing *point de pied*, and those *pirouettes*, being such as never before attempted on a colonial stage.' Apart from having to interpret the meaning of expressions like *'pas de fascination'*, what were the standards by which the writer judged Mlle Dimier? Few will deny the likelihood that she may well have done things 'never before attempted on a colonial stage', but what was her dancing really like and, even more to the point, what was this version of *La fille mal gardée* like? It needs no detective to discover that a bare recitation of the facts as stated in the colonial press of the time hardly gives a true picture of ballet in the 1850s in Australia.

The dancer in question, the 'star' in question, had been trained at the Paris Opera under the guidance of teachers like Jean Coralli, the creator of *Giselle* fourteen years earlier. She did dance beside genuine stars like Fanny Elssler, Lucille Grahn and Carlotta Grisi, first in the corps de ballet and then in small roles. The list of ballets in which she appeared in Paris is not that long, but it includes some works which are still played, including *Giselle*. So, Aurelia Dimier danced a small part in *Giselle*. In fact, she was one of the Giselle's friends!

In Sydney Dimier also danced the leading role in *Le diable a quatre,* in the Paris premiere of which she claimed she had appeared. If she appeared at all, it was in the corps de ballet, because her name is not listed in the original cast! Let us be realistic: Dimier danced roles in Paris, but not as a *prima ballerina*. Her claims to fame lay in her face and her figure, both of which stood her in good stead during a nine year stint of touring America before she came to Australia. Only if American standards of the 1850s were acceptable as a rule of thumb, would Dimier have been a ballerina worthy of *La fille mal gardée*. Unfortunately, most of the United States was balletically little more advanced than Australia at that time.

My purpose in dwelling on the virtues, or otherwise, of Mlle Dimier is to be, frankly, evasive. A detailed history of the dancers and ballets which were seen in Australia in the nineteenth century may have historic value, but not a great deal of interest to the average balletomane. I propose to gloss over the period fairly quickly. If there were indeed artistic highlights, as there well may have been, we cannot rely on the evidence available to us to decide what dancers or what ballets affected the history of dance in this country. Academic research into the chronology of Terpsichorean episodes in the history of Australia does not belong in these pages. We are concerned with the overall picture, rather than the detail, until we come to that part of our past which can be discussed at first or second hand with some authority.

Ballet in the Colonies

2

In the nineteenth century ballet in Australia was inextricably attached to opera. Just as opera was the most important form of theatre in Europe a hundred years ago, so it was in Australia. And ballet, as in Europe, was usually attached to an opera company, to provide an essential part of the performance. Paris was the artistic capital of Europe and Paris demanded ballet in its operas. But there is not very much doubt that the rise of ballet in Paris in the days of Meyerbeer and Halévy was brought about by the demands of the flesh rather than the soul. At the risk of upsetting some of the more delicately artistic souls among my readers, the facts which brought ballet as we know it into being must be briefly reviewed; it will also help to bring the Australian scene into perspective.

The court ballets of Louis XIV were indeed art in the true sense of the word, though they may have been very far from what we consider ballet today. A hundred years later Jean Georges Noverre laid down the principles of ballet which apply to this day, just as Gluck established the *raison d'être* of opera. Yet, by the time a further hundred years had passed the Paris Opera and its patrons had begun to popularize both arts to an extent which neither Noverre nor Gluck could have foreseen. From a historical point of view this bringing art to the people as popular entertainment was undoubtedly the best thing that ever happened, but the corruption of France's Second and Third Empires also extended into the arts.

The importance of ballet at the Opera in Paris was not, repeat not, based on its artistic values. Mlle Dimier, soon to be hailed in Australia, also had her admirers there, though she was only in the corps de ballet. Actresses and opera singers were thought to be, and often were, high-class prostitutes, though their behaviour on stage was decorous in the extreme. Only in the ballet were they at liberty to do the otherwise unforgivable, to show legs and (if you managed to get the much sought after front row seats) even the frilly knickers into which those extremities disappeared. The reality is there for all to see, though few are willing to admit it: the ballet in Paris, the same ballet which, via Italy and Russia, has come down to us as the art we love, was the nineteenth century equivalent of the modern girlie show, made respectable under the thin disguise of art for art's sake. People went to the opera to see the ballet! If proof is needed, read the history of the *Tannhäuser* scandal; Wagner's opera had to be taken off because he placed his Venusberg ballet in the first act and when the bulk of the audience arrived in time to see the usual second act ballet, they found they had missed their favourite leg show. The riots which followed are well and truly chronicled.

It is, therefore, not surprising that Australia followed in the footsteps of Europe. Performances of opera contained some dancing whenever possible. If the action of the opera

La Cachucha The most commonly danced 'ballet' of colonial times was no more than another Spanish dance, which is rarely performed these days. Madame Céline Céleste hardly looked like this when she performed it nightly in Australia in 1867; she had been retired from the ballet for twenty-four years and was then a fifty-six year old actress – which didn't stop her from contributing *La Cachucha* to Australia's ballet history.

made any kind of leg show inadmissible, the ballet was staged after the opera, but before the straight play or farce which always ended the evening's entertainment. It was opera, ballet, play, for decade after decade. All three were judiciously cut and standards were not the highest. Initially, the ballets were no more than dances; Irish jigs, Scottish reels, polkas, *La cachucha* or perhaps some dimly remembered solo, *pas de deux* or *pas de trois* from a famous ballet. The dancers who presented them were hardly what even the European audiences of the day would have called first class; more often than not they appeared in both the opera and the play as well, and you may be sure that their principal employment was as singers and actors rather than as dancers. Reading the fine print in our history, it is doubtful whether many of our most notable 'dancers' could ever have danced in ballet in Australia. What, for example, does one make of Madame Céline Céleste, a famous Paris-born dancer who, in 1867, after a twenty-four year career as a straight actress in London, toured Australia at the age of fifty-six and danced *La cachucha* after each performance of *The Woman in Red*? (With great success, I hasten to add.) Are we to accept Madame Céleste as a pioneer of ballet in Australia? Whatever her virtues during her early years in ballet, an elderly *actress* doing a Spanish dance added little to our history.

Artists, be they dancers or singers or actors (or all three), had to be versatile in colonial days. In the case of dancers, the circus was never very far away and why should it have been? The Russian technique on which all modern and classical ballet is based is an amalgam of the French theatre and Italian circus traditions. Thirty-two *fouettés* hardly constitutes an aesthetic experience; they are a circus trick and it shows, however much applause they may raise. When we come to dancers seen in Australia in the nineteenth century, we often find that they are mountebanks of some sort. In 1841 a French dancer named Charrière made a sensational first appearance in a *pas seul* on stilts (!) and the public was just as delighted with J. H. Flexmore, 'danseur pantomimist and trapeze artist extraordinaire'. Others were more candid about the true nature of their art; presumably Monsieur delle Case (surely Signor delle Case) will have a place in the history of dance in Australia, even though his company was billed as a 'Pantomimic and Gymnastic Troupe'.

That word 'pantomime' plays a very large part in the early balletic history of the country. Next to appearing in opera, dancers appeared most often in pantomime in pantomime, if you see what I mean; the former word is taken in its real sense – the acting of a part without the use of words – and the latter is the good old English Christmas show for children of all ages, which invariably features a traditional harlequinade staged in mime and dance.

It is almost impossible to state that ballet or even dance began at any one point in Australia. A year after the sup-

THE CACHUCHA
as danced by
CELESTE
with
UNE VALSE SENTIMENTALE
NEW YORK
Published by FIRTH & HALL *No 1 Franklin Sqre*

posed first opera, Bishop's *Clari, or The Maid of Milan* (in 1834), Barnett Levey in the same Theatre Royal in Sydney presented *The Fair Maid of Perth, or The Rival Lovers,* which may or may not have been a ballet, as *Clari* may or may not have been an opera. The principal dancers were Mrs Jones and Mr Fitzgerald and neither is heard from again in balletic terms, unless you count their efforts at running a dancing academy in those early years. One presumes (does anybody *know* what really happened in those days in the colonies?) that they taught ladies and gentlemen to dance quadrilles and the like; it seems extremely unlikely that Sydney would have sported an academy of theatrical dancing in the 1830s.

The first genuine dancer whose public appearance is recorded was not exactly typical either. Rachel Lazar was all of ten years old when she arrived in Sydney with her father, the only survivors of a big family from a shipwreck en route from England. Rachel had been learning ballet in London and she entertained audiences during plays in which her father appeared at the Theatre Royal in 1837. Whether the *Cinderella* in which she played Cinders was ballet or pantomime is a moot point, however, and the inability of the Press to judge what she was doing already points to things to come; Rachel Lazar's Cinderella was preferred because 'Sydney is not yet sufficiently *Italianized* to relish the lascivious motions of foreign figurantes'. How close could ten year old Rachel have come to being lascivious?

Thereafter dancers appearing in the colonies came and went with monotonous regularity. In the early years their income came mainly from teaching, but stage performers began gradually to settle on a permanent basis and some names began to appear more and more regularly. Rachel and her colleagues mainly provided interludes before, during or after operas or plays. Hornpipes, jigs and the like were the most common, but there was the occasional appearance of dance forms, the existence of which nobody in Europe would have suspected. Whatever was the *Cracoquick* which a Mr Phillips performed in *Fidelio* (!?) in 1839?

The early 'ballets', like the early 'operas' of those days, were primitive indeed – more notable for their inventive titles than any choreographic originality. The motto was: anything to get the public to pay for its entertainment – and it was indeed entertainment rather than art which the public sought. The box office value of titles like *The Freaks of Milor Plum Podin, Polichinelle Vampire* or *Tawny in a Galloping Consumption* obviously owed more to farce or melodrama than to ballet.

The Tasmanian adventures which launched the Carandinis on the Australian opera scene in the 1830s should be mentioned again (see also Opera section), since Count Gerome Carandini was stated to be a dancer, though he made his debut as a singer in Boieldieu's opera *Jean de Paris*. Count Gerome and his colleagues danced as well as they sang (or sang as badly as they danced), but Carandini himself appears to have been the exception rather than the rule, though to what extent his mazurkas and tarantellas extended into the ballet field is not known. Carandini married a Hobart girl, who also took part in the performances as Madame Carandini. Two other multi-talented artists were Frank Howson and his wife. Indications are that in later years Mrs Howson, whose dancing was much admired, tagged along with Carandini, while Madame Carandini went off with Mr Howson to sing in grand opera, each in time also turning impresario. All four pop up all over the place for the next few decades, though there appears to be no direct evidence that other than professional reasons were behind the separate careers which, at times, merged as they met in the limited venues open to all four.

The word 'copyright' existed as little in Australia as in America in the mid-1800s. The name of any attraction was flagrantly plagiarized, and there is no evidence that in the case of ballets there was very much relation between the various presentations bearing the same title, specially when that title belonged to a known literary classic. Hence, the reappearance of *The Fair Maid of Perth* in Hobart and Melbourne, as arranged by the English dancer Charles Young in 1843, would hardly have had any connection with that supposed first ballet in Sydney eight years earlier. (Come to that, we have no evidence that Young's 'ballet' was a proper ballet either!) The meaning of titles becomes a little more important when it comes to works that still survive. Was *La Sylphide* as presented by Young in many of our cities over several years the ballet created for Marie Taglioni by her father in 1832, or was it some concoction of Young's own? I am afraid we shall never know. In any case, Filippo Taglioni's choreography did not survive even in Europe. It is possible, even likely, that some section – a *pas seul* or *pas de deux* – from the ballet might have been reconstructed by Young if he danced in it in London, but we do not know even that.

Dancing appears to have been a family business in those days, possibly another link with the circus background. The first blood-related group to make a name in Australia was the Chambers family, father Joe, daughter Amy and two sons, Joseph and Sydney. Joe, a former member of the corps de ballet of the Royal Italian Opera in London, made a 'sensational' debut in 1842 with a Highland Fling! A few years later he was ready to step in when Young was suddenly dismissed by his impresario, George Coppin. Though he never danced with Young, Chambers staged what must have been yet another *Fair Maid of Perth;* it could not possibly have been Young's. Still, in those days choreography was almost certainly as haphazard as opera production; that is, dancers would more often than not make up their own steps, under the rough guidance of the leader of the group, in this case Chambers.

To quote once again the doubtful value of the reports on which any Australian historian must rely, as late as 1851 *The South Australian Register* in reviewing the Chambers family blandly stated: 'The novelty of real stage dancing has been much desired.' If stage dancing was still a novelty, how could the same writer then continue to assess Chambers' 'aerial steps and pirouettes (in which) he stands unrivalled in the Australian Colonies'? Whatever operatic standards were in Australia in the 1850s, at least the singers sang the music which London and Paris heard. Ballet in Australia at that time must been extremely primitive by comparison.

The Chambers family was followed by many other family groups, some originating in Australia, but most imported *en bloc,* sometimes even by accident. If Melbourne impresario George Coppin had not lost his way in a London fog in 1857, mistaking the Marylebone for the Haymarket Theatre (it must have been a pretty thick fog for him to go quite that far astray), Australia would never have seen the Leopolds, three brothers and Fräulein Fannie, the latter being the wife of Henry Leopold; Coppin was looking for the famous Perea Neña Spanish dancing troupe! It so happened that the Leopolds were more balletically minded, having travelled throughout Europe where they had even attended classes with the famous teacher August Bournonville in Copenhagen. They were able to reassure Coppin when he discovered his mistake by duplicating (?) *The Spanish Dancers, or Galician Fête,* which had brought such fame to Perea Neña in London. More to the point, they were launched in Melbourne in 1857 in the pantomime *Dick Whittington,* which was 'redeemed from partial failure' by their presence. Perea Neña would hardly have been suitable for saving Dick Whittington with or without his cat.

The Leopolds broke up after the death of brother Tom, though the others, and their children, pop up all over the place in later years. Brother George finally went into operetta as a singer, with some success; most probably it was a craft he also practised in his dancing years when the occasion demanded. The Edouins, the Martinettis, the Lehmanns, the Duvalli Sisters ('operatic and acrobatic danseuses'), not to mention the many soloists, often with partners, like Thérèse Strebinger, Carandini, Dimier and the rest, crisscrossed the continent, joining, splitting, filling in and generally establishing a following for dance, though ballet (as we know it) was not yet the correct word for it. They were the great days of the gold rushes, of an avalanche of immigrants hungry for entertainment. The dancing segment of a night at the theatre was quite often also its highlight, not least when it happened to be performed by Lola Montes, whose impact on Australia was quite out of all proportion to her own abilities as a dancer, as we shall see.

Lola Montes to Lyster

The short six months Lola Montes spent in Australia in 1855 contain more than just the abundance of scandal and adventure which have turned the lady into a legend second only to Ned Kelly. Montes (for reasons which are not clear, she was always billed as Montes in Australia and Montez in Europe) was the kind of fake which was not uncommon in colonial days – an artistic confidence trickster imposing a curtain of publicity between herself and the true judgement she should have received. Adverse criticism in Australia was moral, not artistic in her case. Local journalists, who had no standards of comparison beyond what they had seen prior to 1855, probably thought her dancing ability as good as the advertisements claimed; it was her scandalous behaviour on and off the stage to which they objected, and which they reported at great lengths!

Lola Montes was not even a dancer; she was an actress! Or, at least, acting was her livelihood when she was not busy extracting money from unsuspecting men, including various husbands and at least one king – poor mad Ludwig of Bavaria, the champion of Wagner. In any other context it would be reported that Lola Montes came to Australia and appeared in a series of plays, starting with one specially written for her, to capitalize on her association with King Ludwig, *Lola Montes in Bavaria,* and following with anything from *School for Scandal,* in which she played Lady Teazle, to long-forgotten plays like *Morning Call* and *Maidens Beware!* Possibly wary of a repetition of the scandals which had followed her around the world, Montes appears to have played things quietly at first, only resurrecting her infamous *Spider Dance* after a full month of performances during which any dancing she did raised little comment.

Lola was no Spanish harridan (much as she tried to pretend she was) but a Limerick Lass, born Eliza Gilbert in 1818, who had married a captain in the British army in India. It was only after she returned to London at the age of twenty-four, having left her husband, that she began to act and decided to learn some Spanish dances to go with her Latin good looks. Her subsequent career was far from notable, except for the off-stage scandals that followed her wherever she went.

An indication of Paris theatre standards of the time may be gained from the fact that she made her debut at the Paris Opera by performing two Spanish dances in Mozart's *Don Giovanni*! And it was here in Paris that an all-embracing criticism of Lola Montes, the dancer, was written by a man who knew what dancing was all about, Théophile Gautier, the greatest ballet critic of the romantic era and author of the *Giselle* libretto. Wrote Gautier: 'Mlle Lola Montes has nothing Andalusian about her except a magnificent pair of black eyes . . . one can say that she has a small foot and pretty legs. But the manner in which she uses them, that is quite another thing!'

Lola left Paris in disgrace. Lola left Bavaria in disgrace. But Lola was a success in Australia; an artistic success, if hardly a moral one. She left the manuscript and rights of *Lola Montes in Bavaria* to Andrew Torning, the licensee of the theatre in which she made her first and last appearances in Australia, Sydney's Royal Victoria, and consequently her name was kept before the public long after she left. Nobody before had ever had quite so much personal publicity and anything to do with Lola Montes filled the house long after she had died in, of all places, Brooklyn, New York, U.S.A.

What continued to fill the house more than *Lola Montes in Bavaria* was the famous *Spider Dance*, which was Lola's way of stirring things up at the box office when the mere mention of her name was not enough. It cannot be established when Lola started to use the dance, or even the title, but the suggestiveness of her dancing seems to have started only with its use. In 1845 she had other methods to scandalize Paris – the shedding of undergarments, to name but one.

It seems more than likely that the *Spider Dance* was nothing more than a simple tarantella, suitably enhanced by the shaking of skirts, legs, bottom and bust, all of which Lola possessed in amplitude. Reports clearly describe a dance in which violent attempts are made to shake one or more spiders from the skirts of the dancer and the killing of the spider(s) by stamping of the feet. The tarantella comes from Southern Italy and is said to be based on the effects of the bite of a tarantula on a person. Lola's pretended nationality was Spanish and Spanish dancing involves skirt-shaking and foot-stamping galore; it seems but a short logical progression from tarantella to *Spider Dance,* specially when considering that Lola herself was able to present a *Spider's Dance* fitting the same description before the staid Adelaide audiences without raising an eyebrow. If eyebrows must be raised on balletic grounds it should be at Lola's use of castanets, yet music in tarantella rhythm often uses the Spanish instrument for this Italian dance.

Lola's non-dancing adventures in Australia have been recounted elsewhere in much detail. One can but admire a woman who, in the midst of the Victorian age, managed to faze a bailiff by defying him to arrest her when she greeted him in the nude, a true and much better story than the horse whipping of the editor of the *Ballaarat Times;* she could do that with impunity in a city of goldminers who revelled in Lola's antics on stage and showered her with nuggets instead of bouquets. If Lola managed to retire to New York and devote herself to assisting needy women, it may well have been through the generosity of the Australian mining towns.

While Lola Montes was scandalizing Australia, ballet (or dance) went on as before and the premiere on 29 October 1855 of *Giselle* in Melbourne should be recorded, though it was very much a premature attempt to follow the grand tradition. Only one thing paralleled the Paris original: it was, like all other ballet of the time and of many years to come, part of a multi-media bill. In Paris the premiere of *Giselle* fourteen years earlier had been given in tandem with the third act of Rossini's opera *Mosé*. In Melbourne it joined Bellini's *La Sonnambula*. The great difference between the two occasions lay in the quality of performances. The local opera may not have been a patch on the magnificence of Paris' *Mosé*, one of the grandest of grand operas presented at the very height of the opera boom, but it was superb compared with what passed for *Giselle*. The brand new Melbourne Theatre Royal was a fine venue for the experiment, but the fact that Thérèse Strebinger had herself danced Giselle in Madrid prior to coming to Australia hardly qualified her to stage a ballet of this size, specially when the total of the company's ensemble consisted of two dancers and a ballet master (our old friend Carandini). Advertisements went out for twenty young ladies 'as pupils for the corps de ballet'. They were trained (from scratch!) by Carandini, not Strebinger, though the Italian count had arrived in Australia before he could possibly have seen the ballet, let alone have appeared in it. Carandini also danced Albrecht to Strebinger's Giselle! The public and the Press were not impressed. *Giselle* was presented at the end of a long evening '. . . and a most lame and impotent conclusion it was!'. There was no second performance.

Three years later, in 1858, Jules and Thérèse Schmidt, a pair of French dancers, tried again, presumably using the Theatre Royal's costumes from Strebinger's abortive earlier production. (Costumes and scenery belonged to the theatre in the days when licensees employed the artists to perform.) This time *Giselle* was the expected hit and the Schmidts restaged it in Sydney during the following year.

Ballet was still no more than an attachment to mixed performances. Lola Montes' friend Torning for some years ran an opera company of sorts with ballet attached in Sydney, but the real chance for ballet came with the arrival of William Saurin Lyster and his Opera Company from America. Primitive as it was by our standards, it was vastly better than anything seen before in Australia (see Opera section) and a serious attempt was made to follow the fashions of Paris, meaning that Lyster had to present his operas with suitable ballets. For the first time something resembling a ballet company came into being in Australia. (Just to keep our values straight: in 1861 not even Paris saw complete evenings devoted to ballet very often, if at all. The next ballet milestone in that city, *Coppélia* in 1870, was presented as a double bill with Weber's opera *Der Freischütz*! Let us remember this when evaluating the endeavours of the next few decades of our own balletic history.)

Lola Montes lecturing John Bull on the United States A caricature of the most famous dancer to visit Australia in the nineteenth century, which demonstrates the political power she was able to wield even after leaving this country. She is lathering John Bull's face with 'soft soap' under a picture of Ludwig of Bavaria hanging on the wall. The purpose of the drawing is to warn the Americans that Lola's imminent arrival in 1859 is a threat to their security. But Lola had reformed by then. The woman who had faced an Australian bailiff in the nude died two years later in Brooklyn while running a home for needy women!

Lyster's 'ballet company' was headed by Jules Schmidt and included Thérèse, his ballerina wife, Joseph Chambers, Thérèse Strebinger, the 'trapeze artist extraordinaire', J. H. Flexmore, and a corps de ballet of twelve. Guest artists were added as required and most of the dancers in Australia at some time or another appeared with Lyster.

The year 1867 proved to be an early peak in Australian ballet to which all before had been only a prelude. Two American groups arrived simultaneously and opened in Melbourne and Sydney. The Martinetti Troupe and the Lehmann Ballet followed the pattern of earlier family groups, but were a lot more ambitious. Though both still played in mixed bills, they did try to present something close to real ballets – in fact, the Martinettis prior to departing for New Zealand gave what may well have been the first complete evening of ballet in Australia. On 29 November 1867 they played a triple bill at the Theatre Royal in Sydney of *L'étoile du marin, Jocko, the Brazilian Ape* and *La Viviandière*. There were no less than twenty-six dancers in the company and standards appear to have been reasonably high – at least, audiences and critics were enthusiastic. *Jocko* in particular was an instant hit and, during the Melbourne season, was seen eighteen times in six weeks. As had happened previously with popular ballets, copies of *Jocko, the Brazilian Ape* (a ballet directly – if perhaps not very accurately – descending from a Paris original by Fillipo Taglioni) were to multiply over the years. Coincidentally, it was also in the repertoire of the Lehmann Ballet which, arriving at the same time, but in a different city, clearly had not copied it from the Martinettis. Paul Martinetti's Jocko enchanted one and all. 'His imitation of a monkey is marvellous; he runs, leaps, bounds and chatters ... etc. etc.' Chatters? Obviously we are still dealing with echoes of the circus-cum-variety-act kind of ballet. There was also some criticism that there was more pantomime than dancing.

The Lehmanns in Sydney were possibly an even greater success, because they were more ambitious. The company numbered thirty-five after adding a fair share of local talent, including the two Schmidts, who had left Lyster. Again the circus aspect came forth; John Haslam (known as 'Young America') was described as a pantomimist-gymnast. The Lehmanns offered Sydney *La Sylphide* in what must have been the first Australian presentation to resemble the original ballet in areas other than name alone. When the company moved to Melbourne it joined a remarkable conglomerate of dancing ensembles for a small colonial city in 1867. The Lehmann Ballet opened at the Royal Haymarket Theatre, while the Martinettis were at the Theatre Royal. Lyster's Opera Company was playing Meyerbeer's *Robert the Devil* at the Princess with a corps de ballet and principals totalling eighteen, and two other minor theatres had variety bills which included dancing groups, not to mention Madame Céline Céleste, whose play was on the same bill with the Lehmanns and who was still dancing her nightly *Cachucha!*

The Lehmann season at the Haymarket was so successful that the company transferred to another theatre, The Varieties, where they played continuously for five months in 1868, without, however, giving any complete evenings of ballet. Some of the principals of the Martinetti Troupe returned from New Zealand to the fleshpots of Australia independently, and joined the Lehmann Ballet, strengthening it even further. When the company finally decided that the local market had been exhausted and departed from these shores, some of its dancers in turn decided to stay behind. The two Schmidts were well and truly residents by then and had no wish to wander further afield and John Haslam joined a circus as a trapeze artist. Gustav Massartic, originally principal dancer of the Martinettis, created a small touring company known as Le Ballet Massartic. But the fleshy temptations of the dance were still to produce more sensations than any ballet, no matter how artistic!

Ballet Improper to Ballet Proper

4

If Lola Montes scandalized Australia with her *Spider Dance,* the arrival of the *Cancan* did more. In Hobart police officers patrolled the Theatre Royal 'in the hope of preventing ANY performance of the *Cancan* taking place'. The performers, the Duvalli Sisters, saw the writing on the wall and got their applause by more legitimate means than their infamous predecessor; they were loudly applauded for their dancing skills alone. At least, one must assume it was the latter, unless one were to take literally what the *Hobart Town Mercury* reported in April 1874. Wrote the Mercury: 'The *Cancan* dance was performed during the evening, *the stage costume usually worn on the occasion having been discarded by the Sisters'.* (The italics are mine.)

The *Cancan* was a symptom of other than moral turpitude; it heralded the age of operetta and the temporary demise of what passed for ballet in those days. Dance is an essential part of operetta and from the 1870s onward the works of Offenbach and Strauss and their many colleagues passed across Australian stages. It was the chorus line rather than the Terpsichorean spectacles seen during the grand opera seasons which held the public's undivided attention.

The sensations of those years were not great dancers, but great tragedies. Fire took as fearsome a toll of Australian theatres as of European and American ones. Practically all the old theatres burnt down at some stage or the other; little wonder, in an age of open oil or gas stage lighting. There were also the local equivalents of the famous European dancers whose skirts caught alight. Fifteen year old dancer Fanny Lloyd died on 3 January 1873 as a result of burns sustained during a performance of *The Yellow Dwarf* (a pantomime) and two thousand people attended her funeral in Sydney. Pages can be recovered from contemporary newspapers about tragedies such as these, but comment on performances was still sadly deficient, if present at all.

Grand opera continued to be performed, of course, but the ballet content deteriorated rapidly. We do not know how good the Italian dancer Emilia Pasta was, but she was a niece of the soprano Giuditta Pasta, who was the original Norma in Bellini's opera in 1831. The dancing Pasta must have been well advanced in years and, for one *Aida* in the Sydney Opera House (no, not the one created by Utzon!) in 1877 she gained great applause 'not because she danced better than usual, but because she was better dressed'! Make of that what you will, but Madame Pasta became a great teacher — of dancers for pantomime. She also appeared as soloist with fifty or sixty of her own pupils at a time, in these family entertainments. It was a time of popular theatre.

The occasional imported dancing troupe seems to have deteriorated too — or had the public finally woken up to the fact that the kind of dancing managements still presented under the name of ballet was not really up to very much? When Martin Simonson brought some Spanish dancers

'from the Royal Court in Madrid', critics and public alike found little to praise. Objections were raised that the Spanish dancers were really Italian (such discernment!), that their costumes were an offence against decency (righteous indignation) and that principal dancer, Emilia Righnetti, 'hopped about with cow-like gracefulness' (the dance critic finally surfacing).

The original J. C. Williamson started his Australian entrepreneurial activities in 1874 by presenting plays. In 1879 he added Gilbert and Sullivan and then, in 1888, pantomimes — and he knew the value of dance to the latter. With true American showmanship he created the Royal Ballerinas, led by his own locally created 'star of the dance', Mary Weir. Williamson's Royal Comic Opera Company and its Royal Ballerinas presented a varied diet of pantomimes and operettas for many years. In line with Williamson's high principles, they were fine clean family entertainment. The only thing improper about them was the ballet and that only in the precise dictionary definition of improper — 'inaccurate'. Ultimately, it was Williamson himself who brought Australia the first taste of proper ballet in the classical sense.

It was when the American showman branched out into grand opera that he quite rightly decided that the pantomime dances of Emilia Pasta (who had taken over the Royal Ballerinas) were not suitable. Oddly enough, his grand operas initially were not the French monsters, which needed ballets at strategic points, but three short operas of the then new *verismo* school, *Cavalleria Rusticana* and *L'amico Fritz* by Mascagni and *Pagliacci* by Leoncavallo. He chose to offer only one opera on each evening and to couple this with a full-size classical ballet, intended to be the real thing at last.

Turquoisette, or A Study in Blue was probably the first proper classical ballet ever created in Australia. It ran with the three operas in repertoire for fully six weeks in Melbourne, after its opening night on 9 September 1893. There were no less than one hundred dancers in the company. Catherine Bartho (from Moscow) and Enrichetta d'Argo (from Naples) were the two *ballerine assolute,* though Bartho appears to have been more *assoluta* than d'Argo. Eight other dancers were imported from London and a corps de ballet of ninety was selected from the best available dancers in Australia and New Zealand. The choreography was by Rosalie Phillipini (from London) and the music was unnamed, though at least one of the dances was performed to a piece by Mozart. (Music and designs were not considered of great importance in ballet in those days when it came to publicizing a work.)

That first Australian ballet appears to have been in the tradition of late nineteenth century French rather than Russian ballet. There were no male dancers and a super abundance of tulle and pretty colours. *Turquoisette* was in fact what its alternative title implied: a study in blue. Dresses were various shades of blue, the scenery was blue and, up to a point, the critics were blue; they do not seem to have understood this strange new beast. The *Argus* critic, reviewing the first performance, gives a rather clear indication of the revolution which *Turquoisette* must have brought to local tastes. He wrote: 'It would not need many repetitions of *Turquoisette* to wean the public's taste from the seductions of skirt dancing ...' It can be assumed that the decidedly skirt-clad dancers moved somewhat differently from the exponents of 'skirt dancing', which is what had previously passed for ballet in Australia.

The public appears to have taken to *Turquoisette*. Though the success of the operas was great, it seems unlikely that opera lovers forced to sit through *Turquoisette* three times to see all the works would not have protested in some way if the ballet had not been acceptable. At any rate, the season was repeated in Adelaide and Sydney, giving two performances in Ballarat on the way. At the end of the Sydney season

The first Australian Coppélia From the first this famous ballet about a girl pretending to be a doll coming to life has been a perennial favourite. In 1913 the great star of the Empire Theatre in London, Adeline Genée, brought *Coppélia* to instant success here. The pertness of Genée's personality was the greatest asset of her Swanilda.

Australia's first international ballet star Ivy Schilling (*right*) represents the sum total of exported Australian dance talent prior to 1933. She was J. C. Williamson's 'ballerina' before World War I and appeared in London musicals before reputedly retiring to the bedroom of the King of Spain.

the singers staged Gounod's *Faust,* with the required ballet led by Bartho. By then it was pantomime time and Williamson split his ballet company between Melbourne and Sydney, in which two cities the two *prime ballerine assolute* was each finally *assoluta* in her own right, though d'Argo in Melbourne's *Little Red Riding Hood* had to compete with little Mary Weir and the Royal Ballerinas, who were still around and under contract to J.C.W.

In February 1894 Bartho and d'Argo departed for Italy. The whole glorious first age of Australian ballet had lasted all of five months. Madame Phillipini remained behind to improve the quality of the pantomime ballets until 1899. The nineteenth century closed rather limply with more of the kind of 'acts' which had represented dance in Australia for so long. In 1896 Hoyt's Comedians were imported direct from Hoyt's Madison Square Gardens in New York and featured Bessie Clayton, 'the celebrated back-kick dancer'! 'Nough said.

'Nough said also about the first decade of the twentieth century. There was no follow-up for *Turquoisette,* but the popular variety bills began to include miniature Russian folk dance groups, whose acrobatic *pirouettes* delighted audiences then as they still do today. There is a solid gap of twenty years between Williamson's solitary ballet venture and the next 'proper' ballet to be seen in Australia. This was performed by the first of the imported companies, led by Adeline Genée. But her arrival was preceded by the appearance of the only Australian dancer to leave a mark outside this country prior to the departure of Robert Helpmann, yet another twenty years away.

The first J. C. Williamson 'revue' (in its most primitive form) was *Come Over Here,* staged early in 1913. Its principal dancers were Fred Leslie and Ivy Schilling, who dazzled their audiences with a *Spider and the Fly* routine. (It is curious that the three local dance celebrities before native ballet began in this country all got involved with spiders. Lola had her *Spider Dance,* Ivy was the Spider or the Fly and one of Helpmann's last appearances before going to England was also as a Spider in the pantomime *Sinbad the Sailor* in 1931.)

Ivy Schilling ultimately went to England, where she danced in other revues before following in Lola Montes' sexual footsteps, which, legend has it, led to another royal bed; Ivy became the mistress of Alfonso XIII of Spain. This was the lady who in her solitary glory encompasses the sum total of all that anyone outside Australia ever heard of Terpsichore Down Under before the 1930s!

While Ivy Schilling was busy doing her own thing with Williamson's and Alfonso, ballet as an art took its first serious steps in Australia – with imported feet.

Adeline Genée was, in her day, as great a star in England as Margot Fonteyn was fifty years later. Danish-born, she

led the Empire Theatre ballet in London and retired from dancing in 1914. (She settled in England and became a great force in British ballet, finally being made a Dame of the British Empire in 1950 at the age of seventy-two.) In 1913 she came to Australia with her own company, which included quite a number of dancers from the Imperial Russian Ballet, including Alexander Volinine, who had come West with Diaghilev's Ballet Russe and was later to become Pavlova's partner. Here indeed was ballet of the kind we can recognize as 'proper' ballet, perhaps not quite in the Diaghilev class, but certainly ballet as good as that presented later in this country by Pavlova. (I am comparing the companies and not the dancers who led them.)

It is from 1913 that we can trace some kind of continuous ballet tradition in Australia, though the interruptions initially were frequent. Genée's eight principals and corps de ballet of twelve were Russians, but Volinine auditioned some local girls and added ten of them to the ensemble. His glowing tributes to their ability can perhaps be put down in part to good manners; they would hardly have been capable of competing directly with even the weakest ex-members of the

greatest ballet company in the world at the time, the Imperial Ballet in St Petersburg.

The first full evening of ballet properly planned, prepared and executed in Australia was seen on 21 June 1913. (The 1867 triple bill by the Martinettis was hardly in the same class and, in any case, it was but a single performance, while Melbourne now was offered eight performances a week, without a single spoken or sung word anywhere within hearing distance.) The principal ballet of the evening was the usual two act version of *Coppélia,* followed by various *divertissements,* which included Fokine's *Dying Swan,* oddly enough not danced by Genée, as might be expected. Genée was no ballerina in the traditional sense. She was quite the opposite to Pavlova, excelling in lighter roles and having a more traditionally Victorian figure than her Russian colleague. At any rate, she rightly left the *Swan* to Halina Schmolz and topped the evening's entertainment instead with the Polka from Drigo's *Les Millions d'Harlequin,* a brilliant *pas de deux,* which she danced with Volinine to public acclaim.

The thirty-three performances of that first Melbourne season also included performances of Fokine's *Les Sylphides* and *La Camargo,* a ballet built around a famous dancer of Louis XV's time, in which Genée had danced at the Empire Theatre in London. (In 1930 Genée was one of the founders of the Camargo Society in London, which was to be the cornerstone of British ballet as we know it today. Its ballets were all taken over by the company first named the Vic-Wells, later the Sadler's Wells and, finally, the Royal Ballet.) Seasons in Adelaide and Sydney followed, which were equally successful; full house notices were common throughout the tour, which ended at Her Majesty's Theatre in Sydney on 7 October 1913.

Adeline Genée and 'The Imperial Russian Ballet' left a deep impression on Australian audiences and announcements that Anna Pavlova would head a company to tour Australia in 1914 appeared almost immediately. The First World War put a stop to that, but the magic of Genée and her dancers had started a slow fuse which was to burst into flame only with the visit of Anna Pavlova in 1926. Genée gave Australians the taste for ballet, but it was Pavlova who started the rush into the ballet studios which began a tradition of native ballet that would need many a long decade to come to fruition.

The gap between the departure of Adeline Genée and the arrival of Anna Pavlova in 1926 was barren indeed. Largely this was the fault of the 1914–18 war. There was no material of any kind on which to build indigenous ballet productions, let alone permanent companies. The difference between ballet and opera was spectacular indeed. Opera, however primitive, had been a part of Australian life (and specially of Australian social life) for more than half a century, but two solitary specimens of the new art form, Williamson's *Turquoisette* and the Genée tour, were hardly enough to create a great new public or an improvement in local dancing standards to encourage emulation. Anybody can sing in a fashion if born with a good voice, but the years of training needed for ballet require teachers able to pass on their knowledge and students prepared to undergo the rigours of daily classes.

Dancers in 1914 had one aim and one only: to become 'stage artistes' and few shows had room for dancers alone. What was required was what came to be known as *soubrettes* – girls who could sing a little, dance a little and speak the occasional line. The original chorus line did a lot more than dance; the day of the 'hoofer' was yet to come. As for the men, anything other than straight acting or singing was tainted with an image which is only now, sixty years later, beginning to die out: it was not a case of 'boys will be boys', but 'boys will be girls' and the deep-seated Australian conviction that dancing is for the sissies is soundly based on the generation that followed the acrobat dancer of the nineteenth century. (I shall say no more after this about the sexuality or otherwise of male dancers.)

The standard of local teachers before the First World War is historically more important than the standard of the dancers. The best had learnt their craft from Emilia Pasta. In the 1880s and 1890s Pasta had established a series of dancing schools in each major city. These were attached to the local J. C. Williamson controlled theatres and, while their purpose was to provide dancers for the new musicals (usually unpaid students), Pasta's basic training was sound and, because schools had to continue in cities without her personal supervision, she was forced to engage in a form of teacher-training which ultimately was to provide the link of continuity between visits of imported companies and their teachers in the early twentieth century. Just as Pasta (and her students) provided choreography (and dancers) for pantomimes and operettas, so did Jennie Brenan, Minnie Everett and Minnie Hooper fulfil the same function between 1914 and the arrival of Pavlova, fully twelve years later. It is remarkable that a short fifty years ago Australia had a period of more than twelve years without any kind of ballet, professional or amateur, other than performances in schools (or, if such took place, no record has been kept of them).

After the departure of Adeline Genée there was a brief visit by the Canadian dancer Maude Allan, a follower of the Isadora Duncan style of 'Greek' dancing. She appears to have left little impression and did not capitalize, as Duncan did, on the more sensational kinds of artistic idealism. Had she shed the seventh veil in her *Vision of Salome,* we would surely have heard more about her than we did.

With the outbreak of war in August 1914 Australia became a balletic Sleeping Beauty for a dozen years, until the arrival of Anna Pavlova set a stone rolling which, gathering moss slowly at first, was to end up as the gigantic boulder which is now the Australian Ballet.

The Dying Swan
5

The Dying Swan was Anna Pavlova's most famous part. It was also a reasonable description of the great dancer herself when she came to Australia. There can be no doubt that Pavlova was a major talent in the field of ballet and that her influence in encouraging the art was immense. It may be as well, however, to look at her career in a realistic light; it cannot dim the brightness of her name, but it may help to clarify the historical perspective.

Anna Pavlova was born in St Petersburg in 1881 and quickly became a ballerina with the Imperial Russian Ballet when it was indisputably the greatest company in the world. She first came to Paris with Diaghilev's ballet in 1909 and finally left Russia for good four years later. Pavlova's great virtue was grace rather than technique. It was she who inspired Michel Fokine to expand a single *pas de deux* in the original *Chopiniana* of March 1908 into *Les Sylphides,* which is probably the most famous of his works. The initial creation was a series of mostly Polish dances with only one *sylphide,* Pavlova. It is thus as the ethereal *sylphide* that Pavlova should be remembered; she was never oustanding in purely technical roles and quickly dropped them when she created her own company in England in the fateful year 1914. From that time until her death in 1931 Pavlova was answerable to no one but herself and both the credits and the discredits were her own.

The Dying Swan started dying long before she came to Australia. Pavlova may have been divine, but she was technically insecure, unmusical and lacked taste. Worst of all, she adored money. She left Diaghilev during his second season for many reasons, but two stand out: she would not or could not make head nor tail of Stravinsky's score for *The Firebird,* in which she was to star, and she was offered more money to tour America than Diaghilev could or would give. The former reason is more important to her subsequent career. Pavlova could not even follow the music in *The Dying Swan,* her performance being totally independent of the music, only the final chord by the orchestra coinciding with any of her movements. Her taste in music, painting and dancing was abominable. Even under the discipline of Diaghilev she could not resist adding applause-inducing gestures – the *cabotinage* (hamminess) which ballet has tried to eliminate ever since Diaghilev's appearance on the scene.

The company to which Pavlova gave her name, which was assembled by her personally and managed by her husband, Victor Dandré, was poor. Nobody has ever denied that Pavlova surrounded herself with nonentities and the theory is often put forward that she did this to make herself look better. It could well be so. The fact remains that Pavlova's company as a company was inferior in every way but one, the quality of its star. The ballets which were the company's own were decidedly inferior, the decor was basic, to say the least, and the music mattered very little, since

Pavlova never did understand its importance. One of her greatest admirers and the last of her partners, Serge Lifar, declared that she 'simply ignored the music'.

As for the standard of Pavlova's ballets, it need only be pointed out that Nicholas Sergueeff, who recreated *The Sleeping Beauty* for Diaghilev in 1921 and all the great Russian full-length ballets for Sadler's Wells in the thirties, was dismissed by Pavlova after a few weeks of rehearsals because she considered him *demodé*! (Sergueeff was too polite to comment on Pavlova's ballets, though he was far from reticent about the lady herself.)

By the time Pavlova came to Australia she was forty-five years old, at a time when most dancers retired well before forty. It is hard to establish at what point people began to complain that she was doing her image harm by continuing, but Pavlova danced to the end, in the process partly destroying her own legend, for many who saw her dance during her last years claim that she should not be the legend she still is. They said the same about Sarah Bernhardt! She has been dead longer than Pavlova, but her name also is immortal.

The Pavlova repertoire that came to Australia in 1926 and again in 1929 can perhaps be best described as a huge chocolate box of sugary trifles which happened to be attached to the most famous dancer of the time. Stars have always been the biggest box office winners and that the company had a star was obvious. If Pavlova had failings, large or small, there was no one in Australia who knew enough about it to pick them. Those who had seen Genée and her company (which was not in the Diaghilev class either) would hardly have been disappointed; there was simply no level on which to compare the saucy wench of 1913 and the fairy figure of 1926. Without a shadow of a doubt the very things which European balletomanes regretted in Pavlova's way with ballet were the very things which Australians loved and welcomed with open arms. Her impact was greater here than almost anywhere else because of the complete absence of any ballet at all for twelve years or so. There was a total lack of standards by which she could be judged. No wonder audiences clamoured for more and every mother wanted her daughter to become another Pavlova. And not only every mother, at least one father was convinced as well.

When a South Australian beef baron saw Pavlova in Melbourne he suggested that his young actor son take classes with her. Robert Helpmann and his mother went to Melbourne, saw the company, auditioned for Pavlova and thereby started the most spectacular career of any Australian to date in the dance field. Helpmann was not taught by Pavlova herself, but by the company's ballet master, Ivan Clustine, and joined the company as an extra for the 1926 tour. By the time Pavlova returned in 1929 Helpmann had already been principal dancer in various musical shows around

Pavlova advertising stockings in Sydney. The lady kept up with *haute couture*, if not with the latest in ballet trends. (Souvenir photograph 'With the Compliments of Lustre Hosiery Ltd.')

Australia for two years and he was not to go back to ballet until after he went to England in 1933.

Because Pavlova surrounded herself with nonentities and ballets hardly worth recording, her two tours of Australia hold little interest for ballet historians, beyond the personal impact the lady made here, as she did everywhere else she went. It is almost certainly because of Pavlova's impact that when Eunice Weston arrived in Australia in 1927, the first fully qualified teacher of ballet to visit the country, she met a rapturous reception. Weston taught the Royal Academy of Dancing syllabus. Pavlova's teacher, until his death in 1928, was Enrico Cecchetti, whose method remains the other

Borovansky appears Melbourne June 1929. Pavlova starring in *Don Quixote*, featuring the young Edouard Borovansky as the Inkeeper in Act 1.

ANNA PAVLOVA

HIS MAJESTY'S THEATRE
... MELBOURNE ...

DIRM 1103   J. C. WILLIAMSON LTD.

PRICE · SIXPENCE

PAVLOVA PROGRAMME
for
Saturday Night, Monday Night, Tuesday Night, June 8, 10, 11, 1929.
(Subject to Alteration)

Overture—"Carmen" ... ... Bizet
THE ORCHESTRA

"DON QUIXOTE"
Ballet in Two Acts and a Prologue
Arranged by Laurent Novikoff   Music by Minkus
Scenery by C. Korovine   Painted by C. Korovine and O. Allegri
Costumes by C. Korovine and executed by the Maison Weldy, Paris

PROLOGUE
SCENE: A Room in Don Quixote's House
Don Quixote ... ... M. DOMOSLAVSKI
Sancho-Panza ... ... M. MARKOWSKI

ACT I
SCENE: A Public Market Place in Barcelona
Innkeeper ... ... M. BOROWANSKI
Kitty (his Daughter) ... ... ANNA PAVLOVA
Basil (the Barber) ... ... PIERRE VLADIMIROFF
Gamash (a Rich Nobleman) ... ... M. PIANOWSKI
Espada ... ... M. SLAVINSKI
A Street Dancer ... ... NINA KIRSANOVA
Companions of Kitty ... ... MLLES. FAUCHEUX and BURK
Don Quixote ... ... M. DOMOSLAVSKI
Sancho-Panza ... ... M. MARKOWSKI
Dancers, Toreadors, Street Vendors, etc.

ACT II
SCENE 1: The Enchanted Forest
Don Quixote ... ... M. DOMOSLAVSKI
Sancho-Panza ... ... M. MARKOWSKI

SCENE 2: Dulcinea's Garden
Dulcinea ... ... ANNA PAVLOVA
Knight of the Silver Shield ... ... PIERRE VLADIMIROFF
Cupid ... ... RUTH FRENCH
Don Quixote ... ... M. DOMOSLAVSKI
Sancho-Panza ... ... M. MARKOWSKI
Suite of Dulcinea, Pages, Cupids, Animated Flowers

of the two major influences on the teaching of the art. (Until very recently there has been some parochial bickering between the followers of the two systems in this country, as overseas, which is fortunately dying out.) Actually, Eunice Weston had been anticipated by the dancer Errol Addison, who took over Cecchetti's own school in London and taught in Sydney for a year before Pavlova's arrival. Thus by 1927 both methods had been introduced into Australia and, with the impetus provided by Pavlova, the teaching boom was well under way.

It takes a minimum of six years, and ideally between eight and ten years, to train a dancer, and the benefits which indigenous ballet received from the happenings of the late 1920s were not to be felt until much later. The point is, that after Pavlova's tours there was a stream of students into ballet schools throughout Australia and teachers themselves began to go overseas to improve their own work. They also prompted the first faltering steps toward a native ballet tradition. The first, only and lonely attempt to create any kind of permanent ballet in Australia began in 1931. Historically it must be recorded, though the value of the first 'Australian Ballet' to the history of dance in this country must be said to be nil.

The First Australian and Russian Ballets

6

The sum total of Australian international involvement in ballet prior to the early 1930s is summed up in one long-forgotten name; Ivy Schilling. Her reputed adventures with the King of Spain imply that Ivy was a better mistress than she was a dancer; at least her career in that capacity appears to have been more successful. Still, local ballet was not even the master (or mistress) of its own destiny until after the Second World War. The first 'Australian Ballet' was the concubine of crass amateurs.

A Russian carpenter named Mischa Burlakov and an Australian assistant to the architect Walter Burley Griffin (who was interested in dancing as a hobby), Louise Lightfoot, founded the first Australian 'ballet company', if it can be so described. This so-called Australian Ballet produced *Coppélia* and some *divertissements* at the Savoy Theatre in Sydney in 1931 and continued during the 1930s with programmes which included *Le Carnaval, Les Sylphides, Schéhérazade, Petrouchka, The Nutcracker,* several of Pavlova's ballets and even *Job*! But, reading between the lines, these 'ballets' of the 1930s must have resembled the 'operas' staged in Australia during the 1830s!

Burlakov was an amateur Russian folk dancer who came to Australia about 1913, when he was already over thirty. His knowledge of ballet would have been negligible, but this did not stop him from dancing the leading roles when he was well into his fifties! Louise Lightfoot had the sketchiest of training, first in Greek dancing and then, from Burlakov, in Russian character work. Lightfoot had also taken some classes from a member of Pavlova's corps de ballet during her first visit and later from a pupil of Mary Wigman. Burlakov and/or Lightfoot restaged *Coppélia, Petrouchka* and similar works from memory, after having seen them many years before, or from written descriptions in a book on the Diaghilev ballet! Performances were mostly given on stages constructed in condemned buildings by the carpenter half of the partnership! At best, the first Australian Ballet was the effort of a group of enthusiastic amateurs doing their own thing, without any guidance from professionals even remotely connected with the art. For this latter fact they cannot be blamed, since such professionals did not exist in Australia at the time.

In later years Louise Lightfoot studied dancing in India and acted as the impresario for tours of Indian dancers in Australia. After she left Australia in 1937 Burlakov continued on his own and in 1940 presented a four act *Swan Lake* at the Sydney Conservatorium of Music with Barbara MacDonell as Odette-Odile and himself as Siegfried. Burlakov would have been about sixty then! During the last war the company of forty (including 'children and their mothers') toured in New South Wales, all artists being unpaid. For this tour Burlakov staged what may rank as the first modern Australian Ballet, *Billabong,* to music specially written by James Payton Kimlin. The accompaniment for all ballets was provided at the piano by Fedor Pellac, who worked from conductor scores from which he obtained 'effects' that certainly did not appear in the piano scores of Tchaikovsky and the like! The first Australian Ballet finally petered out during the 1950s, though Burlakov continued to teach until his death in 1965, the year the now Australian Ballet left on its first overseas tour.

The only creative ballet activity in Melbourne during the Burlakov period was a solitary season at the Princess Theatre in 1939, which combined most of the students of major local ballet schools in a well thought out programme of ballets under the reasonably professional direction of the young National Theatre Movement. Jennie Brenan presented her 'Ballet de la Jeunesse Australienne' in *Les Sylphides*, restaged by Laurel Martyn who had just returned from a spell with the Vic-Wells Ballet in London. Edouard Borovansky presented and choreographed two ballets, *Étude* and *Petite Mozartiana*, and Elsie James offered an uncredited 'fairy fantasy' from *A Midsummernight's Dream*. Among the dancers to achieve some reputation later were Edna Busse, Martin Rubinstein and Philippe Perrottet, but Borovansky's *Petite Mozartiana* also featured a number of senior artists like Serge Bousloff, Eunice Weston, Borovansky himself and his wife Xenia. His pianist was Eric Clapham, but the performance was professional enough to require a conductor as well, and the job was done by Gustav Slappoffski, at eighty-two a very senior musician indeed, whose field was really opera. All in all, the whole venture (though undoubtedly amateur in terms of payment or non-payment of fees) was presented with the kind of professionalism absent in the much longer running, Sydney based, Australian Ballet.

In the meantime Australia had seen three international ballet companies which had, for the first time, brought ballet as we know it today to the attention of the public. Nobody was rubbishing Pavlova, whose name was so great that doubting it was inconceivable, but she had left the impression that ballet was something pretty for ladies of both sexes; now the principles of Diaghilev, the father of the modern Russian ballet, were established in Australia through his heirs, if not through himself. Diaghilev died in 1929 and Pavlova in 1931. Their successors were to create the climate out of which Australian indigenous ballet was to emerge.

The pattern, briefly, was this: Pavlova brought an awareness of ballet as an art and created the demand for serious training in ballet. Three imported Russian companies, in 1934, 1936 and, the last, in 1938 and 1940 created the public which, after their departure, longed for more of the same. At the same time, the Russian companies left behind a series of artists who made their home here and brought not only improvements in teaching but expertise in the performing field. (Actually Edouard Borovansky first came to Australia with Pavlova, but he did not 'defect' until 1938.)

The first Russian group to arrive was the anonymous 'Russian Ballet Company' sponsored by Williamson's which toured late in 1934 and early in 1935. Its star was Olga Spessivtseva or Olga Spessiva, as she was billed in Australia and also often in England. Spessivtseva was a direct successor of Pavlova, first in the Imperial Russian Ballet and later with Diaghilev, who revived the full-length *Sleeping Beauty* for her in London in 1921. Spessivtseva was all that Pavlova was and more, except that she was not a star of the same calibre. She stayed within the framework of a company instead of trying to promote herself. Since proper companies do not encourage the kind of adulation Pavlova demanded, Spessivtseva was no more than a *prima ballerina assoluta;* her place in history is great indeed, though her name is not a household word.

Anton Dolin, the famous English dancer, wrote a book about Spessivtseva, with whom he danced extensively. (It was Spessivtseva and Dolin who starred in *Giselle* when the Camargo Society was formed in London by Adeline Genée among others, a performance which was filmed and still exists in some historical archives.) Australia's part in Spessivtseva's life, however, is a tragic one. After Brisbane, the Sydney season was an immense success, but towards its end Spessivtseva began to show signs of mental illness and during the last item on the final evening of the closing programme of the season the balletically impossible happened; she could no longer remember her *enchaînements* and the final curtain had to be lowered before the end. Spessivtseva did not appear in Melbourne, but returned to Europe where she deteriorated slowly, finally being committed to an asylum in America after the outbreak of war. Unlike Nijinsky, with whom she danced early in her career, Spessivtseva's loss of mind did not prove permanent, though twenty-two years behind locked doors is not a fate one would wish on anyone. At any rate, she was discharged in 1962 and is, at the time of writing, still alive and mentally alert. Her Sydney season was her last, except for occasional performances during the early stages of her illness in the thirties.

The thing to remember is that Sydney saw in Spessivtseva a dancer who was undoubtedly much better than Pavlova during either of her visits to Australia. Furthermore, the supporting artists were vastly superior to Pavlova's and so was the repertoire. Anatole Vilzak dancing the Polovtsian Dances from *Prince Igor* must have been as great a revelation to Australia as Adolphe Bolm was when the same ballet was the sensation of Diaghilev's first season in Paris in 1909. And in place of Pavlova's *Autumn Bacchanale* or *The Fairy Doll*, there was *Les Sylphides, Le Carnaval* or *Swan Lake, Act 2*. Since what follows must always be better than what went before, people probably thought that what they were seeing was as good as the Pavlova tours, better though it all was. At any rate, appetites were whetted further and the enthusiasm for ballet grew.

The Kangarussky Ballet

7

In 1936 the 'Russian Ballet Company' was topped by the first visit of what really was the Russian Ballet. Let me just briefly clarify the picture historically: Diaghilev died in 1929 and his company disbanded. Pavlova died in 1931 and her company disbanded. The following year Colonel W. de Basil and René Blum formed the Ballets Russes de Monte Carlo.* During the 1930s this company changed management, name and personnel periodically, making any kind of continuity almost impossible. It was not a great group of dancers, but it was the best there was around, and furthermore, it was a genuine continuation of the Diaghilev tradition and used most of the best Diaghilev ballets and some of his dancers. Its choreographers included Michel Fokine and Leonide Massine, the two twentieth century giants, and their successors.

Ballet standards today are higher, but for about fifteen years this was by far the best ballet to be seen in the world and it came to Australia three times, in 1936–37, 1938–39 and 1939–40. For five years running, some part of Australia had the best ballet company in the world playing in one of its theatres! No wonder it left a lasting effect on the local public.

The first Russian Ballet with Spessivtseva was managed by Victor Dandré, Pavlova's husband who, no longer under his wife's artistic thumb, proved that her standards were not his. His company was more successful than any company at that time, without Pavlova, could be in Australia. But the arrival of Colonel de Basil's Monte Carlo Russian Ballet proved to be the first real Australian ballet sensation. Curiously enough, the company that produced the sensation was not even the genuine article, though it did prove the adaptability of experienced dancers.

In 1936 Col. de Basil's Ballet Russe was playing in London with all the stars who had made it famous since its

---

* To clarify the welter of names of Russian ballet companies which is about to confuse the reader, the following chart may help.

Col. W. de Basil's Companies	Rene Blum's Companies
1932 Ballets Russes de Monte Carlo (with René Blum)	Ballets Russes de Monte Carlo (with de Basil)
1936 Col. W. de Basil's Ballet Russe	Ballet Russe de Monte Carlo
1938 Educational Ballets Limited (without de Basil)	Ballet Russe de Monte Carlo
1939 Educational Ballets Limited (with de Basil)	Ballet Russe de Monte Carlo
1939 Original Ballet Russe	Ballet Russe de Monte Carlo

Australian Tours
1936–37 Monte Carlo Russian Ballet was a scratch company with de Basil Ballet Russe repertoire

1938–39 Covent Garden Russian Ballet was 1938 Educational Ballets Limited

1939–40 Original Ballet Russe was Original Ballet Russe

creation in 1932: Baronova, Toumanova, Riaboushinska, Massine and the rest. The company was about to tour the United States when rumours of a split appeared; half the company was to go to Australia and nobody wanted to be in that half. Finally it transpired that a completely new second company was to be formed, a group which was quickly nick-named the 'Kangarussky Ballet'. Its core was the Léon Woizikowsky Company which had existed all of one year! Woizikowsky had been a defector from de Basil's ballet and now came back with his tail between his legs – which didn't stop him from dancing as superbly as ever, though. Two of his own ballets were kept on, *Port Said* and *L'amour sorcier* and to these his dancers, and a whole new group casually brought together by de Basil, added no less than twenty-two of the ballets of the Ballet Russe repertoire within a time span of three weeks! And it took only three weeks to duplicate costumes and scenery for the twenty-two ballets!

Throughout the long journey via the Suez Canal and the tropics the dancers continued to polish their repertoire and they opened their season in Adelaide on 13 October 1936. How brilliantly this second company, so quickly assembled, did its job can be judged by the fact that de Basil's double-cross was leaked to the Press and actually published prior to the opening date. (The real Ballet Russe was in America by then.) Regardless of any prejudice against the company thus established, the success was immense. What Adelaide and the other Australian cities saw was first-class ballet, of

that there was no possible doubt, no possible doubt whatever. And if de Basil had forged his credentials, they still opened the door to magic of a kind never before seen in Australia.

For the first time the emphasis was on the ballets and not on the dancers. Massine's *Le beau Danube, La boutique fantasque,* the first of his symphonic ballets, *Les Présages,* and *Scuola di ballo,* Balanchine's *Cotillon,* Nijinska's *Les cent baisers* and a whole row of Fokine ballets from *Schéhérazade* to *Petrouchka* were seen in Australia for the first time and the public was as bowled over by the brilliant designs and an orchestra, however scratch, conducted by Jascha Horenstein, as by the dancers. The latter were led by Woizikowski and Hélène Kirsova, while rising stars like Igor Youskevitch and Roland Guerard created their own following. The tour ran well into 1937.

After the company's return to Europe a very major revolution in the artistic and financial ranks took place which knocked out Colonel de Basil and replaced him with Victor Dandré, who headed a new company called (possibly for taxation reasons) Educational Ballets Limited. Dandré lost no time in getting back to the flesh pots of Australia and the Covent Garden Russian Ballet arrived for its 1938–39 season. The Australian public must have wondered about the composition of these companies, always with new titles and new stars, yet always featuring the same ballets in the same settings. Once more the company was able to improve on its previous image. What Australia was offered this time was basically the same company which played at Covent Garden during 1938. The only dancers missing were those who had decided to leave when de Basil departed. They joined René Blum's 'Monte Carlo Ballet' which had played a simultaneous season at Drury Lane that year while the original company had its usual Covent Garden season. Each company had its virtues, but Australia got the better bargain of the two; it saw Baronova, Riabouchinska, David Lichine, Anton Dolin and a whole range of fine artists in the ensemble who were worthy of better things, and soon proved that they were.

Of even greater importance in 1938 was the fact that Michel Fokine was in charge of the company during its Australian season. (Woizikowsky had been *maître de ballet* during the 1936–37 tour.) Fokine staged his own ballets and resident Australian artists were able to study his work at first hand. Since his are the ballets most often revived to this day, the fact of his working here for many months had a profound effect. 1938 also saw the first premiere of a ballet by an international choreographer in Australia. David Lichine staged his *Prodigal Son* in Sydney, but it was hardly what one would call a great ballet.

The outbreak of war in 1939 provided Australia with its greatest and best opportunity to find out what ballet really

The Russians in Australia Colonel de Basil's Monte Carlo Russian Ballet in Melbourne in 1936. Héléne Kirsova and Igor Youskevitch in *Les Sylphides* (*top*). From 1939 to 1945 Kirsova ran her own company in Australia.

The kind of bird we need to be given Tatiana Riaboushinska (*bottom*) in Fokine's *Le coq d'or*, photographed in Melbourne in 1938.

The first Russian ballet premiere in Australia David Lichine's most successful ballet, *Graduation Ball*, was premiered in Sydney on 28 February 1940 with Lichine himself, centre right, and Tatiana Riaboushinska, centre left. The fainting medal winners are Alexandra Denisova, left, and Geneviéve Moulin, right. The was the highlight of Colonel de Basil's Russian Ballet seasons in Astralia.

can do. With London's theatres closed, de Basil (who had miraculously surfaced again) decided to continue the unbroken run of successes in Australia with The Original Ballet Russe. This time Serge Lifar took the place of Dolin and Toumanova replaced Baronova, whose turn it was to make a film in Hollywood. (In the end, Toumanova's good looks led to quite a career as an actress, while Baronova remained just another dancer in films.) Another ex-Diaghilev ballerina, Vera Nemtchinova, was engaged to cover the older ballets such as the inevitable *Swan Lake, Act 2*. Fokine's latest opus, *Paganini*, joined the repertoire and Lichine did a little better than the year before by premiering his immortal *Graduation Ball* Down Under.

Lifar also made history of sorts by inviting Sidney Nolan to design new decor for his music-less ballet *Icare*, portraying the rise and fall of Icarus to the tune (?) of percussion only. The company presented no less than forty-five ballets. It was a glorious season and much of the repertoire was filmed

by an amateur camera buff, the late Dr J. Ringland Anderson. These priceless records are today in the Australian Archives of the Dance; they chronicle the end of the Russian Ballet as far as Australia was concerned. In fact, it was just about the end as far as Russian Ballet outside Russia was concerned. During the 1940s both the Original Ballet Russe and the Ballet Russe de Monte Carlo disappeared into history; one brief attempt to revive the former company after de Basil's death in 1951 failed very quickly.

But apart from the ballet public the company had built in Australia, it left us with a much more valuable heritage, the dancers who stayed behind or returned on their own. Principal of these was Edouard Borovansky, though there were others, such as Raissa Kousnetzova, who came out with the first Russian Ballet and settled in Sydney where she played a large part in the Polish–Australian Ballet, a typical national group trying to fill the ballet drought in Sydney just after the war.

The War of the Ballets

8

The outbreak of war always brings out the best in people. Not only do personal leadership qualities become important, but the creative urge of the human beast attempts to counteract the wastage of life, material possessions and spiritual experiences which are supposed to be plentiful in peacetime, but so very often are not. In more obvious terms this means more babies are born, new inventions proliferate and the old conventions are replaced by new. Whatever the futility of war, and few will claim that it is a desirable part of human evolution, war inevitably advances citilization in victorious and defeated countries alike.

While the arts should, theoretically, suffer in wartime, when all efforts are concentrated on the drive to victory, history proves otherwise. The very fact that mobility of companies and the interchange of artists between nations is severely restricted produces activity at grass roots level which would not have a chance under normal conditions. In London the growth of the Sadler's Wells Ballet into the Royal Ballet was certainly accelerated during the last war, but England had by then had at least a decade of very positive native ballet development. Australia was in a somewhat different situation.

The decade prior to 1939 started with Pavlova's second visit and ended with the years of the regular Russian Ballet tours. The interest in ballet was phenomenal, but it was only seen in terms of international standards which could not be equalled by local artists. Intimate ballet of the Rambert style, out of which British ballet had grown, was completely unknown. The efforts of Burlakov's first Australian Ballet may have been well-intentioned, but they hardly represent the beginning of any kind of standards, let alone tradition; they must, regrettably, be dismissed out of hand.

The war years altered the situation completely, though they did not begin balletically until after the departure of the de Basil company in 1940. But from that moment the public's thirst for ballet produced a plethora of activity which quickly grew from amateur performances staged by various ballet schools into a number of professional companies waging a private war of their own. Each claimed to be the first and only Australian Ballet and many even used the name itself. In the end the Borovansky Australian Ballet Company won out, but only after dropping the 'Australian' part of its title. (The Borovansky Ballet ultimately became the Australian Ballet of today.) But the road was long and hard and during the forties it was far from certain that it would lead anywhere at all.

The number of companies that had varying spans of life, any one of which might have proved the winner of this particular war, was great indeed. Chronologically, and ignoring quality or standing, the 1940s saw the still continuing Burlakov company, Borovansky's initial Australian Ballet, the Kirsova Ballet, the Victorian Ballet Guild, the Polish–

Australian Ballet which became the Kousnetzova Ballet, the West Australian Ballet Caravan, the South Australian Ballet and the Melbourne National Ballet.

There was also the modern dance group of Gertrud Bodenwieser, who had settled in Sydney in 1940 after being caught in Colombia, South America, at the outbreak of war. Bodenwieser spent the rest of her life in Australia, teaching and touring her little dance troupe, first around Australia and then, after the cessation of hostilities, to New Zealand, India and even South Africa. She died in Sydney in 1959, the first and last dancer to attempt the creation of a Central European dance ensemble in this country.

Leaving the efforts of Borovansky for more detailed examination later, the Kirsova Ballet in Sydney and later the National Ballet in Melbourne were the only other contenders who might have made the grade. Kirsova wisely dropped the initial 'Australian National Ballet' title in favour of 'The Kirsova Ballet' for her professional seasons. After all, she herself was far more famous than any new company with which she might be associated. Born in 1911 in Denmark, she had studied with most of the great European teachers and appeared in the original Ballets Russes de Monte Carlo, later visiting Australia with de Basil's first company as *prima ballerina*. She started a ballet school in Sydney in 1940 and ultimately married an Australian. Her dancing days were over, but the Sydney contingent of Russians who had also stayed behind rallied to her cause, and she managed to present a much closer approximation to the kind of ballet the public had only recently seen than Borovansky did in Melbourne. Perhaps it was the more Australian character of Borovansky's group which gave him ultimate victory, but at first Kirsova appeared to have better qualifications (and more backers) to establish a permanent company.

The first short season at the Sydney Conservatorium in July 1941 was little more than a dry run, but one good enough to justify the creation of a fully professional company in the following year. From the first Kirsova herself provided all the original choreography. During the five years of the Kirsova Ballet only three ballets from other sources were ever staged, Fokine's *Les Sylphides,* Massine's *Les Matelots* and the inevitable *Swan Lake, Act 2.* Kirsova's own ballets were ambitious to say the least. Her full-length *Faust* was not some quick cashing in on a famous story or even Gounod's music, but an original work based on a ballet libretto by Heinrich Heine with original music by Henry Krips and decor by Loudon Sainthill.

The principals of the Kirsova Ballet were Tamara Tchinarova, Raissa Kousnetzova, Edouard Sobishevsky and Valery Shaevsky, all ex-members of Russian companies which had visited Australia. Three Australians who were featured initially were Henry Legerton, Rachel Cameron and, in the true fashion of the time, Kirsova's own 'baby' *ballerina,* fif-teen year old Strelsa Heckelman. More notable names came from the ranks of the corps de ballet; Peggy Sager started dancing the Swan Queen while with Kirsova and, though she was never called on to do the seventy-two *fouettés* which were claimed for her, there wasn't much doubt about the strength of her technique.

Some idea of Kirsova's thoroughness can be gleaned from the rise of Paul Clementin, who later became Paul Hammond. Kirsova's husband, Peter Bellew in his book *Pioneering Ballet in Australia* (which is totally concerned with Kirsova and not with ballet in Australia) makes much of the fact that young Paul took over the role of Siegfried in the abridged *Swan Lake* 'with only twelve rehearsals'. Male dancers today, stepping into a rehearsed ballet with an experienced ballerina, would be lucky to get three or four.

At war's end Kirsova went overseas and her company folded, leaving Borovansky to carry the Australian ballet banner. It was Borovansky alone who was able to separate himself and his company from the ballet 'war' that continued to rage on the sidelines, while he was laying the foundations for today's Australian Ballet.

'Boro'
9

Edouard Borovansky was all that a Russian ballet dancer and impresario could be. He belonged to an era which no longer exists, the era of the aura. Books of fiction and non-fiction were written about the Russian Ballet of the thirties and anybody reading one of them today, preferably Caryl Brahms' *Bullet in the Ballet*, will find a composite figure of Mr Borovansky (to his company), Boro (to his equals) and Ted (to the Australian working man, meaning the stage hands).

There was an aura, an aura of awe, surrounding the volatile character who was all things to all men, and I include in this term all three sexes with whom Borovansky had to deal in his daily life. If he did not become a legend in his lifetime, it is only because he died too soon, but it can also be said that his life's work, the Borovansky Ballet, would almost certainly not have survived if he had lived on. Like Caryl Brahms' fictional characters (based on shrewd observation of real people working in the Russian Ballet) Boro was the villain with a heart of gold. He was frightening, lovable, arrogant, loyal, brutish and twenty-five other things. And he could be all of them to one person; it was not a matter of favour or disfavour for this one or that one. The good of the company came first and 'the company, *c'est moi*'. He was the Borovansky Ballet and the part played by J. C. Williamson's Frank Tait in keeping it going was the role of the lion, not the lion-tamer, in Boro's circus. Borovansky ran his company the way he wanted and nothing stood in his way.

It is said, perhaps rightly, that Borovansky was a good businessman. If so, he suffered the handicap of all temperamental people, he often undid all his good work in one thoughtless moment. (He may have been Ted to the stage hands, but that didn't stop them from going on strike one day in 1957 because he had insulted one of their number!) Whatever his motives, which were undoubtedly good, too many people ended up hating him, and working under duress does not always produce the best results. Because people like Frank Tait had faith in the future of the Borovansky Ballet under the direction of the man who created it, the company prospered. But its financial ills were as much Borovansky's fault as its artistic virtues were. He was fortunate in that he came on the scene at a time when Australia was ballet starved and when the competition did not have his ability to survive.

Hélène Kirsova in Sydney or Gertrude Johnson in Melbourne (with a good artistic director) might well have knocked out the ultimate survivor. They did not. Though Kirsova had greater artistic resources, they were weakened by ill-health. Though Miss Johnson had greater financial resources, they were weakened by a total lack of knowledge of ballet and the consequent reliance on advice from quarters which had more pretensions than expertise in the field. The

path of Edouard Borovansky was not easy, but his place above all others is secure in the history of Australian ballet and it is to be hoped that it will be recorded whenever and wherever the Australian Ballet presents itself to a new public.

Borovansky was born in Czechoslovakia in 1902 and was

trained by people with direct lineage to the great masters of the nineteenth century. However, he himself was neither a great dancer nor a great teacher. On stage, during his many years with de Basil, he is remembered only for character roles; he made so much of the Strong Man in Massine's *Le beau Danube* that the tiny role has achieved fame through him. It was not a part that needed dancing ability; it was an almost total case of personality plus. Perhaps his notability in this kind of role brought home to Borovansky that no fortune was to be made as a dancer and his two visits to Australia, first with Pavlova in 1929 and later with de Basil in 1938, showed him a virgin territory without competition in his own field. When the Russians returned to Europe, he remained behind and founded a ballet school in Melbourne. What happened thereafter was surely unplanned, for there is no evidence of any entrepreneurial activity in his past.

The outbreak of war found de Basil's company returning to Australia and Borovansky joined them to dance his old roles again. But, as before, he did not leave when his colleagues departed. Out of mourning audiences, left without ballet in the forseeable future, he encouraged the creation of the Melbourne Ballet Club, or perhaps it encouraged his interest; who can tell at this distance? At any rate, on Monday, 17 December 1940, there was a presumptuously ambitious opening, complete with glossy souvenir programme, of the 'First Season of BOROVANSKY AUSTRALIAN BALLET COMPANY'. Under the patronage and in the presence of His Excellency the Governor of Victoria, Sir Winston Dugan, and Lady Dugan, of course.

In view of what followed, it is nice to think that Borovansky's ambitions came to fruition, but it was really an example of a showmanship which not only set him onto the right path, but made people believe that he was in fact on the right path.

Two performances, on a Monday and Tuesday, even at the comparatively large Comedy Theatre in Melbourne, were about all that could be managed by a school which was hardly established, and following only months after a full season by the best Russian ballet company in the world. But Borovansky's thinking was right. The very name 'Australian Ballet', though dropped later on, made it clear that he was trying to create something for local talent, unlike Kirsova who, in the following year, tried to imitate the style and professionalism of the Russians.

That the new company could survive on local talent alone may surprise, but apart from the large corps de ballet which, well-rehearsed though it was, consisted totally of students, there were enough dancers who proved themselves in later years to show that 'Director-General' Borovansky could both find and train raw material at a time when help from overseas was out of the question. Was Borovansky simply promoting his own school or was he genuinely trying to create a real *Australian* company? It certainly looks like the latter, because he would have had no trouble locating and engaging the Russians who were to lead the Kirsova Ballet in 1941. He chose to build a company from local talent alone.

Apart from Borovansky and Serge Bousloff, all the dancers were Australian and only one had had any experience as a principal overseas. Laurel Martyn had danced leading roles at Sadler's Wells, but had returned to Australia in 1938. More to the point, she had some experience in choreography, though that first programme consisted of only three ballets by Borovansky and one by his 'Professor of the Dance', his wife Xenia. The other principal roles were shared by Edna Busse, Rachel Cameron and also Dorothy Stevenson, who had had a short spell with de Basil. Not what one would call a tremendously impressive line-up of talent, but certainly (with hindsight) a good start. Though four pianists shared the duties of the orchestra, there was a conductor, Eric Clapham, whose name pops up in both the ballet and the opera field over the ensuing years too often to bear repetition. Suffice to say that the gentleman was always to be relied on; and here again Borovansky showed his innate instinct for the right man in the right job.

It is less easy to speak of the ballets performed in this first season, as it is of any creative thing which was not and could not be recorded for posterity. To say that *Pas classique, Autumn Leaves, Vltava* and *L'amour ridicule* made up the programme means nothing at all. A ballet called *Autumn Leaves* was in Pavlova's repertoire, but Borovansky did not claim that his was Pavlova's work. *Vltava* was a Czech ballet, the last a Spanish one and *Pas classique* (with music by Tchaikovsky) is not too difficult to visualize.

The critics were kind, very kind. No doubt they felt that the new venture should be encouraged and encouraged it was. Obviously this man Borovansky was practical and experienced. He did not over extend his raw material (raw in more ways than one) and the need for some kind of ballet through the coming years of a war of uncertain length was great. Borovansky's Australian Ballet Company did not make an instant fortune, but it did not lose enough to cause immediate closure. Not that there was any kind of permanent company; two performances in 1940 and three in 1941 meant no more than a continuity of interest in a possible future on the part of all the participants.

Borovansky's break came after a five night season at the Princess Theatre in 1942. Using the same female principals, but replacing the only other non-Australian, Serge Bousloff, with the young Martin Rubinstein, Borovansky staged a completely new repertoire of six ballets, including *Les Sylphides* and two-and-a-half works by Laurel Martyn; Dorothy Stevenson shared the choreography of *Beethoven Variations* set to music by L.V. Beethoven [*sic*]. *Fantasy on Grieg's Concerto* and some Russian *divertissements* were provided by Borovansky, but it was already obvious that choreography held no great interest for him – he did it from necessity rather than ambition. He encouraged a younger talent, Laurel Martyn, whose *Sigrid* and *En Saga* completed the programme. What followed must have looked like a lottery win to Borovansky.

Tait-à-Tait with Borovansky

10

The large public attending the performances of the Borovansky Australian Ballet Company proved to be less important than the presence of the three Tait brothers, John, Nevin and Frank, meaning J. C. Williamson's. They wanted the baby ballet company out of the competing Princess Theatre and in 1943 the Firm presented Borovansky under its own banner — twice: first for seven nights and a matinee in April at Her Majesty's Theatre and then in November for three consecutive weeks at the Comedy. It began to look as though Borovansky's ballet was here to stay.

Admittedly, it was wartime and the public was as starved of entertainment as the Williamson theatres were of attractions, but the move from self-staged and self-financed ballet to presentation under professional auspices with all the backing of Australia's largest theatrical entrepreneur was a giant step forward. Borovansky's artistic policies worked only too well; even the choice of William Constable to design practically all the ballets for many years was a good one, because the visual aspects of costumes and scenery, skimpy as they may have been, attracted favourable comment from the beginning. How good Borovansky's planning really had been is shown by the fact that the initial two seasons under the Williamson banner were little different from the earlier ones. The replacement of the pianists with an orchestra was a great improvement, but basically what went on on stage did not change. The same ballets were performed and the repertoire enlarged only marginally; only one out of four ballets in each season was new.

Laurel Martyn drew on her English experience to restage Ashton's delightful *Façade* and Dorothy Stevenson added *Sea Legend,* giving a decidedly watery aspect to the second season, when it followed what turned out to be the most popular and lasting of Borovansky's early ballets, *Vltava,* with its Czech river theme. The personnel of the company remained unchanged and, as in any traditional company, principals stepped into ensemble parts in those ballets in which others danced the leads. Of course, it was not the kind of company the Borovansky Ballet later became, but it followed a logical development, closely paralleling that of major overseas groups in their early years and, wisely, Williamson's did not push the infant too much too soon.

Stevenson's *Sea Legend* was hardly a classic ballet of lasting fame, but it was the first Borovansky ballet to be completely native — even its music was composed by an Australian, Esther Rofe. It was also later staged in England for the International Ballet by its creator, thereby becoming the first exported ballet. If it did not set the world on fire, its success here from 1943 to 1947 was substantial. Then, as now, it was not common to have a ballet performed continuously for three weeks with Saturday matinees as well, as *Sea Legend* was, and yet Stevenson and her rapidly improving partner, Martin Rubinstein, were acclaimed at every performance.

Sympathy must be extended to the nine girls in the corps impersonating the Sea itself; they had to toss Rubinstein around like a cork before he was rescued by the Woman from the Sea – the choreographer – who had imposed such an appropriate indignity on him in the first place.

As far back as 1943 the corps de ballet played a major role in Borovansky's theme of things. Knowing full well that his principals could not hope to erase memories of the Russian Ballet, which were still fresh in people's minds, he concentrated on ensemble from the start. Principals and corps worked as one and were rehearsed as one. To the day of his death the father of the Australian Ballet continued this overlap of rank and file; members of the corps de ballet learnt the principal roles, whether they were suitable for them or not. Borovansky had no understudies as such, though roles in later years were shared. When an artist was injured or ill, there was always a selection of minor dancers who could step in. Nobody ever needed twelve rehearsals to take over any role, no matter how big, because everbody was constantly kept on his or her toes by the hardest task-master any company has ever had. Perhaps the dancers were not happy about this, but it paid handsome dividends on stage.

A company managed by a team as shrewd as the Tait brothers was not going to be rushed into any major ventures. The two short 1943 Williamson seasons were clearly planned to measure audience potential, but when three weeks of basic-ally one programme by Borovansky at the Comedy Theatre in Melbourne showed an undiminishing box office, the Taits decided to take the plunge.

The next three years were spectacular justification of their faith in the volatile Czech-Russian-Australian ballet master. It took faith to increase the company and repertoire for 1944, to justify a capital city tour lasting fully eight months. It could not, of course, have been done without Williamson's financial and organizational backing, but it is important to stress that there was no change in the personnel of the company beyond the enlargement of the corps de ballet. The principal dancers remained Laurel Martyn, Dorothy Steven-son, Edna Busse, Borovansky, Martin Rubinstein and Serge Bousloff, whose absence had only been temporary. The pro-grammes still contained every ballet of the pre-Williamson seasons except trifles like *Beethoven Variations*. To these were added three classics, *Giselle*, the usual one-act *Swan Lake*, *Les Sylphides* and *Le Spectre de la Rose*, making a repertoire of twelve ballets plus *divertissements*. No doubt the orchestras still left something to be desired, though the new musical director Gabriel Joffe did a good job. The company did not yet have the lustre of later years, but there was no question whatever of the public's response. Melbourne, Adelaide, Syd-ney and Brisbane had seasons of four weeks or more. Hobart and Launceston had their first taste ever of a full-size ballet

company and the year wound up with a tour of New Zealand in November and December.

Kirsova's departure overseas in 1945 gave a further impetus to Borovansky, who acquired some of her best dancers. However, Tamara Tchinarova, Strelsa Heckelman and Edouard Sobishevsky were not used to demote Borovansky's young old faithfuls and, like good ballet troup-ers, they happily accepted the roles not already the property of Martyn, Stevenson and the rest. Tchinarova danced the Queen of the Wilis to Laurel Martyn's Giselle, but also starred in one of the two additions to the repertoire, Massine's Viennese ballet, *Le beau Danube,* which quickly became the popular favourite it had always been in the Russian Ballet. Fokine's *Le Carnaval* was the other novelty – Laurel Martyn and Sobishevsky dancing Columbine and Harlequin – while Borovansky himself mimed his heart out as Pierrot. Inevitably, he also repeated his Strong Man in *Le beau Danube.*

But new dancers were also coming out of the ranks. Six-teen year old Vassilie Trunoff (Australian in spite of his name) showed tremendous, if uncontrollable, verve and energy and Helen ffrance and Corrie Lodders began to re-ceive favourable notices. The 1945 tour was the same as be-fore, except that Perth replaced New Zealand. Despite all the acclaim in the Press and the box office, expenses proved to be high and difficulties of touring commercially arose constantly; the Sydney season actually had to open with half the scenery missing somewhere between Victoria and New South Wales. 1945 was an unqualified success, but it was also the last such tour for many a long year. Peace breaking out had a dampening effect on J. C. Williamson's ballet plans. The compromise which resulted in 1946 was a unique one.

The year started auspiciously with (apparently) the form-ula as before. In May the Borovansky Ballet (which had lost the 'Australian' from its title without comment half way through 1944) opened at Her Majesty's Theatre in Mel-bourne with the same repertoire as before and two novelties. Fokine's *Schéhérazade* starred Tchinarova and Rubinstein, the latter specially making a great impact as the Golden Slave, and had new designs by Constable which owed little to the original Bakst decor, but were very acceptable substitutes.

The more important novelty was Borovansky's first ballet catering specifically to nationalistic sentiments, *Terra Aus-tralis.* This was one of his less happy inventions, an allegorical picture of the white explorer putting down the Aborigine and feeling sorry about it afterwards. It had Peggy Sager creating her first major role as a symbolic Australia, Martin Rubinstein as the Explorer and Trunoff as Binghi, the Aborigine. Special music was written by Esther Rofe (whatever happened to this Australian composer of so many ballets?) and the decor was by Eve Harris. The success of *Terra Australis* was probably due more to its patriotic impli-

The all-Australian boy From the earliest Borovansky days the athletic young Australian male was an asset to the local ballet scene. Vassilie Trunoff (real name and Australian-born) was the energetic Polovtsian Chief in *Prince Igor* 1954.

cations than its artistic values, but there was no question about the popularity of *Schéhérazade* or Gabriel Joffe's conducting of the orchestra.

The bare statement that the Melbourne season of the Borovansky Ballet, which began on 10 May 1946, continued without interruption in the same theatre until 15 February 1947 may be correct, but it is also an untruth. Yes, the company was continuously employed at Her Majesty's Theatre in Melbourne for nearly eight months, but only as part of a deal Borovansky made with J. C. Williamson's with some reluctance. He could not hope to break away from his powerful ally and had to accept the terms and, balletically, they were not attractive.

Williamson's were about to go back to staging musicals now that the war was over and an international exchange of productions again became possible. Their first effort was Ivor Novello's *The Dancing Years*. If Max Oldaker in the lead was no Ivor Novello, the Australian production in other ways improved on the English version because of Borovansky and his dancers. They appeared in all three acts and ran away with the show leaving Williamson's and the public equally satisfied. It was a virtuoso performance which could not be equalled overseas, where no reputable ballet company would be seen dead supporting singers in a musical. Ironically, the singers Borovansky helped to eclipse included Viola Wilson, who married the boss, Frank Tait.

The Dancing Years ran for three-and-a-half months in Melbourne and was followed by a second season of the ballet proper with most of the same dancers and repertoire plus a new *Coppélia* staged by Borovansky himself. The success of this was tremendous though, probably anticipating the company's demise, Williamson's stinted on the sets which were not of the usual splendour. There had been two major desertions before the excursion into musical comedy – Laurel Martyn to form the Victorian Ballet Guild and Dorothy Stevenson to go overseas. Edna Busse moved up to become *prima ballerina* and in *Coppélia* certainly proved her worth by being substantially better than Bousloff as Franz and, more remarkably, than Borovansky as Dr Coppelius. (It was not one of his greatest roles.) Nevertheless the ballet, relying in the first act on the first-rate corps de ballet and in the second on Busse, was a roaring success. Again, it seemed as if past glories were to be repeated.

Five weeks later it was back to musical comedy, or rather operetta: an updated version of *Die Fledermaus* arrived in Melbourne under the title *Gay Rosalinda*. Again the ballet, this time in the middle act only, made the greatest impact and *Gay Rosalinda* continued until February 1947, at which point the Borovansky Ballet gave a five night Farewell Season prior to its departure for Sydney. It was to be its real farewell to Melbourne for some years. Due to the departure of Peggy Sager (who had danced the Swan Queen briefly with success during the last season) Edna Busse was saddled with both Odette and Coppélia for all five performances and survived with great credit. Then it was off to Sydney.

Williamson's Sydney Theatre Royal plans paralleled those of Melbourne, if in a different order. *Gay Rosalinda* was followed by *The Dancing Years* and only in July 1947 did the first proper season by the Borovansky Ballet take place. It was presented by a somewhat discouraged group, though the plaudits of public and critics continued unabated. The writing was writ large on the wall, however, and only the sudden emergence of a young Kathleen Gorham is worthy of mention historically. The company was disbanded, its repertoire now the property of J. C. Williamson's, and Borovansky had to fall back on his studio productions.

The Ballet War Continued

11

The gap left by the apparent demise of the Borovansky Ballet two short years after the departure of Kirsova needed to be filled quickly, but nobody had an idea how this was to be done. Only the Polish–Australian Ballet in Sydney remained as a continuing body and its function as a means of raising cash for the Polish War Relief Fund had disappeared. Its brief reappearance as the Kousnetzova Ballet, to supplement the National Opera of New South Wales, was too little too late.

By then other events had produced a new contender for top honours in Australian ballet, the hated opponent of the National Opera in Sydney, Melbourne's National Theatre Movement. This had always claimed to cater for ballet as well as opera and drama, though up to 1947 its efforts in ballet had been restricted to a school run by one Jean Alexander, an erstwhile teacher of eurythmics who fancied herself as an amateur Egyptologist. In what way this qualified her to teach ballet has never been clear, but she did employ the grand old lady of the Cecchetti method in Australia, Lucie Saronova, whose abilities were unquestioned.

Any credit the Melbourne National Theatre then obtained in teaching ballet belongs to Saronova, in spite of, and not because of Jean Alexander, who, in time, became a regrettably bad joke in ballet circles. When her boss and close friend Gertrude Johnson, the director of the National Theatre, finally leaped into the professional ballet field it was as a result of a situation parallel to the Russian Ballet dancers remaining in Australia, except that it was an English company which was now the source of new directing talent.

In 1947 the Ballet Rambert came from England to tour Australia. This was Australia's first introduction to English ballet on a smaller scale. Works like Andrée Howard's *Lady into Fox* with the original creators of the leading roles (Sally Gilmour and Charles Boyd) brought a completely new concept of ballet to the notice of local dancers as much as to the public. The public's need for the massed dancers of the Russian ballet was no longer so great and some of Borovansky's smaller works, such as Laurel Martyn's *Sigrid*, suddenly took on a new meaning; perhaps they were not created out of necessity, but could be considered a legitimate art form. The aspect of ballet as an art, as opposed to ballet as a spectacle began to be accepted.

Walter Gore and Paula Hinton starred for Rambert and ultimately were to return to Australia more than once. Gore's personality was perhaps not conducive to leading companies to success, but his experience as one of England's best dancer-mimes was to bring balance to the Russian-orientated ballet thinking in this country at the time.

An even greater benefit to Australia also came from Ballet Rambert via Joyce Graeme, Margaret Scott and Rex Reid, three dancers who created the National Ballet in Melbourne in 1949. Joyce Graeme, as the director of the company during its formative years, played the major role, before returning to England. But Rex Reid and Margaret Scott went on to become tremendous assets to the art in Australia – Scott as creator and principal of the Australian Ballet School, Reid as one of our best choreographers and, for many years, as the director of the West Australian Ballet Company.

Marie Rambert, although Polish-born and an early member of the Diaghilev Ballet, was fiercely and nationalistically British. She had done in England what Borovansky was trying to do in Australia – created a native ballet company. Hers was and still remains the oldest British group, though it has never been the largest. While in Australia Rambert took in a few of the better Borovansky dancers, pretending they were not as good as they thought they were, but quickly acknowledging their worth by promoting them to principal roles, preferably without rehearsal, to test them to the full.

In that immediate post-war period the tendency to give Russian names to dancers was still strong. Stage names as such are not that uncommon and nobody would have thought twice if Harold Algernon Essex had changed his name to Harcourt Essex, but Anna Pavlova turned this English dancer into *Algeranoff* and during his years in Australia (long after the Rambert visit) he was billed as H. Algeranoff, the H. standing for Harcourt, not Harold. I give this as a typical example which was multiplied a hundredfold over the years.

But Rambert was different. She ran an English company and her dancers had to be identifiably English, though she herself spoke with a thick Polish accent! Thus arose the case of an Australian who happened to be born with a Russian name, Vassilie Trunoff, being renamed Basil Truro! (He reverted to his own name after leaving Rambert.)

Less clear is the reason why Rambert renamed Kathleen Gorham; she became Anne Somers for the duration of her stay with the company. For somebody who, Rambert said, was not good enough for her corps de ballet, the casting was remarkable; she danced one of the little Swans in *Swan Lake* on the day she started with the company, the *Pas de trois* the following week and her first Swan Queen not long afterwards. Rambert certainly knew how to make people work. She was a disciplinarian like Borovansky and her aim at the time she was here was to build a major company out of her intimate group. Unfortunately her own principals, trained and experienced in her own kind of chamber ballets, got some rather big ideas in the process.

At the time the National Ballet was created Borovansky was in eclipse; his company had not presented a season for two years. Kirsova had departed. There was no fully professional company on a permanent basis anywhere in Australia and the National Theatre in Melbourne had a policy of presenting opera, drama *and ballet* under the auspices of

its parent body, the *Australian* National Theatre. Its founder, Gertrude Johnson, had good reason to believe that her company would one day become the truly national body in opera, but its previous ventures into ballet under the direction of Jean Alexander had brought little credit to the National Theatre, while its drama presentations never did get off the ground. In 1949 the immense popularity of the National Theatre opera seasons overshadowed the drama and ballet parts of the company's so-called 'Festivals of Theatre Arts' ('Arts' plural!) and something had to be done to bring the other sections up to scratch. A start was made with ballet that year.

The National Theatre held all the cards in 1950. It was the only organization of its type in Australia which was subsidized by a State Government, not to mention half of Melbourne's high society. It had already created what could seriously be considered a native opera company of some quality. It had established annual seasons in the Princess Theatre for which a willing public was waiting. There was no reason why the National Theatre should not equal its operatic success in the field of ballet and, for a start, things went very well indeed.

The originality of the first National Ballet seasons can only be admired. The financial backing which had not been available to Borovansky and Kirsova helped, and the new artistic policies were tempered only by the shortage of quality dancers to fill the ranks. Initially no attempt was made to bring in guest stars; the opera seasons had succeeded with local talent and the ballet was expected to do the same. The only exception was a unique one for a ballet company. The noted Indian dancer Shivaram was in Australia and his manager Louise Lightfoot (of the first Australian Ballet) had become an expert in his oriental art. She produced a Hindu ballet, *Indra Vijayam* starring Shivaram and instructed the whole company in the intricacies of Indian techniques. The exercise was hardly a box office promotion stunt. In a more experienced company it could have been a most valuable asset, but even so, dancers and audiences gained considerable benefit.

Joyce Graeme, Margaret Scott and Rex Reid danced most of the leading roles more than adequately in 1950, but the real value of their policies lay in the encouragement of new choreographic and design talent. Graeme herself staged *Romantic Suite* to music by John Field with designs by Kenneth Rowell, which was a revelation, coming from a newly assembled group like this, partly because the National could provide expert lighting and stage management. Classics like *Prince Igor* were restaged by Serge Bousloff and his wife Kira (Kira also danced in the ballet) and lesser new works were produced by Laurel Martyn, Rex Reid and Joanne Priest. If Rex Reid's first choreographic effort, *Les belles Creoles*, fell into the 'lesser' class, he followed it with what remains a

Corroboree The only successful ballet on Aboriginal themes was *Corroboree*, choreographed by Rex Reid to John Antill's music. Unfortunately it was staged by the short-lived National Ballet in Melbourne in 1950 and has not been seen for many years now.

milestone in Australian ballet, *Corroboree*. It was a spectacular climax to the company's first full year of operation, which included two seasons at the Princess Theare in Melbourne, visits to Perth, Adelaide and Sydney and an extensive country tour, not to mention its participation in a particularly vile pantomime-cum-musical, *The Glass Slipper,* in Melbourne at Christmas time.

Corroboree was not the first Australian ballet, but it was and remains the only major work on Aboriginal themes. The music by John Antill had been written in 1946 but was always intended for ballet. It is to the credit of Joyce Graeme as director of the company and Rex Reid as choreographer that they accepted the challenge and met it so well. William Constable provided the decor and Robin Lovejoy the costumes. None of the contributors took the Aboriginal theme literally; like all good ballet, *Corroboree* was a balletic interpretation of something else. It was good theare and good entertainment. Too few artists can find the happy medium between the real article and travesty. The former – specially when dealing with a primitive culture – becomes simply boring to sophisticated audiences and the latter brings unwonted laughter. Reid and his collaborators managed to strike that happy medium, greatly helped by Antill himself, who conducted the Sydney Sympony Orchestra and its Mel-

bourne counterpart in both seasons.

The Jubilee Year of the Commonwealth (1951) saw Borovansky's company back in full swing presented by J.C. Williamson's, with its usual one-act version of *Swan Lake.* The National Theatre Ballet Company (as it had become) went three better and produced the full four acts of *Swan Lake* in a reasonably faithful reproduction by Joyce Graeme with admirable designs by Ann Church. It was Australia's first taste of a full classical ballet, something which since then has become a staple diet in our ballet fare. It also marked the debut of young Lynne Golding, starting at the very top and getting away with it. Henry Danton's Prince (specially imported from England) was a little more polished, but the whole company still relied on presentation and production rather than major dancing skills. Even so, it was good enough to have an immensely successful tour of New Zealand with *Swan Lake* and *Corroboree* as the highlights.

Joyce Graeme's brief, but admirable reign at the National Theatre ended in 1952 when she resigned. Walter Gore, who had been Gertrude Johnson's original choice in 1949, but had backed out in haste, returned to lead the company. The fact that Graeme and her colleagues had stepped into the breech and had done all the hard work of establishing a company, which in 1951 was still running neck and neck with Borovansky, did not stop Miss Johnson from falling for the star names of Gore and Hinton when they suddenly became available. That Gore should play second fiddle to Graeme was inconceivable, and the National Theatre paid the price.

The director of the parent body and her new star saw eye to eye: they would create the biggest and the best ballet company that Australia had ever seen. The success of the spectacular *Swan Lake* was proof. If young Lynne Golding could fill the house as Odile-Odette, surely Paula Hinton could do the same with *Giselle*. If Ann Church's designs for the Petipa ballet brought thunders of applause, Kenneth Rowell's for *Giselle* must do the same. And if box office ballets brought in that kind of money, then obviously more box office ballets were needed. As for young choreographers, there was no further need for them when the director himself was a world-famous choreographer. (He may have been world-famous, but was he good? Let us be charitable and say he was often not bad.)

The biggest year for the National Theatre Ballet was 1952, but it was also the turning point – away from success. The box office was big, but so was the expense and once the public had seen Walter Gore and Paula Hinton, which it did again and again and again, there was not so much reason to return. They starred in *Giselle* and a whole series of Gore's own ballets: *Theme and Variations, Crucifix, Pastorale for Today* and *Antonia*. Fortunately he also engaged Kira Bousloff to restage many of the Russian Ballet favourites. People wanted to see *Graduation Ball, Protée* and *Prince Igor* again, specially when the latter was even provided with Borodin's required chorus backing from the National Theatre Opera Chorus.

It really was a very big season, followed by the usual big tour. Apart from Gore and Hinton, Henry Danton continued to dance with Lynne Golding in *Swan Lake*, but second casts began to appear, in this case Raymond Trickett and Strelsa Heckelman. Young dancers like Marie Cumisky, Marita Lowden, William Carse and Athol Willoughby began to appear in roles and Leon Kellaway remained a tower of strength as Ballet Master, while also appearing in character roles. It was all too good to last. There was no way in which strong personalities like Walter Gore and Gertrude Johnson could collaborate on a permanent basis, however much their ambitions were of equal size and purpose. Gore's tenure ceased after one year and the bills for 1952 had to be paid. In fact, they were not – at least not for some considerable time.

The following year Valrene Tweedie, an Australian dancer who had spent fourteen years in Russian companies overseas, became the under-staffed and underpaid director of a travesty of the previous year's splendid pretensions. Ballets like Fokine's *Le Carnaval* and a pathetic *Pas de Quatre,* vaguely based on the old lithograph showing Taglioni, Grahn, Grisi and Cerito in their 1845 glory, took the place of four-act *Swan Lakes* or *Graduation Ball.* Maureen Davis, Norma Lowden, Pamela Proud and Gloria May were distant relations indeed of the ancestors they tried to represent and by 1954 the company had become no more than a group of dancers supporting the National Theatre Opera during the Coronation Season. On the occasion of the parent company's 25 Anniversary in 1960, the remnants of the company, which had occasionally assembled to work in the open air for Moomba, gave a nine day season at the huge Palais Theatre in St Kilda. It is doubtful whether the dancers who appeared in the full-length *Swan Lake,* in *Les Sylphides* or *Le Coq d'Or* would wish to be reminded of it. 'The entire productions directed by JEAN ALEXANDER' read the programmes. Let her accept the blame. It was the end of the war of the ballets. By 1960 Edouard Borovansky had died, Peggy van Praagh was in charge of his company and the Australian Ballet was about to be born.

As a footnote to the fate of the National Theatre Ballet it should be recorded that Walter Gore and Paula Hinton returned to Australia in 1955 and formed the Australian Theatre Ballet, a company based in a studio theatre in Adelaide, which toured the country and gave a season at the Union Theatre in Melbourne. All its ballets were by Walter Gore and the first programme consisted of *Hoops, Soft Sorrow, Peepshow* and *Musical Chairs* – it sums up Walter Gore's career in Australia at that time admirably.

The Benevolent Villains

12

Having been responsible for creating the Borovansky Ballet as a viable national touring company, J. C. Williamson Theatres suddenly withdrew its backing in 1947. The logic behind the move was crassly commercial and if ever an example were needed of the selfishness of capitalism in the arts this was certainly it.

The public for ballet had been created slowly and painfully, initially by the Russian companies offering the best and then by building up purely local talent on both sides of the footlights during the war years. In the words of the old song: it takes two to tango. It also takes two to make ballet: performers and audiences, and training the latter can be more difficult than creating a ballet company. Borovansky, Kirsova and various others had shown the way to putting something worthwhile on to our stages, but it was the audience-relying commercial management of Williamson's which created the mass market needed for ballet to survive. The motive may have been to make money, but the end result was good ballet.

In 1947 Williamson's became the villains by commercial necessity. Suddenly the overseas market had been re-opened and it was impossible to ignore the box office attraction of the imported article. What comes from far away must always be better than the local article; it is a sentiment which survives even today. The penalty of importing inferior artists, while relegating Australians to small parts or worse, would in the end spell ruin for the Firm, but the years of competition and decline for the company, which then held a virtual monopoly in Australian theatre, were yet to come. Having made use of Borovansky's group in its first post-war musicals, while casting around for overseas attractions, Williamson's simply dropped the local company and imported the Ballet Rambert from England instead. Its influence on the development of ballet during Borovansky's four year enforced sabbatical was chronicled in the last chapter.

Ballet Rambert made money for Williamson's; twice the company had to send home for more ballets to extend the seasons. Borovansky returned to his dancing school in Melbourne and staged occasional seasons in the tiny confines of the Union Theatre, firmly convinced that his day would come again, as it did. The National Theatre Ballet began its climb (unfortunately in the same city) and Ballet Guild (also in Melbourne) was starting its excellent work, concentrating on the creation of new choreographers in the absence of dancers (apart from Laurel Martyn herself) who could compete with what the public was by now demanding. As always with young companies, the works designed for the dancers were vastly better than revivals of classics like *Les Sylphides* or *Le Carnaval,* which had to stand comparison with earlier and better productions seen here.

In the meantime the ability of the National Theatre in Melbourne to stage full seasons of ballet with the financial backing of the Victorian State Government did not pass unnoticed. The concept of subsidies for the arts was as yet a novelty. In fact, the arts were a major source of revenue to the Federal Government in Canberra. Theatres were full to overflowing and entertainment tax provided a pretty penny, which was not lightly cast aside.

Somewhere along the way Edouard Borovansky, an Australian citizen since 1944, found the way to Williamson's greedy heart by holding out the hope of exemption from entertainment tax. This would result in increased profit or decreased prices (the former probably dominated the minds of the Taits) and would make it possible to revive the Borovansky Ballet as a paying proposition. The last company in 1947 had been better than anything around in 1950. Guest artists could now be imported and a huge repertoire of ballets was available already in costumes and scenery. All it needed was tax exemption, and a way was found to obtain it.

Williamson's Claude Kingston and Prime Minister Ben Chifley found the loophole to by-pass Treasurer Ben Chifley and his tax collectors.

As far as can be discovered, the 'Education in Music and Dramatic Arts Society' was never more than a name appearing on all the programmes of the Borovansky Ballet from 1951 onward. A President and Secretary were religiously listed, but there is no record of anything ever done by the Society, any meeting being held or any members recruited. It was no more and no less than what it was intended to be: a tax dodge. Furthermore the society to further education in music and drama was only ever associated with ballet. Nevertheless, it brought the Borovansky Ballet back to life and it can thus be said to have played an important part in the artistic history of this country.

Practically all the best dancers from Borovansky's earlier seasons had gone overseas. It is an indication of their quality that all ended up in senior positions in European companies. Kathleen Gorham had joined Roland Petit's Ballets de Paris and, later, the Sadler's Wells Ballet; Dorothy Stevenson joined the International and Peggy Sager the Metropolitan Ballet in England. In 1950 Borovansky went to Europe to try and wean them back to the fold, and succeeded! He was still determined to create an Australian company and the only non-Australians he would accept in the new Borovansky Ballet were those commanded by necessity — male principals. Only two Australian men had up to that time shown the makings of truly top dancers, Vassilie Trunoff and Martin Rubinstein. (Helpmann in England was in the big league as a star of stage and screen by then and out of the running as a dancer.) Trunoff was principal dancer with Festival Ballet in England and not ready to return and Rubinstein was already ailing from the tuberculosis which was to bring a most promising career to a premature end that year.

The first of the Borovansky seasons, which were to lead to the creation of the Australian Ballet ten years later, opened at the Empire Theatre in Sydney on 6 April 1951 under the auspices of J. C. Williamson's and the mythical E.M.D.A. Society. The major addition to the ranks of old Borovansky favourites was the Belgian dancer Paul Grinwis, a tall graceful artist who was to be a great asset to the company, though his career overseas never amounted to much. For him, as much as Borovansky, it was a case of being the right man in the right place at the right time.

The repertoire for that tour, which continued without interruption for seventeen months playing in only three cities, Sydney, Melbourne and Adelaide, was worthy of almost any international company; no less than seventeen ballets were staged, including a full-length *Sleeping Beauty*. Most were leftovers from earlier seasons, it is true, but there were four brand new productions and the box office oriented addition of numerous standard classics, like *Petrouchka*, *La boutique fantasque*, *Coppélia*, *Giselle* and so on. Of the older Borovansky works, *L'amour ridicule* resurfaced surprisingly. This ballet, choreographed by Borovansky himself, had been in the very first performance of the original Borovansky Australian Ballet in 1940. The old Constable sets stood the test of time well, but the primitive Spanish tale with uncohesive music by several composers hardly warranted its revival.

Far more important were two ballets on Australian themes, both by Borovansky. Their ultimate failure pointed up again the master builder's shortcomings as a choreographer, but they also proved the man's nationalism. *Black Swan* was no relation to the usual extract from Act 3 of *Swan Lake*, but a very classical interpretation of the landing of Dutch explorers near Perth in 1697. It really was very much a Petipa-style ballet, with Amsterdam taking the place of the Royal Palace of Prince Siegfried and the Swan River that of the famous Swan Lake; hardly something which could be considered Australian. (The music was early Sibelius!)

More to the point, though possibly not better, was *The Outlaw,* an unimaginative interpretation of the Ned Kelly legend. At least it had an original score by Verdon Williams and the Constable designs were based on early Australian prints. There was a spoken prologue delivered by Borovansky's junior Helpmann, John Auld, and Peggy Sager appeared in the final courtroom scene as Justice. Paul Grinwis was an impressive Ned and Gorham/Stevenson alternated as 'Miss X', Ned Kelly's Girl Friend [*sic*]. Dorothy Stevenson also provided one of the more pleasant (meaning less ambitious) new ballets, *Chiaroscuro,* an abstract work set to the Schumann Piano Quintet.

Paul Grinwis from the first season also proved an asset as a choreographer. His *Eternal Lovers,* to Tchaikovsky's *Romeo and Juliet* music, proved to be the most lasting of the com-

Swan River — not Swan Lake Borovansky's Australian *Black Swan*. The Swan River doubled for Swan Lake, the Dutch Lieutenant Brandt (Kenneth Gillespie) for Prince Siegfried and a dark-plumed West Australian bird (Edna Busse) for Odette/Odile 1951.

The life and death of Ned Kelly   It was inevitable that Ned should become the subject of a ballet and it happened early in the history of the Borovansky company. The admirable decor of the resident designer, William Constable, can be judged from the black and white pictures, but Borovansky's choreography was not good enough to let *The Outlaw* survive beyond 1951. Paul Grinwis (*right*) portrayed Ned Kelly, whose armour has failed to protect him. *Below*, Ned Kelly defies the law.

pany's original ballets; it remained in the repertoire until the last weeks of its existence.

If Williamson's wanted proof that local ballet could produce profits, Borovansky certainly provided it. Unfortunately for them, the Government was not interested in having the entertainment tax used to bolster dividends of shareholders and insisted that the benefits be fed back into ballet. Thus, when the company was disbanded in 1952, the Taits made plans to re-start it again and from 1954 to the final curtain after the death of Borovansky, the gaps between seasons only once exceeded a year. Nevertheless, the fact that dancers were not paid during the breaks caused considerable hardship, defections overseas and premature retirement from the profession. It was not an easy period by any means, but Borovansky's labours for his company were herculean indeed.

The company that reassembled in January 1954 had lost four of its principal dancers; Kathleen Gorham and Dorothy Stevenson had gone overseas, as had Kenneth Gillespie,

whose work in Australia had been the introduction to a career which would take off only in England, and Edna Busse had retired without the fuss which should have been made. They were replaced by a variety of imported soloists of varying quality. Pretty Hungarian ballerina, Anna Mariya, was no replacement for Kathleen Gorham; Christiane Hubert and Claudie Algeranova were no replacement for Stevenson and Busse. It all went to prove that home-grown talent even at that early age could out-dance the kind of import the company could afford.

In the male field Grinwis returned, and so did Trunoff. Martin Rubinstein's forced retirement required more strength from abroad and Raoul Celada from Brazil fitted the bill; he was good-looking and could do some spectacular pirouettes, which is about all that was required of a male dancer in those days. More to the point, the company acquired Kiril Vassilkovsky, one of the pre-war de Basil dancers, as Ballet Master. Vassilkovksy proved to be a great asset in many ways, but (no doubt with the contrivance of

Borovansky's best ballet was not by Borovansky, but by Paul Grinwis. *The Eternal Lovers*, to Tchaikovsky's *Romeo and Juliet* music and with magnificent decor by William Constable, was the only original work to survive in the Borovansky repertoire for ten years. Paul Grinwis and Peggy Sager as the dead lovers, with Kiril Vassilkovsky as a very Massine-ish Death, centre.

Borovansky) he almost cost the company dearly; in due course he revived a whole row of Massine ballets without that gentleman's permission and the legal repercussions were still reverberating when Massine himself visited Australia in 1971.

The repertoire was slightly reduced in 1954, but thirteen ballets were staged in the seven months' season which again covered only Melbourne, Adelaide and Sydney. Vassilkovsky reproduced *Symphonie Fantastique,* the best of Massine's symphonic ballets, with Anna Mariya as an ideal leading lady, Fokine's *Prince Igor* and a new ballet of his own, *Candide,* based on the Voltaire story. The small cast was as close to all-star as Borovansky could get: Trunoff as Candide, Peggy Sager as a somewhat untypical Cunegonde, Celada, Hubert and Paul Hammond as Dr Pangloss. Claudie Algeranova doubled for Sager; Vassilkovsky appeared to be determined to make sweet Cunegonde anything but. Frank Tait objected because Candide, after falling on ill times, was dressed in rags (much too tatty for Williamson's), but the ballet failed

for different reasons.

The big event of 1954 was the Australian premiere of *Pineapple Poll,* staged by its creator, John Cranko. Apart from being one of the most delightful ballets and ideal for a young company, it produced an opening night curtain speech from Cranko which deserves immortalizing. Said Mr Cranko:

> Ladies and gentlemen. Before you leave the theatre tonight I want to say something to you. You will probably read in the newspapers in a day or two how this ballet was danced. I understand that one of the critics here this evening is a fellow who writes up the sports page and that the other one does three sorts of things, none of which is related one to the other, and that none of them know anything at all about ballet. But this is my ballet and I've choreographed it and I've been out front and watched the performance and I'd like to say that it was better than any performance of *Pineapple Poll* I have ever seen and this company is really

In days of old when ballet meant gold J. C. Williamson's made money out of the Borovansky Ballet and money makes money, hence their elaborate promotions, such as the decorations of Her Majesty's Theatre in Melbourne for the 1954 premiere of *The Sleeping Beauty*.

rather marvellous. Now, you gentlemen, just go away and write what you like, but these people here have got to know the truth.

The management was outraged, of course, but the critics did not rise to the bait – not one was ready to disagree with Cranko. (Of course, it is perfectly possible that they had all gone home early to meet a deadline and didn't hear the speech.) In deference to the doyen of Australian ballet critics it should be stated that Geoffrey Hutton was overseas at that time.

Pineapple Poll's success was to no small extent due to the unexpected return of Kathleen Gorham toward the end of the season and the twinkling toes of Tom Merrifield, who made Jasper, the Pot Boy, the last of many memorable performances here. Merrifield was a personality plus dancer, who diverted his energies elsewhere when he realized that the big time would never be for him. Today he is a respected sculptor and painter, whose sketches of dancers like Nureyev have

brought him international acclaim.

The company's need for Gorham had become obvious from the very beginning. For all her good looks, Anna Mariya was broad of hip and inclined to be heavy, and Algeranova was really no more than a second-string Peggy Sager. In desperation Borovansky cabled Gorham, who was dancing in Cairo with the Grand Ballet du Marquis de Cuevas. Only just establishing herself after a year in very high-class company indeed, Gorham may well have given up an international career, which a continuance with de Cuevas would have brought, when she decided that loyalty demanded her return. Apart from creating *Pineapple Poll* for Cranko, she was almost immediately thrust into three solid weeks of dancing Giselle – twenty-four performances in a row! The need for Gorham must have been great indeed and she remained *prima ballerina* of the company until the bitter end.

The Prodigal Returns

13

The shift toward native talent became more prominent in 1955–56, but the importance of visiting choreographers who could set high standards was seen to be most important. Borovansky had thrown in the choreographic sponge and no viable new talent in this line had yet appeared. Williamson's also needed the Russian Ballet image to serve the box office and Borovansky's natural inclination lay in that direction anyway. The engagement of David Lichine to return seventeen years after he had been the choreographer of the first locally produced Russian ballet, *The Prodigal Son,* was a coup of sorts.

Lichine was then forty-five years old and, with Balanchine, considered the great white hope of ballet, though his inspiration had almost dried up by then. The company had re-staged his *Graduation Ball* (world premiered in Sydney back in 1940!) the previous year with immense success. He now arrived to stage a brand new *Nutcracker* (which was good enough to be adopted by Festival Ballet in England later), his own *Francesca da Rimini,* a left-over from de Basil's days, which was almost certainly chosen because it was mainly mime and needed few rehearsals, and a new creation, *Corrida.*

A new Lichine ballet should have been a big event, and it was. But successful premieres seldom mean lasting works of art and *Corrida,* like most of Borovansky's new ballets, lasted only the one season. Bullfighting to the strains of Scarlatti is not a logical progression and Kurt Herweg's arrangement attempted to modernize the music via the use of a 'doctored' piano – tissue paper was wound through the strings to give a distorted harpsichord effect. It was all very arty and without the undoubted energy of Paul Grinwis, who specialized in this kind of strong masculine dancing, and Kathleen Gorham, whose death drives the Matador mad, *Corrida* might not have had what little impact it did.

The Nutcracker was substantially better and an instant winner. For once the admirable William Constable (still being used for *Corrida* that year) was replaced by a new designer, Elaine Haxton, whose delicacy contrasted admirably with the boldness of Constable's designs. Historically it may be of some interest that Lichine probably danced his last ballet in Australia; he valiantly trained for three weeks to make a solitary appearance as the Chief Cadet in *Graduation Ball* to show the company, in his words, what *joie de vivre* is. Since he had admired just that very quality among these dancers, it appears to have been a case of sheer bravado: 'look at this middle-aged man who can still pass for nineteen' – and by all accounts he did; though his dancing days were obviously over.

March 1955 extended without interruption into a tour covering Brisbane, Melbourne, Adelaide, Perth, Sydney and a return engagement in Melbourne, ending in April 1956. Instead of Vassilkovsky and his writ-producing Massine piracies, Yurek Shabelevsky staged a ballet called *Fifth Symphony* to Tchaikovsky's music, which was actually Massine's old *Les Présages*. Any difference was certainly unintentional, caused solely by Shabelevsky's inability to remember a ballet in which he had danced at a time when there was no thought of ever having to stage it.

Shabelevsky was one of the better character dancers of de Basil's companies and he had fallen on bad times. Three years earlier, in 1952, he had been approached by Melbourne's National Theatre to become the artistic director of its ballet company at the princely salary of $50 per week. His appointment was, in fact, announced and his picture appeared alongside that of Walter Gore and Paula Hinton in the souvenir programme. The reason why Shabelevsky failed to appear in Australia then is wrapped in mystery, but the Immigration Department refused to issue him with a visa. Nobody will ever know whether this was part of the Petrov spy scandal backlash, but by 1955 Borovansky had no problems getting permission for Shabelevsky to join his company. Shabelevsky at that time was still the best Petrouchka Australia has ever seen. (After his contract expired the following year, he briefly went back to the National Theatre and produced *Les Matelots* and two operas in the tiny theatre at Eastern Hill.)

1955 was also the year of Garth Welch's introduction to ballet. William Akers, originally an unwilling disciple as assistant stage manager with Borovansky, had been won over by his temperamental master (or the master had been won over by him) and began pushing some barrows of his own. Among these was the understudy of principal dancer Kevan Johnston in Williamson's production of *Call Me Madam,* a very young Garth Welch. (Dancing alongside chorus member Jill Perryman!) When the musical closed, Welch went to see Borovansky one Saturday afternoon and was accepted, much to his surprise, without an audition, started work the following Monday and actually danced on the Tuesday in *Pineapple Poll.* Borovansky threatened Akers with dismissal if Welch wasn't a star in three years! There is many a true word spoken in jest, and Akers was not dismissed. (He didn't know at the time that Edward Millar, one of the soloists, had just given notice and Borovansky desperately needed a replacement.)

The need for a new male star had been obvious for a long time. Gorham and Sager were two excellent, strongly contrasted ballerinas, Trunoff was the only *premier danseur* of local origin and there was a wealth of talent among the minor soloists, but none really had the makings to get to the top. John Auld, Paul Hammond, Raymond Trickett and Bruce Morrow each in their own way filled a distinct place in the repertoire. And Grinwis was almost an Australian by then. However, the need for leading men still required imports and each year the pattern repeated itself, though no-

tably few remained for more than one season.

Paul Grinwis continued to be the mainstay principal dancer and produced what was probably the best of the year's new ballets, *Los tres diabolos,* an amusing Offenbach romp with decor again by Elaine Haxton. The huge cast was given ample opportunity to show off their individual talents, the three devils, Grinwis, Vassilkovsky and Auld being outwitted by Poupette, a minxish lady danced by Gorham, a sort of *Orpheus in the Underworld* in reverse, with devils in the Upper World being victimized by a female. The season continued well into 1956.

The arrival of Margot Fonteyn partnered by Michael Somes, her long-time partner at the Royal Ballet, plus a second pair of stars, Bryan Ashbridge and Rowena Jackson, made 1957 a special year for Australia as well as the Borovansky Ballet. It was, after all, the first opportunity balletomanes had had to see genuine top overseas stars since 1940 and the picture internationally had changed completely. English and American companies rather than Russian ones were dominating the scene and these four dancers exemplified all that was best in the new English tradition.

Fonteyn and Somes appeared in *Swan Lake, Act 2* (ironically, in the very year in which Borovansky first produced the full evening *Swan Lake* for the first time), *Aurora's Wedding* (the last act of Borovansky's *Sleeping Beauty*) and the *Nutcracker pas de deux.* Jackson and Ashbridge more than held their own simply by dancing the *Black Swan* (Petipa) and *Don Quixote pas de deux.* The company didn't know it, but it was Williamson's dry run for a year of imported companies the following year, during which Borovansky disbanded as usual.

The state of the ballet was still good in 1957. Its strength had always been in the great corps de ballet, which Borovansky had trained in true Russian discipline and, whatever may be said about the worth of the Australian Ballet, in this field the latter never has equalled the former. The usual principals were supplemented by another Hollywood ballerina, Mary Gelder, a very young almost Marilyn Monroe, with a fantastic technique and a fatal way of putting on weight. In the end, she came into her own during the New Zealand tour, when both Gorham and Sager fell ill. Regardless of size, her brilliant *fouettés* and youthful charm made her the audiences' darling, though her *Swan Lake* proved to be her swan song; like so many imported 'stars' she vanished from the scene after departing from our shores.

A more lasting impression was made by Robert Pomié from Paris, a fine male dancer with a polished technique. He promptly married the *prima ballerina,* Kathleen Gorham, and a fiery relationship on and off stage resulted. With temperament a major asset in artistic creativity, this marriage seems to have brought out the best in both dancers. Gorham went from strength to strength and so did Pomié, though

242

Fonteyn's first night The first of Margot Fonteyn's many appearances in Australia, when she starred with her Royal Ballet partner, Michael Somes, in the 1957 *Sleeping Beauty*. Left to right: Borovansky, Fonteyn, Somes and the then still Mr Frank Tait; extreme right: Kathleen Gorham and Vassilie Trunoff.

occasional excesses, such as appearing in his *Don Quixote* costume with straw hat and cane when Maurice Chevalier was in the house raised some eyebrows.

Elaine Fifield returned after eleven years overseas and stepped into the part she had created for Cranko at Sadler's Wells six years earlier: *Pineapple Poll*. A very young Garth Welch for the first time got his picture into the programme as a soloist, but ended the season as *premier danseur*. Graham Smith still looked as though he would become a future star. Joan Potter (Mrs Vassilie Trunoff) began to be noticed. Laurence Bishop did well in character parts. Dudley Simpson's conducting was superb, scratch orchestras notwithstanding. And no less than four ballerinas were sharing the four act *Swan Lake* – Gorham, Sager, Fifield and Gelder!

The only possible regret about the sixteen months' tour of 1957-58 was that it included not one new production; presumably the risk of bringing out four English stars headed by Fonteyn killed any creative expense. Nevertheless, plans for reassembly late in 1959 were well advanced and augured well for the future. Nobody dreamt that Borovansky would not see another opening night of his company.

The Death of a Ballet

14

Rehearsals for the Gala Opening of the Borovansky Ballet's full-length *Sleeping Beauty* on 11 November 1959 at the Empire Theatre in Sydney went well. Brief visits by the New York City Ballet and the Royal Ballet between the seasons had been exhilarating – now it was up to Borovansky to prove that his audiences had not imagined the excellence of his company. This time there would be new ballets and some new blood from Australia as well as from abroad. Garth Welch had ended the last season as the equal of Grinwis and Pomié, who remained, and young Marilyn Jones, a Newcastle girl freshly returned from leading roles with the Royal Ballet in England and on an American tour, replaced Peggy Sager, who had retired. Kathleen Gorham, with beautiful timing, had produced a son during the break between seasons and was back as *prima ballerina* in better form than ever. They were joined by another 'glamour star', Iovanka Biegovic from Belgrade. (Iovanka who?)

A few weeks before the opening Borovansky began to complain about pains in his chest and just before the premiere he suffered a hefty heart attack and was taken to hospital. For the first time a season opened without 'Boro' in the house.

Distressed as the company was, there was no suspicion that the still young Borovansky (he was fifty-seven) needed more than a well-earned rest and nobody even bothered to call his wife in Melbourne. However, she did ultimately go to Sydney, watched her husband improve day by day and on 18 December helped him to pack his things before being discharged from the hospital. Minutes before leaving, Borovansky collapsed again and this time there was no recovery. Five minutes later he was dead.

In the true 'the show must go on' tradition *The Sleeping Beauty* was performed that evening with the audience unaware of what had happened and a great alternation of smiles and tears as dancers came on and off stage. The final curtain came down and stayed down. Williamson's Sydney director, Harold Bowden, made a short announcement and everybody went home well and truly depressed, not only about the tragic events of the day but about the future of the company.

The Sleeping Beauty had been scheduled for a four week run to open the Sydney season and no repertoire to follow had as yet been planned; programming was Borovansky's prerogative and he was supremely good at it. There had been no thought that he would not again be able to do this, even if only from a hospital bed. Williamson's were theatre people and they had no one to replace the one-man ballet dynamo who had created everything single-handed. Oddly enough, Borovansky himself had approached Peggy van Praagh in the previous year to become Ballet Mistress for the company to take some of the weight off his shoulders. Van Praagh (ultimately to be Borovansky's successor) had declined; she could see no point in coming to Australia unless it meant a position with a future and there could be no future for anybody in a company run by Borovansky. Whatever his great virtues, Borovansky was obviously another of those people who would give up the reins only to death himself, as did in fact happen. In time Williamson's were to remember Borovansky's first choice as Ballet Mistress.

In the meantime the man who had become Ballet Master for the season, Algeranoff, played his part in saving the company's bacon. With his assistant, Leon Kellaway, he took over the running of the company, while William Akers (long ago promoted to stage manager) handled the business side. Three took the place of one – it was a fair comment on Borovansky's abilities. To give credit where credit is due, the triumvirate staged seven more ballets within six weeks of Borovansky's death, including a brand new full evening ballet by Paul Grinwis, *Journey to the Moon*. Grinwis dedicated this, the first full-length ballet created in Australia, to the memory of Borovansky.

Journey to the Moon proved to be a popular spectacle, if rather more of a pantomime than a ballet. The music was a pastiche of Donizetti tunes and the delightful decor was by Elaine Haxton. The elaborate plot (and its delightfully named characters, astronomer Archie Supernick, housekeeper Cranky Sourpuss, her daughter Bonny Sugarbun and astrologer Stuffy Letzterschutz) reads better than it worked, but so much was happening so quickly that there was little time to ponder incomprehensibilities. Marilyn Jones and Christiane Hubert doubled as Bonny, and Grinwis, as usual, danced his own leading role and danced it well.

The year which followed can hardly be described as happy. Frank Tait wasted no time in looking for a successor to Borovansky. The logical people to ask for advice were in turn: Ninette de Valois, Robert Helpmann and Margot Fonteyn. All three came up with the same name, the person Borovansky had already approached, if for different reasons: Peggy van Praagh. In March 1960 van Praagh arrived to take over the running of the Borovansky Ballet for a strictly one year only period – and even that reluctantly; she was forced by Ninette de Valois to make the decision. De Valois simply informed her that the Royal Ballet had no more work for her. Perhaps next year . . . ? It was a form of blackmail for the recipient's own good and it worked.

What didn't work was the Borovansky Ballet under Peggy van Praagh. Her standards were not his and the demoralizing effect of his sudden death accentuated those problems which time might have cured. The company's scenery and costumes were beginning to look faded. In any case, the standards of Borovansky had been those of de Basil; which had been overtaken by new ideas overseas. The corps de ballet, which had had to be whipped into shape after each break by Borovansky, had had none of the usual advance work, because

the boss had collapsed before the season even began. The principals, who would accept anything up to physical violence from Borovansky, were not inclined to take direction from some woman they did not know. There was open revolt when van Praagh suggested that some dance lesser roles on their days off; the ways of the Royal Ballet were not the ways of the Australian company. (That they were not the ways of Borovansky's Russian predecessors either was completely overlooked.)

It is doubtful whether the company was quite as bad as Peggy van Praagh believes it was when she arrived one hot day in March 1960. Brisbane had two performances of *The Sleeping Beauty* that day and the new artistic director took one horrified look at the outdated designs, which made the cavaliers look like fairies, if not vice versa. Between the two performances their wigs suddenly disappeared. The new broom was determined to sweep clean without delay, and a prickly broom it turned out to be.

The true test of the company's qualities proved to be the production of *Coppélia* by van Praagh herself, which was reluctantly approved by Williamson's as a sop to falling attendances. The death of Borovansky had apparently convinced the public that the company also had to die and they proved to be right, if only partially so. Van Praagh argued correctly that an effort had to be made to show that things would improve, but the staging of Frederick Asthon's *Les Rendezvous* proved nothing except that the company had great assets in Marilyn Jones and Garth Welch. It was a pretty and stylish imitation of the original, but hardly something to revive a dying company.

Van Praagh's *Coppélia* was on a different level. It was a ballet in which she herself had been famous, one which she had learned from Ninette de Vaolois and which she had in turn taught to Fonteyn – a ballet which she had staged for several companies overseas. Kenneth Rowell executed the designs with his usual flair and Kathleen Gorham, Robert Pomié and Algeranoff did more than justice to the leading roles. No company without a complement of good artists could have staged a *Coppélia* as good as this and van Praagh should have been well satisfied. In fact, she was, but by then the fates were well and truly against her; the fall in takings since the death of Borovansky had been huge. Audiences found the same old repertoire tiresome after the novelty of the English and American visitors in 1958 and Williamson's had no intention of carrying on the company under its new and (in spite of *Coppélia*) untried director. The *Borovansky Ballet* could not exist without Borovansky and a *Van Praagh Ballet* was clearly ludicrous. The Firm decided to end the life of the Borovansky Ballet in January 1961.

On the last night Peggy van Praagh was asked to make the curtain speech by Frank Tait. She paid a handsome tribute to Borovansky, announced that Williamson's could not afford to go on and appealed to the public to lobby its

The many faces of Kathleen Gorham Australia's first prime ballerina shone in every type of role. She started at the top with Borovansky in 1947 and retired while still at the peak of her abilities as prima ballerina for the Australian Ballet in 1966.

The Soubrette – With Edouard Borovansky (*above*) in his most famous role, as the Strong Man in Massine's *Le beau Danube*. Standing, left to right: Leon Kellaway, Rosalina Kurowska, Robert Pomié, John Auld, Gorham and Borovansky.

The Minx – As Swanilda (*right*) in the Borovansky Ballet's *Coppélia*, with Algeranoff as Dr Coppelius.

The many facets of Kathleen Gorham

The Tragedienne – In her greatest role, as Giselle (*left*). The expression in her Mad Scene needs no close-up to make an impact.

The ballerina – Her technical brilliance in classical roles, like Aurora (*below*) in *The Sleeping Beauty*, was surpassed only by her feathery lightness.

The Goddess – As Tsukiyomi (*bottom*) the Moon Goddess who lost her wings, in Helpmann's Japanese masterpiece *Yugen* with Garth Welch.

The Virago – In Greek tragedy, as Elektra (*right*) in the title role of Helpmann's violent ballet.

M.P.s for the creation of a government-backed national ballet company. Among those who listened was one balletomane who could do something about it and did; after the show a silver-haired gentleman went backstage to talk to Peggy van Praagh. His name was Harold Holt, he was the Deputy Prime Minister of Australia, and he promised to get his boss, Robert Menzies, to back the company for which she was asking – provided that Peggy van Praagh was willing to come back to take charge of it!

Thus, unspectacularly, died the Borovansky Ballet and thus, quietly, was born the Australian Ballet.

The glory of Borovansky — without Borovansky Peggy van Praagh's production of *Coppélia* for the Borovansky Ballet after the death of its founder in 1959. This was the cast as it appeared on the last night of the company in January 1961. Centre: Kathleen Gorham and Robert Pomié; on the balcony right: Algeranoff as Dr Coppelius; extreme left: Leon Kellaway as the Burgomaster. Future Prime Minister Harold Holt heard van Praagh's curtain speech and, within minutes of its end, the first seeds of the Australian Ballet were sown.

The Birth of a Ballet

15

It is not correct to say that the Australian Ballet was a reborn Borovansky Ballet. What continuity there was was little more than coincidental. The older company created audiences and a number of excellent Australian dancers, both of whom ensured the success of the newcomer, but the policies of the Australian Ballet from ts inception were far removed from those of Borovansky. The foundations for the national company were actually laid well before Borovansky died by people who ultimately played only a minor part in the Australian Ballet's history.

There had been criticism of the Borovansky Ballet in many quarters on the grounds that it was a commercial money-making organization which had no artistic aims; financial considerations over-rode all other policy matters. It was fair comment and not necessarily criticism of Borovansky himself. The very nature of the beast depended on the goodwill of a commercial management, J. C. Williamson Theatres, and the Taits were naturally concerned with paying dividends rather than building for posterity.

At least one group of what can reasonably be described as public-spirited citizens made a submission to the Elizabethan Theatre Trust in 1958 that a non-commercial ballet company should be created in parallel with the Elizabethan Trust Opera Company. The submittors included a number of ballet figures — Margaret Scott, Rex Reid and Sally Gilmour — and their convenor, or chairman, was a young man who was to appear again on the scene later, ex-dancer Geoffrey Ingram.

It is a moot point whether this submission from private sources affected the ultimate outcome of the move instigated from above by Harold Holt, but it certainly sowed a seed in the minds of the executives of the Elizabethan Theatre Trust. Its opera company was degenerating rapidly and was quite clearly destined to be a financial liability for as long as it existed; the operatic barometer overseas showed which way the wind was blowing. On the other hand, ballet was still a viable proposition; in fact, only a decade earlier the Covent Garden Opera Company in London had survived solely on the box office receipts of the then Sadler's Wells Ballet. The 1959 Trust Opera season had been cancelled. Anything prosperous enough to be managed by J. C. Williamson's had to be worth its weight in gold. To Trust Executive Director Hugh Hunt, ballet, especially ballet without competition from Williamson's, must have appeared a very attractive proposition.

When Borovansky died and Williamson's declared that they would not continue with his company, the Australian Ballet Foundation came into being as a direct result of action at Prime Ministerial level. On paper it looked a somewhat lop-sided affair, but the end more than justified the means.

A public body headed by Frank Tait, the managing director of J. C. Williamson Theatres? It seemed an unlikely arrangement, but it was quickly made clear that (possibly for the first time) Williamson's were acting in a completely selfless manner. The Foundation was split straight down the centre, with Williamson's and the Trust accepting roles of equal importance, if of totally different character. The Trust, headed by Dr Coombs, became the financier on behalf of the Federal Government and Williamson's supplied the know-how, administration and costumes, scenery, music, theatres and so on, which were needed to run a ballet company. In fact, the Firm continued to act for the Australian Ballet Foundation as they had for the Borovansky Ballet, except that they relinquished the financial risk and profit factors of the venture. There is no evidence to suggest that they made any gain through the operation of the Australian Ballet, other than what the company would normally obtain from any hirer of its theatres or goods.

Sir Frank Tait's chairmanship of the Foundation was nominal and he was close to the end of his professional life. (No doubt his work for the ballet had some bearing on his elevation to the knighthood and few grudged him the honour.) The people who supervised the actual creation and ultimately the running of the Australian Ballet during its first years were the Joint Executive Directors: John McCallum, acting for Williamson's, and Neil Hutchinson, acting for the Elizabethan Theatre Trust.

Peggy van Praagh returned to England in 1961, while the birth pangs of incorporation took place, receiving a pittance of a retainer during the long fifteen months of gestation. Geoffrey Ingram, no doubt as a result of his earlier citizen's committee to promote a national ballet company, was sent overseas with an even smaller retainer to study ballet administration. Both were kept posted of developments and given instructions by John McCallum in Melbourne and Neil Hutchinson in Sydney. The fact that the instructions were often in direct contradiction of each other and that neither consulted Peggy van Praagh, whose job it was to lead the future company, appears to have resulted in none of the flare-ups which commonly accompany this kind of multiplicity of administration. All parties concerned, though in different cities and even different continents, were determined to make the Australian Ballet a reality and all put aside personal irritations for the common good. There appears to have been a quite incredible amount of goodwill in every quarter, a rare thing indeed in the arts, and many years were to pass before the pattern was broken.

In England and on the Continent, Peggy van Praagh was busy earning a precarious living to supplement her retainer from the Foundation. This living was also to help the company later on; she became Professor of the Dance for the Marquis de Cuevas Ballet and taught several new recruits to the company, including Marilyn Jones and Garth Welch

from Australia and a young Russian dancer who had recently fled to the West, one Rudolf Nureyev. Three years later Nureyev was happy to repay his first non-Russian teacher by coming to Australia for the first of many guest appearances.

At the same time van Praagh and Ingram met and discussed possible future policies for the company. The seven points on which they agreed were placed before the Australian Ballet Foundation as a kind of charter and accepted *in toto*.

This policy, in outline, covered the following points:
1. To provide a professional company that would give full-time employment to its dancers.
2. To establish a school, for professional students only, that would develop a national style and provide the main source of trained dancers for the Company.
3. To build a balanced repertoire, including the standard classical ballets, revivals of the best modern works from all over the world, and to create new ballets exclusive to the company.
4. To encourage Australian creative artists, that is, choreographers, composers and painters, already leaders in their own fields, to contribute to the creation of new ballets for the company.
5. To encourage international stars to visit Australia and dance with the company as Guest Artists.
6. To develop an education programme providing lecture demonstrations and special school matinees, to increase the interest and knowledge of ballet in the younger generation, with a view to building future audiences.
7. To attain a high artistic standard within Australia and to merit, by performance and presentation, recognition in the field of international ballet.

Peggy van Praagh estimated that it would take ten to twenty years for all these aims to be realized, particularly the last. It may be a further indication of her underestimation of the Borovansky Ballet she found in 1960, as much as a credit to her own work, that the goal was reached within a short four years!

The schools education programme was implemented almost immediately and its successful execution contributed very heavily to the future of the company. The emergence of a vital male dancing generation in particular can be traced to the lectures and demonstrations in schools, which began almost as soon as the company was created. Geoffrey Ingram was largely responsible for this activity, and the breaking down of prejudice among the non-converted was a direct result of this programme. Male dancing is considered a respectable career today and Australia is second to no other nation in this area.

In the meantime the Ballet Foundation had finally completed its bureaucratic procedures and van Praagh was

Ah, yes, I remember her well! Toynbee Hall in the East End of London, 5 December 1938. Anthony Tudor's new London Ballet premiered his *Gala Performance,* built around its three ballerinas, Peggy van Praagh, Maud Lloyd and Gerd Larsen. Van Praagh was a pretty little thing, stocky by modern standards, but her strong technique and steely point work left a lasting impression on one fan in the cheapest seats, John Cargher.

given the green light to commence recruiting her dancers. Travelling the length and breadth of Europe, she saw and individually spoke to every Australian dancer in the profession over there and attempted to talk them into returning home. Some resisted, but when the company finally assembled for rehearsals in 1962 at least Marilyn Jones and Garth Welch were there to rejoin Kathleen Gorham. On a lower level, Heather Macrae and Barbara Chambers also left overseas companies to return.

There was a notable absence of the kind of second-rate imported 'star', who was billed above better Australian dancers in Borovansky's time, in the new company. Initially, the only addition to the Australian roster was in the male principal field, where the new generation was still to come. Still, there was no attempt to give preferential treatment to Karl Welander; he had come to Australia as a migrant on an assisted passage and joined the rank and file like any other leading cast member. In the second year Bryan Lawrence, a very major talent indeed, followed in his footsteps. Both proved great assets to the Australian scene during and after their careers in the Australian Ballet.

The thinking was: anybody can join the company if they want to become Australians. After all, if migrants can become top architects or plumbers, why not dancers; all three are needed. When it came to guest stars, van Praagh aimed for the top: Erik Bruhn and Sonia Arova were the guests during the first season of the Australian Ballet and their presence was a lesson to the company members and also to the public, who immediately saw the difference between them and the kind of secondary dancer Borovansky had been passing off as imported stars.

The preparation was good. That what resulted was artistically viable can be proved very readily (with a little luck in the coming pages), but what is more important is that from November 1962 to the present, without even one day's interruption, every dancer and employee of the Australian Ballet has been paid a wage, which has made it worth his or her while to be a truly permanent member of a company which has a limitless future before it. And it wasn't done with mirrors, but with good will. Compare the creation of the Australian Ballet with the struggles of the Australian Opera elsewhere in this book and you will see what I mean.

However smooth the creation of the new Australian Ballet may have been, its success with audiences and its financial future were far from secure at first. The acceptance of the company by the critics and the public was instantaneous and, in the light of the continuity of policies, dancers and repertoire in the years to come, this is not surprising. But the financial problems which caused Williamson's to drop their support of the Borovansky Ballet did not disappear, nor did pockets of resistance at the box office.

It became obvious very quickly that the overseas pattern of continuous subsidies for ballet would have to be repeated in Australia. If there was any illusion at the Trust that the ballet would make up the opera's losses, it was quickly dispelled. The company lost money from the start and the spectre of early closure hung over its head for many years. That this at no time affected artistic standards must be to the everlasting credit of Peggy van Praagh.

The first signs of audience troubles began during the New Zealand tour which came toward the end of the company's first year. The most enthusiastic reviews failed to attract audiences in Auckland and other cities and three of the planned eight weeks were abandoned. In Australia a similar picture presented itself in many country centres which the company visited as part of its required programme to bring ballet to all parts of the nation. The cities gave reasonable support, if not the sold-out houses of later years, but identical programmes with identical casts often attracted audiences of less than a hundred in cities like Ballarat, Bendigo or Lismore. It was to take a few years before the triumph of the Australian Ballet were to make it the box office draw it is today.

There was no reason to believe that audiences would see anything very much better than the last Borovansky season and to Australians not even Erik Bruhn and Sonia Arova meant a great deal; for all they knew, Bruhn and Arova were no better than the much publicized imports of Borovansky. The uphill struggle to create new audiences began almost before the first performance of the Australian Ballet and it involved its share of heartbreak. There is a danger that nostalgia may blind us to the realities of the early years; the headlines across the nation when Marilyn Jones returned from overseas were not a true reflection of her qualities as a dancer in 1962 and the great Australian ballet launched with such a fanfare, *Melbourne Cup*, has a place in history only because it accidentally notched up more performances than better ballets staged later, when a wider range of repertoire gave each work a shorter life.

The Australian Ballet started with a standard well above that of the last Borovansky seasons, but it was not the traumatic realization of everbody's dreams of balletic glories in the Antipodes. Among other things, it suffered comparison with the first of the visiting companies which appeared during the period between the closure of Borovansky and the start of the new company. The Elizabethan Theatre Trust itself was instrumental in bringing the majority of these groups to Australia in an attempt to keep a continuity of interest in the dance. It was a good thought, but it back-fired in giving the public a look at standards which were not to be attained by the Australian Ballet for many years.

The Leningrad Maly Ballet was not in the Kirov or Bolshoi class, but it had the discipline of Russian dancers with a lifetime of good training. The French duo Claude Bessy and Atilio Labis had little to offer, but an ensemble

SWAN LAKE

BALLET IN FOUR ACTS

Choreography by Marius Petipa and Lev Ivanov
Present production revised by Peggy van Praagh and Ray Powell
Music by Peter Ilich Tchaikovsky
Scenery by Production Division of The Australian Elizabethan Theatre Trust and J. C. Williamson Theatres Ltd.

ODETTE/ODILE .... Sonia Arova
SIEGFRIED .... Erik Bruhn
PRINCESS MOTHER .... Meredith Kinmont
BENNO .... Douglas Gilchrist
VON ROTHBART .... Ron Paul

ACT I

WOLFGANG—SIEGFRIED'S TUTOR .... Leon Kellaway
PAS DE TROIS .... Kathleen Geldard, Heather Macrae, Karl Welander
PAS DE SIX .... Beverley Dean, Leonie Leahy, Suzanne Musitz,
Douglas Gilchrist, Max Hansen, Robert Olup
COURT LADIES ... Beverley Dean, Carol Ann Ford, Rhyl Kennell, Gillian Collinson
HUNTSMEN .... Ian Rannard, Leslie Sinclair, Robert Smith, Kenneth Tillson
PEASANTS .... Margaret Akerman, Mercia Barden, Joan Boler,
Patrina Coates, Lexie Kunze, Helen Magner, Jan Melvin,
Carmel Nolan, Ramona Ratas, Rhonda Russell, Gailene Stock,
Barry Kitcher, Colin Peaseley, Peter Condon, Paul Wright,
Kelvin Coe, Wally Bourke
A GIRL .... Jan Melvin

INTERVAL

ACT II

TWO SWANS .... Rosemary Mildner, Leonie Leahy
CYGNETS .... Patrina Coates, Robyn Croft, Jan Melvin, Rhonda Russell
SWANS .... Margaret Akerman, Mercia Barden, Joan Boler, Beverley Dean,
Carol Ann Ford, Meredith Kinmont, Rhyl Kennell, Lexie Kunze,
Helen Magner, Carmel Nolan, Ramona Ratas, Gailene Stock

INTERVAL

ACT III

MASTER OF CEREMONIES .... Leon Kellaway
THE SIX PRINCESSES ... Margaret Akerman, Patrina Coates, Carol Ann Ford,
Lexie Kunze, Helen Magner, Gailene Stock
CZARDAS .... Sandra Bingham, Barry Kitcher,
Joan Boler, Robyn Croft, Mercia Barden, Jan Melvin,
Wally Bourke, Peter Condon, Colin Peaseley, Paul Wright
SPANISH DANCE .... Rosemary Mildner, Suzanne Musitz,
Kenneth Tillson, Barry Moreland
NEAPOLITAN .... Kathleen Geldard, Karl Welander
MAZURKA .... Beverley Dean, Rhyl Kennell, Ramona Ratas,
Douglas Gilchrist, Leslie Sinclair, Robert Olup
HERALDS .... Ian Rannard, Robert Smith, Kelvin Coe
PAGES .... Gillian Collinson, Leona Woodnutt

INTERVAL

ACT IV

TWO SWANS .... Rosemary Mildner, Leonie Leahy
CYGNETS .... Patrina Coates, Mercia Barden, Jan Melvin, Rhonda Russell
SWANS .... Margaret Akerman, Joan Boler, Beverley Dean, Carol Ann Ford,
Meredith Kinmont, Rhyll Kennell, Lexie Kunze, Heather Macrae,
Helen Magner, Carmel Nolan, Ramona Ratas, Gailene Stock

Musical Director: NOEL SMITH
Deputy Conductor: REUBEN FINEBERG   Leader: DAN SCULLY

Curtain up! The first performance of the Australian Ballet on 2 November 1962 needed guest stars Sonia Arova and Erik Bruhn to attract its gala audience. Local stars like Gorham, Jones and Welch were not in sight, but among the ensemble were many to achieve fame in later years. (Note Kelvin Coe and Walter Bourke getting bottom billing among the Peasants.)

of dancers from the Bolshoi, and Margot Fonteyn with a group from the Royal Ballet, were both seen in Australia in 1962 and the memory of their work was very fresh indeed in the public's mind when comparisons had to be made. Unfortunately the public then, as now, had and has a nasty habit of not believing its own eyes. Fonteyn, Royal and Bolshoi meant something better than Erik Bruhn and Sonia Arova, possibly because they were publicized as stars in their own right, while the latter were 'only' guests with a local company. Thus even the best which the Australian Ballet could offer failed to impress many of its first audiences.

The public took a wait and see attitude. Fortunately it didn't have to wait long before it began to see.

The Fledgling Takes Off

16

Melbourne has always been the ballet capital of Australia. Borovansky started in this city, his prime backer, J. C. Williamson's, had its head office there and the Australian Ballet continued the tradition. Rehearsals for the first season of the new company began in Melbourne and administrative offices were opened in East Melbourne. Since 1962 the ballet has continued to live in the capital of Victoria, yet since 1962 practically all its major productions have been premiered elsewhere! Circumstance rather than planning, fate rather than foresight were responsible, but the very first performance of the Australian Ballet took place on 2 November 1962 at Her Majesty's Theatre in Sydney.

It was a glittering affair, completely in line with past traditions of diamonds and mink gala premieres. There was an official pre-ballet dinner and an official post-ballet supper, both hosted by the top brass of the Elizabethan Theatre Trust and the papers were full of socialites in all their glory. To pander to the wealthy and the powerful able to provide financial sponsorship via banks (N.S.W.), oil (B.P.), beer (C.U.B.) or cigarettes (Rothman's), the full four acts of *Swan Lake* were unearthed from the archives as a setting for the two guest stars, Erik Bruhn and Sonia Arova. However good the performance — and it was far from bad — it was a vehicle for social rather than balletic glorification and obviously chosen for that purpose.

'Sonia Arova and Erik Bruhn in *Swan Lake*' would have been a more appropriate title for the Australian Ballet's first programme. Its own dancers were no more than a frame for the two guests, the ballet was not exactly a novelty and no estimate could be made from its performance as to what the future would bring. The Press was understandably kind, though the *Sydney Morning Herald* used the slightly patronizing 'high level of competence' and probably hit the nail squarely on the head. It was too early to judge the new infant on the basis of a soundly trained corps de ballet and a few soloists in roles which required no great demonstration of skills.

The inevitable 'stirrers' created their inevitable storms in teacups before the grand opening. Some of the dancers were unwisely exposed to a press photographer while engaged in replenishing much needed calories with sandwiches and *beer*! 'Are Our Ballet Dancers Too Fat?' screamed the headline and poor Erik Bruhn was conned into saying that he had danced with slimmer girls. The management promptly exacerbated the situation by ordering no more photographs during meal breaks.

The alternative Australian casts for *Swan Lake* could hardly be accused of being overweight. Kathleen Gorham and Garth Welch more than held their own against the foreign usurpers and (an exceptionally slim) Marilyn Jones already had the classical line and technique, if not the experience, to compete. She was partnered by the Swede, Caj Selling,

256

How Australian can you get? The first Australian ballet by the Australian Ballet was built around the only horse race in the world which warrants a public holiday, *Melbourne Cup*.

The Odds – Elaine Fifield (The Debutante) has placed her bet with Barry Kitcher (The Bookie) and Bryan Lawrence (The Jackeroo) and is a bit doubtful about the odds being offered.

who was getting ready to replace Bruhn when his short contract ran out.

The real debut of the company came with the second programme and a most ambitious undertaking, the balletic interpretation of the first running of the Melbourne Cup, the world's only horse race for which a public holiday is gazetted. *Melbourne Cup* was big news, though Ray Powell's comic gem *One in Five* on the same bill was the better ballet. (*One in Five* was notable for Marilyn Jones' debut as a comedienne, an aspect of her art she shamefully neglected later during long years as the very classical *prima ballerina* of the company.)

Audiences had their first glimpse of *Melbourne Cup* via A.B.C. television and a show called *Woman's World,* compered by one (Dr) Jean Battersby. It was the new Australian work, and not *Swan Lake*, which was featured to introduce the Australian Ballet to the public, but plans to present the premiere on Melbourne Cup Day (in Sydney) were scrapped to make way for the blue rinse brigade's glorious *Swan Lake*.

Melbourne Cup was perhaps too much for a young company. It was by far the most ambitious ballet to be staged and it set out to emulate lighter classics like *Pineapple Poll* or *Le beau Danube*. Its principal weakness lay in the non-existence of Australian light music on which choreographer Rex Reid could draw. To capture the mood of the first great Australian race meeting in 1861, the son of a jockey, Harold Badger, arranged some music of the period, of European

How Australian can you get?

The Runners – Some excellent hurdling (*left*) by the Jockeys (Karl Welander and Walter Bourke), while their pretty steeds (Robyn Croft and Barbara Chamber) appear to be holding the reins . . . Jockeys being raced by horses?

The Barrackers – The Pink Bonnet Girls (*below left*), led by Rhyl Kennell, seem to be on the winning streak which the Australian Ballet started with *Melbourne Cup*.

The Winner – First, second and third place-getters in the original Melbourne Cup of 1861 in the shapely forms (*below*) of Barbara Chambers (Archer), Kathleen Geldard (Twilight) and Heather Macrae (Tory Boy) with their jockeys, Karl Welander, Walter Bourke and Robert Okell.

origin. Unfortunately, the medley of styles and the familiarity of the tunes by Suppé, Offenbach and others, that were used proved to be lively but unconducive to creating a viable whole. Only the excellent decor by Ann Church and the lively performances of the many dancers in a multitude of parts made *Melbourne Cup* the success it remained until better ballets took its place in the repertoire.

A remarkable number of the dancers who appeared in this literally Australian ballet were to leave a lasting mark on the company's history. The excellence of Kathleen Gorham as a very equine Archer (the first winner of the Cup) and Karl Welander as her jockey may have been expected, but in the many smaller roles were dancers like Walter Bourke, Barbara Chambers, Kelvin Coe, Warren de Maria, Kathleen Geldard, Rhyl Kennell, Barry Kitcher, Leonie Leahy, Heather Macrae, Barry Moreland, Robert Olup, Colin Peasley and Gailene Stock, not to mention Garth Welch and Leon Kellaway.

The strength of the male contingent was already coming to the fore during that first season, though the ranks of the top men still had to be fortified with imports.

After revivals of *Les Rendezvous* and *Coppélia* (with Algeranoff guesting as Dr Coppelius), a second programme of novelties was not quite up to the standard of the first. A modern English classic, John Cranko's *The Lady and the Fool* eclipsed the smaller *Just for Fun* and *The Night is a Sorceress*. Ray Powell, the company's Ballet Master on loan on a temporary basis (which extends to this day) from the Royal Ballet, danced the part of Bootface, which he had created at Covent Garden seven years earlier. *The Lady and the Fool* remains the only ballet from that first year still in the repertoire and, amazingly enough, its leading lady now as then is and was Marilyn Jones; La Capricciosa is a part made for her and she has, if anything, grown better in it over the years.

While *One in Five* was an established success before Ray Powell restaged it for the Australian Ballet, his *Just for Fun* was a new creation for the company. The title summarizes its virtues and failings admirably. *The Night is a Sorceress,* on the other hand, was a reversion to the early Borovansky principle of acquiring the best work of local choreographers previously seen in Australia. Again, the source was the Victorian Ballet Guild. Unfortunately, Rex Reid's minor piece of *grand guignol* to the music of Sidney Bechet lost in the transition to a full-size company.

Arova and Bruhn continued to add classical *pas de deux* to keep faith with their public, which was already beginning to show some preference for balletic integration against the harsh concentration on technique which the guest artists were providing.

The tour that followed the Sydney season started on 27 December 1962 and continued with the same repertoire until late the following year. Adelaide, Perth, Melbourne and Brisbane were followed by the fateful New Zealand Tour and the trip around the Australian backwoods, both of which showed that not everybody was ready for the brand new company's wares. Audiences and Press may have been enthusiastic, but the former often stayed away *en masse,* and to enjoy ballet it is necessary to see it first. The financial implications of these box office set-backs proved to be severe.

Artistically, on the other hand, the Australian Ballet took off from the start. Perhaps its repertoire was a little slow in developing originality, perhaps its wardrobe and scenery still reflected budgetary rather than artistic considerations (much still came from the old Borovansky warehouse), perhaps the scratch orchestras conducted with great skill by Noel Smith were still on the scratchy side, but the dancers themselves showed discipline and promise in the ensembles and they had been admirably chosen and obviously trained for the maximum development of their potential. Peggy van Praagh had indeed done her homework.

The charge is made to this day that van Praagh moulded the company in the image of the Royal Ballet. There is some truth in this, but it must be remembered that she came to Australia from England and had herself taken part in the emergence of English ballet as a major world force in the art. It was not simply a matter of aping the Royal Ballet, but of following the pattern which had successfully led to the creation of that company. This meant incorporating much that had been done by a whole range of companies in England outside the confines of the original Sadler's Wells Ballet, which became the Royal Ballet in 1956. Van Praagh had danced herself with many of these companies and was familiar with the work of them all. Ballet Rambert, the London Ballet, the Festival Ballet and many minor companies all contributed to the emergence of *English ballet*. The Australian Ballet was created in the image of English ballet and if this led to a similar end result, we should not really be surprised. The only question is whether this is a good thing.

Ballet in England began in a most primitive manner during the twenties, developed rapidly in the intimate ballet field during the thirties, began to enlarge during the war years due to the immense demand for escapist entertainment at that time and, finally, the many components and years of work by hundreds of people resulted in the Royal Ballet and the various other groups in England today, many of them no more and no less shadows of the Covent Garden company than the Australian Ballet is.

Peggy van Praagh was asked more or less to produce the end result without the years of preliminaries. Borovansky had filled a great need, but the historical facts are there: he left behind him no recognizable Australian style in danc-

The Lady and the Fool The first of John Cranko's superb ballets to be staged by the Australian Ballet. It has been continuously in the repertoire since 1962. The mixture of spectacle and pathos has proved to be irresistible to Australian audiences and Marilyn Jones continues to shine as La Capricciosa.

The Fool (*top*) thinks he has made it into society, the fool! Marilyn Jones and John Meehan in the 1975 revival.

The Lady meets the Fool – and his friend – on the way to the ball (*bottom*). Marilyn Jones and, on the bench, John Meehan as Moondog and Paul Saliba as Bootface; Colin Peasley as The Footman.

ing, let alone repertoire. His early adventurousness, which paralleled the work of the likes of Rambert in England, went by the board as soon as Williamson's invested in his company with the profit motive uppermost in mind. In recent years the Australian Ballet has on occasion been forced to follow suit when subsidies have not kept pace with cost increases. Yet at no time has the company ceased producing new works; it is constantly trying to broaden the repertoire. It is too easy to forget the appearance of Tetley and Butler and Moreland, or young local choreographers, in the blaze of publicity which surrounds the big box office ballets.

The Australian Ballet's policies may well be in the pattern of the Royal Ballet, but Australia would not today have a place in the international ballet scene if in 1962 van Praagh had started à la Ninette de Valois with six dancers performing with an opera company. The creation of a sound corps de ballet was possible in 1962 because of work done by others before her arrival. The availability of three major Australian principals (Gorham, Jones and Welch) enabled her to at least claim an Australianism for the dancers from the top down. But putting all that into a frame which was identifiably Australian was impossible and, to a lesser degree, is still impossible today. It is all very well to speak of an Australian school of dancing; without the constant cross-fertilization which takes place overseas not enough influences can be brought to bear on artists so far from the epicentre of balletic activities. The creation of new choreographers alone is almost impossible, unless they can work regularly with other companies before settling in their own environment to become genuine originals.

In 1963 the Australian Ballet had begun to exist as a pale shadow of the Royal Ballet. In 1976, at the end of the first creative period, the age of van Praagh and Helpmann, it had become a bright shadow of the Royal Ballet with some decidedly individualistic overtones. But it was still in the pattern in which it began in that first season and the company's gradual development over the intervening thirteen years was neither forced nor hindered by factors other than purely financial ones. The highlights exceed the lowlights, but the daily grind of the good average output has predominated. If in the process some of the excitement of the more flamboyant companies has been missing, we have also been spared the temperamental explosions and the major crises which normally abound in the ballet world. Perhaps the very complacency of almost unbroken excellence in performance has been a handicap. If so, it is not yet being felt at the box office.

It took Peggy van Praagh one year to create a viable ballet company which was not as large as Borovansky's, but was acceptable to Margot Fonteyn and Rudolf Nureyev, the world's most celebrated dancers in 1964, as a vehicle for their talents. Topping Bruhn and Arova could not have been easy, but faith in van Praagh on the part of her erstwhile colleagues overseas made the impossible possible and ballet in Australia received a greater shot in the arm in 1964 than the creation of the company itself had been during the previous year. The excitement created by the appearance of Nureyev and Fonteyn was phenomenal.

The Turning Point
17

It may seem ridiculous to refer to the second year of a company as the 'turning point', but the foundations laid were artistically so sound that by the end of Year Two (1964) the Australian Ballet was so well established that the government seriously suggested, and ultimately insisted, that it represent Australia at the Commonwealth Festival of the Arts in England in 1965. It was a remarkable achievement and it did not occur without teething troubles.

By the end of the first year (November 1963) the losses from the tours in New Zealand and the country towns in Australia nearly proved to be the end of the Australian Ballet. The capital cities were not exactly rapturous about the company, but at least there was enough hard cash at the box office to break even. The company's first General Manager, Louis van Eyssen, originally a colleague of and now directed by the far from business-like administration of the Elizabethan Theatre Trust was obviously a little short on managerial abilities.

The Trust's answer to the problems was to seek to follow the fortunes, or misfortunes, of its opera company: disband and reassemble every year. Peggy van Praagh protested loudly that continuity in a ballet company is more important than in an opera company. 'If you interrupt the work of the company now', she said, 'forget it!' They didn't. The first year's results had been impressive – Canberra was clearly interested in the future of the company and the possibility of countering the Trust's operatic disasters with balletic successes was very real. A sacrificial lamb had to be found nevertheless and van Eyssen departed – to be replaced by Geoffrey Ingram, who, in typical Trust fashion, was given a different title; the General Manager was replaced by an Administrator.

The role of Geoffrey Ingram during the next two years is curious. He came from the same mould as Louis van Eyssen in that he saw the role of the Administrator largely as that of Artistic Director rather than General Manager. He was not qualified in business matters and made up for his inexperience with an enthusiasm which was infectious. In the face of Peggy van Praagh's rightly unyielding artistic directorship and the Trust's holding of the purse strings, Ingram was unable to develop any natural abilities he may have possessed. Fortunately for him, his time in charge coincided with some most spectacular artistic achievements, which were reflected at the box office.

The influence of the Trust at this time was very strong in the Australian Ballet. Unfortunately, the policies which it forced onto the company proved to be the only failures of 1964. It was the Trust's new Executive Director, Stefan Haag's, idea to duplicate the Covent Garden opera/ballet system, which was, of course, what had attracted the Trust to going into the ballet field in the first place. That something which worked in one theatre with permanent facilities

and (for its time) lavish grants might not work under touring conditions with very limited backing did not occur to Stefan Haag or even that financial wizard, Dr Coombs. At any rate, plans were made for a joint ballet and opera season late in 1964. It was as well from the ballet's point of view that its two big events of the year came before the merger.

The Adelaide Festival of 1964 remains to this day the most memorable from the Australian Ballet's point of view. It was the first appearance of the company at the Festival, it appeared without any guest artists and it presented the world premiere of Robert Helpmann's *The Display,* the most notable of all the ballets ever produced entirely by Australians. The fact that the company managed to present a season up to festival standards without any guest artists is, in the context of this history, even more important than the creation of *The Display.* A new version of *Aurora's Wedding,* restaged by Peggy van Praagh with designs by Kristian Frederickson, extended the company to the fullest and it came through with flying colours. The other addition to the repertoire for the festival, Betty Pounder's *Jazz Spectrum,* was a most suitable curtain raiser and balanced the programme admirably, but it was hardly more than an extension of the kind of television ensemble ballet so popular at that time, an impression strengthened by the music specially written by Les Patching, a television band leader!

Robert Helpmann in 1964 was riding the crest of the wave internationally. He had been equally successful in ballet, drama and films. He had danced, acted and even sung with success. He had produced ballets, plays and opera. Nothing appeared to be outside his capabilities and, like most people in the ballet world in England, he had worked with Peggy van Praagh. As the leading Australian in her field, he was the logical choice to stage a work for the Australian Ballet, and particularly for the Adelaide Festival, for he was South Australian by birth. What he produced was certainly more genuinely Australian than anything seen before, or after, *The Display.*

Original music was commissioned from the best known of the expatriate Australian composers, Malcolm Williamson. Sidney Nolan provided the designs and at one stage Australia's leading author, Patrick White, actually produced a scenario for *The Display,* although this was discarded very quickly, since White knew nothing about ballet and provided the most unballetic situations. (Some people never got used to the football and beer-drinking; what would they have done if faced with Patrick White's policemen arriving to arrest all and sundry?)

The key to *The Display* lay in that most Australian creature, the lyrebird. Helpmann, who had recently toured Australia, performing Shakespeare with Katherine Hepburn, had been fascinated by his first view of the bird's mating dance and now built a complex piece of symbolism around its sex-ual habits, running parallel to and ultimately intermingling with some genuinely Australian young people at play. The lyrebird itself was billed (no pun intended) as The Male and the leading girl as The Female and there was a most realistic rape scene between the two to scandalize the Adelaide matrons.

Good as *The Display* is as a ballet pure and simple, a major part of its success came from other areas. Helpmann's concept of the lyrebird itself was uncannily true to nature, but it could not have been realized without the truly remarkable costume which was created in London by an elderly, uncredited master builder named Hugh Skillen. He built a huge – five metres from tip to tip – lyrebird tail onto something closely resembling a parachute harness. It was originally made of bamboo spines, but the actions of the dancer broke these too quickly; the poor man (Barry Kitcher) was finally expected to move and dance in this constricting harness weighed down with shafts of steel! But the end justified the means; the lyrebird in *The Display* is one of the most successful recreations of reality ever seen in the theatre.

Credit must also be given to William Akers, at that time the Production Director of the company, for his (again uncredited) lighting of the ballet. Anything as atmospheric as *The Display* needed something little short of genius in the way of lighting and Akers in this, as in so many later ballets, achieved miracles in visual illusion, recreating the lyrebird's natural habitat.

Yet ultimately it is the dancers who make a ballet and Helpmann, in true Sadler's Wells or Royal Ballet fashion, built his choreography around his raw material. Kathleen Gorham's Female was the highlight of her career; Bryan Lawrence, though only just arrived in Australia, was an uncomfortably convincing gang leader and Garth Welch an equally convincing gang victim. Van Praagh's policy of 'unstarring' her principals paid handsome dividends; most of them appeared in the crowd scenes.

The Nureyev–Fonteyn seasons followed immediately in Sydney and Melbourne. Fonteyn was probably talking with a small tongue in her cheek when she explained that she felt obliged to come, because it was her fault that Peggy van Praagh had been landed with the Australian Ballet; had she not recommended her for the job? As for Nureyev, his career had really only taken off after his partnership with Fonteyn began in 1962 and apart from keeping the team together, he also owed a debt to van Praagh. Their success in 1964 was great indeed. An English management joined the Trust, Williamson's and the Australian Ballet Foundation in presenting the season, which also featured two more guest stars, Royes Fernandez and Lupe Serrano, to ensure that the public paying high prices should have imported back-stops if either Fonteyn or Nureyev were prevented from appearing. *Giselle* and *Swan Lake* (four acts) were their vehicles and the returns were spectacular – so spectacular that James Laurie, the English impresario, immediately made plans to use the Australian company in 1965, plans which were to materialize in spectacular fashion.

The July Brisbane season produced little more than confusion in the public's mind. It opened in July with a so-called Gala Performance of Carl Orff's *The Wise Woman (Die Kluge)* coupled with *The Display*. Since the general public in Queensland had never heard of either, nobody knew whether they were opera or ballet or both. Fortunately, it was a 'Gala' and people who attend galas rarely care what goes on, provided that they are seen in the intervals. Less fortunate was the solitary Saturday matinee in which the Trust attempted to marry the two arts again. *The Wise Woman* plus *Jazz Spectrum* (of all things!) attracted about a hundred customers paying reduced matinee prices! More to the point, the publics for opera and ballet were confused as to whether one or the other was playing each night and many stayed away altogether, particularly when the reviews failed to glow with enthusiasm. The dancers in the company may or may not have become infected with the spirit of defeatism; suffice to say that they did not exactly reach the heights of superlativity.

The solitary premiere did not exactly help either. *Roundelay* was Ray Powell's third ballet for the company and hardly an advance on *Just for Fun*. Somehow, Powell never realized the immense promise of *One in Five* and the fact that the latter masterpiece (so cheap to stage too!) did not remain in the repertoire may have imbued him with the idea that something bigger would also be better. Unfortunately the miniaturist failed to provide good large canvases, though his *Symphony in Gold* six years later (to Mendelssohn's *Italian Symphony*) was far from bad; but by then it was probably too late.

The Sydney season which followed was financially even less rewarding than the Brisbane one because it was here that the full impact of the opera/ballet integration attempt was felt. The apparent independence of the company in the earlier part of 1964 was an illusion; though Administrator Ingram had fought against it, the joint season proceeded and went far beyond anything Covent Garden had ever tried. There, at least, each company played (and plays) its own evenings, if in tandem. But the Trust was ruling the Australian Ballet Foundation, since the participation of Williamson's was never more than token. In any case, the Foundation's members met only intermittently, principally to rubber-stamp the plans worked out between meetings of the Trust and the Administrators of the company.

Something which might have worked for the Adelaide Festival earlier in 1964 saw the light of day in Sydney. The coupling of Orff's opera *The Wise Woman* and his cantata-cum-ballet *Catulli Carmina* made artistic sense, but ignored the fact that Orff always has been and still is a non-event in Australia. The general public does not know him and the high-brow critic hates him. Actually, both works have a considerable following among the *cognoscenti,* but they failed to rise to the bait. For once, the opera company outshone the ballet. *Catulli Carmina,* an earthy medieval sex romp was choreographed by Joanne Priest as some kind of Sunday School harvest festival. She gave the best choreography to the singers, who mixed with the dancers on stage, meaning that there was very little dancing of any kind. The whole thing didn't work and attempts to couple *The Wise Woman* with other ballets were no more successful.

A more sensible, but less exploitable, use of the opera company's resources for ballet came with the revival of Fokine's *Prince Igor*. The music here calls for a chorus off-stage and the ballet was certainly enhanced by this. Bryan Lawrence's Polovtsian Chief was fine and the passive female lead was entrusted to Elaine Fifield. (Fifield had been a very major international ballerina until she married and retired to Papua-New Guinea to raise a family. When this did not work out too well, she came back to Australia and joined the Australian Ballet in 1964.) Apart from the revival of another Fokine work, *Le Carnaval,* in which her Columbine retained all her original charm, casting her in *Prince Igor* could hardly be said to make the best use of her talents. In any case, two Fokine revivals plus *Catulli Carmina* (not to mention one or two classical *pas de deux*) were hardly a great step forward for the company. But then, it was economy time as losses continued to mount and the company sank lower and lower in its own estimation.

When the Trust's balance sheet for 1964 appeared it showed that the Australian Ballet had lost $135,306, an incredible figure, for it was stated in Dr Coombs' report that in Melbourne alone, ten performances with Nureyev and Fonteyn had netted $185,956 at the box office and Sydney was not far behind. *The Display* had proved a winner from the start and attendances during the subsequent tour, while not on a par with the Nureyev performances, were not really bad. Unfortunately the ill-fated combined tour of opera and ballet companies had proceeded as planned and the shape things to come looked decidedly unpleasant. It can be said that only the hopes for 1965 kept heart and soul together.

Divide To Rule

18

Divide et impera is a Latin proverb meaning 'divide and rule'. It had long been obvious that Peggy van Praagh was determined to get her way and that she had very little respect for the ill-informed advice which was being offered by her Trust-dominated board of directors. Admittedly, she could not control the money, but she was unwilling to permit interference in artistic matters. That she had access to Fonteyn, Nureyev, Helpmann and anybody else she needed and was able to get within budget specifications, mattered very little. She ruled alone; there were none who could say her nay, though there were many who would.

For quite some time waves were being made in several directions, all with the worst intentions but, fortunately, none with really bad results. The creation of the Australian Ballet School in 1964, in line with van Praagh's policies laid down before the company even began to be assembled, was greeted with howls of protest by the National Theatre and Ballet Guild, both situated in Melbourne and both engaged in ballet training. The ridiculous claims of the former were easily dismissed, but Laurel Martyn's objections had a sounder foundation; after all, she had been around a lot longer than anybody at the Australian Ballet. The possibility of Martyn's becoming the school for the Australian Ballet was probably never mooted and it seems unlikely that such a proposition would have been entertained. It was almost certainly van Praagh's choice of Margaret Scott as director of the school which caused most of the waves; she had been a colleague of Laurel Martyn's and had also been associated with the National Theatre, during its better days. Fortunately in the light of history, van Praagh stuck to her guns and nobody today will argue with the excellent job Margaret Scott has done with her school.

(In fairness to the National Theatre it should be mentioned here that, after the death of Jean Alexander in 1972, its 'ridiculous' ballet school engaged a new Director, Marilyn Jones, in temporary retirement from the Australian Ballet after having had her second child. With the move to the new National Theatre building in St Kilda, and its huge modern studios, Jones had no problem in establishing a sound and basically new school, which was strongly reinforced in 1974 when her old friend and predecessor as *prima ballerina* of the Australian Ballet, Kathleen Gorham, brought her own huge and successful ballet school into the National Theatre. With Australia's two leading ballerinas — who had by then both been awarded O.B.E.s for services to the dance — the National Theatre Ballet School of the 1970s bears no relation to that mentioned earlier in these pages.)

The next attack centred on van Praagh herself. The administrative upheavals which were so much a part of the Elizabethan Theatre Trust's history began to affect the Australian Ballet. Peggy van Praagh's initial contract was for two years and this was due for renewal late in 1964. Van Eyssen had been replaced by Geoffrey Ingram, whose tenure was still too new to judge his long-term prospects as Administrator of the company. The financial disasters of the combined opera/ballet seasons had wiped out any hope of a balanced budget for the ballet; not that anybody had expected a profit. The fact remained that the company had been threatened with closure at the end of van Praagh's first year and that now a similar situation existed.

But for the fact that the company was committed to representing Australia at the Commonwealth Arts Festival in London in 1965 the Australian Ballet might well have perished there and then. To allow it to continue without some sacrificial goat being offered was inconceivable. The public service mentality demanded that blame be apportioned. It was decided that Ingram had not been there long enough to take the blame, the Trust management was clearly not at fault, since it allowed the company complete autonomy (except in matters of policy), and that new blood had to be infused into the company's direction. If blood had to be shed in the process, well this was nothing abnormal in the ever-changing structure of the Trust. It was decided that Peggy van Praagh would have to go!

The idea of bringing Helpmann back on a regular basis had been proposed by van Praagh herself, who favoured such a move. She was basically a teacher, a trainer of dancers, while he was a showman with tremendous flair in matters theatrical and the two clearly complemented each other. The immense success of the company notwithstanding, a campaign was mounted that van Praagh's two year contract, which was about to expire, should not be renewed. At least one member of the Press fed the fires by publishing an attack suggesting that 'this foreign woman' be sent home on the grounds that the Australian Ballet was a failure!

Negotiations were begun with Helpmann to bring him into the company administration. Stefan Haag rightly argued that anybody who could produce *The Display* would be an asset to the company, but Helpmann was not interested in a full-time job in Australia; he had too many profitable (artistic as well as financial) commitments overseas. Suitable candidates to replace van Praagh completely were clearly not obtainable and finally she was faced with an ultimatum: stay and share the artistic directorship with Helpmann or . . . Van Praagh accepted, as much for the sake of the company, because she knew that Helpmann would be an asset, as for herself, for she also knew that he was not interested in her primary interests – the donkey work of the day to day artistic administration. Her decision proved to be the right one, for the partnership worked well enough for a great number of years and by the time it began to crumble, the people who had sought to gain a greater say through the division of power had long departed from the scene.

Helpmann, if anything, had even more friends and connections than van Praagh and, as things turned out, he had even less respect for the directors than his colleague. At first the very coup of having obtained his services, and his name, to put at the masthead of the stationery, made him the blue-eyed idol of the board, (which began to grow alarmingly as the company's future brightened). Helpmann says now that he never once attended a board meeting. If he had, it would hardly have been a momentous occasion, for Helpmann's disdain for amateur administrators was always amply displayed. He was more interested in producing more ballets and more income for himself. The former proved to be a boon to the company as well as to ballet in Australia as such. The latter irritated only those who were unable to obtain comparable terms.

The ballets which Helpmann began to produce for the company are a subject on their own. Criticism of his choreography has always been strong and, up to a point, Helpmann the choreographer may not be in the top class. Yet there is a combination of professionalism and perfectionism in his work which always makes it worthwhile. Most of his ballets do not survive the ravages of time too well and that, in a closed community like Australia, is not a good thing. Ballet companies necessarily rely on repertory – the repeating of the same works at regular intervals – and much of Helpmann's work relies on impact and sensation which, once seen, loses impetus. Few of his overseas works are revived regularly, though some – like *Hamlet* – are minor masterpieces. His work for the Australian Ballet has been significant, forming the backbone of the repertoire for a number of years. Yet here again it is one work – *The Display* in this case – that stands out above the others.

His next ballet (already in the production planning stage at the time of his appointment in 1965) was *Yūgen*, a piece of delicate Japanese balletic Noh theatre with some most beautiful decor by Desmond Heeley. While hardly pleasing the encore brigade and its demands for *pirouettes* and *entrechats* galore, it is the most likely of Helpmann's ballets to endure. *Sun Music* (1968) was another attempt at the all-Australian definitive work, built around Peter Sculthorpe's music of the same name. Largely attacked for its pretentiousness in attempting to imitate creation itself or at least the sun's influence on it, it may have been a little long and over elaborate, but hardly worthless (though a revival appears unlikely). Like most of Helpmann's ballets it is not easily forgotten by those who saw it, whether they liked it or not.

On the other hand the tremendously theatrical and dramatic *Elektra* (staged by the company in 1966) was not an original, but one of his English ballets with a well-established reputation, and *Hamlet,* produced here in 1970 with Nureyev in the title role (the kind of theatrical coup at which Helpmann excels) had proved its worth world-wide

over a period of twenty-eight years. His swan song was *Perisynthyon,* which was so much abused that it may well have discouraged Helpmann from trying again. Anyway, by then (1974) the honeymoon was over and his moon ballet was allowed its run without the first-aid which might well have given it a longer life. Having to change from a commissioned musical score to a Sibelius symphony (two Australian composers failed to meet agreed deadlines) was unlikely to encourage good choreography, but there was much in this ballet which was too clever by half.

Adding the scores fairly, though, Helpmann comes out of the exercise rather well. Two first-class originals, two excellent revivals, one glorious failure and one simple failure. Few choreographers today could provide six such works in eight years for any one company and no Australian choreographer is anywhere within reach of Helpmann's achievement. There can be no doubt that his contribution to the company's repertoire, combined with his ability to bring his influence to bear on outside choreographers during his years

as co-Artistic Director, helped very substantially to consolidate the work of Peggy van Praagh. The parting of their ways in the end was affected by matters other than those which may have been feared on his appointment in 1965. I shall deal with this in a later chapter.

In the meantime plans for 1965 proceeded, everything being angled toward the company's first world tour. That it should have even attempted such a venture so early in its existence is remarkable and van Praagh was dead set against it. However, Harold Holt put it to her squarely that it was up to the Australian Ballet to carry the banner at the Commonwealth Arts Festival, and she reluctantly agreed to go ahead with the plans. The Trust, licking its wounds from the 1964 record deficits of both companies, was delighted. The opera company was in recess while the Sutherland-Williamson Grand Opera Season of 1965 played and, with the ballet overseas for much of the year under government and private patronage, the chances of losses in the ballet field were remote.

271

Australia's Rite of Spring *Sun Music* was the Australian Ballet's most ambitious production at the time of its creation, 1968; an attempt to duplicate in dance Peter Sculthorpe's very successful musical scores of the same name. Though it toured the United States and England successfully in 1970 and 1973, it was too big and too costly a work to survive only partly justified criticism. Pictorially Helpmann's brilliant groupings and Kenneth Rowell's designs combined with Akers' lighting left a deep impression.

Josephine Jason (*left*) being 'born' at the creation of Helpmann's sun-inspired world.

One reason why Sun Music failed Karl Welander bouncing on a symbolic Earth ball, a somewhat ludicrous interlude in an otherwise most serious ballet.

Today Australia, Tomorrow the World

19

The only Prime Minister in the world to die while surfing, Harold Holt left no impression on the political history of Australia, but the part he played in creating the Australian Ballet and supporting it during its early years assures him of a place in any history of the arts in this country. It was Holt who arranged the participation of the Australian Ballet in the 1965 Commonwealth Arts Festival in London. Holt had more faith in the company than Peggy van Praagh, who felt it was too much too soon, and Holt proved to be right. One thing led to another and what started as a token appearance in a private British arts club, grew into an international tour of enormous impact.

Sir Robert Menzies (shortly to be succeeded as Prime Minister by Harold Holt) authorized extensive financial backing to cover the $200,000 which it was estimated that the tour would cost. Another later Prime Minister, Senator John Gorton, was in charge of the Australia Council's ancestor, Federal Activities in Education and Research. (What a title!) Gorton advanced $90,000 and every State government, with the exception only of the company's home State, Victoria, provided guarantees of $40,000 each, which the Federal Government agreed to meet dollar for dollar. But once the ball had been set rolling it began to bounce in some unexpected places. James Laurie surfaced again with a proposal for further tours with Fonteyn and Nureyev, and festivals in Paris and Baalbek (in the Lebanon) suddenly issued invitations to the company.

The troubles of the Middle East in the 1970s have pushed the once renowned annual arts festivals at Baalbek into oblivion. In the hills one hundred kilometres from Beirut, this Lebanese archaeologically important group of ruins has in recent years become a battleground of war rather than of the arts. In 1965 to be invited to appear at Baalbek was an honour. Fonteyn had danced at the Festival with the Royal Ballet in 1961, and in 1965 the same company returned with Nureyev as well as Fonteyn. Though both had recently danced in Australia, the Australian Ballet received an invitation on its own, without these box office guest stars. Helpmann, the new co-Artistic Director, did his share in arranging the appearance of the company which was built around his first two Australian ballets, *The Display* and *Yūgen*.

It was an impressive sight, performing ballet in the open air surrounded by the splendours of antiquity. Audiences were large, comments were favourable and altogether it was an auspicious start for a tour which grew like topsy, thanks to James Laurie, who had Fonteyn and Nureyev under contract and promptly used the Australian dancers as their backing to fill the lengthy gap between the non-commercial commitments in Baalbek and London. And suddenly it was no longer a matter of filling gaps, suddenly there were return engagements, additional seasons and dates to fill on the way

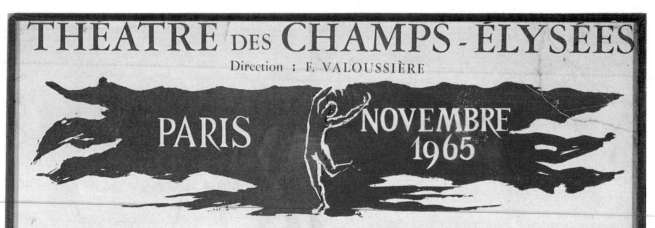

THÉATRE DES CHAMPS - ÉLYSÉES

Direction : F. VALOUSSIÈRE

PARIS NOVEMBRE 1965

3ᵉ FESTIVAL INTERNATIONAL de DANSE

Sous la Présidence d'Honneur
de M. le Président du CONSEIL MUNICIPAL de PARIS
de M. le Président de la CHAMBRE de COMMERCE et d'INDUSTRIE de PARIS
Président : JANINE ALEXANDRE - DEBRAY

NOVEMBRE 3.4.5.6 A 20ʰ30	**ALLEMAGNE**	**BALLET DE L'OPÉRA DE HAMBOURG**
NOVEMBRE 10.11.12.13 A 20ʰ30	**ROUMANIE**	**BALLET DE L'OPÉRA DE BUCAREST**
NOVEMBRE DU 15 AU 22 A 20ʰ30 ET LE 21 A 14ʰ30	**AUSTRALIE**	**AUSTRALIAN BALLET**
NOVEMBRE 24.25.26.27 A 20ʰ30	**BELGIQUE**	**BALLET DU XXᵉ SIÈCLE**
29 NOVEMBRE ET DU 1ᵉʳ AU 12 DÉCEMBRE RELACHE LE 7 A 20ʰ30 ET LES 5 ET 12 A 14ʰ30	**U.R.S.S.**	**BALLET DU THÉATRE KIROV DE LENINGRAD**

ORCHESTRE DE LA SOCIÉTÉ
DES CONCERTS DU CONSERVATOIRE

DIRECTEUR GÉNÉRAL DU FESTIVAL : JEAN ROBIN

RENSEIGNEMENTS : COMITÉ DE TOURISME 7, RUE BALZAC - PARIS 8ᵉ - BAL. 68-46
COMITÉ OFFICIEL DES FETES DE PARIS : 7, RUE BALZAC
COMMISSARIAT GÉNÉRAL : TH. DES CHAMPS-ÉLYSÉES - BAL. 90-45
LOCATION AU THÉATRE ELY 72-42 ET AGENCES

ets saint martin imp. paris

Tour de force Within ten years of its first international tour in 1965 the Australian Ballet visited 56 cities in 29 countries outside Australia.

Paris 1965 – The original poster (*left*) advertising the International Dance Festival during which Peggy van Praagh's new *Giselle* won the Grand Prix of the City of Paris.

Moscow – The Australian Ballet in Moscow (*above*), the home of the Bolshoi Ballet.

Bucharest – Posters in the Romanian capital featured pictures (*above right*) of two leading ladies: Marilyn Jones and Ray Powell!

First steps abroad Helpmann's ballet *Yūgen* in rehearsal and performance among the ruins of Baalbeck, Lebanon, during the 1965 Festival. Kathleen Gorham and Francis Croese with Robert Okell among the billowing silk waves (*top*) of the ballet sea. Moon Goddess Gorham (*bottom*) in rehearsal with one of her attendants, Roger Myers (today a not so skinny Victorian Manager for the Elizabethan Theatre Trust). Fisherman Garth Welch (*right*) with Gorham in the background.

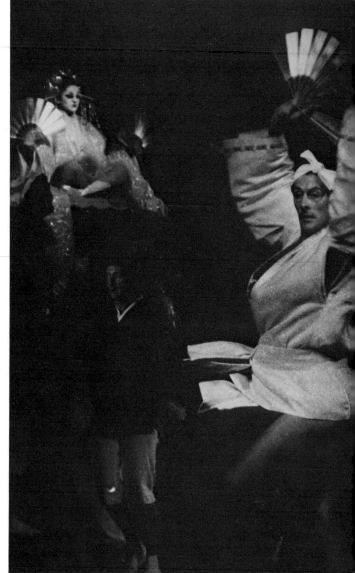

home. Minor cities on the French Riviera, like Nice and Cannes, were played while rehearsals began for the major works which Laurie demanded as part of his deal. This was shortly after Nureyev's first ventures into choreography. *Raymonda* and *Don Quixote* were scheduled to be staged by him, but the latter proved not to be financially viable and ultimately Peggy van Praagh threw a new *Giselle* together in three weeks in Birmingham to provide the second major work which the contract demanded.

The Australian Ballet opened at Covent Garden on 1 October 1965, the only company to play in England's major theatre during the Festival. The Ballets were *Le Conservatoire*, the *Namouna pas de deux, Yūgen* and *The Display*. Fonteyn and Nureyev were conspicuous by their absence;

they were no part of a Commonwealth ballet company, invited for its own merits. The original trio from Borovansky's time, Kathleen Gorham, Marilyn Jones and Garth Welch were now supplemented by Elaine Fifield, Bryan Lawrence and Karl Welander. Barbara Chambers, Kathleen Geldard and Janet Karin led the soloists, who were still a little short on male talent, though Alan Alder and Walter Bourke stood out. It was in the corps de ballet that the future of the company could already be seen. Marilyn Rowe, Gailene Stock, Carolyn Rappel, Kelvin Coe, Warren de Maria, Gerard Sibbritt, Frank Croese, Colin Peasley . . . again, the men were beginning to outnumber the girls on the way up.

While some of the critics praised with faint damns — the Australian content of *The Display* was a strange thing

The ballet Paris booed Ray Powell's *Just for Fun* was considered too irreverent for the 1965 Paris International Dance Festival, but the second part of the programme, *Giselle*, carried off the Grand Prix of the City of Paris. Left to right: Douglas Gilchrist, Kathleen Geldard, Karl Welander, Barbara Chambers and, at right, Robert Olup.

indeed to those who had never seen a lyrebird – the most surprising hit with public and critics alike was the stylized *Conservatoire,* a reconstruction by Poul Gnatt of a Bournonville classical ballet, which demanded great style and professional polish from the ensemble led by Fifield, Welander and Chambers. It was a good test indeed for the company, because you cannot hide imperfections in technique in Bournonville; he was the purest of all the choreographers, relying neither on dramatic effect nor on show-stopping technical feats.

The Covent Garden season was followed by James Laurie's launching of 'his' Australian Ballet tour. On 14 December 1965 a Gala Performance in the presence of the Queen Mother and Princess Margaret, not to mention her husband, the Earl of Snowdon, saw the London premiere of Rudolf Nureyev's *Raymonda* at the New Victoria Theatre. Nureyev and Fonteyn danced the leading roles, with Bryan Lawrence outstanding as the villainous Abderachman. The full company, including all principals, appeared in lesser roles.

The Paris season which followed is a story on its own and, fortunately, one which has a happy end. The directors had declined to accept Nureyev's advice as to what would please Paris and the season at the Théâtre des Champs-Elysées opened with *Just for Fun,* which was roundly booed by the uninhibited Paris public. It was, perhaps, entitled to expect something better, because this season was a part of the *Troisième Festival International de Danse de Paris,* in which the Australian Ballet competed with the Leningrad Kirov Ballet, Maurice Béjart's Twentieth Century Ballet from Brussels and other long-established companies from Hamburg and Bucharest. Guest stars were not permitted (much to Nureyev's annoyance) to qualify for the prizes, though they could and did dance during the rest of the season. Clearly *Just for Fun* was hardly a suitable work to win friends and influence audiences, let alone judges, in such a context.

The other works presented for consideration were, hopefully, *The Display, Yūgen, Le Conservatoire, Raymonda* and the late and quickly slapped together *Giselle. The Display* was certainly the most original and *Yūgen* the most beautiful, while *Le Conservatoire* showed the company at its best and *Raymonda* was, of course, the latest opus of Nureyev himself. Perhaps it was the fairy tale ending which sentimental French judges thought would be popular, perhaps the city in which the original ballet first saw the light of day in 1841 was trying to pat itself on the back, but Peggy van Praagh herself was more surprised than anybody else when the jury awarded to her Cinderella of the repertoire, *Giselle,* the *Grand Prix of the City of Paris.* It was an honour which the company has not yet equalled in its long history since then. Coming, as it did, at a crucial period of its young life, the effect on the Australian Ballet's future was incalculable. For one thing, it immediately put the company into a different class

from the Elizabethan Trust Opera back home, and in terms of subsidies and governmental approval it has not looked back since.

Regardless of the bitching of some Paris critics and the star-oriented gala audiences, the public flocked to see the dancers from Down Under and a return season at the Palais des Sports, an arena seating well over 6,000, was quickly arranged to follow seasons in Berlin and Copenhagen.

Nureyev and Fonteyn danced in all cities, the former muttering darkly about the injustice of not having been part of the award-winning *Giselle,* which had featured Gorham, Welch and Janet Karin's superb Queen of the Wilis. During a *Raymonda* rehearsal in Berlin he screamed at the dancers in a fit of pique: 'Dance, you bastards, dance, and you might win another competition!' Kathleen Geldard, with typical Australian spunk, was heard to tell him: 'Don't knock it, sport, we won it, you didn't!'

On the way home the company gave three charity performances at the then un-named Dorothy Chandler Pavilion in the Los Angeles Music Center. While the company here,

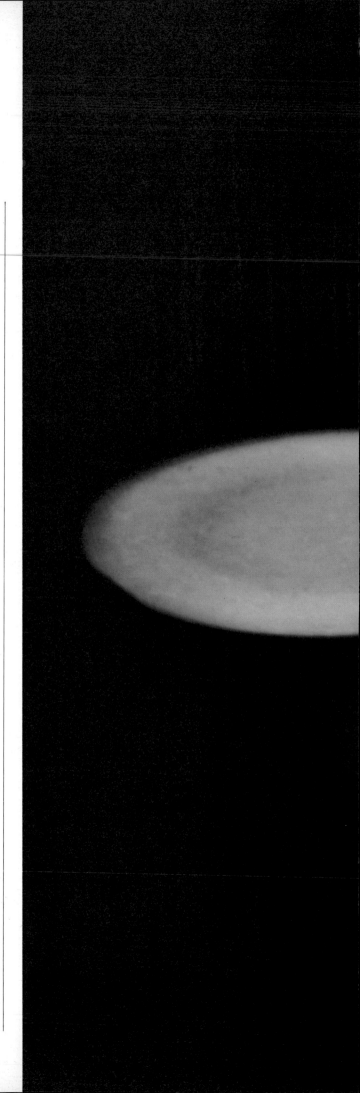

The pace begins to tell Overworked dancers rushing around the world as well as Australia begin to show the strain, though it takes a picture to tell the story. The cast of Butler's *Threshold* not managing to work within the lighting plot during a performance.

as in all its Laurie dates, was guaranteed only its fee, the proceeds must have been astronomical at $75 a ticket in a 3,250 seat theatre! The cause appeared to be a good one: The Western Ballet Association, which had and, I believe, still has as its aim the creation of a ballet company in California. What exactly happened to the money raised by the Australian Ballet's performances in 1966 is not clear, but no such permanent company has yet come into being, though many attempts have been made. The Gala committees (plural) totalled 137 officers, counting Mr & Mrs in dozens of cases as one! They started with the Bing Crosbys, Bob Hopes and Danny Kayes and went on via Marlene Dietrich and Noah Dietrich (of Howard Hughes fame and no relation to Marlene) to lesser lights like Dame Judith Anderson, Burt Lancaster, Peggy Lee and George Balanchine, apart from Eugene Loring the only ballet man on the list. They do things in style in the United States, though they don't always produce the goods. They certainly have not in this case, at the time of writing.

Overseas tours became an almost annual event for the Australian Ballet after this. Expo '67 in Montreal was the excuse to tack Honolulu and a wide swing through the Carribean and South America on to the artistic flag-waving in Canada. Both this tour in 1967 and the Asian tour in 1968, which covered Singapore, Kuala Lumpur, Bangkok, Manila, Taipei, Seoul, Tokyo and Cambodia, required no help from guest stars. Principal dancers and repertoire were identical to what Australia saw each year, with Marilyn Jones taking over as *prima ballerina* from Kathleen Gorham, who had announced her intention to retire before the first tour and was ready to open her Melbourne ballet school on her return.

America retains its star complex to this day and as late as 1976 Fonteyn was engaged for the American tour of *The Merry Widow*. Therefore, when Nureyev finally got around to producing *Don Quixote* for the Australian Ballet in 1970, and another American tour was arranged and accepted, it was unthinkable to omit Nureyev and Helpmann (who played the title role). Lucette Aldous, who had created Kitri in *Don Quixote* as a guest artist in Australia, also went along, indirectly contributing waves of discontent which caused a minor palace revolution at home among the other principals (see page 319). The point is that, thanks to Nureyev, the company played successfully in no less than eighteen different cities of the United States in 1970, with return engagements in two and a detour to Toronto in Canada. It was a gruelling tour and left the dancers exhausted, but it established a standing for the company abroad which people at home find hard to comprehend. After this nobody could say that the Australian Ballet did not belong on the international scene. (Specially after Nureyev and the company made a film of *Don Quixote* which, while not the immense

success everybody had hoped for, nevertheless compares favourably with many other ballet films around.)

Returning to Australia in 1971, the ballet almost immediately was off to Singapore and Manila again, this time with Fonteyn as guest artist. After that the overseas tours became less frequent. Two years were to pass before Moscow and most of Eastern Europe plus London and India saw the company in 1973 and it was 1976 before the immensely successful *Merry Widow* brought instantaneous offers from America as well as London.

The Australian Ballet has undoubtedly overworked its dancers; in 1973 they returned from the strenuous tour of Russia and Europe to find that the Canberra season opened forty-eight hours after their arrival back in Melbourne! No wonder two of the best principals, Gary Norman and Gailene Stock, decided that there are easier ways of making a living by dancing overseas. It is a penalty which has to be paid for being good, for perhaps having become good too quickly. Yet excellence is its own reward, not only in artistic, but in financial terms. No doubt, dancers will always feel underpaid; a successful company is bound to have union troubles and the sight of dancers carrying placards while picketing a theatre has been one of the less uplifting spectacles of the company's history.

In 1968 the Australian Ballet's subsidies were actually $70,000 more ($263,000 against $193,000) than those of the Australian Opera. Since it is vastly more expensive to produce opera than ballet, the imbalance was due solely to the much greater number of performances per annum, to the overseas tours and to the regard with which the ballet was held by the subsidising bodies. The opera has long overtaken the ballet in its annual expenditure, principally because of the much greater production and running costs, now that it is approaching the ballet's annual number of performances. It is a rare thing to have a ballet cost $300,000 as *The Merry Widow* did, but that is an expenditure which covers not simply the local market, but the overseas one as well, and is the exception rather than the rule.

It is rightly said that the Australian Ballet should 'service' Australia first. But it also should carry the banner of the nation which created it and eight overseas tours in eleven years should be ample evidence that what we see here is indeed world-class ballet and not something which we simply believe is good or bad or indifferent. Only by international standards can any artistic endeavour be judged. Perhaps the Australian Ballet has not yet created a truly national image for itself. Perhaps it should try harder toward that goal. Perhaps. (It is a handy word.) Just the same, I know of no ballet company in the world that has done as much as this company did in as short a time and the contents of this chapter should prove beyond doubt.

W dniach 29 i 30 VIII o godz. 19⁰⁰
w sali Opery Poznańskiej
wystąpi gościnnie

THE AUSTRALIAN BALLET

w repertuarze pełnospektaklowym balet
„*Córka źle strzeżona*"
wieczór baletów japońskich

Przedsprzedaż biletów zbiorowych i indywidualnych od 8 VIII 1973 w godz. 10—13 i 16—19

Tour de force Berlin – Fonteyn and Nureyev were the guests when the Australian Ballet visited the divided capital of Germany.

Buenos Aires – The largest theatre in the Argentine is the Colón, which seats 2,500 and has standing room for 1,000 more. The Australian Ballet filled it without needing any guest stars in 1967.

A Presentation by J & M LAURIE for CONCERTS MANAGEMENT (London) Ltd and THE AUSTRALIAN BALLET FOUNDATION

THE AUSTRALIAN BALLET

ARTISTIC DIRECTORS
PEGGY VAN PRAAGH
ROBERT HELPMANN C.B.E.

MARGOT FONTEYN

RUDOLF NUREYEV

GASTSPIEL vom 30. Novemb. bis 5. Dezemb. 1965 tägl. 20 Uhr

Vorverkauf an der Kasse des Theater des Westens täglich von 11 bis 19 Uhr
(Telefon 32 10 20 oder 32 10 50) sowie an den bekannten Vorverkaufsstellen

THEATER DES WESTENS

Veranstalter: Concerts Management (London) Ltd. in Zusammenarbeit mit Christian Wölfter

TEATRO COLON
TEMPORADA 1967
SEGUNDA FUNCION DEL ABONO "B"
EL TEATRO COLON, CON EL AUSPICIO DEL GOBIERNO AUSTRALIANO
Y THE AUSTRALIAN ELIZABETHAN THEATRE TRUST, PRESENTA AL

BALLET AUSTRALIANO
Directores Artisticos
PEGGY van PRAAGH
ROBERT HELPMANN

Programa
MELBOURNE CUP
de BADGER-REID
THE DISPLAY
de WILLIAMSON-HELPMANN
RAYMONDA (acto III)
de GLAZUNOV-NUREYEV

ORQUESTA FILARMONICA DE BUENOS AIRES
Director
NOEL SMITH
VIERNES 30 DE JUNIO. **21.00 HS.**
PLATEA $ 2.000.- Sobrantes de abonos en venta.

Politics and Policies

20

The history of the Australian Ballet at home after the first international tour in 1965 was remarkably smooth, all things considered. Of course, there were crises; an artistic operation without some mud-slinging is almost unthinkable. After all, it is a fact that for some time the company was under the direction of the Elizabethan Theatre Trust, which had trouble keeping its own house in order for a considerable number of years after the ballet had already settled into some form of orderly existence.

The first tour started ominously enough. It had been planned by van Praagh with her protégé administrator, Geoffrey Ingram, and considerable help from her new partner, Helpmann. Ex-dancer Ingram understood the artistic problems better than the financial and technical ones and the Trust administration was, as in the case of the opera company, only too ready to pounce on shortcomings, real or imaginary. The Trust's own administrator, Bruce Scott, arrived in London for reasons which are not clear, though the results were: as Ingram's technical superior, Scott felt it his duty to interfere, Ingram resigned on the spot and that was that. The rest of the tour was managed by Scott in name, if not totally in fact; James Laurie was the promoter of most of the tour and his tour manager was Joan Thring (ex-wife of actor Frank Thring). Mrs Thring provided the day to day management which was so badly needed. The dancers objected strenuously to the departure of the popular Ingram, but any kind of serious trouble was submerged in the common need to get the tour and two major new productions on the road.

In the meantime the Trust back home was desperately casting around for a third business manager of the ballet in four years. J. C. Williamson's, however inactive in practice, were still part of the Australian Ballet Foundation and it was John McCallum who came up with a practical suggestion, a young man who had worked his way up inside their own organization, Peter F. Bahen. Bahen had been Williamson's paymaster in Borovansky's time and had graduated to managing some of their tours. In 1966 he was appointed Manager of the Australian Ballet under Bruce Scott, who remained as the Administrator of both the Trust and the ballet. Scott's fall from grace in the Trust left Bahen in full charge of the company's business affairs from 1967 onwards, though politics prevented his name appearing prominently in the programmes until 1969.

Bahen's reign has been long and superficially smooth, yet it may be fairly described as a period of war and peace; war within the ranks on artistic matters and peace within the board room and financially. There is little doubt that Bahen has been an efficient manager of the company's affairs; the course of the Australian Ballet has been smoother than that of any other theatrical organization in Australia during the last ten years. (A possible exception is the Melbourne

All together now . . . The team which made the Australian Ballet what it is, in the boardroom of the company's headquarters in Flemington, Victoria, in 1974. Left to right: N. R. Seddon, C.B.E., the Chairman of the Australian Ballet Foundation; Peter F. Bahen, the Administrator; and Sir Robert Helpmann, C.B.E., with Dame Peggy van Praagh D.B.E., the then joint Artistic Directors.

Garth Welch, the choreographer Welch's best work, *Othello*, in performance (*right*), with Marilyn Jones as Desdemona, the choreographer as Othello and Alan Alder's writhing Iago on the floor, 1971.

Theatre Company.) The wars in which Bahen has been engaged have been skirmishes behind the scenes which never see the light of day. Bahen is shrewd enough to pretend that his place is in the accounting office, that policy matters are for his Board of Directors to decide and that his Artistic Directors have a completely free hand. In fact, in the immortal words of Ira Gershwin, it ain't necessarily so.

Bahen wields far greater power than he cares to admit, because he holds the purse strings and does not hesitate to use them in influencing every aspect of running the company. As far as his Board, the Trust, the Australia Council and the Press have been concerned over the years, Bahen has produced results financially and administratively which are above reproach. Money doesn't make headlines and complaints aired publicly were always the concern of the two Artistic Directors, Sir (since 1967) Robert Helpmann, C.B.E. and Dame (since 1971) Peggy van Praagh, D.B.E. Nobody has seen any significance in the fact that since 1968 it has been Peter Bahen whose signature graces the introductory remarks in each year's programmes and since 1970, when the company became autonomous and no longer tied to the Trust, Bahen has been responsible only to the Australian Ballet Foundation, a part-time body, the Secretary of which is – Peter Bahen!

Popularity has never been the hallmark of the successful administrator and Bahen is not afraid to make himself unpopular. To his credit, he has not opposed some fairly expensive contracts to attract the right kind of man to help the company's standing; the coup of luring the Musical Director of the Royal Ballet, John Lanchbery, away from Covent Garden deserved more headlines than it got and Bahen correctly assessed his worth when Lanchbery's name was put forward. On the other hand, he is capable of penny-pinching and squeezing contract artists to an extent that breeds dissatisfaction in the ranks, and his real or imagined influence on strictly non-administrative matters, like casting, is deeply resented.

The division of power between van Praagh and Helpmann helped Peter Bahen to build his own little empire. He is surrounded with people in key positions who do their own jobs extremely well, yet are not strong enough to stand up to the Administrator when he wants to have his way. This situation makes nobody very happy, but what counts in the end is the success of the company, and while this is not always total, the face it presents to the public remains high and, whether axes are ground or not, much of the credit must go to Peter Bahen, and, perhaps, his political shock-absorber, Noel Pelly.

Pelly's title today is Deputy Administrator. In 1965 he was the company's Director of Publicity and, though he has never held such a title, he has been and still is a superb Director of Public Relations, the diplomat *par excellence* inside as well as outside the organization. The perfect foil for Bahen's necessary toughness, Pelly's art of preventing ripples from becoming waves is legendary.

The conflict between money and art is ever present in ballet. When the present Artistic Director, Anne Woolliams, was appointed in 1976 she expressed bewilderment at the subscription system on which ticket sales of the company have been based for so many years. In merchandising terms, bulk sales of tickets or soap or meat balls make sense, but in artistic terms rather less so. It is hard to sell meat balls if some are made of offal, though the latter could be the most expensive kind of pâté de fois gras, and it is difficult to sell ballet subscriptions if the buyer objects to some part of the package being offered. Overseas companies, and the Australian Opera in this country, have long explored ways to cater for minorities outside the subscription series and the Australian Ballet will undoubtedly follow suit in due course. But its programming policies at the time of writing are coming under attack.

The company created in the image of the Royal Ballet

by Peggy van Praagh has certainly done its share of exploring the new and the esoteric. Whatever the criticism of Helpmann as a choreographer, his ballets are always adventurous and the many visiting choreographers the company has employed over the years have given the dancers and the public a taste of things as varied as anything the average overseas company presents. There has been a superabundance of box office ballets, but lesser, often meaning artistically more valuable, works have been thrown together quickly and as part of a schedule of performances so heavy that dancers have been unable to do them justice. Experimental works have been relegated to the annual 'Ballet '74, '75, '76, etc.' put on in Canberra under the sponsorship of the *Canberra Times,* or to the graduation performances of the Australian Ballet School. (The Canberra 'specials' differ from the school productions only in that young choreographers can use the professional dancers of the Australian Ballet instead of students.)

There has been a will, but the way has often been destructive rather than constructive. When Garth Welch staged *Othello* for the Australian Ballet School in 1971, its success was immediate, because he was given the time to develop and fully rehearse the work with dancers, however inexperienced, who were at his disposal for the full time he needed

How to ruin a good ballet The original Ballet '74 production of John Meehan's *Night Episode* in Canberra (*below*). An experimental ballet staged by a young choreographer with a minimum of expense, it impressed critics and audiences immensely. Chrisa Keramides, Mark Brinkley, Jack Callick and Paul Saliba, with Christine Walsh and Gary Norman on the floor.

The same artists (*right*, minus Gary Norman) in the hurriedly 'improved' *Night Episode* which was added to the current season of the Australian Ballet. Note the cheap costuming and indiscipline of the under-rehearsed dancers — and that was the end of a potentially first-rate addition to the repertoire.

to be as creative as he could; and that can be a very variable period indeed! When the ballet was taken into the parent company's repertoire it lost little of its impact and possibly gained by some stronger performances. Yet, like almost all the company's own new ballets, its impact lessened as time progressed because the time given to its re-study between seasons was limited and audiences who first applauded *Othello* did not look on it later as the strong centre piece it should have been in any bill.

The annual Canberra experimental programmes have been presented by more experienced dancers used by young choreographers. Some fine talent has been discovered, but it has been dissipated and put down instead of being launched with a hail of publicity. John Meehan, for example, demonstrated amazing potential as a choreographer. One of the ballets he created, *Night Episode,* was accepted into the main repertoire, but it was staged quickly and cheaply, and under-rehearsal

ensured its quick demise. The bare stage and lack of costumes in Canberra were more effective than the cheap trimmings which were added later on. Like *Othello, Night Episode* needed building and the erroneous idea that something from a young choreographer cannot be good box office killed both in the end.

On the other hand, an audience pleaser like *Superman,* produced in Canberra in 1974, was given the full publicity treatment before it was ready. Choreographer Julia Cotton had dreamt up just the kind of ballet the company needed, a send-up of the twenties vogue of the day. The concept was brilliant, the execution, using any old costumes and scenery that could be dug up, was very good for an experimental affair like Ballet '74. Because the audience loved it, *Superman* was accepted unchanged by the parent company, had its expected 'Gee, what good fun' reaction and disappeared into limbo. Both financially and artistically, this was

an opportunity to create a lasting addition to the repertoire, by giving Cotton a chance to polish her raw work, by having it properly designed, and staging it with a flourish as a major new ballet. Refreshing as it was, *Superman* was not worthy of the company that performed it. There was a lack of planning in throwing it on as it was, which had causes that should have been investigated, but were not. Was it a matter of: why spend money on something the public already likes? Or was it: anything will do for the public?

The Australian Ballet at present prefers to save its resources to stage *The Merry Widow* and *Eugene Onegin* in truly grand style. It is a moot point whether this should be done at the expense of works which may or may not ultimately result in establishing a truly Australian ballet style. While subsidies remain limited, the company must cater for box office. Administrator Bahen sees to that and without that source of cash the company might well decline. It remains to be seen whether Anne Woolliams will or can do something about this problem.

Air on a shoe string   Julia Cotton's satire of the nostalgia vogue for the Twenties, *Superman,* was thrown together brilliantly, if haphazardly, using only odd costumes and props assembled from stock for Ballet '74 in Canberra. (Note Superman's telephone kiosk changing room at the left and Galapogus Duck playing on the band-stand behind the dancers.)

Air on a shoe string Superman, unlike John Meehan's *Night Episode*, was transferred unchanged from the 1974 choreographic competition in Canberra to the Australian Ballet's repertoire, a credit to young Julia Cotton's enterprise in begging and borrowing an ideal collection of nostalgia items for the costumes and decor.

The Fringe and Beyond the Fringe

21

It is a lot easier to start a ballet company than to start an opera company. Not only does it need a lot less money, not only can you use recorded music, not only can you perform in almost any kind of a hall, but you need not even have any balletic skills. Anybody can (and often does) set himself or herself up as a self-appointed apostle of the dance and, if what is presented bears little or no resemblance to anything ever seen before, well, we then have an 'original' new choreographer being innovative. It would be quite literally impossible to list, let alone cover, all the dance groups that have ever appeared in Australia or even all those that exist at this moment. I can but attempt to touch those who seem to have left an impression, however small, which deserves recording; and I hasten to add that omission definitely does not imply inferiority, only ignorance on the part of the author.

It is perhaps unfair to include Ballet Victoria in any chapter headed The Fringe. The work done by Laurel Martyn continuously over a period of thirty years was remarkable by any standards and Ballet Victoria, in spite of its many ups and downs, must have a prominent place in any history of ballet in Australia. The company produced no less than ninety-four ballets, thirty with choreography by Laurel Martyn herself, and if many of these were little more than minor *divertissements* danced by sometimes only two or three dancers, the fact remains that the great majority were original works and not second-rate revivals, though the company had a few of those also.

Ballet Victoria first began without even a name in November 1946, when the Melbourne Ballet Club (which had launched Borovansky six years earlier) asked the director of its new school, Laurel Martyn, to stage a season of four ballets at the Melbourne Repertory Theatre (later the Arrow Theatre, Middle Park). Martyn was no novice to choreography, having a number of successful ballets to her credit, some of which had helped to launch the Borovansky Ballet, with the choreographer herself in leading roles.

From the very first, the Victorian Ballet Guild, as the new company quickly called itself, concentrated on chamber ballets of the Rambert style, with fully commissioned new music and designs. The initial programme contained works to music by Dorian Le Gallienne (*Contes heraldiques,* one of Martyn's most successful works) and Margaret Sutherland (*Dithyramb*). The list of Australian composers who followed in their footsteps is almost endless and includes John Antill, Esther Rofe, Verdon Williams, John Tallis, Clive Douglas, Peter Sculthorpe, Harold Badger, and others, while designers offered work, however ill-paid, if paid at all, ranged all the way from John Truscott, Charles Bush, Leonard French and Ann Church to Raymond Trickett, Gerard Sibbritt and Jeoffry Monk — again, the omissions are many.

It is a hopeless task to do justice to the huge output

The dead have few friends For thirty years before its collapse in 1976 Ballet Victoria produced more original works than any other ballet company in Australia. Even in its worst years it balanced new and classical ballets to keep its dancers and audiences together. Nobody wants to know about the company's ninety-four ballets now.

Laurel Martyn's *Voyageur*, with a commissioned score from Dorian le Gallienne and original designs by Douglas Smith. Janet Karin and Antonio Rodriguez, formerly Katherine Dunham's principal dancer.

The beginning with no end *Giselle*, the ballet in which Laurel Martyn, Ballet Victoria's moving spirit, excelled in her dancing days, as staged in a primitive Bourke Street, Melbourne, studio (*above left*). While space ruled out a full corps de ballet, the production was a close replica of authentic classical ballet. Martyn with Max Collis and, at right, Eve King as the Queen of the Wilis.

The Sentimental Bloke would be nostalgic rather than sentimental today. The lead in this 1952 Victorian Ballet Guild production (*below left*), was Geoffrey Ingram who became the first Administrator of the Australian Ballet when it was formed ten years later. Ingram with Laurel Martyn as Doreen.

of this tiny company. Martyn's own best ballets were probably *En Saga* and *Sigrid,* both also performed by Borovansky. In *The Sentimental Bloke* (1952) she tried to take her native Australianism to its logical peak. *Voyageur* is remembered mostly because of Dorian Le Gallienne's excellent music, which was recorded. Martyn staged the first full-length *Sylvia* in Australia (her own choreography) and balletized Keats in *The Eve of St Agnes.* Some of the company's ballets were staged in a tiny studio theatre in Bouverie Street, Carlton, others in the huge Palais Theatre in St Kilda. Some day a book will be written about Laurel Martyn and the Victorian Ballet Guild, which in 1967 was finally acknowledged by subsidies at State and Federal levels, when it officially became Ballet Victoria. Ballet Guild remained the name of the parent body, which also ran a large ballet school, whose graduates found a place in the professional company. This company for many years spent the major part of each year in taking ballet to schools; its *Let's Make a Ballet* series was a model of what ballet education for children should be.

In 1974 Garth Welch retired as *premier danseur* of the Australian Ballet and became co-Artistic Director of Ballet Victoria with Laurel Martyn. He also applied his talents as a choreographer and used the company to stage a large-scale modern work, *Images,* to Rachmaninov's *Paganini Variations,* followed by *Ritual* and his successful *Othello.* Apart from continuing the encouragement of local choreographers, like John Meehan, Gail Ferguson and Margaret Scott (who staged a pleasant, if lightweight *Recollections of a Beloved Place*), Ballet Victoria brought the English choreographer Jonathan Taylor out from England to produce a new work and one of his established successes. The former, *Star's End,* turned out to be one of the best ballets ever produced by anybody in Australia, a brilliant concept of worlds in collision in outer space.

The list of dancers who went through the ranks of Ballet Victoria over the years is as long as the list of works it produced. Some, like Janet Karin, Heather Macrae, Ian Spink and the company's ballerina for so many years, Diane Parrington, began their careers in the school of the Victorian Ballet Guild and Laurence Bishop, its Ballet Master, was one of the company's principals for years. Laurel Martyn never sought to import stars (except Russians, of course) and her ensemble was not top heavy on principals. Ballet Victoria's strength lay in its artistic policies, which were aimed squarely at producing new works. In this it succeeded far beyond anything any company, the Australian Ballet included, had done in this country before 1975.

The company's biggest success ultimately was the recipe for disaster. Mikhail Barishnikov and Natalia Makarova, the world's most desirable Russian stars in 1974, came to Australia and used Ballet Victoria as a background for their Act 2 of *Giselle;* some *pas de deux* and *The Dying Swan* were

sandwiched between *Star's End, Images,* Balanchine's *Concerto Barocco* and a travesty of Walter Gore's *Simple Symphony,* restaged by Gore himself. So successful was this Australia-wide tour that it was followed by a similar venture in 1975, when Valery and Galina Panov, the much publicized and much over-rated Russian Jewish exiles, were the stars for whom the company revived *Petrouchka,* no less. The tour was a financial disaster!

'Let the cobbler stick to his last', like all proverbs, contains more than a grain of truth. Ballet Victoria spent nearly thirty years in establishing a pattern which clearly worked and which had been accepted by both State and Federal subsidizing bodies. It abandoned its balletic last because its association with Barishnikov and Makarova seemed to point to an easier financial path, a path which (in theory) could benefit the artistic development of the company. Unfortunately the cobbler knew nothing about the mass production of shoes. There was no lack of warnings, all of them ignored, but just four short weeks before its thirtieth birthday, Laurel Martyn's carefully nurtured brainchild died an unnatural death at the hands of a receiver, ironically, just after Martyn had been awarded an O.B.E. for services to the dance.

The Victorian Government agreed to support the Ballet Guild's schools as an interim measure, while Garth Welch was commissioned to make a report on the viability of a State ballet company in October 1976. Since the need for such a company is undisputed, it will no doubt materialize some time in 1977, probably under the direction of Welch himself, who is an obvious choice, though he has yet to prove himself as an administrator. One can only hope that he will learn from the mistakes of the past and that he will, perhaps, continue some of the principles of Ballet Victoria; its work should not be totally forgotten.

The minor Melbourne companies leave classical ballet well alone. Most prominent is the Kolobok Dance Company of Australia, founded in 1970 by Marina Berezowsky. Kolobok is a folk dance group which endeavours to fill a largely educational place in the community, specializing in Russian and Eastern European dances, but ready to include Chinese or Latin American dances if and when suitable choreographers are available. Its activities extend beyond Victoria through tours to the other states.

There are two modern groups, both of an intermittent nature, Margaret Lasica's Modern Dance Ensemble and Shirley McKechnie's Australian Contemporary Dance Theatre, both typically self-help 'expressive' groups, Lasica having greater pretensions à la Martha Graham and McKechnie being more realistic in keeping within the limitations of her students and dancers. Fringe activities in Melbourne include the Spanish Ballet Company of Carimina and the impossibly over-ambitious Australian Ballet Comique of Kalman Solymossy, a local dance teacher in the habit of announcing seasons by his pupils with blurbs like 'Never before has an Australian ballet company reached such splendid entertaining heights . . .'

Sydney never has been as active as Melbourne in dance companies, though it does have a fractionally larger population. When the Elizabethan Trust Opera Company decided to acquire some dancers for its 1957 opera season, it ambitiously created the Elizabethan Opera Ballet Company, which staged local classics like Laurel Martyn's *Sigrid,* and even a commissioned new ballet by John Antill, *Wakooka,* with choreography by Valrene Tweedie and designs by Elaine Haxton – a real Australian ballet set on a sheep station. With the full backing of the Trust and the use of the A.B.C. Symphony Orchestras this could have turned into something big. It did not. Nor did the company which, however indirectly, sprang from it.

Five years later Tweedie's *Wakooka* re-emerged in the first programme of the ambitiously titled Ballet Australia; President: Valrene Tweedie. Ballet Australia basically tried to do in Sydney what Laurel Martyn had done in Melbourne – to create genuine Australian works within severely restricted financial limits. Unlike Martyn, Tweedie aimed too high and some of the company's claims, including one that it was doing the job at which the Australian Ballet was failing, were presumptuous, to say the least. Nevertheless, the actual work of the company was far from worthless and its ballets were mostly original, using undoubted talent, such as the young composer Richard Meale and choreographers Desmond Meyers, Keith Little and James Upshaw, the latter an American at that time prominent in Australian television production.

The major Sydney dance group today is the Dance Company (N.S.W.), founded in 1965 by Suzanne Muzitz, an ex-soloist with the Australian Ballet. First vaguely associated with the Australian Ballet itself and then assisted by just about every subsidising body in New South Wales, the company has been presenting modern works of a pretty high standard, obtaining some glowing testimonials from hardened critics like Kevon Kemp and Brian Hoad. The former produced a headline in 1973, 'At last, an alternative Australian Ballet', in *The National Times* and audience response did indeed back him up. Dance Company (N.S.W.) had by then become a highly professional group with an enterprising and original repertoire. If *Australia, Australia* (music by Cool Bananas – from Southern Queensland?) was the work of a Dutchman, Frans Vervenne, from the Nederlands Dans Theater, it was an effective work nevertheless. The inspiration of the Dutch company has been very much in evidence throughout and in 1975 the artistic direction was taken over by Jaap Flier, one of the founders of the Nederlands Dans Theater. Flier in turn was followed, in 1977, by Graeme Murphy.

The recent loose association between the Dance Company (N.S.W.) and the Australian Opera has unfortunately been no more successful than previous attempts to weld the two arts; their joint *Madrigal Comedy* (Orazio Vecchi's *L'Amfiparnaso*) in 1976 was a disastrous failure.

Jaap Flier came to the New South Wales company from Adelaide, where he had presided over the collapse (after a burst of glory) of the so-called Australian Dance Theatre. Growing out of a small dance group founded in 1965 by Elizabeth Dalman, the Australian Dance Theatre distinguished itself initially at the Adelaide Festivals of the sixties. Dalman tried, with some success, to create a modern style of her own, backing the ballets she created herself with ample outside talent, not only local, but also from overseas. She was fortunate in having substantial backing from the Adelaide Establishment and, starting in 1968, the company even undertook a series of overseas tours which, if Press reports are any indication, were a substantial success. It had a repertoire of over thirty ballets with Dalman herself, Eleo Pomare, Don Asker, Ray Cook and Frans Vervenne as principal choreographers. By 1973 the Australian Dance Theatre was well and truly established and gaining a reputation outside Adelaide. Subsidies increased rapidly as the company improved and ambitions increased. In July of that year it was announced that Flier had been appointed co-Artistic Director with Dalman for a period of two years.

Many things then happened. Flier certainly implanted the discipline of the Dutch school in the Australian group. He also added a nucleus of his own dancers, creating an at first hardly perceptible division in the company. But this was glossed over as work poured in, most notably the engagement of the company to provide the main attraction in the Australian Opera's premiere at the Sydney Opera House of Peter Sculthorpe's excellent non-opera, *Rites of Passage,* which was actually produced by Flier. His undoubted success in this (late in 1974) laid the foundations of his move to the Dance Company (N.S.W.) after his contract in Adelaide expired in the following year. The division between Dalman and Flier had become stronger as Flier tried to change the company. When he left, the majority of the dancers left with him and Dalman found herself with the bare bones of what had been a pretty good ensemble before Flier's arrival. Unfortunately, she was unable to recover the company's fortunes, standards fell and in 1976 the company ostensibly disbanded. Jonathan Taylor, the brilliant English choreographer, whose ballets helped Ballet Victoria to new artistic peaks before its untimely demise, has now taken over the direction of the Australian Dance Theatre. It is as yet too early to know what success he will have, but he is assured of sound financial backing by the South Australian Government, and that is no small thing for a start.

Earlier attempts at regional companies in Adelaide have

The model which failed   The perfection of (ex)Kirov dancers Mikhail Barishnikov and Natalia Markarova, who used Ballet Victoria as a backing for their 1975 tour of Australia, proved to be the model which killed a company just reaching artistic maturity. The success of the tour prompted the management to undertake a similar tour in 1976 with Valery and Galina Panov. In six short months the disasters of that tour wiped out thirty years of hard work.

left no mark on the history of dance in South Australia. Immediately after the war Joanne Priest founded the South Australian Ballet and Arts Club, which existed for some years, and in 1967 Dorothy Simpson started the South Australian Ballet Company to provide more traditional kinds of ballets, though it also commissioned some unusual works, notably Leon Kellaway's *The Nightingale and the Rose,* based on Oscar Wilde, and *Henkei,* a Buddhist ballet by Harvey Collins.

Western Australia has always been served well by its own companies, mostly because distance prevents too frequent visits from other groups. The West Australian Ballet Company came into being in 1952 through the efforts of Kira Bousloff, an ex-de Basil dancer who had settled in Perth. This company originally followed the principles of Borovansky, mixing established classics with modern works and using a variety of choreographers, including Kiril Vassilkovsky and Poul Gnatt. After Bousloff's retirement, the company was directed by Rex Reid for some years and developed an extensive repertoire of modern and classical ballets, even undertaking a full Australian tour. Its guest artists have been rather more extensive than is usual for a regional company; they have included Kathleen Gorham, Robert Pomié, Vassilie Trunoff, Patricia Cox, Karl Welander, Marilyn Jones and Elaine Fifield.

The company which works farthest north in Australia is the North Queensland Ballet Company, based in Townsville. Under the direction of Ann Roberts, it concentrates on providing basic reproductions of classics like *Les Sylphides* or the ballets of Laurel Martyn for what is hardly a specialist market. Incredibly, the Queensland capital, Brisbane, has two ballet companies; Ballet Theatre of Queensland has been in existence since 1953 and the Queensland Ballet Company since 1962. The former sticks to presenting standard classics using mostly local ballet students, but the latter can be seriously considered as a proper company, though its seasons are intermittent. Its standing is mainly due to the work of its founder and original Artistic Director, Charles Lisner, but he has recently retired and Harry Haythorne of the Scottish Ballet has taken over. Original works by choreographers like Water Gore and Rex Reid are produced regularly and the company is filling a very necessary place in this part of Australia.

Lastly, poor little Tasmania down south is struggling to support the Tasmanian State Ballet Company, much under-financed and under-supported. It is proud of having played a season at the Wrest Point Casino in Hobart! This in itself is probably a reflection on its standards. It is the pet of Tasmanian born dancer Kenneth Gillespie who, as happens so often with small companies, tries to do too much at once and all by himself. The Tasmanian company is a one man band and its productions of classics like *Petrouchka, The*

Nutcracker, and the like, are poor cousins of the originals. An attempt is being made to introduce ballets by young choreographers like Julia Cotton and Graeme Murphy, but until such time as some major subsidising body throws its weight behind the company, it will remain at its present low level, no matter how hard its Director may work.

This chapter shows clearly that the regional field of ballet in Australia is hardly under-supplied. While standards vary immensely, the potential talent is enormous and the fact that most companies are attached to, or have attached to them, schools, is probably a very good thing. It cannot be said that young Australians do not have the opportunity to become dancers if they have the ability to succeed.

Edgley & Co.
22

The only non-balletic personality to have left a lasting mark on the ballet scene in Australia is the once *Wunderkind* of the theatre, Michael Edgley. Taking over his family empire of theatres in Perth in his early twenties, Edgley quickly built a niche for himself by continuing the family tradition of negotiating with the Russians for visiting companies at a time when anyone who knew the difference between *da* and *nyet* was considered distinctly un-Australian. What is even more remarkable is that Edgley, a died-in-the-wool capitalist, has won the trust of the Soviet officials controlling the Russian artists. The benefits we have received balletically through the courtesy of Michael Edgley and his associates cannot be underestimated.

The Australian Ballet rightly chose to bring out guests like Nureyev and Fonteyn so that our dancers could see their work at first hand. Edgley has managed to let them (and the public) see the grand tradition of Russian ballet as it is still practised in the land from which the great ballet renaissance sprang seventy years ago.

The Edgley family have been in show business for generations. They have sawdust in their veins and know that every attraction must be better than the last. If Edgley's imports have varied from time to time, he has seldom failed to catch the public's imagination, nor has he failed to make his artists and teachers available to companies and schools throughout Australia so that the maximum benefits should acrue to Australia in every sphere. Edgley may not have the image of a philanthropist, but he has been broadminded enough to see that not keeping everything in the family can ultimately bring ever bigger rewards. Not for him the 'this is mine' attitude, which has been the policy of just about every other importer of artists to Australia for generations.

The first Bolshoi Ballet Ensemble imported by the Edgleys in 1962 was little more than a group of Russian dancers picked from the middle ranks of the Bolshoi. Ludmilla Bogomolova and Gennady Ledvakh may have been Bolshoi dancers and at that time were a wondrous thing for local audiences, but they were only a foretaste of the kind of thing Michael Edgley was to bring in later years. In the early sixties the Edgley family did better in bringing out the first of the great folk ensembles, the Georgian State Dance Theatre, since followed by the Omsk Siberian Dance Company, the Beriozska Company of Russia, the Mazowsze Dance Company of Poland and two companies presented by Igor Moiseyev.

Moiseyev was a respected independent dance man in Russia — as far as any artistic endeavour can be independent in Russia. His Moiseyev Dance Company, which came to Australia in 1968, was the first company brought out from Russia by Michael Edgley after he had taken charge of the family business (aged all of twenty-four years), and it was no more than yet another folk dance troupe. However, in the following year Moiseyev returned in a different guise.

The Russian marriage-go-round Ai-Gul Gaisina was one of the 'Forty Stars of the Russian Ballet' imported by Michael Edgley's company in 1908. In spite of dire warnings all round, Edgley's director Andrew Guild married Gaisina, obtained permission for her to leave Russia and added a shining light to the ballet scene in Australia.

The 'Forty Stars of the Russian Ballet' consisted of one of the other Moiseyev companies, the Moscow Young Ballet, with guest artists from the Bolshoi in Moscow, Elena Tcherkasskaya and Alexander Godounov (who later danced Vronsky in the Bolshoi film *Anna Karenina*) and from the Kirov in Leningrad, Kaleria Fedicheva and Yuri Soloviev, while a very young Ai-Gul Gaisina offered as yet little more than charm and grace. Within a few years she was to marry one of the Edgley directors, Andrew Guild, and become a leading dancer of the Australian Ballet. Edgley at this early stage already began to shine up his selfless knight's image by allowing Moiseyev to choreograph a short work for the Australian Ballet. The fact that *The Last Vision* was a miserable little thing of no value was certainly not Edgley's fault, but Moiseyev working with the Australian Ballet certainly did it no harm.

In 1970 Edgley outdid himself. Not only was there a return of the Georgian Dancers, but he imported Russia's greatest ballerina, Maya Plisetskaya, with another ensemble of dancers from the Bolshoi. The highlight of this tour was the presentation of the *Carmen Ballet,* which the Cuban Alberto Alonso had choreographed for Plisetskaya. Australia saw virtually the original cast, for Nicolai Fadeyechev danced Don José and Sergei Radchenko Escamillo. It was, however, again a case of stars from the Bolshoi Ballet rather than The Bolshoi Ballet, and the stars (apart from Plisetskaya and Fadeyechev) were spectacular youngsters on the way up, some of whom Australia was to see again. Nina Sorokina and Yuri Vladimirov offered some fantastic technical tricks, including sixty-four *fouettés*! They returned with the full Bolshoi Ballet in 1976 as caricatures of athletic non-dancers. (One wonders whether the Bolshoi is so bureaucratic that dancers retain their status, once promoted, regardless of their abilities.) However, in 1970 these dancers were a sensation.

The Novosibirsk Ballet in the following year was a distinct step backwards. Supposedly the third best company in Russia it turned out to be a group of almost children from the wilds of Central Asia. But then, this was not the company Edgley had booked; the Kirov Ballet was supposed to come to Australia for the first time in 1971, but fate in the form of Natalia Makarova had intervened. Makarova, one of the greatest dancers of the Kirov, had defected from the company in London in September 1970 and the Russian authorities were taking no chances with mature artists of independent minds and ambitions.

For a brief moment in 1972 Michael Edgley became Managing Director of a joint Williamson–Edgley Theatres Limited. Williamson's had had a financial interest in most of the Edgley tours and, having fallen on hard times, the Firm had decided that this vital youngster might turn the tide of fortune for it. Balletically this meant the importation of The Royal Winnipeg Ballet from Canada and the Neder-

lands Dans Theater from Holland. The former involved a great deal of tub-thumping when it was revealed that the Australia Council had guaranteed the Canadians' tour to the tune of $40,000. The high point of the season was an excellent presentation of Agnes de Mille's masterpiece, *Fall River Legend.* Whether giving Australian audiences and dancers the chance to see such a work warranted risking this kind of money remains a moot point. I doubt whether it is an exercise which will be repeated. The experience was a great one, though the dancers as a whole and the balance of the repertoire were nothing special.

The Nederlands Dans Theater proved to be a different kettle of fish entirely and one which was to influence the Australian Ballet scene quite substantially. The sensational aspect of a nude ballet, *Mutations* by Glen Tetley and Hans van Manen, somewhat overshadowed the impact of an ultra-modern dance group based on balletic movement, yet rejecting all that ballet stands for. The concept was so revolutionary that for some years every Australian choreographer copied these Dutch novelties *ad infinitum,* and the Australian Ballet promptly commissioned Tetley to create a ballet for it. *Gemini,* produced in 1973, remains one of the best and most popular of the company's modern ballets, though the Australian dancers are not asked to perform in the nude; the by now obligatory lycra tights give almost the same illusion.

While there has not been a Russian defector from a company under the Edgley banner, the Nederlands Dans Theater provided one. Jaap Flier, its Artistic Director, left the company to work in Australia and became a substantial asset to the regional ballet field, first in Adelaide and then in Sydney.

If Michael Edgley were never to import another company, the visit of the Kirov Ballet of Leningrad in 1973 would ensure him a place in the history of ballet in this country. This was no collection of 'stars of', but a full ballet company from Russia, the direct descendent of the original Maryinsky Ballet of Tsarist days, the company of Petipa and *Swan Lake, Sleeping Beauty* and the rest. In some respects it was unspectacular, but it was ballet pure and simple, a model of good taste with only faint traces of old-fashioned sentiment. And then there was Mikhail Barishnikov, giving Australia a superb chance to know what it was all about when he defected in Canada a year later; a dancer possibly greater than Nureyev, if not as king-size a personality.

The one lesson the Kirov taught, which Actors' Equity is not likely to allow the Australian Ballet to learn, was the value of principals in minor parts. Barishnikov, Irina Kolpakova and Ninela Kurgapkina dancing the *Pas de trois* in *Swan Lake*! Russia values its stars, but the stars are interested more in ballet than in star billing.

1974 saw the Georgian Dancers again and Fonteyn, much

The greatness of Russia   One picture speaks a thousand words and ballet will always be associated with Russia, though it did not originate in that country. The sheer perfection of the Russian technique and the personality of Russian dancers are shown by Maya Plisetskaya (*left*) in the Bolshoi Ballet's *Carmen Ballet*, which was seen twice in Australia, in 1970 and again in 1976.

The naked truth   Sir Robert Helpmann claims that parts of the nude human body can not keep time with the music needed for dancing. True enough, but the Nederlands Dans Theater's *Mutations* in 1972 aroused only admiration for its nudity, though Brisbane refused to look on it — naturally. Anja Licher and Gerard Lemaître.

Barishnikov on the way up A superb action shot of Mikhail Barishnikov in Australia. His effortless *elevation* impressed local audiences long before his name became a household word overseas. (In the *Don Quixote pas de deux* in Melbourne.)

reduced in technique now, returned with the Scottish Ballet and Ivan Nagy. And Edgley imported the Stuttgart Ballet, a revelation to Australians unused to looking for excellence in a ballet from an obscure German city; Richard Cragun and Marcia Haydée perpetuating the great traditions of the late John Cranko in *The Taming of the Shrew,* surely one of the greatest ballets of all time! And with the company came one of Cranko's heirs, Anne Woolliams, once his deputy, and in 1974 deputy to his successor, Glen Tetley. (Was this when negotiations to engage her as Artistic Director for the Australian Ballet started?)

And Edgley has continued the good work. 1975: the London Festival Ballet with Nureyev in his own *Sleeping Beauty.* 1976: the actual full company of the Bolshoi with Plisetskaya and ballets which hardly did the great Russian tradition proud. Never mind, the activities of Michael Edgley over the years have placed us in his debt and if we have helped to boost his profits, we have certainly received value for money. In this case he even provided Australia with a Bolshoi world premiere, Maurice Béjart's *Boléro,* slipped past the Russian censors by Maya Plisetskaya with the help of Edgley!

Not that Edgley is the only one to bring dance companies to Australia over the years. There has indeed been ample competition for the Australian Ballet and the fact that so very often the local company more than holds its own is significant! We have had Luisillo and his Spanish Dance Theatre, the Chitrasena Ballet of Ceylon, José Limon's Company from America, the Bayanihan Phillipine Dance Company, Alvin Ailey's group from the States, José Greco, the Ballet Folklorico of Mexico, the Paris Opera Ballet with Yvette Chauviré, Les Ballets Africains, Antonio and his Spanish Dancers, a Brazilian Dance Company, El Sali Flamenco Company, the National Ballet of Senegal, Alice Reyes from the Phillipines and that great innovator, Merce Cunningham, stunning us with John Cage's so-called music and ballet performed in total darkness!

There are few things we have not experienced in Australia in dance during the years since the Australian Ballet was formed, yet there remains an impression that we are away from the main stream of the art. The forty-five dance groups that have visited Australia during the last fifteen years represent only an average of three per year. Add the Australian Ballet's seasons each year and you get enough to satisfy the average public, but not the balletomane. But at least he is beginning to know the standards against which he must judge his own ballet company. How many times in those years has the local article been better than the imported one? Quite often, I am pleased to say. But let us also remember that a ballet company rushing half way around the world does not always present its best feet forward; the Bolshoi Ballet of ninety dancers which visited us in 1976 was hardly

The beauty of being ugly One of the world's great ballerinas, Marcia Haydée (Kate), being swept off her feet by Richard Cragun (Petruchio) in John Cranko's *The Taming of the Shrew*, staged in Australia by the Stuttgart Ballet in 1974. Not to be afraid to sacrifice an image for the sake of artistic integrity is the secret of greatness. Cragun as well as Haydée are among the giants of this century's world of ballet.

The Australian Bolshoi premiere Melbourne 4 August 1976. Forty Men and one Girl — Maya Plisetskaya in the Bolshoi Ballet's premiere of Maurice Béjart's *Boléro*. To the insistent rhythms of Ravel's music she drives her admirers to a spectacular pack rape — after the curtain falls. There is a question whether Moscow will accept this kind of sexuality in ballet. In 1973 it refused Helpmann's *The Display* on moral grounds!

Too big for Sydney or Melbourne Only Adelaide had a threatre large enough to accomodate a full-size, full-length Soviet ballet when the Bolshoi Ballet visited Australia in 1976. None of the other cities saw the Race Scene or any other part of *Anna Karenina*. (Note that in Russian ballets horse races are run by the jockeys and not the horses!)

Here come de judge! Or so the young lady might have cried had this shot been taken in Brisbane. Les Ballets Africains' dancers had to wear brassieres when performing in Queensland. The rest of Australia was more liberal in meeting this very realistic dance company — not even the genuine jungle odours were missing!

Pavlova dances again! No relation to her famous namesake, Nadezhda Pavlova (*right*) is Russia's newest ballet star. Born in 1955, she won the Gold Medal at the International Dance Competition in Moscow in 1973 and visited Australia with the Bolshoi Ballet in 1976.

what people see at the Bolshoi in Moscow! Except, of course, for Nadezhda Pavlova, no relation to her famous namesake, who had won the Gold Medal at the prestigious International Dance Competition in Moscow in 1973, had danced the title role in the disastrous film of Maeterlinck's *The Blue Bird* (made in Russia with an aging Elizabeth Taylor) and was now ready to show the world that Russia could still produce the greatest dancers of all.

In 1976 Michael Edgley joined Australia's shrewdest theatre fox, Kenn Brodziak, Lady Tait, the widow of Williamson's last real showman, Sir Frank Tait, and a few others in buying the name of the dead, but unmourned, J. C. Williamson organization. It remains to be seen whether J. C. Williamson Productions Ltd is going to enter the dance field or whether Edgley will keep this corner of the market to himself. If he can continue to produce rabbits like Pavlova and Barishnikov out of the hat he never wears, he may not need his new partners. And the public will always have ballet stars in its eyes!

Consolidating a Success

23

Between overseas tours in the late sixties the Australian Ballet developed its repertoire, which was varied and amply adventurous in every way but one: very little attempt was made to develop native choreographers, though principal dancer Garth Welch was given some half-hearted backing. His initial efforts, *Illyria* and *Jeunesse* were little more than pretty *divertissements* and, despite the undoubted success of his best work to date, the stark *Othello* (originally created for the Australian Ballet School), he was obviously anxious to seek greater freedom than his duties as a dancer permitted. (Ultimately he left to join Ballet Victoria, which offered more scope for a choreographer.)

No, the successes of the Australian Ballet have not come from native choreographers to date. The company has as yet to throw its full weight behind even one young choreographer. It may well be that such a step would be a futile act of faith, but sooner or later it will have to be taken; probably more than once. And Australian choreographers will have to be backed by Australian composers.

The company is quite willing to commission elaborate designs which produce enough spectacle to justify high seat prices in the eyes of the uninitiated, but there has not been a commissioned score since 1969; and Nehama Patkin's *Arena* in that year can hardly be considered seriously in ballet terms. But four years before that there was the Japanese Yuzo Toyama's magnificent music for Helpmann's *Yūgen* and in 1964 no less than three new ballet scores saw the light of day; *The Display* is musical history by now, but music was also commissioned from James Penberthy for *Roundelay* and from Les Patching for *Jazz Spectrum*. Two winners out of five is not a bad average, but there has been little attempt to follow up. Not even the creation of the Music Board of the Australia Council has produced one ballet by an Australian composer for the national company.

Helpmann's unfortunate experiences in 1973–74 were admittedly discouraging; first Richard Meale and then Malcolm Williamson failed to meet agreed deadlines to provide music for the same ballet, *Perisynthion,* while elsewhere Peter Sculthorpe was letting down the Australian Opera in a similar manner. Frustrating as this may have been for Helpmann, it does not in the least affect the fact that music specially written for ballet is part and parcel of the creative process and one failure is no reason to abandon the principle. Composers and choreographers in this country have not had time to establish any kind of tradition and it is not to the credit of the Australian Ballet that they have received so little encouragement since its creation.

If local talent could not (or was not allowed to) create an original repertoire out of the blue, the availability of the Royal Ballet's proven successes provided a quick way to satisfy the demands of Australian audiences. Experimentation should have run parallel with proven recipes, but it was not

Fly away Garth Garth Welch in his last year with the Australian Ballet (1973), which he led as *premier danseur* since its first performance in 1962. He chose to cease dancing while still at the top of his form, as this picture shows beyond doubt. With Marilyn Rowe in Kenneth MacMillan's *Concerto*.

really surprising that the former became the Cinderella of the piece. It was just too easy to star the excellent dancers available in established successes like Cranko's *Pineapple Poll* and Ashton's *La fille mal gardée*. The former became an obvious addition to the repertoire in 1964 when Elaine Fifield joined the company after some years of retirement. She had created the title role at Sadler's Wells in 1951 and her performance had contributed largely to its initial success. Now she recreated Poll in Australia, Bryan Lawrence at his brilliant best danced Captain Belaye and Gerard Sibbritt's Jasper was a marvel of precision. What hope had any local choreographic talent against competition of this kind?

A different kind of import was Helpmann's brutal piece of theatre, *Elektra,* the last ballet in which Kathleen Gorham created the leading part in Australia. The year was 1966 and she retired at the end of the season, reappearing briefly a few months later to dance a final series of *Giselles.*

But *La fille mal gardée* in 1967 was the great triumph of those years, the forerunner of a whole series of full-length ballets which seem to attract the Australian public so much more than the more flexible triple bills which Diaghilev had established half a century earlier and which still make up the major part of the repertoire of almost every company in the world. Ashton's *Fille* is a masterpiece, combining the virtues of all modern developments in ballet with the charm of its period setting. It was a milestone for Ashton also, who followed the same principle with success in many later works of almost unvarying excellence.

313

La fille bien gardée The Australian Ballet's most popular ballet has been well looked after by the company. Since its premiere in 1967 *La fille* has been revived many times and always with success. Its secret lies in ample doses of comedy alternating with superb dance sequences and Alan Alder's Alain (*below*) remains one of the great comic creations of the Australian theatre. He is seen here with (left to right) Roger Myers, Ray Powell and Marilyn Jones.

The other end of Marilyn Jones Mother Simone (*right*) takes time off from her (be)labours, while Lise's bottom has a spanking time. Ray Powell and Marilyn Jones in *La fille mal gardée*.

The school of body language The innovations of Glen Tetley and John Butler brought a welcome change from full-length classical works to the Australian Ballet in the seventies, though the limitations of earth-bound twisting bodies soon became apparent. John Meehan, centre, and Mark Brinkley in Butler's *Night Encounter.*

The Australian Ballet's production of *La fille mal gardée* was restaged by Elphine Allen and used Osbert Lancaster's original designs. With a humanized Marilyn Jones coming down from her icy classical image as a delightfully mischievous Lise, Bryan Lawrence's magnificent dancing and Alan Alder as the dumb suitor Alain, one of the greatest comic ballet creations of all time, *La fille mal gardée* was a runaway winner and remains one to this day. It far outshone the other 1967 premiere, *Ballet Imperial,* more notable for the playing of the Tchaikovsky Piano Concerto No. 2 by Wendy Pomroy in the pit than for its worth as a ballet. This Balanchine work relies on personality rather than technique and only Marilyn Jones had that; young Warren de Maria was shooting up well over the 180 cm mark and not adjusting physically to the combination of muscle and lankiness. Importing works by Balanchine may have seemed like a good idea, but neither *Ballet Imperial* nor the later (1970) *Serenade* were what the company needed.

The very prettiness of the 1967 repertoire resulted in a strong reversal the following year, which saw Helpmann's spectacular *Sun Music* and the arrival of John Butler in Australia. Butler's *Threshold* introduced the kind of absolute modern ballet which, after a while, was to become too much of a good thing. Human bodies dressed in lycra tights entwining their limbs in endless convolutions brought into close-up the kind of thing Helpmann did *en masse* in *Sun Music.* Less ambitious than the Helpmann work, *Threshold* made a much greater impact. (Oddly enough Kenneth Rowell provided the decor for both ballets, which were often programmed together and, in spite of their superficial resemblance, balanced each other rather well.) Garth Welch and Alan Alder were the athletic men showing off their glistening muscles, while Kathleen Geldard and Josephine Jason provided the somewhat sex-less ladies. Jason, still a member of the corps de ballet, had been used by Helpmann in a key role in *Sun Music* and was immediately pushed into an even more difficult part by Butler. The company was still desperately trying to build up new principals. This did not always work; Jason never went beyond having great promise.

The pattern of pushing young dancers into modern ballets continued with Jack Manuel's *Arena,* which suffered as a result. That inexperienced choreographers need experienced dancers to assist them in interpreting their half-formed ideas somehow did not get through to van Praagh, who appeared to think that youth should interpret youth. The appearance of Frederick Ashton's *The Dream,* another of the Royal Ballet's established successes, this one based on Shakespeare's *Midsummernight's Dream,* showed what an experienced choreographer can do with young talent: Paul Saliba and Graeme Murphy, alternating as Puck, achieved successes out of all proportion to their abilities at that stage of their ca-

The school of body language The remarkable adaptability of the Australian dancers showed most clearly in modern works like Butler's *Night Encounter*. That perfect example of classical haughtiness, Marilyn Jones, seen here with John Meehan, was a sensation in this work.

reers, though both proved themselves in later years. As an Ashton work, *The Dream* was given V.I.P. treatment compared with poor Manuel's work. Peter Farmer's decor and costumes were superbly lit by William Akers and Fifield was a lovely Titania. The sensation was Kelvin Coe as Oberon, however, creating his first leading role with dazzling virtuosity.

With no overseas tour in 1969 the company let its head go in building the repertoire. The arrival of Antony Tudor in person was quite a coup. Tudor is an English choreographer whose roots go back to the pre-war Rambert days. He has created a whole series of masterpieces which are still making the rounds in overseas companies. One of these, *Pillar of Fire,* he now came to stage for the Australian Ballet. Better yet, he undertook to create a completely new work for the company as well. His visit should have been a very major event, but hopes were only partly realized. *Pillar of Fire* almost fulfilled expectations but, good as Kathleen Geldard was in the leading role of the neurotic American spinster, she was no great personality like Nora Kaye, the role's creator. With Tudor himself in charge, the large cast caught the spirit of the occasion, but the public did not go overboard for what is considered to be Tudor's best ballet.

The Divine Horseman was the work Tudor produced specially for the Australian Ballet. Based on a Caribbean legend of voodoo and possession, it proved to be a very weak mixture of sensationalism and sexual symbolism, though Gailene Stock and Karl Welander won notable personal successes. Stock in particular did admirable work during this period, taking over many of Kathleen Gorham's old roles, including the Female in *The Display*; and that was no easy task! With Marilyn Jones absent, having her first child, Kathleen Gorham, Bryan Lawrence and the admirable Janet Karin retired, and no guest artists, 1969 was a year of consolidation which brought a great number of dancers into leading roles who might not otherwise have found themselves there. Some went on to greater strength (Kelvin Coe and Marilyn Rowe), others were fully extended and believed that their day of glory would never end. One of the results of this situation was the personality crisis of the following year when Warren de Maria, Barbara Chambers, Kathleen Geldard and a few others departed on the grounds (freely reported in the Press) that they felt the company was not doing enough to promote their image as stars. Whatever their virtues (and they were many) few of them were star material and they were replaced with remarkable promptness by graduates from the ranks and the Australian Ballet School.

The monopoly that the Australian Ballet (as much as the Australian Opera) enjoys, makes the fate of any dancer, rightly or wrongly unhappy with his fate in the company, very difficult. Young choreographers like Ian Spink and

Who do voodoo? The Australian Ballet did do in *The Divine Horseman*, an original ballet commissioned from Anthony Tudor in 1969, but not even the best danced calypso could overcome the curse of weak choreography. Karl Welander with Gailene Stock; Janet Vernon at right.

Blood and guts There is nothing sissy about a John Butler ballet. This American choreographer has left a deep impression on the style and repertoire of the Australian Ballet and on the young artists of this country. Alan Alder and Gailene Stock (*right*) in *Sebastian*, 1971.

Don Quixote on stage Designer Barry Kay's stunning costumes and sets and Nureyev's wonderful updating of a very old ballet produced a superb impact at the 1970 Adelaide Festival and during world-wide tours which followed.
The duel (*top left*) between Don Quixote (Helpmann) and Gamache (Colin Peasley). At the back: Alan Alder.
Don Quixote sets out on his quest (*bottom left*) led by Sancho Panza (Ray Powell).

Graeme Murphy left, and suffered grievous financial hazards, to develop talents for which there was no opening in the company. Dancers, such as those who departed in 1970, are unable to improve their art outside the Australian Ballet; none of the regional ballet companies in Australia can yet offer permanent or rewarding employment to dancers really dedicated to their art.

Karl Welander and Barbara Chambers joined the so-called Sydney Festival Ballet, an attempt by William Gill, an ex-Borovansky corps de ballet dancer, to revert to the Borovansky way of commercial exploitation of ballet – at the Orpheum Theatre in Cremorne! He imported several quite major stars like Ivan Nagy and Marilyn Burr from the Washington Ballet, Georgina Parkinson from the Royal Ballet and Zsu Zsu Kun from Budapest. Welander and Chambers were in good company, but not for long; after two brief seasons the Sydney Festival Ballet folded its wings and was heard from no longer. Their colleague Warren de Maria, the most vocal with demands for star billing, met a balletic fate almost worse than death; he became the male lead for Les Girls at Kings Cross!

The Adelaide Festival of 1970 brought Rudolf Nureyev back to the company to provide a shot in the arm. The marking time of the previous year was suddenly forgotten in the excitement of getting ready for the long-awaited *Don Quixote,* the production that was timed to coincide with the next tour of the United States under the direction of Sol Hurok. Hurok, the showman, demanded a star name and Nureyev was willing to oblige. Helpmann was happy to play (rather than dance; he was sixty-one!) the title role and a fine Sancho Panza, Ray Powell, was in the company. A ballerina of good standing was all that had to be found. Jones was obviously wrong for the small Spanish spitfire the part required and, over the loud protests of other dancers far from qualified to be chosen, New Zealand-born and Australian-educated Lucette Aldous from the Royal Ballet was engaged. She, as well as Nureyev, came to dance in the premiere of the ballet at the Adelaide Festival.

Little need be said about the success of *Don Quixote,* a full-length classical ballet up-dated by Nureyev to modern standards, as *Fille mal gardée* was updated by Ashton. It remains Nureyev's best work as a choreographer and can be seen at will on film, showing the Australian Ballet exactly as it was in the early seventies, except that many of the smaller roles are danced by major artists who had, by then, often taken both the Nureyev and Aldous roles.

Helpmann also achieved the remarkable coup of getting Nureyev to dance the title role in his own best ballet, *Hamlet,* in Australia. Outside of Helpmann himself in his prime, no better choice than the moody Russian for this part could be imagined. Josephine Jason's youthful Ophelia and Paul Saliba's Gravedigger also stood out. Ray Powell's

323

Don Quixote on film   Nureyev talked some money men into filming his ballet with himself as director as well as star. Using the Australian Ballet's full complement of soloists, he employed no other outside artist. Thus the world saw the actual Australian production of *Don Quixote* in toto. *Opposite*, right to left, Lucette Aldous, Nureyev, Gailene Stock and Carolyn Rappel. The whole of the *Don Quixote* film was made in one set constructed in an old hangar at Essendon Airport in Melbourne. The model (*inset*), shows how it was done. Nancy Austin, the company's press representative, and Edward H. Pask, its Archivist.

Rudi, the Comedian   Nureyev's Basilio (*below*) faking a very funny suicide in *Don Quixote*.

pleasant, but unmemorable *Symphony in Gold,* an indifferent revival of *Petrouchka* with designs by Raymond Boyce, Ashton's delightful *Les Patineurs* and Balanchine's *Serenade* completed the huge new repertoire created in 1970. Why, after all that, only *Symphony in Gold* made the trip to America is not very clear, unless the management was trying to make *Don Quixote* look better. Nureyev certainly saw to it that his brain child got ample exposure; on occasion he (and Aldous) were not above dancing the full ballet four times on two days!

Some unexpected side benefits came to the company from the American tour. Not only did Aldous ultimately become ballerina for the Australian Ballet, a role she has filled with tremendous verve and vitality ever since, but John Lanchbery, the Musical Director of the Royal Ballet in London was engaged to conduct *Don Quixote* in America. Lanchbery had arranged the original score when Nureyev first produced the ballet in Vienna in 1966 and he was given permission by the Royal Ballet to join the tour. The early conductors for the Australian Ballet, like Robert Rosen, an admirable musician with extensive experience in opera who adapted himself well to ballet, had provided little more than accompaniment for the dancers. Lanchbery was a musical director – in a different category altogether; somebody who could contribute a lot to every aspect of the artistic policies of a company. He made many friends during the American tour and finally decided to leave the Royal Ballet which, at that time, was going through some changes in artistic policies after the retirement of Sir Frederick Ashton. He came to Australia to take charge of the Australian Ballet's musical complexities and his influence on the company's standards and on those of the two orchestras, which are run by the Elizabethan Theatre Trust for the use of the Australian Ballet and Opera, has been immense. Lanchbery has spent a lifetime in the service of ballet and it shows.

The returned expatriate An Australian ballerina who did not mature at home is Lucette Aldous. While having her basic training in Australia, she fought her way to the top against strong competition in London's Royal Ballet. She joined the Australian Ballet in 1970 to star with Nureyev in *Don Quixote* and stayed.

Above left, with Kelvin Coe and one of the protagonists of the title, who upstages even Aldous, in *The Two Pigeons*; *left*, with Gary Norman in Roland Petit's *Carmen*; *right*, with Kelvin Coe in the sensational short *pas de deux Spring Waters.*

The corps of the apple   The unsung heroes of seasons past, the corps de ballet at the mid-point of the Australian Ballet's history to date, 1969.

Alida Chase   Juliette Solley   Ronald Bekker   Graham Murphy   Janet Vernon   William Pepper   Julie da Costa   Judy Donovan   Gary Hill   Graeme Hudson   Jo-Anne Endicott   Renee Valent   Robert Barlow

Frederic Werner

Roslyn Anderson

Colin Peasley

Wendy Moyle

Paul Saliba

Suzanne Neumann

Joseph Janusaitis

Lucyna Sevitsky

Rex McNeill
Cheryl Mallinson

Leigh Rowles

Wendy Walker

Andris Toppe

The End of the Beginning

24

The end is drawing nigh — not mine, or the Australian Ballet's, but this book's. The last five years of the Australian Ballet have been a consolidation of resources. Margaret Scott's admirable Australian Ballet School has filled the ranks of principals with youngsters who started their training under her direction. One of her first graduates, Marilyn Rowe, is a leading ballerina with the company. One of her best boys, Gary Norman, has achieved principal status, danced all the leading roles and is already lost to us overseas. Another, John Meehan, may well have departed by the time this book is in the reader's hand, his appearances in America and England in *The Merry Widow* have brought offers galore and he would be foolish indeed to ignore them. As we import the occasional principal, like Aldous, so must we lose some of our own. Blessedly, we have an apparently inexhaustible pool of talent which, through the improvement in training in many schools and the final polish available in the Australian Ballet School's full-time course, can and does reach standards as high as can be found anywhere in the world.

And the occasional outsider who is accepted into the ranks of the principals really has to be something special. Ai-Gul Gaisina's fortuitous arrival via her marriage brought a touch of genuine Russian style into the company and only stiff competition prevents her from dancing more of those brilliant Auroras and Kitris so much admired by the *cognoscenti*. On the male side Jonathan Kelly is not only a fine male dancer, but tall and handsome to boot. No, there is no longer any need to import second-raters and pretend they are stars.

The new ballets of recent years have, on the whole, been less interesting than the emergence of so many fine dancers, who keep our interest alive. Production standards have risen and going to the ballet has become a theatrical experience. New Ashton ballets have been added to the repertoire, including the full-length *Cinderella* in 1972 for which Sir Frederick himself arrived, not only to oversee final rehearsals, but to make some appearances with his old partner, Sir Robert Helpmann, as the two Ugly Sisters. Leonide Massine belatedly produced a ballet for the company and afterwards himself admitted that *Mam'zelle Angot* was the wrong choice; 'but I had no idea it would be a company of such quality', he later explained. On the other hand, no excuses were needed for Anne Woolliams' reconstruction of John Cranko's *Romeo and Juliet* in 1974, a feast of dance and colour which brought the loss the ballet world suffered by Cranko's early death home to Australians. Marilyn Jones and John Meehan were the immortal lovers and matriarch of the Edgley family, Mrs Edna Edgley, made her debut in ballet playing the Nurse, putting an unusual strain on various Romeos used to less weighty dancing partners.

Helpmann put his personal stamp on two spectacle ballets,

The unknown extra 1968 Appearing among the unlisted dancers in the Trust Opera's production of *Tannhäuser* (*right*) was this seventeen year old student on leave of absence from the Australian Ballet School, Gary Norman.

The known star 1974 The polished star performer, the finished product of the Australian Ballet School, the corps de ballet of the Australian Ballet and three years as a principal. Gary Norman (*below*) in Barry Moreland's *Sacred Space*, his last leading role before he left Australia to gain experience as principal dancer with the National Ballet of Canada and then the Royal Winnipeg Ballet.

with somewhat different end results. *The Sleeping Beauty* suffered from the unexpectedly abominable designs of that usual master of colour and taste, Kenneth Rowell, but *The Merry Widow*, Helpmann's swan song for the company, completed during his last months as Artistic Director, has conceivably been the company's greatest success. Designed superbly by Desmond Heeley, with choreography by Ronald Hynes and Lehàr's familiar music arranged by Lanchbery, it made a sensational debut on 13 November 1975 in Melbourne. Within days the offers from overseas rolled in and yet another world tour was thrown together for 1976.

Fonteyn had to dance in place of Marilyn Rowe in America, where the 'star' mentality demanded more than just a fine spectacle. In London the critics took unkindly to the Australian upstart and Fonteyn again had to make some, this time unplanned, appearances to save the season. Of course, *The Merry Widow* is not a good ballet; it is a magnificent spectacle with a considerable amount of fine dancing and the Australian Ballet had the dancers to do it justice. Significantly, there were no complaints about the company, and if the choice of ballet to show off Australia was considered unsuitable, that is fair criticism. Sour grapes also may have something to do with it; imitations are already being planned in quarters where the whole thing was openly panned. Ah, yes, that's show business!

I'm going to Maxim's The Australian Ballet's most spectacular production and Sir Robert Helpmann's swan song, *The Merry Widow.*

The merrily dancing widow Helpmann's adaptation of Franz Lehár's *The Merry Widow*, arranged by John Lanchbery for ballet, was seen not only in Australia, but in Washington, New York, London and Manila within eleven months of its premiere in 1975. As sheer spectacle and escapist entertainment it is an unquestioned success — and it is not a bad ballet either!

Below, the Ball Scene;
Below left, the Pavilion Scene. Left: John Meehan as Danilo; centre: Marilyn Rowe as Hanna and Kelvin Coe as Camille; right: Lucette Aldous as Valencienne, fainted dead away, and Ray Powell as Njegus.
Left, the inevitable Happy End — Danilo finds Hanna. John Meehan and Marilyn Rowe.

The trial of Anne Woolliams In 1974 Anne Woolliams, the late John Cranko's assistant in the Stuttgart Ballet, came to Australia to stage his *Romeo and Juliet* for the Australian Ballet.

A brawl in the market place of Verona.

The most recent ventures into repertoire have been varied in the extreme, from the conventional *Les Sylphides,* restaged for the company by one of Fokine's own dancers, Alicia Markova, to Ashton's severe exercise in discipline, *Monotones,* and a television romp to music by the Beatles, *The Fool on the Hill.* Produced for the Australian Broadcasting Commission by Gillian Lynne, the latter was foolishly put into the normal repertoire, where it fell amusingly, and confusingly, flat on its very prettily designed face. (Tim Goodchild's costumes alone remain in unbeatable glory, a joy forever, if only on videotape.)

After fourteen years of existence few of the original dancers remain in the company. Only Marilyn Jones, after two retirements to raise some off-spring, remains of the original principals and (in the footsteps of Fonteyn) is dancing better in her late thirties than in her early twenties. Her Merry Widow in London received rave notices and she excels as much in modern as in classical roles. From the original ensemble Kelvin Coe and Robert Olup remain, while Colin Peasley has become the company's leading mime. (Coe shares the honour of having won a Silver Medal at the Second Moscow International Dance Competition in 1972 with Marilyn Rowe, the first graduate to emerge from the Australian Ballet School, who is now among the best principals of the company.) Walter Bourke, who grew up in the company, has returned to it after many years abroad and has not, therefore, had the continuity of service the others have.

As for the original administrators and staff of the company, none remain except for the 'temporary' ballet master of the very first season, Ray Powell, who has quietly worked in the background all these years, only emerging into the limelight whenever there has been a major mime role, in which he excels, such as Bootface in *The Lady and the Fool,* which he created for the Royal Ballet in 1955. With Bryan Ashbridge, who joined the company as Assistant Artistic Director in 1968 to take some of the weight off the ailing Peggy van Praagh's shoulders, Powell has shared the administrative burden since 1972, when he also was appointed Assistant Artistic Director. The need for Ashbridge and Powell was very real during the last years of van Praagh's tenure, for her health kept her in and out of hospitals for many years. Ultimately she was to read about her own retirement in the daily Press in 1974, an unforgivable *faux pas* on the part of the management, since she had made it clear that she realized that physical incapacity would not allow her to continue. It was the first public sign of ill-relations or non-relations between the administration and the Artistic Directors since their original appointment.

Sir Robert Helpmann remained as sole Artistic Director for eighteen months after van Praagh's retirement, during which he planned and created *The Merry Widow.* Long before

The trial of Anne Woolliams 'Not another full-length ballet!', the critics complained when *Romeo and Juliet* was staged in 1974. But, like most of Cranko's ballets, it proved to be a winner. Did the success of *Romeo and Juliet* prompt the engagement of Anne Woolliams as Artistic Director of the Australian Ballet? Was this her 'trial'? If so, she needed no judge to acquit her — she acquitted herself. With honours!

A full-scale fight (*below*) between the Capulets and the Montagues (Alan Alder as Tybalt and Kelvin Coe as Romeo) ends in the death of Tybalt. *Right*, Alder with Mary Duchesne as Lady Capulet.

Romeo and Juliet John Cranko found things to do with his dancers, props, scenery or costumes which created the most original effects. A simple kiss (*left*) in the right kind of costume . . . (Kelvin Coe and Lucette Aldous in the Wedding Scene in Friar Laurence's Garden.)

The Balcony Scene – without the balcony! It is easier for Juliet to dance with Romeo in the courtyard (*below*) than for Romeo to dance with Juliet on her balcony. (John Meehan and Marilyn Jones.)

its premiere he was summarily notified that the Board of Directors did not intend to renew his contract after August 1976. The rights and wrongs of the affair made headlines throughout Australia and the whole world. I do not propose to re-open the controversy, beyond stating that all the noise was being made by supporters of Sir Robert, of whom there was a legion. In no way can the manner of Sir Robert's departure be taken to reflect on his successor, Anne Woolliams, who commences her work with the company as these lines are being written. Hers will be no easy task, to continue to run a company that is often criticized, but rarely justly. Of course, we would all like matters to improve even further. Still, she has been left a far from ailing infant.

Anne Woolliams has some very definite ideas of what she would like the Australian Ballet to be, but she is realistic enough to know that there are practical reasons why everything cannot be done overnight. She appears to have an iron hand in a velvet glove. How hard the iron is, if or when it meets an immovable object, remains to be seen. She is intent on developing new choreographers at any price, and that alone is a good thing. She would prefer to use the repertory system of nightly changes of programme, as practised overseas, and, contrary to past practice, she wants to build stars in the company so that the need for box office names on overseas tours will disappear. Quite rightly, she feels the company should be able to stand on its own feet. The big obstacle lies not abroad, but at home; Australians are not so ready to acclaim their own, and convincing them of the excellence of homegrown stars will be an uphill battle, but one which Woolliams thinks she can win. Guest stars will be welcome, but only to supplement the company's own dancers, not to replace them.

It appears that Anne Woolliams has all the right answers to all the right questions. The only one remaining is: will she be given the chance to pass the test of time and give those answers? No company can stand still; the Australian Ballet has not done so since its inception. But sooner or later there must be changes in direction and a major one is about to take place. For what it is worth, I feel that there is more than hope that enough will happen to the Australian Ballet to demand another history of the company before too many years have passed.

Ring out the old, ring in the new Whatever the controversy surrounding the changes in the artistic direction of the Australian Ballet in 1976, the worth of Sir Robert Helpmann's twelve years with the company has been great indeed and his successor, Anne Woolliams, certainly had no part in the decision to end his term as sole Artistic Director. Dare one hope that the amicable scene pictured here will be repeated if and when Sir Robert returns to produce a successor to *The Display* for the company to which he gave so much?

credits

My thanks to the following for permission to reproduce illustrations. Every effort has been made to trace all copyright holders; however advice of any omissions would be appreciated.

The Australian Ballet: 189–92, 207–12, 218–20, 228, 236–40, 244–8 left top and bottom, 250–73, 276–80, 282 bottom–96, 313, 317–25, 326 bottom, 327, 331 bottom, 43.

The Australian Opera: endpapers, x, xiv–xv, 32, 33 top, 37, 38 bottom, 39 bottom, 41, 49–51, 52 right top and bottom, 53–6, 60–72, 73, 79 bottom, 83 top, 85, 86, 88–9, 100–3, 109–15, 124–86, 331 top.

Dance Collection, New York Public Library at Lincoln Center; Astor, Lennox and Tilden Foundations: 196, 199, 204

La Trobe Collection, State Library of Victoria: 5, 6, 7, 8, 9, 15, 19, 20.

William Baxter: 93, 94 top, 243, 248 top right, 249, 274, 282 top, 299, 302, 305, 306, 307, 308, 310, 311, 314, 315, 326 top, 328.

Australian National Memorial Theatre Limited: 22, 24, 25, 26–7, 30, 31, 35, 36, 38 top, 39 top, 40, 44–5, 52 left, 59, 232.

New Opera, South Australia: 74, 76, 77, 79 top, 80, 104–5.

William Akers: 224.

J. C. Williamson Theatres Limited: 12, 13, 18, 214.

Victoria Opera Company: 94 bottom, 95.

National Library, Canberra: 2, 3, 17, 213.

Norman L. Danvers: 57.

Australian Consolidated Press: 83 bottom.

Max Dupain: 120.

opera

index

347

ballet index

References in **bold** type indicate fuller references, and in *italic* indicate illustrations.

Order of credits after the title of each ballet: Choreographer/Composer/Designer.

Choreography: All works re-staged 'after' an original choreographer have been credited to the latter only, unless the production varies substantially from the original.

Designs: Works usually associated with one designer are credited to him (even though different designs have been used in some revivals) except when the text refers solely to one specific revival using a new designer.

Abbreviations:

(a)   Administrator/Manager
(act)   Actor
(ch)   Choreographer
(comp)   Composer/Arranger
(cond)   Conductor
(d)   Dancer
(des)   Designer
(lib)   Librettist/Author
(o)   Opera/Operetta/Musical
(pant)   Pantomime
(tea)   Teacher

351